KU-434-723

PENGUIN BOOKS

Religion and Magic in Ancient Egypt

Rosalie David took a BA degree in Ancient History with Egyptology at University College London. Her doctoral thesis at the University of Liverpool explored the ritual use and function of the ancient Egyptian temple.

In 1972 she began her academic career at the Manchester Museum, University of Manchester, where she is currently Professor and Keeper of Egyptology. Her work has focused on the initiation and development of biomedical studies in the field of Egyptology, and in 1973 she inaugurated and has continued to direct the internationally renowned Manchester Egyptian Mummy Research Project. For many years she has also taught university courses on ancient Egyptian religion.

Professor David has lectured in many countries and on cruises in Egypt and the Middle East, and has also been consultant and presenter for scientific television documentary films. She has published many articles, and has edited or authored over twenty books of which the most recent are *The Experience of Ancient Egypt* (Routledge, 1999), *Handbook to Life in Ancient Egypt* (FactsOnFile, 1999; second revised edition, 2002), and (with Rick Archbold) *Conversations with Mummies* (HarperCollins/Madison Press, 2000).

Religion and Magic in Ancient Egypt

ROSALIE DAVID

PENGUIN BOOKS

PENGUIN BOOKS

Published by the Penguin Group
Penguin Books Ltd, 80 Strand, London WC2R ORL, England
Penguin Putnam Inc., 375 Hudson Street, New York, New York 10014, USA
Penguin Books Australia Ltd, 250 Camberwell Road, Camberwell, Victoria 3124, Australia
Penguin Books Canada Ltd, 10 Alcorn Avenue, Toronto, Ontario, Canada M4V 3B2
Penguin Books India (P) Ltd, 11 Community Centre, Panchsheel Park, New Delhi – 110 017, India
Penguin Books (NZ) Ltd, Cnr Rosedale and Airborne Roads, Albany, Auckland, New Zealand
Penguin Books (South Africa) (Pty) Ltd, 24 Sturdee Avenue, Rosebank 2196, South Africa

Penguin Books Ltd, Registered Offices: 80 Strand, London WC2R ORL, England

www.penguin.com

First published 2002
2

Set in 10.5/12.5 pt PostScript Monotype Fournier
Typeset by Rowland Phototypesetting Ltd, Bury St Edmunds, Suffolk
Printed in England by Clays Ltd, St Ives plc

Contents

List of Figures and Maps

FIGURES

The figures are after: J. G. Wilkinson, *A Popular Account of the Ancient Egyptians*, 2 vols (London, 1878); A. Erman, *Life in Ancient Egypt* (transl. by H. M. Tirard) (New York, 1971); and W. B. Emery, *Archaic Egypt* (Harmondsworth, 1963).

Thoth, god of writing, and Seshat, goddess of writing, who inscribe his name on the Persea tree. Each leaf represented a year of the king's life that the gods had allotted him. 206

17. Most tombs contained wall scenes depicting food production (as here), to ensure a perpetual food supply for the deceased owner. 209

18. King Horemheb, carried here in procession by his soldiers, used his powers as head of the army to take over the kingship and restore the traditional religion. 247

19. A tomb scene shows scribes writing on papyrus. They have pushed spare pens behind their ears. 265

20. A tomb scene illustrates some stages in the production of mudbricks. An overseer is shown, carrying a whip. 268

21. A tomb scene shows the transportation of a colossal statue, probably to a temple location. A man pours milk in front of the sledge to lubricate the runners. 275

22. A tomb scene shows a workshop where men bandage mummies and make coffins. 299

23. A tomb scene shows stages in a funeral: a man pours a libation over two mummies and they are then dragged on sledges to a kiosk. 300

24. A tomb scene shows funerary preparations: men pour milk in front of a sledge that transports the owner's mummy on a bier, accompanied by two attendants. 301

MAPS

List of Illustrations

Acknowledgements

I am grateful to Professor J. R. Hinnells, who encouraged me to embark on this book and subsequently offered many helpful suggestions.

For permission to use the photographs, I should like to thank and acknowledge Robert Partridge: the Ancient Egypt Picture Library; and the Manchester Museum, University of Manchester (especially Mr G. Thompson for producing these images). I am grateful to Mr A. Andrew for producing the maps; Mrs Audrey Johnson and Mrs Sue McDade for typing the manuscript; and the publishers, particularly Caroline Pretty and all the members of the production team, for their comments and advice.

Finally, I should especially like to thank my husband for all his help and support throughout the process of writing the book.

A Chronological Table
of Egyptian History

Period	Date	Dynasty	
Predynastic Period	c.5000–c.3100 BCE		
Archaic Period	c.3100–c.2890 BCE	I	
	c.2890–c.2686 BCE	II	
Old Kingdom	c.2686–c.2613 BCE	III	
	c.2613–c.2494 BCE	IV	
	c.2494–c.2345 BCE	V	
	c.2345–c.2181 BCE	VI	
First Intermediate Period	c.2181–c.2173 BCE	VII	Memphite
	c.2173–c.2160 BCE	VIII	
	c.2160–c.2130 BCE	IX	Heracleopolitan
	c.2130–c.2040 BCE	X	
	c.2133–c.1991 BCE	XI	Theban
Middle Kingdom	1991–1786 BCE	XII	

Second Intermediate	1786–1633 BCE	XIII	
Period	1786–c.1603 BCE	XIV	Xois
	1674–1567 BCE	XV	Hyksos
	c.1684–1567 BCE	XVI	Hyksos
	c.1650–1567 BCE	XVII	Theban
New Kingdom	1567–1320 BCE	XVIII	
	1320–1200 BCE	XIX	
	1200–1085 BCE	XX	
Third Intermediate	1085–945 BCE	XXI	Tanis
Period	945–730 BCE	XXII	Bubastis
	817(?)–730 BCE	XXIII	Leontopolis
	720–715 BCE	XXIV	Sais
	715–668 BCE	XXV	Ethiopian
Late Period	664–525 BCE	XXVI	Sais
	525–404 BCE	XXVII	Persian
	404–399 BCE	XXVIII	Sais
	399–380 BCE	XXIX	Mendes
	380–343 BCE	XXX	Sebennytos
	343–332 BCE	XXXI	Persian

Conquest by		Graeco-
Alexander the Great	332 BCE	Roman
Ptolemaic Period	332–30 BCE	Period
Conquest by Romans	30 BCE	
Roman Period	30 BCE – Fourth Century ACE	

CHAPTER I

The Creation of Egyptian Civilization

THE ENVIRONMENTAL BACKGROUND

Egypt is a land of marked contrasts, and the environment and the natural forces have always had a strong impact on the lives and beliefs of the people. Every day, they observed the unchanging cycle of the sun's passage: each night it died but was reborn on the horizon at dawn and continued its celestial course throughout the day, creating and sustaining life on earth. Similarly, in the annual cycle of the seasons, they saw the regular death and destruction of the vegetation, due to the parching of the land, which in turn was followed by the inundation of the River Nile, which revived and restored the plants and the crops. Both these great life-forces – the sun and the river – followed patterns of life, death and rebirth which probably inspired in the Egyptians a very early belief that individual human existence reflected these natural cycles and involved life, death and continuation after death.

The ancient Egyptians believed that the Nile – their life source – originated in the netherworld. The inundation of the river was regarded as a divine gift although, since its level could not be controlled artificially, each rising was awaited with trepidation: if the river did not rise at all (although this never happened), they feared that there would be widespread famine and death; and certainly there were excessive floods which swept away homes and crops, and low Nile levels that resulted in drought, famine and disaster.

The Nile's blessing was capricious and uncontrollable, a situation only rectified in modern times by the construction of a series of dams along the river, culminating with the High Dam at Aswan. This allows a vast volume of water to be held back in Lake Nasser behind the dam, and then released as required for irrigation of the land and to supply electricity to the towns and villages in the Valley.

In antiquity, it is evident that the people's religious beliefs were profoundly influenced not only by the challenging nature of this environment, but also by the general predictability of the climate. There is almost perpetual sunshine in the south, with virtually non-existent rainfall (apart from the few freak storms that can cause destruction), and milder temperatures in the north, accompanied by some winter rainfall in the northern Delta. Even when high summer temperatures are reached in the south, the climate is bearable because of the dryness of the atmosphere. Between March and May, winds from the south or south-west (the *Khamasin*) can bring sandstorms.

Evidently, this generally pleasant climate which held few surprises, together with the regularity of the inundation of the Nile and its consequences, strongly influenced the type of religion which emerged: a structured pattern of ideas which was designed to perpetuate the principle of Ma'at, the goddess of order and equilibrium in the universe, and to continually challenge and overthrow the forces of chaos.

The earliest evidence for religion occurs amongst the Neolithic communities (*c*.5000 to *c*.4000 BCE) who had established and developed settlements, and supported themselves by growing grain and domesticating animals. The area had been inhabited earlier, during the Palaeolithic Period (before *c*.5000 BCE), and archaeological evidence indicates that at this time people occupied the desert spurs on the periphery of the Nile Valley where they hunted game. No conclusions can be drawn, however, about their social organization or religious beliefs and customs at this period.

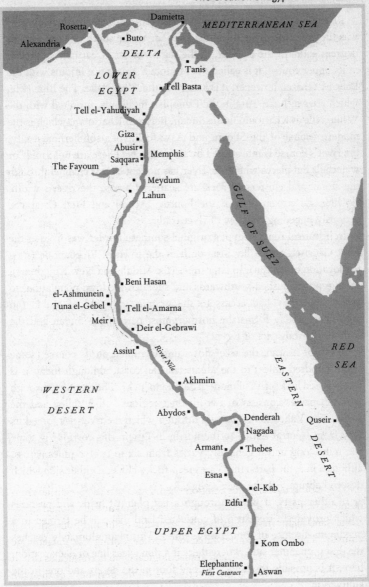

Map of Egypt

Probably the most important single factor in Egypt's development was the Nile, the great river that rises far to the south of Egypt, three degrees south of the equator, in the region of the Great Lakes. Today, in its upper course, it is called the Mountain Nile; once it joins with the Bahr El-Ghazel, however, it is known as the White Nile. The Blue Nile, which rises in Lake Tara in the Ethiopian highlands, is united with the White Nile at Khartoum in the Sudan. Between Khartoum, which is the modern capital of the Sudan, and Aswan, Egypt's southernmost city, the river's course is interrupted by six cataracts. These are not rapids or waterfalls but places where the river has not cut a clear channel through the stone, and clusters of rock are scattered across the river's width, slowing the stream and, at the Fourth, Second and First Cataracts, seriously impeding the flow of river traffic.

In historical times, Egypt's original southern border was fixed at the First Cataract, which lay just south of the town of Elephantine (now the location of Aswan). In later times (the Middle and New Kingdoms), the Egyptians pushed southwards and subdued the local population, to ensure that they had access to the granite and gold of Nubia (an area which today forms the northernmost part of the Sudan and the southernmost district of Egypt).

North of Aswan, the river flows uninterrupted on its course (some seven hundred miles) to the Mediterranean coast, although today it is interspersed by a series of modern dams and locks. The territory through which it passes consists of two distinct regions – the Valley and the Delta. The Valley is the passage through which the river has forced its way from Central Africa to the north; in Egypt, this corridor is some 500 miles long and it generally varies from six to twelve miles across, although in some parts, there are steep rocky cliffs on either side which descend abruptly to the river's edge.

In other parts, it passes through a flat plain of fields and pastures which provides a rich strip of cultivated land that can be farmed to a maximum distance of some twelve miles. This plain ultimately reaches the desert on either side, where there is a thin, clear line of demarcation: here, it is possible to stand with one foot in the desert and one in the cultivation.

At the apex of the Delta, where the Arab conquerors later founded

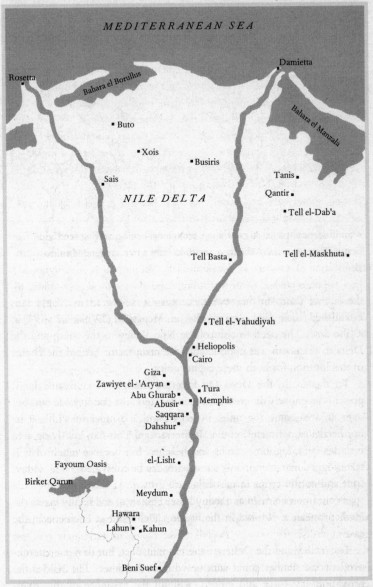

MEDITERRANEAN SEA

Rosetta

Damietta

Bahara el Borullus

Bahara el Manzala

Buto

Xois

Busiris

Sais

Tanis

Qantir

Tell el-Dab'a

NILE DELTA

Tell Basta

Tell el-Maskhuta

Tell el-Yahudiyah

Heliopolis

Cairo

Giza

Zawiyet el- 'Aryan

Tura

Abu Ghurab

Abusir

Memphis

Saqqara

Dahshur

el-Lisht

Fayoum Oasis

Birket Qarun

Meydum

Hawara

Lahun   Kahun

Beni Suef

Map of Lower Egypt

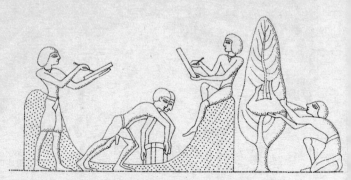

A tomb scene shows crop cultivation: ploughing, hoeing, sowing seed and beating it into the soil. A thirsty man drinks from a tree-suspended animal skin.

the city of Cairo in the seventh century ACE, the ancient Egyptians established their first capital city at Memphis ('White Walls') in c.3100 BCE. The need to control the Nile Valley to the south and the Delta to the north was undoubtedly the main factor behind the choice of this location for both these capital cities.

To the north, the Delta (an inverted triangle of cultivated land) presents an entirely different perspective. Here, the countryside fans out over an area some 100 miles in length and 200 miles in width at its northernmost perimeter on the Mediterranean. This flat, low-lying area includes land, lagoons, canals and beaches, but because much of it is waterlogged marshland, only some parts can be cultivated. Here, today, fruit and cotton crops in particular are grown. At this point, the Nile spans out into two main and many lesser branches, and finally meets the Mediterranean at Rosetta in the western Delta and at Damietta in the east.

The Valley and the Delta are therefore distinct, but they are interdependent and neither could survive without the other. The Nile is the great unifying force and indeed, without the existence of this river, Egypt would simply be a desert. The political borders of modern Egypt

form a large rectangular area, but apart from the Delta and the cultivated land on either side of the Nile the rest is desert. The rainfall in Egypt has always been negligible: the winter rains of the Mediterranean reach the northern part of the Delta, but in the south of the country rain is an exceptional occurrence.

In antiquity, agriculture was dependent on the annual inundation of the Nile; this flood made Egypt habitable and enabled crops to be grown and animals to be reared along the riverbanks and in parts of the Delta. Here, in these regions, the earliest centres of habitation were established. Indeed, Egypt's situation was most aptly described in the words of the ancient writer Hecataeus who claimed that the country was literally 'the gift of the Nile'. As a river, the Nile has always intrigued historians and geographers. The longest river in Africa, it runs from south to north, and the location of its source and the cause of its inundation puzzled many ancient writers and explorers. When the Greeks and Romans began to visit Egypt as tourists and explorers, they speculated about the source of the river and the cause of the inundation.

The most famous of these writers, Herodotus, expressed his ignorance of the facts: 'About why the Nile behaves precisely as it does I could get no information from the priests or anyone else. What I particularly wished to know was why the water begins to rise at the summer solstice, continues to do so for a hundred days, and then falls again at the end of

A tomb scene shows a man and his family on a fowling excursion in the marshes. Areas of Egypt, fed by canals, had dense plant growth where wealthy people could hunt and fish.

that period, so that it remains low throughout the winter until the summer solstice comes round again the following year.' However, he was informed by the Egyptian priests (and his own observations led him to agree with this conclusion) that most of the country had been built up by silt from the river.

Today, it is known that the inundation has always been caused by the rains falling on the highlands of Ethiopia which feed into the Nile, causing it to rise and swell. Until this century, the subsequent flooding of the river banks deposited a rich black silt across the parched soil which created excellent fertile conditions for growing crops. This annual miracle is started by the heavy rains in Ethiopia from June to September; until the latter part of the twentieth century, as the inundation moved northwards, it reached the First Cataract in the fourth week of June. The full height of the water was visible at the Delta apex towards the end of September, and two weeks later, the inundation began to subside. By the end of October, the river had returned to the confines of its own banks and, in the following April, it would have reached its lowest level. The countryside again became parched and dry until the cycle repeated itself.

In antiquity, it was believed that the Nile flood was controlled from two 'caverns' or 'sources', and two nilometers (devices to measure and record the levels of the flood) were positioned at the two sources, at Aswan and to the south of Cairo. Other nilometers were positioned along the Nile; at some of these places, an annual ritual was performed to ensure a satisfactory inundation, when food, jewellery and sacrificial animals were cast into the river; in addition, to ensure the country's fertility, female 'dolls' were thrown to the Nile.

Although the Nile was a bringer of life to Egypt, the Egyptians do not appear to have deified the river at any time in their history. The god Hapy was a personification of the inundation and not of the Nile. The obese fecundity figures, which have survived in the form of statues and as carved deities on offering tables and in temple wall reliefs during the period from the Old Kingdom to the Roman Period, represent offering bearers who bring the products of the land.' By contrast, the other great life force – the sun – became one of Egypt's greatest deities. However, the Egyptians were acutely aware that a successful harvest was entirely

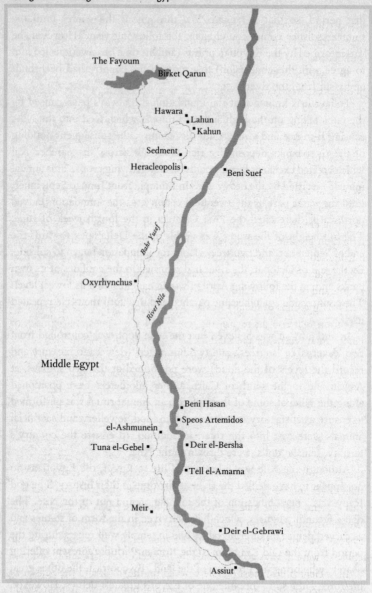

The Fayoum
Birket Qarun

Hawara
Lahun
Kahun

Sedment
Heracleopolis
Beni Suef

Bahr Yusef

Oxyrhynchus

River Nile

Middle Egypt

Beni Hasan
Speos Artemidos
el-Ashmunein
Tuna el-Gebel
Deir el-Bersha
Tell el-Amarna

Meir
Deir el-Gebrawi

Assiut

Map of Middle Egypt

dependent on divine beneficence, and Hapy and Osiris (the god of vegetation and rebirth) were worshipped and petitioned for a favourable inundation.

The Nile and the inundation had a profound effect upon the history, political organization and religion of Egypt. Very early in their history, the scattered communities realized that they had to act together and undertake measures that would control and regulate the flood. In order to bring benefit to all the settlements in the Delta and Nile Valley, it was essential that they helped each other to organize an efficient irrigation system. Although the geography of Egypt dictated that the communities were scattered along the length of the river, the common goal of irrigation provided a unifying force and certainly contributed to the eventual creation of a political state in $c.3100$ BCE. The exact date when irrigation became a central feature of Nile agriculture is uncertain, but a King Scorpion who preceded Menes, the unifier of Egypt, is shown in scenes carved on a ceremonial macehead from Hieraconpolis, undertaking and perhaps initiating the irrigation process.

The Egyptians gradually evolved a complex and effective system of irrigation that sought to use the water and the associated deposits of black silt to cultivate the land as far as possible on either side of the river. Known as the 'basin' system, this was used continuously until about the middle of the nineteenth century ACE. Earth banks were built to divide the land into compartments or 'basins' of different sizes.

When the river rose, a series of canals directed the water into these basins, so that the land was flooded; it was then retained there so that the silt that it carried would be deposited on the land. Once the river fell again, any remaining water was drained off, and the farmers could then plough the land and plant their crops. Complex organization of manpower and resources was required in order to construct and maintain this system, and the kings devoted considerable effort to ensuring that the dams and dykes were built and the canals were dug, and that the system was properly maintained. Periods of political and economic collapse were always accompanied by neglect of the irrigation system.

In ancient times, most people worked on the land, and the peasantry represented perhaps 80 per cent of the total population. A man would work either with his family or in a group, to cultivate crops for their own needs and to pay their taxes to the state, which controlled the irrigation system and stored these food supplies in granaries for future use.

As soon as the Nile waters had receded, the land was simultaneously ploughed and sown. Water had to be distributed as evenly as possible across the land, and a water-hoist (known today as a *shaduf*) was used to guide the water into channels so that all areas could be reached. The peasants then scattered seed on the fertile soil and, using a wooden hoe or a plough dragged by two cows, ensured that they were firmly planted into the ground. Sheep and pigs were brought in to trample the sown ground, and in the following spring, the harvest of spelt, emmer and barley was gathered. By the Graeco-Roman Period, it was customary to try to cultivate a two-fold harvest, although the second crop required even more arduous attention because the level of the river water was lower.

In pharaonic times, the flora and fauna of the Delta and Nile Valley were very different from today's environment: in early times, there were belts of marshes and swamps in the south where papyrus and lotus grew, and vast papyrus swamps grew in the Delta, creating a habitat for a variety of water-birds, crocodiles, hippopotami and the sacred ibis. The wildlife of the desert included lions, leopards, ostriches, ibex and oryx. During the course of history, many of these creatures disappeared from Egypt and retreated into the southern Nilotic regions, but there is ample evidence that plants, animals and birds had a profound influence on the religious concepts and symbolism of early Egypt.

The ancient Egyptians would have been keenly aware that, in their physical surroundings, life and death were always sharply contrasted and juxtaposed. This was aptly represented by the close relationship between the desert and the cultivation, reminding them of the balance and proximity of life and death.

They called their country 'Kemet', which is translated as the 'Black Land', a reference to the colour of the black silt brought by the inundation in which the crops were grown. From this association, the colour black came to represent life and rebirth. Beyond the cultivation lay the desert, a place of terror and death, where wild animals and marauding tribesmen posed a threat to all travellers. The predominant colour of the landscape

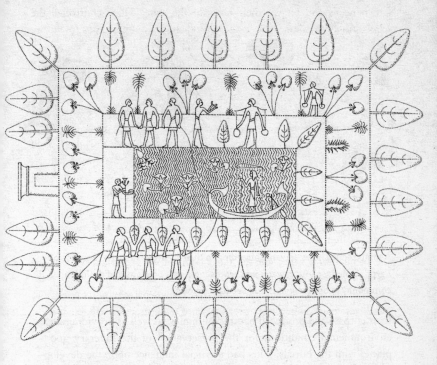

A tomb scene shows men pulling a barque on an ornamental lake in a garden (demonstrating the principles of aspective art). Landscaped gardens usually contained water features and selected trees, shrubs and plants.

was red, and so the Egyptians called this region 'Deshret' (from which our own word 'desert' is derived), meaning the 'Red Land'. According to Egyptian symbolism, red was the colour of danger and death.

These geographical features also had a profoundly practical influence upon the daily customs and funerary practices of the communities. As the available cultivated area was so scarce, its use had to be limited to growing crops, rearing animals and housing the population. There was no spare capacity here for the burial of the dead and so, even in the earliest communities, the dead were interred in shallow graves on the edges of the desert. Here, the heat and dryness of the sand desiccated

A tomb scene shows servants attending to their mistress's toilette. Because of Egypt's hot, dry climate, water was represented as a precious and desirable commodity in both religious and secular contexts.

their corpses and produced natural mummies, as well as providing ideal environmental conditions for the preservation of the funerary goods placed with the burials. This had a crucial influence upon the development of religious beliefs and customs.

THE EMERGENCE OF EGYPTIAN CIVILIZATION

Egyptian civilization lasted over 3,000 years and during that period, although there were changes and developments, there was also a superficial continuity of style in the art, architecture, decoration, funerary customs, religious beliefs, and articles of everyday use. This was underpinned by beliefs and concepts that had been developed in the earliest historical periods and remained unchanged for most of Egypt's history. A visit to look at a collection of Egyptian artifacts in a museum, or to view the ancient monuments in Egypt, confirms the distinctive nature of the civilization – until the Graeco-Roman Period, there is little outward evidence of any impact from other peoples, although Egypt was conquered and ruled by the Hyksos, Assyrians and Persians at different stages of history. However, by the time these foreign rulers arrived, Egyptian culture was so strongly established that the cultural impact of the newcomers was minimal, and instead, foreign elements tended to be absorbed and Egyptianized.

The country was protected from external threat for many centuries during its formative period by natural geographical barriers. Unlike some other contemporary ancient civilizations in the Near East, it was not constantly overrun and conquered. The Delta and the Nile Valley were encompassed by seas and deserts on all sides. The Mediterranean formed the northern border and, although it eventually opened up trading routes for Egypt with countries to the north, it was initially an effective deterrent to invaders.

To the south lay Nubia, which Egypt had effectively controlled since the Old Kingdom so that there was unimpeded access to local commodities such as stone. By the Middle and New Kingdoms, Egypt's military action had established fortresses in the region, to subdue the population and ensure that they could gain possession of the local gold supplies. The area's population adopted Egyptian customs and beliefs, and it was not until Dynasty 25 that this relationship was reversed when the rulers of a Nubian kingdom succeeded in conquering Egypt.

To the west of Egypt lies the Libyan desert with its scattering of oases. The Egyptians traded with the two peoples of this area, the Tjehenyu and Tjemehu, and sent expeditions to quell any minor conflicts. Until Dynasty 20, when there were attempted invasions by coalitions of the Libu and the Sea-peoples, Egypt had little difficulty in controlling this neighbour. One of the oases, the Fayoum, which lies closest to the Nile Valley, played an important part in Egyptian history from early times, and during the Middle Kingdom, it became the seat of royal government and residence. Fed by a tributary of the Nile known today as the Bahr Yusef, the Fayoum is not a true oasis, and it has been much more closely integrated into Egyptian history than the other five western oases.

Egypt was always at its most vulnerable to external attack on its eastern flank. To the south of this area, the Red Sea provided another natural barrier, but across the north of the Sinai peninsula there lay the route which linked Egypt with Palestine. It has been suggested that, if invaders penetrated Egypt around 3400 BCE, they may have taken this means of entry. In later times, the Egyptians sent their own armies in this direction, and conquerors such as the Assyrians, Persians, and Alexander the Great probably entered the Delta along this road. The desert-dwellers who roamed the area also constantly harassed this border.

Without the urgent need to ward off waves of invaders or to contend with the vicissitudes of an unpredictable climate, the Egyptians were able to establish settled communities, produce ample food, and devote considerable time and effort to developing a unique and distinctive civilization. Natural resources such as supplies of stone and raw metals encouraged them to construct monumental buildings, and make fine quality tools, weapons and jewellery. They also had sufficient surplus materials to enable them to trade for commodities which included best quality timber from Syria/Palestine, which Egypt itself lacked.

With their essential requirements satisfied by the natural ample resources of their own country, the Egyptians had sufficient leisure time to speculate about the origin of the universe and the creation of the gods and mankind, and to engage in theorizing about how and where life continued after death. They also had the freedom to devote considerable time to the production of monuments and sacred artifacts to meet their religious requirements. This whole system rested on a relatively stable and well-ordered political structure that centred around the concept of divine kingship.

HOW WE CONSTRUCT THE HISTORICAL CONTEXT

An Egyptian priest, Manetho (323–245 BCE), compiled a chronicle of Egyptian kings between c.3100 and 332 BCE, dividing his King-list into dynasties. Although Manetho's records are sometimes unreliable and inaccurate (and have only survived in the writings of later historians), nevertheless Egyptologists have accepted his division of reigns into thirty dynasties (plus a thirty-first dynasty added by a later chronographer). Essentially, the chronology of ancient Egypt that is used today is based on the record of Manetho.

In modern histories, these dynasties are grouped together in major historical periods which include the Archaic Period (Dynasties 1 and 2, c.3100 – c.2686 BCE), the Old Kingdom (Dynasties 3 to 6, c.2686 – c.2181 BCE), the First Intermediate Period (Dynasties 7 to 11, c.2181–1991 BCE), the Middle Kingdom (Dynasty 12, 1991–1786 BCE), the Second Intermediate Period (Dynasties 13 to 17, 1786–1567 BCE), the New Kingdom (Dynasties 18 to 20, 1567–1085 BCE), the Third Intermediate Period (Dynasties 21 to 25, 1085–668 BCE), and the Late Period (Dynasties 26 to 31, 664–332 BCE).

In 332 BCE, Alexander the Great of Macedon conquered Egypt. The country was subsequently ruled by a line of Macedonian Greeks known as the Ptolemies, who were the descendants of Alexander's general Ptolemy (who became King Ptolemy I). With the death of the last of this dynasty, Cleopatra VII, Egypt became part of the Roman Empire in 30 BCE, and was subsequently ruled as a province from Rome. The whole era is often referred to as the 'Graeco-Roman Period'.

Before the establishment of a united kingdom of Egypt in c.3100 BCE and the introduction of dynasties, people lived in a series of scattered communities in the Delta and along the Nile. These communities gradually developed into larger groups and eventually evolved into two kingdoms, one in the north and the other in the south. Today, this whole era (c.5000 – c.3100 BCE) is described as the 'Predynastic Period'.

HOW WE ACQUIRE KNOWLEDGE ABOUT EGYPTIAN RELIGION

The ancient Egyptians have left a rich legacy which, in addition to well-preserved monuments, artifacts, and human remains, also includes an extensive religious and secular literature. All these sources enable us to understand and interpret ideas and concepts that, in some cases, originated over 5,000 years ago. However, there are few uncontested facts in the study of Egyptian civilization: at the best, we can gain only a partial view and comprehension of a civilization that is separated from the modern world by such a timespan, and in many instances, only imprecise conclusions can be drawn. The difficulties posed by the source material include the unevenness and fragmentary nature of the archaeological remains, problems with translation and interpretation of the textual sources, and the effect of individual bias in understanding the evidence.

For example, successive generations of scholars have approached the subject with a range of presuppositions. Early Classical travellers who went to Egypt sometimes suggested fantastic theories to explain monuments such as the pyramids. Later, Christians who encountered the Egyptian civilization in medieval and Renaissance times often interpreted the architecture and beliefs in terms of the Bible.

More recently, scholars have offered different explanations of the 'facts' associated with the Biblical account of the Exodus; similarly, the religious 'revolution' of Akhenaten (Amenhotep IV) has continued to be the subject of lively debate. In the late twentieth century, there was a much greater attempt to assess Egyptian religious beliefs and practices within the context of their own culture rather than to explain them from the historian's own religious or social standpoint, but difficulties of interpretation still remain.

There are four main sources of evidence for Egyptian religion.

The Monuments

Many of the archaeological sites, especially the pyramids, tombs and temples, have survived remarkably well, and have always remained partially visible above ground. They were seen and recorded (although often wrongly interpreted) by travellers who visited Egypt during the Roman Empire and the medieval and Renaissance periods. In addition, since the establishment of Egyptology as an academic discipline some two hundred years ago, excavation has revealed many more sites. There have also been clearing programmes to remove sand, debris and modern dwellings from the tombs and temples which have revealed the interior wall scenes and enabled further study of the accompanying inscriptions to be undertaken. This work has greatly increased current knowledge of the religious uses of these buildings.

However, the evidence that has survived is fragmentary and uneven, partly due to environmental and geographical factors and partly because of the location and specific construction and use of particular buildings within this society. Two main types of archaeological sites have survived. First, there are 'settlement sites' – the villages, towns, cities, and fortresses where people lived – which were situated in the cultivation, close to the crops and animals. Secondly, there are the cemeteries (for which the term *necropolis/necropolises* is often used), which included royal burial places (pyramid complexes and other tombs) and private (nonroyal) tombs or graves for the nobles, officials, craftsmen and peasants.

An abundance of information has survived about these buildings, funerary goods, and the bodies of the dead because of the ideal environmental conditions of these desert burial places. Also, since they were situated well away from the river, the tombs did not suffer damage from the annual Nile flood which sometimes affected the towns and villages. In addition, religious buildings (pyramids, tombs and temples) were largely constructed of stone because they were intended to last 'for eternity', whereas houses, municipal buildings, and military fortifications were mainly constructed of perishable materials such as wood and mudbrick. It was envisaged that they could be readily replaced, and even royal palaces were built in the same way, since it was customary for each ruler to construct a new residence.

There is another factor that has had an impact on the availability of evidence. The environmental and climatic conditions are different in the north and south of Egypt: the hot, dry climate of the south has ensured that archaeological sites are better preserved here than in the Delta, and consequently, archaeologists have tended to concentrate on the southern sites, although current interest in the Delta is beginning to address this imbalance.

Nevertheless, because of these variations between burial and settlement sites, there is a marked inequality in the preservation of archaeological evidence. This has produced a somewhat one-sided view of Egyptian civilization, particularly in relation to their religious beliefs and practices.

For example, information about the state religion (as exemplified by the temples) is more extensive than knowledge about people's religious observances in their own homes and communities. Also, it is essential to understand that the Egyptians were not obsessed with death and funerary observances. The preponderance of information relating to their funerary practices merely reflects the imbalance in the preservation of evidence from burial and settlement sites.

Artifacts

In addition to the standing monuments, archaeologists have uncovered a wide range of manmade objects (artifacts) which were either placed in the tombs or left behind by their owners at the domestic sites. The Egyptians believed that people would require many articles for use in their continuing existence after death, and therefore equipped the burials of both rich and poor with a variety of goods.

Some of these – items of everyday use such as pottery, make-up and cosmetic equipment, clothing, jewellery, food and drink, tools, weapons, and toys and games – provide information about their everyday lives, and the advances and developments in technology and craftsmanship. Other items were purely funerary in purpose, and inform us about the beliefs and customs that surrounded death and burial.

By the Middle Kingdom, the democratization of religion resulted in a greatly expanded range and variety of funerary goods for private as well as royal burials. These major items included the coffin or nest of coffins which housed the mummified body and also provided a location for the Coffin Texts (spells inscribed on the sides and lid of the coffin which were intended to assist the passage of the deceased into the next world).

There were also canopic jars which were sometimes housed in a canopic chest. Canopic jars contained the viscera (internal organs) removed from the thoracic and abdominal cavities by the embalmer during the mummification process. These jars are distinguished by lids made to represent the heads of four deities known as the 'Four Sons of Horus', but the use of the term 'canopic' has a somewhat tortuous explanation. The Greeks had given the name of one of their legendary heroes, Canopus, to the Egyptian port of Abukir where, in the later periods, the god Osiris was worshipped in the form of a jar with the head of a god. Because of the tenuous connection between the appearance of these Egyptian lidded funerary vessels and this form of Osiris at Canopus, the term 'canopic' was given to these jars by early European antiquarians.

From the Middle Kingdom onwards, it was customary to place a variety of wooden models in the tombs. These often represented a three-dimensional version of the subject matter which was painted or sculpted in the scenes that decorated the interior walls of the tomb. These included statuettes of the tomb-owner and sometimes other members of his family, servants engaged in food production and preparation, soldiers, musicians, concubines, and animals.

Their main purpose was to provide the deceased owner with adequate and eternal food supplies, military protection if required, and entertainment. His own statuette was included in order that, if his mummified body was damaged or destroyed, the statuette could act on his behalf to receive sustenance from the food offerings placed in the tomb. One special category of model was the *ushabti* (or *shabti*). This word meant 'the answerer', since it was expected that this figurine (represented as a mummiform agricultural worker) would respond to the tomb-owner's requests to undertake menial labouring tasks on his behalf when he entered the kingdom of Osiris (the realm of the dead).

Additionally, model boats were included in the tomb to allow the owner to travel to Abydos, the burial place of the god Osiris, so that the owner could enhance his chances of his own resurrection. All these models were believed to have the innate properties of the originals, including the ability to become full-sized, and, once special rituals had been carried out, it was expected that they would be able to serve the owner in his afterlife.

The body of the deceased was mummified in order that the owner's spirit would have a locus to which it could return on earth, allowing it to derive sustenance from the food offerings and menu inscribed on the tomb walls. Within the layers of linen bandaging that enclosed the mummy, the embalmers placed artifacts which endowed the owner with magical powers, and sometimes gave additional physical protection to parts of the mummy. These included a face mask (often made of cartonnage, a mixture of gum and linen or papyrus) which protected the face and also provided another locus for the spirit if the mummy or statuette were destroyed. In the Graeco-Roman Period, these masks which carried stylized representations of the human face were replaced with portraits painted on thin wooden panels. In many cases, these seem to have provided true likenesses of the individuals when alive. Cartonnage chest and foot covers were also placed beneath the bandages in order to give special protection to those areas of the body.

Between the layers of linen, the embalmers inserted sacred jewellery (amulets), which were intended to provide magical and spiritual protection for the owner during his passage to the next world. The shapes, design, and materials of these pieces all had an important symbolism: they represented gods, sacred signs, and parts of the human body which would attract good influences to help the deceased and ward off evil influences. One special category of amulet – the scarab – represented the dung-beetle, a creature which was believed to constantly regenerate itself, and thus came to symbolize eternal renewal of life.

The tomb contents provide a wealth of information about funerary beliefs and customs and also about the contemporary daily life. However, the religious practices which people observed in their everyday lives are less well represented by the artifacts, although altars, offering stands, stelae (inscribed stones) and statuettes of deities have been discovered in domestic contexts.

Literary Sources

We have a more profound understanding of Egyptian civilization than of many other early societies because, in addition to the archaeological evidence, there is an extensive secular and religious literature. From this, we can gain insight into their ideas, thoughts and beliefs. Written sources that can be translated and understood exist from the beginning of the historical period (c.3100 BCE); texts from the earlier (Predynastic) periods have eluded full interpretation although sometimes it has been possible to explain some aspects of the Predynastic culture by extrapolating information from the written evidence of later times.

The main sources which supply information about their religious beliefs include Egyptian texts inscribed on papyri, stelae, ostraca (pottery sherds or limestone flakes), writing boards, and tomb and temple walls, and also the accounts written by Egyptian and Classical authors. However, even the most conscientious Classical authors sometimes reached ludicrous conclusions about the significance and meaning of monuments; for example, the pyramids were variously identified as Joseph's granaries, astronomical structures, and royal burial places.

In earlier centuries, a major impediment in attempting to understand Egyptian civilization has been scholars' inability to read and translate Egyptian Hieroglyphs. This knowledge had been lost by the latter part of the Graeco-Roman Period, and Hieroglyphs came to be regarded merely as magical symbols rather than as a writing system which was designed to convey the syntax, grammar and vocabulary of a language that had been spoken for over 3,000 years.

This totally erroneous concept was first promoted by Classical writers, but since European travellers and scholars who visited Egypt in medieval and Renaissance times still relied substantially on the Classical accounts, most of them continued to accept and promote this idea. Their adherence to this belief considerably impeded attempts to decipher Hieroglyphs in a logical and accurate manner.

The breakthrough in decipherment was finally achieved by the French scholar Champollion in the early nineteenth century, and this finally enabled Egyptologists to understand and translate the texts. Once they could do this, they soon revised the earlier belief that Egypt was an awesome but mysterious civilization that had produced vast monuments, strange art forms and quaint religious beliefs and customs. As knowledge of Hieroglyphs, and of the related scripts of Hieratic and Demotic, increased, it became possible to translate most texts, and a rich literary tradition was revealed. However, particularly with regard to religious texts, even today there are some areas of translation and interpretation that still remain a matter of discussion and debate.

The value of the literary sources is that they can amplify the archaeological evidence and sometimes they can even offer a different perspective. At best, archaeology can only provide a limited and sometimes unbalanced view of a society, whereas literary sources give us direct access to its ideas, beliefs, wit, humour, joys and sorrows. Occasionally, the literature presents a viewpoint that appears to be almost diametrically opposed to the material evidence.

For example, the archaeological finds from Egypt give the impression that a belief in a continued existence after death was universal and unchallenged. To achieve this end, the society allocated considerable human and material resources. However, some of the texts indicate that, in times of social upheaval and collapse, some people questioned this certainty. Despite elaborate and expensive funerary preparations, some literary sources posed a question about man's immortality, stating that no one had actually returned from the realm of the dead to confirm the reality of survival. In view of this, they indicated that it was preferable to enjoy the pleasures of life while they were available.

There are several ancient *Histories* that have contributed to the modern understanding of the chronology and history of Egypt. The most important of these is the work of Manetho, an Egyptian priest in the temple of Sebennytos in the Delta. His knowledge of Egyptian Hieroglyphs and Greek, and his firsthand experience of religious beliefs and customs, provided him with the requisite skills and information to write a number of books that covered a range of subjects including religion, rituals and festivals. However, his most important work, the *Aegyptiaca* (*History of Egypt*), was a chronicle of the Egyptian kings, written in Greek in the reign of Ptolemy II.

As a priest, Manetho had access to the original lists and registers compiled by the priests and kept in the temples, which he was able to use as the basis for his book. Unfortunately, there is no extant, complete account of the *Aegyptiaca*; it is only preserved in edited extracts in the writings of the Jewish historian Flavius Josephus (*c.*70 ACE), and in an abridged form in the works of the Christian chronographer Africanus (*c.*220 ACE), and the Christian writers Eusebius (*c.*320 ACE) and Syncellus (*c.*800 ACE) who included a partial record of Manetho's writings in his book *History of the World from Creation to Diocletian*. Unfortunately, the details recounted by Eusebius and Africanus are often at variance, and so Manetho cannot be regarded as an accurate source in all areas. In addition to preserving the work of Manetho, Josephus also commented on the Hyksos, Joseph, Moses and the Exodus.

Apart from Manetho's history, the ancient Egyptian King-lists, originally inscribed on the walls of tombs and temples, provide partial or damaged evidence about Egyptian chronology. These include the Turin Canon of Kings (reign of Ramesses II, c.1250 BCE), the Palermo Stone (Dynasty 5), the Table of Abydos (reign of Sethos I, c.1300 BCE), the Table of Karnak (reign of Tuthmosis III, c.1450 BCE), and the Table of Saqqara (reign of Ramesses II). The purpose of these lists was religious and ritual, and they were never intended to be historical records; therefore, unfortunately, they do not preserve a complete and accurate list of rulers. Some have also suffered damage, which has obliterated some of the kings' names.

Classical travellers visited Egypt in large numbers, attracted by a civilization that was already over 3,000 years old at the time of the Roman Empire. Some of their accounts, based on firsthand observations, provide a unique view of Egypt. Since they visited Egypt at a time when many of the monuments were still largely intact, and because they saw ancient Egyptian traditions and customs still being practised, their descriptions often provide important information that is not available from other sources.

The most famous of these writers, Herodotus, visited Egypt in c.450 BCE. In his works, he made an unprecedented attempt to distinguish between accurate, historical facts, and fantastic explanations. In his renowned account of the conflict between Greece and Persia, known as *The Histories*,[2] he digresses in Book II to discuss Egypt and its civilization. This account of the country's history and geography provides the first extant comprehensive study by a foreign observer.

Despite some shortcomings and inaccuracies, the book remains a major source for the study of ancient Egypt, particularly where it discusses mummification and some aspects of religion. In later times, European travellers used Herodotus as their major authority on ancient Egypt, and his work was the inspiration for other Classical writers such as Diodorus Siculus who visited Egypt in 59 BCE. Diodorus Siculus used his own firsthand experience as well as information provided by earlier Classical writers to discuss ancient Egypt in the first of twelve volumes which comprised his *Universal History*.

The geographer Strabo wrote a short work about the geography of Egypt. This was the last of seventeen volumes of his *Geographia*, which presented a mass of facts about the Roman world in which he lived. He accompanied his friend, the Roman Prefect Aelius Gallus, on a visit to Egypt in 25/24 BCE when he probably travelled as far as the First Cataract. His book included a topographic list of ninety-nine towns and settlements, as well as a description of the country's natural resources. He recounted information about the pyramids, tombs and temples and commented on religious cults. He also famously described the Colossi of Memnon, two massive statues in the Theban plain which had once flanked the temple of Amenhotep III, and commented on the 'wonder' of the northernmost statue which was reputed to 'sing' at dawn.

Another writer, Pliny the Elder (23-79 ACE), also discussed Egypt in his *Historia Naturalis*, which provided one of the earliest Classical descriptions of the Great Sphinx at Giza. The Greek author Plutarch (*c*.50-120 ACE) supplies a different type of information about Egyptian religion. In his *Moralia*, he concentrates on one aspect of the subject, and today this provides the most complete extant version of the Egyptian myth of Osiris and Isis (*De Iside et Osiride*).

Although there are references to the myth elsewhere in Egyptian texts found on the walls of tombs and temples, no extant, complete account of the story survives in the Egyptian language. Therefore, although Plutarch's version may provide a Greek rather than a purely Egyptian account, it probably represents a fairly accurate outline of the myth. Medieval and Renaissance scholars used it as a unique source for the study of Egyptian religious beliefs.

The ancient Egyptians have also bequeathed us a wealth of *Religious Texts* that developed over some 3,000 years. The main groups (which will be discussed in much greater detail in subsequent chapters) include *Funerary Texts*, which took the form of a series of spells or utterances, designed to ensure individual survival in the afterlife; *Myths*, which attempted to explain the creation of the universe and the role of the gods; *Wisdom Literature*, which provided young scholars with instruction in morals and ethics; *Pessimistic Literature*, which questioned the Egyptians' belief in survival after death; *Temple Inscriptions*, which preserve details of the ritual and other uses of the temples; the *Aten Hymns*, which provide information about the Amarna 'heresy'; and texts which illuminate personal religious beliefs and the application of magic within medicine and other contexts.

The earliest examples of writing (Hieroglyphs) are found in religious contexts. In addition to providing a written version of the Egyptian language, it was believed that Hieroglyphs could be used to bring concepts or events into existence, through the agency of magic. The hieroglyphic forms are themselves visually attractive, often depicting the natural beauty of Egypt's flora and fauna, and they were usually drawn or sculpted with great skill.

However, the essential purpose of writing was not decorative since texts were frequently inscribed in places within the tombs and on funerary goods where they would not be visible once the burial was sealed. Similarly, although the cursive forms of the script, known as Hieratic and Demotic, were widely used for secular and commercial purposes, the intrinsic religious value of writing was never ignored; the act of writing, regarded as a spiritual function, was always expected to benefit the scribe and the recipient of the text.

With regard to the *Funerary Texts*, the earliest examples can be traced to the Old Kingdom. Towards the end of this period (Dynasties 5 and 6), when the pyramids were reduced in size and quality, the kings introduced sets of spells into their burials, perhaps to provide an alternative means by which they could secure their tombs and gain access to heaven where they would be received and accepted by the gods. These magical texts were inscribed on the interior walls of the pyramids of Dynasties 5, 6, and 7 at Saqqara. Known today as the Pyramid Texts, they form the world's oldest substantial body of religious writings. It is probable that the Pyramid Texts were intended exclusively for royal use, to ensure that the king would attain individual immortality.

However, in the Middle Kingdom, when democratization of religious and funerary beliefs occurred, other spells were developed for the use of non-royal owners. Inscribed on coffins, these are known today as 'Coffin Texts'. Again, they were designed to assist the owner with a safe passage into the next world, and to ensure his immortality and continued well-being in the realm of the dead. During the New Kingdom, the function of the Pyramid Texts and the Coffin Texts was largely replaced by the so-called 'Funerary Books'. The Egyptians entitled the most famous of these, known today as the 'Book of the Dead', as the 'Book of Coming Forth by Day'.

The spells contained in these books provided magical measures to ensure the resurrection of the deceased and his safety in the next world. They were also associated with the rituals enacted at the burial and in the subsequent mortuary cult performed for the deceased owner. Scenes and inscriptions from the books provided the subject matter for the wall scenes inside the rock-cut tombs of this period. In non-royal burials, the owner was supplied with a papyrus roll inscribed with the Book of the Dead which protected him on his difficult journey into the next world. The inscribed papyrus scroll was a much cheaper version of the earlier Pyramid and Coffin Texts, which now made these religious privileges and benefits available to many more people.

Other texts first introduced into the non-royal tombs of nobles and officials in the Old Kingdom were intended to protect the status of the deceased owner in the next world, and provide him with an eternal food supply. The Autobiography recorded the owner's rank, titles and family connections, and also summarized his various virtues, to ensure that he enjoyed an equal status in the next world. The Offering List requested food and other requirements for the deceased, through the agency of the god Anubis or the king's bounty, and provided an eternal and indestructible source of sustenance in the form of a written menu.

Egyptian literature also contains a wealth of *Myths*, of which some of the oldest and most significant are the cosmogonies (Creation Myths). The Egyptians believed that the creation of the universe had been brought about through divine thought and speech. Some religious centres had powerful priesthoods who, in the Old Kingdom, promoted the cults of their own gods and developed individual theologies. Each of these included a mythological explanation of the role of the cult-centre's chief god in creating the universe, other deities, and mankind.

The most important of these cosmogonies flourished at Heliopolis, Memphis, Hermopolis and, in the New Kingdom, at Thebes. They explained the origin of the universe and outlined the means by which creation was thought to have occurred. Other important myths are centred round the sun-god Re, and the life, death and resurrection of Osiris.

The *Wisdom Literature* was a major genre first developed in the Old Kingdom and continued until the Late Period. It provides the earliest written evidence of a code of morals and ethics. These 'Instructions in Wisdom' were authorized by the gods. In the Old and Middle Kingdoms, they were usually couched as an address by a king, vizier or great sage to his charges – young boys of upper-class families who trained as future courtiers and officials. In later times, when the Instructions were also used for educating middle-class children, they were presented as advice given by a father to his son. The texts give a detailed account of how people were expected to act and gain advancement in society, and emphasized the importance of kindness, moderation, good judgement and polite behaviour in other people's homes and at the table.

Egyptologists use the term *'Pessimistic Literature'* for a series of texts that express an attitude towards life and death which appears to be at variance with the archaeological evidence. Whereas confidence in eternal life is expressed in the funerary monuments and burial goods, these texts question the certainty of an individual immortality. Some describe appalling social and economic conditions (which perhaps existed during the First Intermediate Period), and one text is a unique example of an individual's reaction to personal problems and the unbearable general circumstances of the country. Some of the funerary hymns that formed part of the burial service during the Middle and New Kingdoms are also included here.

In the great temple complexes, particularly of the New Kingdom and Graeco-Roman Periods, there is a wealth of inscriptional evidence about the rituals that were once performed there. Scenes and accompanying texts on the walls of these buildings depict not only the regular rituals offered to the gods and kings, but also the divine festivals, coronation of the ruler, and temple foundation and consecration ceremonies. In addition, there are scenes showing the king's great military victories. Some wall inscriptions include the hymns that were sung during the rituals and festivals.

During one reign – that of King Akhenaten – there was a break with traditional religion, and hymns inscribed on the walls of courtiers' tombs at Akhetaten (Amarna), the new capital city built by Akhenaten, have preserved some details of the doctrine and worship of the Aten, the god honoured exclusively during this period. Although these incorporated ideas which occurred in earlier hymns to other gods, they also express the uniquely monotheistic aspects of the Aten cult.

Inscriptional evidence about personal religion is relatively scarce, but a unique set of votive hymns, found mainly on stelae from the royal necropolis workmen's village at Deir el-Medina, preserves information about personal piety, humility, and the concept of divine retribution and salvation.

Magic also played a significant role, not only in ensuring the survival of the king and state but also in allowing people to achieve particular goals. One important source, the Medical Papyri, indicates that patients sought treatment by both 'rational' and 'magical' methods.

Most of the above religious texts are preserved on funerary monuments, temples, burial goods, stelae or papyri. One important group of papyri, the Schoolboy Exercises from the New Kingdom, sometimes provide the only extant copies of earlier works. These exercises were designed to improve the literary and ethical standards of the pupils. The models chosen for them to copy included classical texts such as the Wisdom Instructions, prayers, and hymns to the gods, but additionally, their tutors introduced model letters. This new form, which represented a correspondence between teachers and pupils, provided the instructors with an opportunity to extol educational and moral values.

Mummies

Since the mid-nineteenth century ACE, the scientific study of Egyptian mummified human[3] and animal[4] remains has added considerably to our knowledge of mummification techniques and funerary practices, as well as disease patterns, diet, and familial relationships. From the Renaissance Period (sixteenth–seventeenth centuries ACE) onwards, wealthy travellers brought mummies to Europe and America as souvenirs and curiosities, and these were sometimes 'unrolled' for frivolous entertainment in front of the owner's specially invited guests. There were, however, a few serious researchers who sought information about the mummification process and ancient funerary customs.

One of these pioneers, the surgeon Thomas Joseph Pettigrew (1791–1865 ACE), unrolled and investigated many mummies. His demonstrations were performed at various London venues, in front of titled, medical, scientific and literary audiences, and his meticulously observed procedures and findings were published in 1842 ACE, in his work entitled *History of Egyptian Mummies and an Account of the Worship and Embalming of Sacred Animals*.

Another early, significant account was published in 1828 ACE, by the members of the Leeds Philosophical and Literary Society. In 1824 ACE, they had acquired a mummy from Henry Salt, the British Consul-General in Egypt, which, with a specially assembled team, they subsequently autopsied and studied. Other pioneering work was carried out by Grafton Elliot Smith (1871–1937 ACE), Professor of Anatomy in the Cairo School of Medicine. He undertook a scientific study of thousands of human remains discovered during the Archaeological Survey of Nubia,[5] and also the collection of royal mummies in the Cairo Museum.[6] From this work, he was able to make the first comprehensive and scientific contribution to the study of mummification, and to identify the main stages in this procedure.[7] Another major project was undertaken by the research team at the University of Manchester, led by Dr Margaret Murray, which in 1908 ACE unwrapped and autopsied two of the mummies in the University Museum's collection.[8]

These early investigations were important because they established that mummies could be studied scientifically instead of merely being 'unrolled' as curiosities; also, they demonstrated that this work could reveal evidence about disease, living conditions, and funerary beliefs. Subsequently, other scientists and scholars built on this foundation, and there have been radiological surveys of the royal mummies in the Cairo Museum, and detailed investigations of individual rulers, including Ramesses II,[9] Tutankhamun,[10] and the body found in Tomb 55[11] at Thebes (Luxor). Studies of mummies have been greatly facilitated in the twentieth century ACE because of the expertise which various multidisciplinary teams have developed, and because they now have access to a wide range of medical and scientific techniques; in addition, excavation has provided these scientists with a greatly expanded source of human and animal mummies on which to carry out their investigations.

Since 1973 ACE, one team, the Manchester Egyptian Mummy Research Project, has pioneered and developed a methodology for examining mummified remains that has been adopted by many other workers.[12] One of the main aims of this project has been to discover evidence from the mummies about disease, diet, and funerary practices. Various techniques have been employed to detect disease: samples of tissue taken from inside the mummies, using the virtually non-destructive method of endoscopy, have been examined histologically, in order to study the microscopic structure of the tissue and identify any evidence of disease. Immunohistochemistry and electron microscopy have provided additional tools for this work, by greatly enhancing the opportunity to identify cell constituents, and allowing the histologist to visualize a much greater resolution of the detailed structure of the cells in the sample or specimen.[13]

In 1995 ACE, the Manchester team established a joint project with the Egyptian Ministry of Health in Cairo, to construct the epidemiologic profile of one particular disease, schistosomiasis, by comparing its pattern in ancient and modern times. In order to obtain a wide range of samples for this study, the world's first International Ancient Egyptian Mummy Tissue Bank has been set up at Manchester to be used as a major resource for studies on this and other diseases. One particlcuar technique – immunocytochemistry – has been developed and used for the first time as a diagnostic tool to detect whether schistosomiasis is present in these minute samples of mummified tissue.

Dental studies have also been carried out on various collections of complete mummies, mummified heads, and dry skulls. These have provided interesting evidence about disease and diet. It has been possible to demonstrate that the flour used for making the bread contained many impurities (including sand and fragments of the querns) that caused attrition of the cusps of the teeth – a common condition found in ancient Egyptian dentitions.

Other techniques have been employed in an attempt to establish familial relationships in pairs or groups of mummies. Palaeoserology (the study of blood groups in ancient human remains) has achieved limited success in this area; however, this technique has its problems and limitations, and it has now largely been replaced by DNA identification. It was pioneering work in the mid-1980s ACE that first enabled DNA to be identified in mummies, and this procedure can now sometimes be used to confirm or refute proposed familial relationships between specific mummies. In future, there may be the opportunity to explore population origins and migrations, and in terms of disease studies, it may be possible to identify viral, bacterial and parasite DNA in mummies, thus revealing the presence of parasitic or hitherto undetected infectious diseases.

Mummies have also been specifically examined to augment knowledge about religious and funerary customs, and the mummification procedure itself. Scientific studies have been undertaken to investigate the use of natron as a dehydrating agent in mummification, and radiology has been employed to examine the bodies and their associated funerary artifacts. Laboratory experiments on the carcasses of pigeons, chickens, rats and mice have helped to validate the account of mummification given in the writings of Herodotus.[14] This research has also indicated that high levels of impurities in the natron samples, the use of fresh or recycled natron, and the optimum period of time required for mummification are all factors that may have affected the varying results achieved in different mummies.[15]

Radiology – a totally non-destructive technique – has been widely used in the investigation of mummies. It provides a means not only of studying disease in the skeleton and any remaining soft tissue, but also supplies evidence of archaeological features associated with the mummy, indicating how each mummy relates to its historical and cultural context. The radiographs can indicate if resin or natron (natural substances used in mummification) are present, and can demonstrate if amulets (sacred jewellery) have been placed between the bandages that encase the mummy. Also, other details, such as an embalmer's restorations (false limbs, false eyes, or subcutaneous packing to enhance the rounded, bodily shape of the mummy), may be detected, and it is usually possible to determine if the abdominal and thoracic cavities have been eviscerated and subsequently filled either with linen packages or the returned, mummified viscera.

Other scientific studies have included projects on the textiles associated with the mummies: the bandages have been examined, and thin layer and gas liquid chromatography have been used to isolate and characterize the substances applied to the bandages during the mummification process. These have shown that the Egyptians used different qualities of linen for the wrappings, and that these were impregnated with a variety of substances, including resin, galbanum and beeswax. Also, investigation of plants and plant remains discovered inside the mummies have shown that, although they probably had little effect in helping to preserve the body, they may have obliterated some of the odours associated with mummification, and possibly delayed insect attack on the body.

Generally, scientific studies on the mummies add new information to existing knowledge of ancient Egypt. Sometimes, archaeological or literary evidence may present a biased or incomplete picture of life in ancient Egypt, but the physical facts provided by scientific studies can give a more balanced viewpoint, and can help to rectify the idealized and glamorized version of the Egyptians' lives that is often given in modern interpretations of the civilization.

This book will attempt to show how all these sources of evidence can be combined to illustrate the lives, and religious beliefs and customs of the Egyptians. Even with this wealth of evidence, however, it is difficult – and perhaps ultimately impossible – to understand the motives and concepts which drove and formed the religious beliefs and principles of people who are separated from us by a timespan of thousands of years, and whose ideas are conveyed to us through the complexities of a very different language system.

There is no one way in which to approach the subject of Egyptian religion: some studies have adopted a thematic scheme, concentrating on specific subject areas such as the gods, mythology, funerary customs, pyramids, temples and so forth, whereas others have provided an in-depth account of a particular deity. Each method has its advantages and drawbacks, but in this book, the subject is considered within a chronological framework, demonstrating how the various concepts, beliefs and practices emerged and continued over some five thousand years. In this way, it is possible to show how religion was an integrated part of the historical and political system of ancient Egypt, but by adopting this linear approach to describe and discuss the religion, it becomes apparent that there was not any true progression from a 'primitive' to a more sophisticated set of beliefs. Most of the main concepts were already established in the Old Kingdom, although democratization of religion in the Middle Kingdom, making individual immortality universally available, and a brief interlude of monotheism during the Amarna Period, were later major developments. Even the arrival of the Greeks and Romans, and the profound political and social changes which accompanied their rulership, did not substantially affect the religious customs of the indigenous Egyptians. In fact, these foreign dynasts chose to support Egyptian religion, in order to confirm themselves as pharaohs, and it was not until the advent of Christianity, and subsequently of Islam, that the ancient gods and cults were finally set aside.

The Emergence of Religion

Predynastic and Early Dynastic Periods, *c*.5000–2686 BCE

THE DISCOVERY OF PREDYNASTIC EGYPT

The Predynastic Period is a term that Egyptologists use to define the time-span between *c*.5000 and *c*.3100 BCE when King Menes united the two kingdoms in the north and the south and established Dynasty 1 and the beginning of Dynastic Egypt. According to the Egyptian writer Manetho, the unification brought to an end a period of rule by a line of gods, succeeded by several demi-gods (known as the Followers of Horus). It is probable that the Followers of Horus were the rulers of the predynastic kingdoms whose capitals were respectively located at Buto and Hieraconpolis. However, later generations of Egyptians evidently retained no historical knowledge of the origin of their history and culture, and chose to explain them in mythological terms.

During the Predynastic Period, climatic changes, when the floor of the Nile Valley became drier, made it possible for neolithic communities to settle in the Delta and the Nile Valley. It was the discovery of several sites in Egypt during the late nineteenth and early twentieth centuries

ACE that first revealed the existence of the predynastic cultures, and indicated that there were scattered communities which fell into two geographical groups, one in the Delta (Lower Egypt) and one in the Nile Valley (Upper Egypt). The social and political organization of these communities appears to have had some features in common, although the lack of translatable written evidence limits our interpretation of the archaeological discoveries.

However, it can be deduced that they practised mixed farming, cultivating their land and domesticating their animals; they produced pottery, domestic articles, and tools and weapons; and they have left evidence of religious beliefs and customs, including funerary preparations, which indicate a reverence for the dead and perhaps a belief in a continued individual existence after death. However, even the length of the Predynastic Period remains uncertain. For example, the archaeologist who discovered predynastic Egypt, Sir William Flinders Petrie, assessed that it lasted from c.9000 down to 4326 BCE (his date for the unification of the Two Lands), whereas another estimate has placed all the predynastic cultures within a time-span of a thousand years.

Also, it is only in Upper Egypt that a well-established chronological sequence can be traced, culminating in Dynasty I, which archaeologists have divided into several periods known as Tasian, Badarian, Naqada I and Naqada II. The Badarian, Naqada I and Naqada II periods are quite distinctive, but some scholars do not believe that it is possible to differentiate between the Tasian and Badarian because excavation of the village and cemetery sites at Deir Tasa and Badari (after which the periods are named), which lie near each other, have both revealed objects which cannot be readily distinguished from each other, although the Tasian pottery and other objects appear to be less sophisticated and there is a total absence of metal goods.

A major difficulty has been to assess whether the various communities formed part of an overall culture or whether there were distinct local variations. Generally, it seems that there was not a uniform culture across the communities of the north and south, but questions such as whether the two groups came from different racial backgrounds and which culture is earlier continue to be the subject of discussion. The evidence is often confusing, but some tentative conclusions can be drawn.

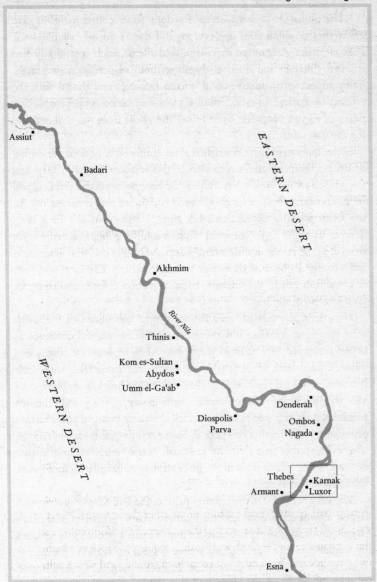

Map of Upper Egypt (North)

There must have been some freedom from constant fighting to allow these communities to develop, and they evidently shared some characteristics. Organized as village settlements, each community had its own chieftain and lived in dwellings built of perishable materials. They supported themselves with mixed farming, and traded with the African hinterland for ivory, while they also obtained copper from areas north of Egypt, turquoise from Sinai, and shells from the Red Sea and the Persian Gulf.

Some important cities flourished even at this early period: the capital of the northern kingdom consisted of the adjacent towns of Dep and Pe, while Sais and Heliopolis – cities that became important political and religious centres in later times – already had flourishing communities. In the south, an early capital existed at Nubt, a name that may have been derived from the Egyptian word 'Nub' meaning 'gold'. Situated not far from the gold mines in the eastern desert, Nubt was probably important and prosperous because of its role as a gold centre. The local god Seth is sometimes called 'the Ombite' because Nubt was later known by its Greek name of Ombos.

Generally, the climatic and environmental conditions of the south were more favourable, and therefore the archaeological evidence is better preserved here than in the north. Also, because the towns and villages were built of perishable materials, the cemeteries with their human and animal remains, together with associated grave foods, provide the richest information about contemporary history and religious practices. As mentioned previously, lack of written material poses further problems in interpreting this period. However, despite these limitations, it is evident that many of the political, social, religious and artistic developments, which formed the basis of the civilization in later times, were already emerging.

The very existence of the cultures prior to the Old Kingdom remained largely unsuspected until about a hundred years ago, when Manetho's largely mythological explanation of Egypt's earliest periods was replaced by factual evidence provided by archaeological excavations. In 1894–5 ACE, the British Egyptologists W. M. F. Petrie and J. E. Quibell started to excavate cemeteries near the modern village of Naqada in southern

Egypt where they discovered evidence that was very different from the material found elsewhere which belonged to the dynastic era.

At first, the excavators concluded that these remains were not Egyptian in origin and attributed them to the advent of a 'new race' who could have arrived in the First Intermediate Period (*c.*2200 BCE), when internal chaos and disruption would have made the country vulnerable to incursions by foreigners. However, the French archaeologist J. de Morgan had found evidence of similar burials at other southern sites and he disputed Petrie's theory. Eventually, Petrie was persuaded that his own interpretation was wrong, and was forced to accept de Morgan's conclusion that in fact the cemeteries were indigenous in origin and belonged to the last two cultures of the Predynastic Period.

SEQUENCE DATING

Once he had recognized their significance, Petrie undertook pioneering studies on these predynastic cultures that enabled the foundation of Egyptian civilization to be revealed for the first time. One of his great contributions to the whole field of Egyptology was the introduction of a system he called Sequence Dating (SD). This is a method of relative dating for excavated material that is based on a comparison of groups of a particular type of pottery found in a series of graves which he excavated at a number of sites. This pottery (known as 'wavy-handled') showed a particular sequence of developments with regard to the form of the handles, and Petrie gave a Sequence Dating number to each stage of the pottery's development. Other types of objects discovered in association with the wavy-handled pots in the burials were then placed sequentially within the system, and finally, each tomb-group was allocated a place within the overall scheme, based on the evidence of the SD numbers of all the objects within each tomb-group.'

THE PREDYNASTIC CULTURES

Petrie divided the predynastic cultures into three groups, which he classified as Amratian, Gerzean and Semainian – terms which he derived from the names of modern villages near to his excavation sites. Today, these have been replaced by other terms: Badarian, Naqada I and Naqada II. The Badarian Period (named after the modern village of el-Badari where important excavations were undertaken) defines the earliest identified predynastic culture, while the terms Naqada I and Naqada II have replaced Petrie's Amratian and Gerzean periods (Amratian-type objects were only found at the site of el-Amra, and Gerzean products were only found at Gerza, whereas objects of both types were discovered at Naqada). The term 'Semainian' is now only used for the earliest dynasties.

The pattern of development and progress at the various sites appears to vary considerably. Clearly, the periods were not entirely distinct from each other and there is evidence that there was cultural evolution from one stage to the next. Between the Badarian and Naqada I periods (c.5000 – c.3400 BCE), there is no indication of a well-defined cultural break. However, there were major innovations introduced at the start of Naqada II (c.3400 BCE), when the evidence of painted pottery and metalwork indicates that there was increased contact with other areas of the Near East. At the same time, the apparent first evidence of writing and monumental brick architecture, together with changes in burial customs and advances in arts and crafts, led Petrie to explain these developments in terms of the arrival in Egypt of a hypothetical, racially distinct group of foreign invaders whom he termed the 'Dynastic Race'.

The 'Dynastic Race'

Some writers[2] now regard this theory as untenable, but it has been widely discussed.[3] At a certain stage (c.3400 BCE), developments occurred in Egypt which Petrie and his supporters claimed were without direct precedent there. They argued that the Dynastic Race could have brought these new ideas and advanced technology into Egypt from an area where such ideas already flourished. One possible place is Mesopotamia, either as the original homeland of the Dynastic Race or as a stage on their journey, perhaps from Syria, Iran, or an as yet undiscovered location that ultimately influenced both Egypt and Mesopotamia.

At this period, Mesopotamia (the 'Land between Two Rivers', the Tigris and the Euphrates) occupied an area roughly equivalent to modern Iraq and was inhabited by the Sumerians. They lived in scattered city-states but nevertheless shared a culture that already included the use of writing and monumental brick architecture. Cuneiform writing predates any known examples of hieroglyphic texts found in Egypt, but this could be due to the difference in the writing materials which the two peoples employed: early examples of cuneiform were inscribed on clay tablets whereas hieroglyphs were usually written on papyrus or wood, so this may explain why the cuneiform texts have survived from earlier times. However, the two languages are very different in appearance and grammatical structure, although both are derived from pictographs. Even if a link could be proved, it would probably only indicate a transfer of the concept of writing because, even if the two languages ever had any association, they evidently diverged at a very early stage.

The burial customs introduced at the commencement of Naqada II provided the leaders of the communities with distinctive, superior burials whereas previously all classes had been buried in simple, shallow graves. Although most of the population continued to build these pit-graves, their leaders were now interred in monumental brick tombs that incorporated a bench-shaped superstructure, decorated with recessed brick panelling on the façade, which housed the burial goods in a series of chambers, and an underground substructure where the body was placed. Because of the shape of the superstructure, these are now called *mastaba* tombs, from the Arabic word for 'bench' or 'bench-shaped'. Brick architecture appeared earlier in Mesopotamia, but there it was used for temples rather than tombs, so again, if there was a link, it was perhaps only the concept that travelled to Egypt.

The new artistic developments included inscribed cylinder seals and stone mace-heads, which occur in both areas (with parallels found in other parts of the world). However, since they are easily transportable, they may have entered Egypt as the result of trading connections. The slate palettes which now appeared in Egypt are perhaps more interesting. Although the concept of the slate palette, which was used at first for grinding and mixing eye make-up and then developed into a ceremonial form, is undoubtedly Egyptian in origin, some examples are carved with figures of composite animals with entwined necks. This motif is not found in earlier or later Egyptian art but may have been derived from forms found in Mesopotamia.

Petrie's theory proposed that this external influence on Egypt came about as the result of an armed conflict, since no parallel evidence of Egyptian culture of this date has ever been discovered in Mesopotamia or any other centre. To support the theory of armed invasion, scholars have often quoted the evidence provided by the Gebel el-Arak knife. The knife has a flint blade and an ivory handle that is carved with scenes that depict some kind of sea-battle between two types of ship, tentatively identified as craft of Mesopotamian and Egyptian origin. These appear to be engaged in some kind of conflict, which perhaps represents an attempted invasion. However, Hassan[4] regards this as a battle between two groups of local Nilotic people, and claims that the ships could be two types of Egyptian craft.

Even if the knife does represent a conflict against foreign invaders, it may depict an isolated instance, and cannot be taken as definitive proof that a horde invasion or major conquest ever occurred. There is no conclusive evidence that a mass of newcomers arrived in Egypt at this time. Even Egyptologists who support the theory of the Dynastic Race have to accept that incomers probably used a variety of routes to enter the country, with some passing across the Red Sea into the Eastern Desert before infiltrating the southern part of the Nile Valley, while others perhaps took the land route from Palestine across the Sinai Peninsula and into the Delta. Again, whereas some may have engaged in armed conflict, others perhaps entered the country as traders.

Claims that the bodies in the two types of Naqada II burials show differences that identify them as distinct racial groups are unproven. Similarly, the proposal that the 'rulers' and 'ruled' of the early Dynastic Period and even the Old Kingdom were direct descendants of these two racial groups, and that the distinction is still evident in the human remains of those later periods, has not yet been confirmed. Today, there are many unanswered questions about this theory that a new race entered Egypt, subdued the indigenous population, imposed their own ideas and concepts, including a two-tiered burial system, and that their descendants eventually became the royalty and nobility of later times.

Instead of attempting to explain these innovations in terms of any external influence, an alternative approach is to regard them as natural developments brought about purely through the efforts of the indigenous population. A general cultural continuity can be demonstrated from the predynastic through to the early dynastic communities, and their economy and political organization developed along lines that could have provided the background against which these dramatic changes occurred. As well as favourable conditions within Egypt that would have fostered this growth and development, it has been argued[5] that Mesopotamia would hardly have been capable of supporting an army or promoting invasion of another country when its own culture was at a formative stage.

Even the proponents of the Dynastic Race theory have had to concede that any foreign incursions must have been discontinued after the beginning of the Dynastic Period. By this time, the architectural innovations of Naqada II had started to develop into the more sophisticated tombs which in turn laid the foundations for the pyramid forms of the Old Kingdom, and artistic motifs such as the composite animals on the slate palettes had already completely disappeared. Also, the forms of the hieroglyphs and the structure of the language, which had emerged by the beginning of Dynasty 1, were distinctively and uniquely Egyptian.

Political and Social Organization

Very little is known about the political and social organization of the Badarian period, except that most people probably lived in scattered village communities. The cemeteries, situated away from the dwellings, provide most information about this period. Evidence about the subsequent Naqada I and Naqada II cultures is derived from the excavation site which lies in the neighbourhood of the modern village of Naqada, between Tukh and el-Ballas. Again, here, most information is derived from the cemeteries rather than the domestic settlement.

As already discussed, during the Naqada II period, profound changes occurred in both cultural and religious areas. These developed against a background of political and social growth, when isolated village communities drew together into larger units. This undoubtedly provided them with greater protection against the intermittent conflicts that must have existed, but almost certainly, the most potent factor was the need to work together in order to harness the annual inundation and irrigate the land. This essential common aim was one of the main forces in unifying the whole country. It required constant diligence and co-operation between the communities along the Nile to make this a successful venture. Each of the larger units had its own capital city, chieftain and deity, and gradually these emerged as even larger coalitions that probably reflected the geographical areas which became the adminis-trative units (*nomes*) in later periods. Finally, two independent kingdoms were formed from these units and these established the political structure of Egypt during the Naqada II period until they were brought together in *c.*3100 BCE with the unification of Egypt.

The two independent kingdoms that emerged were situated in the north and in the south. The northern one – known as the Red Land – was centred in the Delta but extended southwards into the Nile Valley, perhaps as far as Atfih. As a political entity, this was quite distinct from the other 'Red Land' (*Deshret*), a term which described a geographical area. The capital of the Red Land was situated at a Delta site known in modern times as Tell el-Fara'in ('The Mound of the Pharaohs'). It originally consisted of two areas – Pe and Dep – and later, the site was generally known as Buto (derived from the ancient Egyptian name of Per-Wadjet which meant 'The House of Wadjet'). Wadjet (alternative reading Edjo), a cobra-goddess, was the patron deity of the Red Land who spat venom to defend the king against his enemies. The ruler of this land wore the distinctive Red Crown.

The southern realm, the White Land, probably stretched from Atfih to Gebel el-Silsileh, and its capital was at Nekhen (later known as Hieraconpolis), near Edfu. As at Buto, this site consisted of two impor-tant settlements known as Nekhen and Nekheb.[6] Nekhen, on the west

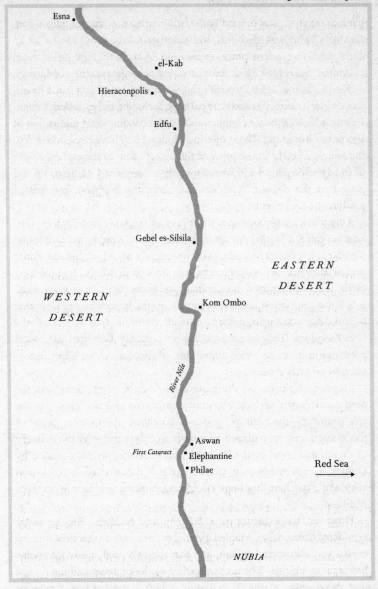

Esna

el-Kab

Hieraconpolis

Edfu

Gebel es-Silsila

EASTERN
DESERT

WESTERN
DESERT

Kom Ombo

River Nile

Aswan
First Cataract
Elephantine
Philae

Red Sea

NUBIA

Map of Upper Egypt (South)

bank of the river, was originally the cult-centre of an ancient falcon-god, Nekheny, who was identified with another falcon deity, Horus, at an early date. In modern times, excavation of the site, now called Kom el-Ahmar, has revealed a temple that contained a great cache of offerings.

Known as the 'Main Deposit', this was found to contain mace-heads, stone vessels, statuettes and slate palettes, including the so-called Narmer Palette which probably commemorated the conquest and unification of Egypt in c.3100 BCE. These offerings appeared to have been donated to the temple in early times; most of the objects date to the earliest reigns of the dynastic period and were probably subsequently gathered up and placed in the deposit. The site also contains extensive remains of predynastic settlements.

One particularly important discovery in the late nineteenth century ACE revealed a brick-built underground tomb. Known as 'Decorated Tomb 100', its exact location has subsequently been lost, but the extant record of its wall-scenes preserves important evidence. A large painting on the west wall depicted men, animals and boats but these were arranged in a loose association and not organized in the horizontal registers that became the standardized form of wall decoration in tombs of the Old Kingdom. This monument, which probably belonged to a local predynastic ruler, provided important information about tomb decoration of an early date.[7]

Opposite Nekhen, on the eastern side of the river, there was the predynastic town of Nekheb, known today as el-Kab. This was the cult-centre of the vulture goddess Nekhbet, the patron deity of the White Land, who played an important role assisting at the delivery of divine and royal births. Nekhen was excavated in 1897–9 ACE by Quibell, Green and Somers Clarke; Quibell also worked at Nekheb in 1897 ACE, but here his hope of finding important evidence was not realized.[8]

However, the excavations at Nekhen and Nekheb were generally significant because they enabled Quibell to demonstrate that the southern capital was a historical reality, and that the two predynastic kingdoms had actually existed. The archaeological evidence disproved the theory that the dualism of the Two Lands, which is retained as a concept throughout the historical period, was simply a fiction, based on the

Egyptians' love of symmetry and balance. The excavations also supported the claim that the two kingdoms had been united by a real historical ruler.

Whereas the northern king wore the Red Crown, the southern ruler had the distinctive White Crown. After the unification of the two kingdoms, the king of Egypt still wore the White and the Red Crowns, either separately on different occasions or in combination as the Double Crown, to signify his power over both areas. Similarly, the two patron goddesses, Wadjet and Nekhbet, became the dual protectresses of Egyptian kingship, while the bee and papyrus plant (symbols of the Red Land) and the sedge (symbol of the White Land) were retained and used to represent the unified kingdom.

There is no doubt that the Red and White Lands were historical realities in predynastic times but, even after Egypt became a united realm, the 'Two Lands' were retained as potent images of balance and unity in art and literature throughout the historic period. The terms 'Lower Egypt' and 'Upper Egypt' are sometimes used for the Red and White Lands, reflecting the fact that the Nile flows from south to north. In modern times, there are still distinct geographical and cultural differences between these areas: the north is now the location for the leading cities of Cairo and Alexandria and, as in antiquity, is affected by more external influences than the south where, hemmed in by the desert, long-established agricultural and traditional customs still prevail.

Religion amongst the Living

Archaeology provides little evidence of the religious organization and worship in the earliest communities. Sacred centres and places of worship, which would have been built of perishable materials, have not been found, but some information can be derived from scenes painted on pottery found in graves of the Naqada II period. Known as 'Decorated Ware', this pottery depicts boats carrying gods' shrines and deities; since some gods appear in more than one place, on pottery found at sites both in the north and south, this indicates that they enjoyed more than merely local significance. Some gods are represented with animal forms, while others are shown as fetishes or symbols.

Evidence from the earliest dynasties and later periods provides depictions of early places of worship, and indicates that statues or symbols of the gods were kept in shrines in the villages during the Predynastic Period. Each deity was probably regarded as a vital and fully integrated part of the local community, and the shrine, built of wood, wickerwork, reeds and mud, would have been a slightly larger version of the people's own dwellings.

This shrine, which protected the deity's image and provided a sacred 'house' where humans could approach the god, formed the basis from which the later stone-built temples developed. Here, the local chieftain probably brought food and perhaps other offerings to the god on behalf of the community, possibly performing this as a regular ritual on a daily basis. Again, this would have foreshadowed the temple rituals of the historic period, in which the king or high priest made offerings to the god's statue in the hope of obtaining divine benefits for the king and his people.

In earliest times, the scattered communities probably had their own localized cults, and each deity was the focus of worship by a discrete population, within a limited geographical area. However, as the political scene changed, and villages joined together to become larger units, the same process (known as 'syncretism') was probably reflected within the sphere of religion.

Local gods gradually evolved to become the deities of larger districts and, as one community conquered or absorbed its neighbours, the victor's god would take over any significant features or characteristics of the deity of the subordinated group. Sometimes, the conquered god probably became an assistant or follower in the mythology of the omnipotent deity or, on other occasions, he disappeared altogether. Some gods thus acquired significant powers, and emerged as chief deities of the nomes (political and geographical units) where, represented by the ensign or symbol of the nome, they protected the chieftain from his enemies.

This amalgamation of the gods presents a confusing picture which shows an apparent expansion of the pantheon, the whole 'family' of gods whom the Egyptians worshipped; it also suggests that people who had once offered their devotions to one local god now had access to a multitude of deities. However, this is probably a distorted view of the situation. The individual worshipper may have still remained loyal to his local god, but some deities appear to have developed additional and more universal roles and powers. This confusing situation was addressed by the Egyptians themselves in the Old Kingdom, when the priesthoods of pre-eminent gods attempted to organize the pantheon either into smaller family groups, or into an *ogdoad* (group of eight gods), or an *ennead* (group of nine gods), each of which had its own mythology and cult centre.

The formative stages of Egyptian religion have received less attention than developments in later times. This is probably because the early evidence is less complete and more difficult to interpret. Archaeological remains, however, indicate that the earliest communities venerated animals, had special locations that were used for rituals, worshipped cult objects, and buried their dead with reverence. Although, today, the remains of their settlement sites are scanty, the burial goods are well preserved and indicate that they had already developed funerary beliefs and customs. Their religious concepts may well have extended beyond this to a belief in a divine being or beings. There have been various theories that have attempted to explain what form their concept of divinity took and how it may have come about.[9]

In some studies of Egyptian religion,[10] it has been suggested that the earliest and most primitive type of worship was fetishism in which a sign or symbol such as a flag or wrapped staff became the cult object. These objects are often enigmatic and cannot always be recognized or explained as human, animal, or natural forms. They were probably manifestations of divine power but it is difficult to gain any further insight into this early conception of divinity. Jéquier suggested that zoolatry (the veneration of deities in animal form) was the second stage in the development of Egyptian religion, and that this was followed by anthropomorphism (the worship of deities in human form). However, although there is some evidence that the fetish and animal forms predated the conceptualization of the divine in terms of human images, there has been much debate regarding whether anthropomorphism was indeed a more advanced form of religious belief that evolved later in Egypt.[11]

Early evidence for the veneration of animals occurs in the animal burials associated with some of the villages of the Badarian Period. These burials most often included gazelles or dogs (or jackals), but cattle and rams were also interred. Buried separately but near to the human graves, the animals were carefully wrapped in linen or matting covers. They provide evidence that there was already a cult of sacred animals or perhaps of the divine powers believed to be present in animal forms. It is unclear why particular animals were venerated, but their qualities of strength, success as hunters and food-gatherers, or usefulness to humans as a food source may have influenced the Egyptians' choice.

In addition to the animal burials, contemporary human burials included animal-shaped amulets (small magical charms); some were perhaps intended to provide a food supply for the deceased which could be activated by means of magic, but others may have been placed in the grave to give the owner the strength and power associated with particular animals. Some slate cosmetic palettes now also had animal forms or decoration; from Naqada I onwards, clay statuettes in the form of animals were placed with human burials, and scenes on Decorated Ware clearly indicate that animal gods were worshipped in different districts throughout the country. Generally, by the end of the Predynastic Period, most divine powers were represented or worshipped in animals' forms, although other images were also found alongside these.

It is uncertain if anthropomorphism started in predynastic times. It has been suggested that some human clay and ivory figures found in Badarian graves, which increase in number in the later Naqada cultures, may have represented gods but, equally, they could be dolls, magic images or votive offerings. It was in the beginning of the dynastic period that a small number of gods first appeared with purely human forms. These existed alongside the much larger group of deities represented entirely as animals. However, towards the end of Dynasty 2, some gods began to incorporate animal heads with human bodies, and although this mixed type never replaced the purely human or animal representations, they added a new form that became the most characteristic way of depicting Egyptian deities.

In his major discussion of the nature of Egyptian gods, Hornung concluded that each god could have several forms that reflected different aspects of his nature and his various attributes and functions. However, the deity's true and complete nature was never fully revealed, but remained 'hidden' and 'unknown', although a variety of body forms allowed the god to inhabit a range of images at different times, so that he could perform a multitude of functions. The visual representations (or indeed the literary descriptions) of the gods do not, therefore, depict or describe the god's complete appearance, but allude to different aspects of his nature and functions.

The forms and dress of the gods were always shown in a fairly uniform manner, providing no indication of the historical date of the figure; the god's individuality or particular function was represented by his distinctive headwear or animal head. A reversed example of the mixture of animal and human features occurs in later periods, in the form of the sphinx, where a human head is placed on an animal body. Whenever animal and human features were united in one body, any details which might appear ludicrous or grotesque, such as the place where the head and the body joined, were masked: in this instance, the neck area was concealed with the lappets of the headdress.

There are no extant literary sources which throw light on either the predynastic practice of zoolatry or anthropomorphism which occurred c.3000 – c.2800 BCE. We can only speculate about the reasons for these developments. As stated previously, some animals may have been deified because they were helpful to mankind, whereas the Egyptians perhaps sought to placate others through acts of worship because they feared them. On the *recto* of the Battlefield Palette (fragments of which are in London and Oxford), where a scene shows defeated enemies on a battlefield, the victors are represented as animal powers. This may provide some insight into the predynastic mind, emphasizing the concept that animals possessed some powers which were far superior to those of men.

This may have formed the Egyptian basis for zoolatry, but by the start of the historic period, people had become more self-aware and had taken control of their own world and circumstances to a much greater extent. This new confidence, inspired by military success, may have prompted the belief that the gods could now be attributed with human as well as animal characteristics, and may have led to the introduction of anthropomorphism.

In this process, some deities originally represented with complete animal forms now acquired animal or bird heads attached to human bodies; others were given completely human forms and were identically clothed (all males wore kilts and females had dresses), but expressed their individuality through the symbols they wore on their heads and other attributes. However, a few deities, such as Ptah of Memphis, always had an entirely human appearance.

Early Gods

Some deities known later in historic times may also have been significant in the Predynastic Period. These include Wadjet and Nekhbet, the goddesses who protected the Two Lands prior to unification, and perhaps some gods who assisted the southern kings in the conquest of the north, including the fertility god Min; Wepwawet, a wolf-god; Anubis, the jackal-god who was noted for protecting the dead in later times; and Thoth, the ibis-headed moon-god who was patron of writing and science in the historic period. The sun-god Re, who had close associations with Horus in the early dynastic period and took over Iwnw (later known by its Greek name of Heliopolis) as his cult-centre from its original owner, Atum, may also have been worshipped in predynastic times.

It has been suggested that some evidence from predynastic graves may indicate that there was an important and widespread cult of a mother-goddess, represented as a cow. For example, there are female figurines that may have been votive offerings to the mother-goddess in request for children, or to beg the goddess for the owner's re-birth in the next world. Again, Decorated Ware pottery has scenes that, according to one interpretation, depict rituals associated with the mother-goddess and a fertility cult, and these may also have been intended to ensure individual immortality. The scenes represent boats, which possibly carry the ensign of the goddess, and also depict a male figure who has tentatively been identified as the goddess's son and lover, a deity known in later times as the 'Bull-of-his-Mother'.

It is possible that these were fertility deities whose union was believed not only to rejuvenate the land, its crops and its people, but also to enhance the chances of individual human rebirth in the afterlife. Some Egyptologists, however, have rejected the idea of an early cult of a mother-goddess and consort, and generally, because information about prehistoric cults is sparse and ambiguous, very few historical deities can be accurately traced back before the Unification.

Cosmic and Local Deities

Early studies of Egyptian religion tended to explain the organization of the gods in simplistic terms. They claimed that there were two distinct, major groups of gods who had existed in predynastic times and continued to be worshipped throughout the historic period; these were described as (1) tribal or local gods, and (2) cosmic gods. They attributed particular geographical centres of worship (cult-centres) to the local gods, and claimed that they had certain physical characteristics, including animal forms. On the other hand, they believed that the cosmic gods represented the forces of nature such as the sun, moon, stars and other elements, which were remote from mankind and yet of universal importance. It was suggested that, although at first they had no cult-centres or physical forms, some cosmic deities later took over the characteristics and cult-centres of local gods whose personae and powers they had absorbed.

It was even proposed that the cosmic gods might have had a different origin from the local gods – possibly being introduced into Egypt by the Dynastic Race – whereas the local gods had always been worshipped by the indigenous population. Possibly, when the newcomers conquered the country, some of their deities may have assimilated the local gods and taken over their centres.

Another interpretation suggested that the indigenous population had originally worshipped both cosmic and local gods but that, because cosmic gods were regarded as remote and inaccessible, their worshippers did not at first give them names and forms. A later fusion of the cosmic and local gods would have enabled the cosmic deities to gain names and attributes. By dynastic times, the cosmic deities had acquired their distinctive forms and were represented with human forms and identifying symbols worn on their heads.

It is now recognized that this approach is too simplistic, and that 'local' and 'cosmic' gods cannot be distinguished and explained in these terms. Hornung's[12] significant exploration of the nature of Egyptian divinity has suggested that there was a 'multiplicity of approaches' and that the whole can only be comprehended through taking all of these into account. Egyptian gods could extend their being endlessly, achieving this through a range of different names, manifestations, and actions, or through combining with other gods. The deity often used various names to express the different facets of his personality or emphasize his special powers, while his presence on earth was made visible through his cult-statue or the animals that represented him; also, he was able to make his will evident through his actions and, by amalgamating some of his characteristics and functions with those of certain other gods, he could use their spheres of influence to reach an even wider audience.

However, simultaneously, the core of an individual god's nature and existence remained limited and distinct from other deities. A god was never a finished entity; he was always in the process of construction, undergoing change and continuing to add new aspects to his nature and experience. In this way, each god could express himself through a confusing multiplicity of forms, each of which was a powerful but limited and imperfect expression of his nature and reality. Important gods hardly ever restricted themselves to one form but changed their manifestations at will; however, the same animal form or object could be used to represent the separate manifestations of several different gods.

The Egyptians carefully distinguished between the image of the god (whether statue or animal) and the god's 'true form', which was only infrequently revealed to mankind. Although this complete and perfect physical manifestation of a god could sometimes be revealed to a worshipper in the next world, this could never happen here on earth, where the divine images and intermediaries could provide only a partial and ultimately unsatisfactory revelation of some aspects of the god's physical attributes and nature.

The earthly images and sacred animals that acted as manifestations of the god served to make the god more accessible to the believer. Thus, in later historical periods, a god might possess different animal forms, and could be worshipped not only through the manifestation of the cult-animal that was sometimes kept at the god's temple, but through all the members of that species. Against this background, the older theories that Egyptian religion developed from fetishism to zoolatry and then to anthropomorphism, or that cosmic and local gods had distinct origins and developed along separate lines, are too simplistic. A more convincing explanation is that gods had different forms and countless images which were present in the environment. At the beginning of their history, the Egyptians may have worshipped some gods in particular locations, but other gods such as Re, Osiris, Ptah and Amun appear to have always had universal powers and to have been unrestricted in terms of any special geographical area or aspects of their nature.

Even from the very earliest times, the nature of the gods and the geography of their worship were complex. Some gods were connected to particular locations, but this was a secondary feature of their cults, and any association with a special place may simply emphasize a facet of the god's nature at one stage in his history and development. The degree of association with one particular geographical area also varies: some gods were closely identified with a town or area whereas others had more tenuous connections.

Earlier theories, which proposed that the identification of a god's original cult-centre would explain his origin and historical importance, have now been largely discounted, and it is recognized that some gods could be universal and transcendent while still retaining strong links with a geographical location; however, other deities never developed their role beyond a local significance. Again, there was a clear distinction drawn between those gods who were truly local, i.e. only worshipped at a particular location, and the local manifestations of great gods which existed to emphasize a special aspect of that deity's nature.

The association between cosmic deities and gods of nature is also difficult to unravel. The natural world that surrounded the ancient Egyptians played an important role in their religious concepts and beliefs, but there are some surprising aspects. For example, there was no god of the Nile, the larger lakes or the sea (until the New Kingdom, when Yamm, a Semitic god, was incorporated into the Egyptian pantheon). Hapy was the god of the inundation, and Khnum was the patron god of a particular area of the river, at the First Cataract. In addition to the lack of a god of 'water', there were no individual deities for the other elements – fire, earth and air. Seth – god of storms, chaos, confusion and evil – joined Shu who represented 'empty space' and Amun who personified 'air in motion' or 'breath of wind', to represent the air, while Geb, Aker and Tatenen ('depths of the earth') personified the Earth. Again surprisingly, there was no specific god of the desert.

Also, some of the main features of the cosmos were not individually deified: 'Night' does not occur as a deity until the Persian Period and only a few significant stars and constellations became gods. There were cults of Sothis and Orion, but generally planets were regarded as manifestations of the god Horus, and stars were considered to be the embodiment of the souls of the dead. In some cases, elements in the cosmos were not given the same names as the gods who represented them; for example, the Egyptian word for sky was *pt* while the name of the sky goddess was 'Nut'.

Several gods were linked to the moon and the sun: Khonsu and Thoth became moon-gods, and Osiris, Min, Shu and Khnum had lunar associations; the god Re embodied the sun, and was also present in his forms of Re-Harakhte, Re-Atum and Amen-Re. The different stages in the sun's daily circle were also represented by separate gods – Khepri symbolized the sun in the morning, Re at midday, and Atum in the evening.[13]

The Egyptians believed that the gods inhabited the next world, but were also present on earth in the form of certain physical manifestations such as the person of the king, statues, and particular sacred plants, animals and objects. These manifestations provided the worshippers with a tangible divine presence, which could be visualized and approached through rituals at the god's shrine or temple. In the Old Kingdom, the gods' abode was believed to exist in the sky. After death, each king aimed to join all the gods in the heavens but, by the Middle Kingdom, when the king's omnipotence had declined, another location for the afterlife was conceptualized, which was located in the underworld. Later literary sources describe how the god was present in his *ba* (soul, *see* further pp. 117–18) in the sky, in his image on earth and in his corpse in the underworld (where the *ba* and corpse united every night), so that the god's various manifestations were present throughout the universe.

Because of the lack of literary sources from the Predynastic Period, information about the gods and any concept of divinity has been mainly derived from later evidence, but this can provide an inaccurate and sometimes over-simplified view of the earliest practices. The need to perceive the complexity of the nature of the gods and of man's approaches towards them during this formative period is now considered essential to our understanding of the foundations of Egyptian religion.

Funerary Practices in the Predynastic Period

Most information about religious practices is available from the archaeological material excavated from cemeteries, but even here, lack of contemporary texts limits current knowledge of this period. Generally, there appears to have been a widespread and commonly held regard for the dead, possibly indicating a belief in a continued existence after death. Grave goods included implements, personal adornments and the provision of food. The concern for the welfare of the dead may have been prompted by a number of factors which cannot now be certainly identified: it is conceivable that the Egyptians sought to propitiate the dead because they feared their revenge or because they hoped that the dead would intercede with the gods on their behalf.

In the Badarian Period, the cemeteries were generally situated away from the settlement sites, on the edge of the desert. Most of the graves were oval in shape, and contained single burials although occasionally two bodies were interred in the same grave. Some of the larger graves, rectangular with rounded corners, were first used for female burials although males were also included in some of them later. Placed only a few feet deep in the sand, the body lay in the foetal position on its left side, with the head to the south. It thus faced the west, which was identified in later texts as the land of the dead.

The body, encased only in coarse matting, a basket woven of twigs, or an animal skin, was in direct contact with the hot, dry sand which provided the ideal environment for the protection of the corpse and the grave goods. Through the natural process of desiccation, these bodies became unintentionally preserved, a process that profoundly affected later religious developments. There is no indication that any artificial methods were used at this date to preserve the body, or that it was dismembered. The location of the grave was probably marked with a small pile of sand or stones.

Within the grave, the body was dressed in linen garments, and sometimes wore a turban as well as a decorative beaded belt and jewellery. The grave goods included elegant ivory combs, spoons and cosmetic vases, slate palettes and cosmetics. Green malachite seems to have had a special significance: it was ground on a palette and then mixed with oil or fat, and applied directly to the skin. Green was the colour associated with life in later times, and may have been used here to assist the deceased owner to renew his life-force. The graves also contained flint tools, but the discovery of some copper beads and a copper tool at this period indicates that metalworking was known, and metal items may have already been used to some extent alongside stone tools and implements.

Some of the finest pottery was produced at this time, and the graves included fine ware vessels and bowls, particularly the 'black-top' pottery which has a distinctive brown or red ware body with a blackened rim and interior. Amulets, often in the shape of animals, were frequently included in the burial, and nude female figurines were found in the graves of both men and women. In the animal burials that existed near to the human cemeteries, jackals or dogs, sheep and cows were encased in linen or matting covers.

In the apparently uninterrupted progression from the Badarian to the Naqada I periods, oval-shaped graves continued in use, although there are some examples of multiple burials (up to seven bodies) in a single grave. The same types of grave goods also continued, but the styles and materials (such as imported turquoise and lapis lazuli) indicate an increased foreign influence, probably due to more active trading contacts.

There were also stone vases, and ivory and earthenware figurines of men and women, as well as ivory combs. Distinctive types of pottery included the continuation of 'black-top' ware; red polished pottery, known as 'white cross-lined' ware, which was decorated with white paint in geometric patterns and sometimes included human, animal and tree forms; black pots with incised ornamentation highlighted with white paint; and the earliest examples of 'wavy-handled' pots which Petrie used as the basis for his Sequence Dating (although most examples date to the Naqada II period). The continued importance of animal cults is evident in the slate palettes, which sometimes take the shape of animals, and in the animal amulets and statuettes.

The start of Naqada II witnessed major changes in the burial customs. Whereas, previously, chieftains of communities seem to have been regarded as ordinary people who acted on behalf of their society and may have been accredited with special magical powers, now there emerged a new pattern. In the earlier communities, leaders had been buried in the same type of grave as the rest of their people, but during Naqada II, a new type of tomb was introduced. Most of the population continued to be interred in shallow round or oval pit-graves, but brick-built tombs were now provided for the ruling classes. Known today as *mastabas* or *mastaba tombs*, these established the pattern for royal and noble tombs in later times, and marked a clear distinction between the rulers and the ruled.

Above ground, the rectangular superstructure of the mastaba has the appearance of the bench found outside village houses in modern Egypt. This superstructure accommodated the burial goods, often in a complex of rooms. The burial was placed below ground in the substructure, where the walls were sometimes lined with matting or strengthened with wooden planks. In the royal tombs of Dynasty 1, this had developed into a wood-lined burial chamber or a wooden coffin that replaced the matting body cover.

The grave goods of this period continued earlier ideas, but there were noticeable innovations in the pottery. Most of the wavy-handled pots date to this period, but the 'Decorated Ware' is the most significant introduction. It is a distinctive buff-coloured pottery that is decorated with red zigzag lines, spirals, or figures of men, animals and birds. In Naqada II, there are also noticeable advances in the arts and crafts: innovations included the use of a wide variety of stone in the production of vessels; a change from disc-shaped to pear-shaped mace-heads; the use of composite animal motifs to decorate slate palettes; and a considerable increase in the use of copper for tools, weapons and toilette equipment.

Some general conclusions can perhaps be drawn from the archaeological evidence. In particular, new information is now becoming available from sites that are being reworked after many decades. For example, the cemeteries at Armant (which lie 9 km to the south-west of Luxor, on the west bank of the Nile) were originally excavated by Mond and Myers in the early 1930s, but have now been re-evaluated with reference to cemetery evolution in the Predynastic Period, and the social organization and changes that can be observed over this time-span.[14]

Here, most of the graves were single pits, although there were several instances of multiple burials in single graves. In some, matting or wood were used as grave linings, and some bodies were wrapped in matting or, more rarely, linen. The most common item placed with the deceased was pottery, but other grave goods included palettes, cosmetic pigments including galena, malachite and red ochre, stone tools and vessels, combs, jewellery and baskets.

The interpretation of the evidence suggests that this was a hierarchical society; since the largest burial discovered was that of a child, and symbols of authority have been found in both adult and infant burials, the evidence appears to indicate that status and wealth were inherited. Generally, the grave goods infer that there was a two-tiered society. However, a major change occurred with the introduction of two large mastaba tombs, built in a style that appears to have been developed elsewhere and then introduced to Armant. This small cemetery probably only served a modest agricultural community, and there is no evidence that an elite class emerged from the indigenous population at Armant and developed this new type of tomb for themselves. The available information suggests that an elite group with distinctive burial practices may have been imposed on the area by rulers who were engaged in unifying Egypt.

Another site of great importance, Hieraconpolis, is currently being more extensively excavated.[15] Archival records left by the original excavator, F. W. Green, at Cambridge and at the British Museum, and by Klaus Baer at the Oriental Institute, Chicago, provide additional information about the site, while archaeology has revealed new evidence from the Predynastic Period to the New Kingdom. One of the most fascinating discoveries are two unique but incomplete pottery masks found in the elite cemetery in the Wadi Abu Suffian; identification of their exact date and religious or funerary use awaits further study.[16] Generally, however, the excavations of predynastic burials, undisturbed since ancient times although plundered in antiquity, will provide new evidence about this formative period of Egyptian religion.

In general, evidence from the predynastic cemeteries indicates that the Egyptians attempted to give power to the deceased, and to obtain his support and influence on behalf of the living. Amulets were probably provided to endow the deceased with special powers: animal forms included the gazelle, hippopotamus, cow, pig, bull's head, crocodile, fly, fish, serpent, lion, and the Seth-animal, a strange creature which represented the god Seth but cannot be identified with any known species of animal. Some of these would have provided an eternal, magical food supply for the deceased, whereas others were doubtless intended to give him the necessary animal skills and strength which would have enhanced his hunting powers.

Because of the lack of firm evidence, many conclusions remain speculative, but it is possible that other grave goods were included to enhance the owner's fertility and thus improve his chances of rebirth after death. Female figurines, found in graves of women in the Badarian Period and in graves of both sexes in later times, could have been placed either in the graves of the men to act as concubines or in the graves of both sexes, as servants or votives made to the gods either for children or for the rebirth of the deceased owner.

Other figurines of the hippopotamus found in women's graves were probably also associated with fertility and rebirth, while figures of cattle on trays may have been intended to increase the fertility of the herd and provide an abundance of food either for the living or the deceased. Similarly, some scenes depicted on the 'Decorated Ware' were probably connected with fertility rites and were placed in the grave to perpetuate individual rebirth.

Again, grave goods indicate that some of the owners were regarded as leaders with special powers to guarantee the fertility of mankind, animals and crops. Small receptacles which may have contained 'medicine', ivory tusks, slates and figurines of men and women were found in some burials and may have been used by their owners in divination rites or to attempt to influence the gods to ensure the prosperity of the land and its inhabitants.

In general, however, the lack of literary evidence severely limits our ability to interpret the archaeological discoveries of this formative period, but it is apparent that the Egyptians already revered their dead and treated them with respect. It is also significant that, as each community increased its status and prosperity, this was reflected in the quality of its burials and grave goods. The provision of articles of daily use within the burials indicates that a concept of an individual afterlife already existed, and the grave may also have been regarded as a gateway to the underworld through which the living could gain access to the dead and the gods.

EARLY DYNASTIC TIMES

During the Archaic Period (Dynasties 1 and 2), many major political, social and religious traditions were established, and the basis of the administration, political institutions, and the judicial system was put in place. This process was assisted by the development of writing, and matched by experimentation and development in architecture and arts and crafts. There was also some attempt to organize and rationalize the religious practices.

The Unification of Egypt

One of the most crucial events in Egyptian history was the unification of the Two Lands under the rulership of a powerful southern leader in c.3100 BCE. An earlier ruler of Upper Egypt, apparently named 'Scorpion', had taken steps to initiate the subjugation of the north. A ceremonial limestone mace-head discovered by archaeologists at Hieraconpolis in 1898 ACE is carved with scenes that may depict Scorpion undertaking an irrigation programme and pursuing military activities, perhaps commemorating his peaceful reorganization of Egypt after some major military engagement. However, it was a successor, whom the historian Manetho identified as Menes, the first king of Dynasty 1, who finally unified the north and south and established historic Egypt. There has been a debate over whether Menes should be identified either with

Narmer or with Horaha as the founder of the Egyptian state, but Egyptologists now generally equate Menes with Horaha.

In the temple of Horus at Nekhen, in the 'Main Deposit', the archaeologists Quibell, Somers Clarke and Green found the famous cache that contained votive offerings from several periods. Amongst these was the so-called Narmer Palette, now housed in the Cairo Museum, which may have been placed in the temple to commemorate the king's gratitude to the god for his victorious campaign against the north.

This particularly fine slate palette is a good example of the late predynastic development in which plain slabs used for grinding eye-paint evolved into large ceremonial pieces, carved with scenes that sometimes recorded historical events. The Narmer Palette, which probably commemorates the Unification of Egypt and, for the first time, shows the king as ruler of the whole country, is a piece of great historical significance.

On the obverse, the king is shown wearing the White Crown of Upper Egypt and smiting a captive northern chieftain who cowers in front of him, while on the reverse, the sequel depicts the conquest of Lower Egypt, in which the king wears the Red Crown of Lower Egypt to symbolize his subordination of the north. This scene appears to depict a ceremony at which the king inspects ten slain northerners, either on the battlefield or at the temple at Nekhen where the sacrifice of selected captives may have formed part of a victory ceremony. The general theme of the palette scene is to depict the ruler both as a southern conqueror and as the acknowledged and victorious king of a united land.

The Political Institutions of Archaic Egypt

Menes (Horaha) and his successors established the country's main political systems during the first two dynasties. A new capital city came into existence in the north at the apex of the Delta, providing a prime location from which the new rulers could control the whole kingdom and subdue any attempted resurgence in the north. Originally named 'White Wall' or 'White Walls' (perhaps as a reference to the white

The slate palette of Narmer (*reverse*), commemorating the unification of the Two Lands (*c.* 3100 BCE). The king (*top left*), preceded by standard-bearers, inspects slain enemies (*right*). The Egyptian Museum, Cairo.

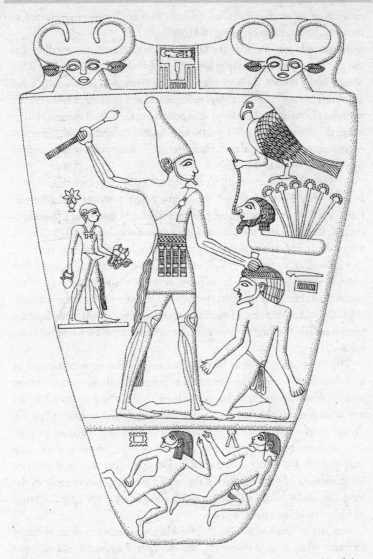

The slate palette of Narmer (*obverse*) shows the king with arm upraised to club his enemy. It was discovered in a foundation deposit in the temple at Hieraconpolis. The Egyptian Museum, Cairo.

coating on its mudbrick walls), this city is more frequently referred to today by its later Greek name of Memphis.

In the fifth century BCE, the Greek historian Herodotus recalled that the priests of Ptah (the patron god of Memphis) had told him that King Menes had founded their city and temple. Memphis became the main royal residence city and bureaucratic centre, and continued to dominate the administrative and political spheres during the Old Kingdom. However, the ancient city of This (near Abydos) remained the foremost religious centre during the Archaic Period, a status that was promoted by the early dynastic kings.

At Memphis, there would have been a mudbrick palace that housed both the royal residence and the centre of government and administration, a dual use which royal palaces retained in later times. Administration, foreign trade, the judiciary, and the treasuries of the Two Lands, which dealt with the collection and redistribution of domestic revenue, were based at Memphis. However, a system of local government had also been established in the provinces, which was strongly linked to the centralized administration at Memphis. The role of the king and the royal family became crucial during the Archaic Period, when the foundations were laid for their future development in both political and religious spheres.

The Egyptian state was intended to sustain the cosmos as well as human beings; without this force, it was believed that cosmic and human society would disintegrate at every level. Nature and mankind could not alone provide the structure and stability required to ensure that the divine order continued and flourished, and therefore the state became the indispensable institution that underpinned the whole system. The state provided a secure framework and ensured that mankind enjoyed an abundance of life's benefits. Crucial to this vision was the role of the king. Studies of kingship[7] have attempted to analyse the characteristics of Egyptian kingship.

As early as the Archaic Period, the king was regarded as an absolute monarch who, as 'god-on-earth', was considered to be the embodiment of whichever royal state-god was supreme at any one period. The gods chose the king to act on their behalf, but he was not only a mediator between gods and mankind; he was himself divine, although he was never the equal of the gods and always retained many human characteristics. In the Archaic Period, he embodied the supreme deity, the hawk Horus, and in succeeding periods, the living king always carried the title of Horus, which was ultimately passed to his successor.

The queens, and particularly the king's mother, already wielded considerable power during the early dynasties, and probably played an important role in the order of royal succession and inheritance. The exact meaning of the title 'Great Royal Wife', which was held in later times by the king's principal wife, remains unclear (*see* below p. 305), but from earliest times, the royal women were undeniably significant.

The king, whose role and many duties were derived from those of the predynastic village chieftains, undoubtedly delegated some of his authority to trusted followers who probably included members of his own family and representatives of the communities who had allied themselves with the conqueror and unifier of the Two Lands. Offices and titles known in the Old Kingdom had already been established in the earliest dynasties, including the post of vizier (chief minister) who acted as the king's delegate in important areas of state administration.

Religious Organization of the Living

As in the Predynastic Period, the evidence for funerary religious practices is far better preserved than information relating to the divine cults and worship. One important type of religious building which existed in the earliest dynasties were the 'Fortresses of the gods' and these played a significant role in the early state.[18] They may have been places where groups of gods, present in the form of their standards, emblems or banners, were gathered to participate in major ceremonies.

The 'fortress' consisted of a large, mainly empty court enclosed inside mudbrick, panelled walls; a sacred mound within the enclosure provided the king with a place to stand in the midst of the gods. These deities, known collectively as the 'Followers of Horus', acted as the earthly embodiments of the ancient sky- and falcon-gods, and followed the king as his devoted supporters.

The god's symbols were probably brought by boat from the various provinces to the fortresses that may have existed at key centres such as

Abydos, Heliopolis and Hieraconpolis. These journeys were perhaps made in association with the biennial collection of taxes, when the revenue was brought to the fortresses. The assembly of gods probably participated in the redistribution of the goods, and was present to receive the king's offerings and worship in return for which they gave their continuing support. The 'Followers of Horus' perhaps also played a significant role in the Sed-festival which marked the king's jubilee and regenerated his life and reign. Again, the gods and their accompanying priests probably travelled by river to the fortress so that they could play a major ritual role in renewing the king's powers in this world and the next life. The fortresses may have had an additional function as a location for the ritual slaughter of prisoners-of-war and desert animals.

Some deities who received worship in later times already had cults in archaic Egypt. The goddesses Wadjet and Nekhbet, the patron deities of the two predynastic kingdoms, continued to protect the king; Seshat, goddess of writing, already received worship; and Ptah's cult-centre at Memphis had probably been established. The falcon-god Horus was the supreme royal patron in the Archaic Period, and Re (whose cult predominated in the Old Kingdom) may have already taken over the centre at Heliopolis, which was originally dedicated to the god Atum. There was also a flourishing cult of the goddess Neith, a goddess of hunting and warfare; a representation of her early temple on a tag from the tomb of Horaha at Abydos[19] shows the features of these early cult shrines. It has been interpreted as a shrine made of wattle work, although this artistic convention may in fact indicate a more solid construction.[20]

Such representations, on ivory or ebony tablets and cylinder seals, provide limited evidence about these shrines and early temples, although traces of actual buildings have been found at Abydos and Hieraconpolis. Continuing in the predynastic tradition, these buildings were probably constructed of mixed materials (which, in the Archaic Period, may have included brickwork, roofs made of wooden beams, and wooden doors).

Each shrine, which contained the cult-image, had a hooped roof and stood at the rear of an open courtyard enclosed by a fence. Two poles with attached banners stood at the entrance to the enclosure and the god's emblem was displayed on another pole in the centre of the courtyard, in front of the shrine. The flagpole eventually became the hieroglyphic sign representing the word *ntr* which meant 'god'. Later stone temples reproduced the main architectural layout and features seen in these early shrines.

These cult-centres probably existed in most villages, towns and communities in the Archaic Period, and provided a locus where the community leaders could perform rites on behalf of the resident deities. Although there is a shortage of hard evidence, it seems likely that these took the same form as later rituals, when the priests, as the king's delegates, offered food and clothing to gods' statues in the temples, in order to obtain material benefits for the king and his people. As in the later temples, the early rites were probably carried out on a regular, daily basis, but there is also evidence from the Palermo Stone records that there were well-established festivals when the divine statues were paraded amongst the worshippers.

Funerary Customs in the Archaic Period

The main architectural development in funerary architecture at this period was the emergence of the mastaba tomb as a 'house' for the deceased. There were six main stages of progression in tomb design during the Archaic Period,[1] and within these, there were further subdivisions which reflected the status of the owner – royal, noble, aristocrat, minor official, artisan, or peasant.

Every effort was made to protect the tomb equipment from robbers: the substructure was deepened, and because the owner now amassed more elaborate and extensive tomb equipment, the superstructure was increased in size and a stairway was built on to its east side, which gave direct access to the burial chamber. However, because the storerooms in the superstructure were very vulnerable to robbers, they were eventually discontinued, and all the goods were placed in the burial chamber, except for the food provisions, which were kept in the subsidiary rooms.

The type of tomb that was used for royalty and the nobility became standardized by the end of Dynasty 2. Funerary goods in the royal tombs continued to be elaborate, but in non-royal tombs the standard declined, and instead the owners chose to express their status and wealth in terms of the tomb structure itself rather than in the contents. In the substructure, there was often the equivalent of a reception hall, guest rooms, a master bedroom represented by the burial chamber, a living room, and women's quarters, with a bathroom and lavatory which could be reached from both the master's bedroom and the women's quarters. The tomb was clearly intended as a 'house' for its deceased owner, and probably reflected the accommodation used by the upper classes in life.

Mudbrick continued to be the main building material, although limestone was abundant and available, but studies of stone construction, such as the series of stone tombs of the Archaic Period which were excavated in 1942–54 ACE by Zaki Saad, emphasize that stone was only infrequently used during this period.[22] The technical ability to work in stone and the motivation to provide durable and secure tombs obviously existed as early as Dynasty 1, but tombs built entirely of stone do not occur until the end of the Archaic Period or the beginning of the Old Kingdom. This can possibly be explained by the fact that mudbrick was regarded as a particularly sacred material for housing the burial. Building in stone may have advanced more rapidly in other religious contexts; for example, it is recorded on the Palermo Stone that a stone temple was built during Dynasty 2, and granite reliefs and other stone architectural fragments have been recovered from Hieraconpolis and el-Kab, indicating that there was early progress in using stone for temple architecture.

In the tomb, provision continued to be made for the owner's afterlife. This ranged from placing simple possessions in the pit-graves of the peasants to the elaborate equipment found in the royal and noble tombs. Every attempt was made to supply a continuing source of food for the deceased, and some burials included complete meals set out on dishes, and reserve supplies stored in the subsidiary rooms. In addition, relatives of the deceased brought food offerings that were placed outside the niches set into the outer wall of the tomb. However, even these sources of food could fail to materialize if the living relatives neglected their duties, and therefore, to protect the deceased against eternal starvation, 'magical' provisions were made available by inscribing a 'menu' of items on a stela (round-topped stone) that was set up inside the tomb.

In order to gain spiritual sustenance from these offerings, the Egyptians believed that the owner's spirit or life-force needed to return to the tomb periodically to partake of these provisions. Therefore, it was essential for the owner's corpse to be preserved in a perfect and recognizable form so that the spirit could readily identify it. In the early pit-grave (which most of the population still used), the heat and dryness of the sand surrounding the corpse had preserved the body naturally by desiccating the tissues before they had time to decompose. However, with the construction of brick burial chambers in the mastabas, the bodies no longer survived intact, and for several hundred years, the Egyptians sought an alternative method of preserving the body, eventually developing the use of a chemical dehydrating agent.

In the Archaic Period, various experimental stages in the process can be traced from the natural to artificial preservation of the body. For the royal family and great nobles, there were attempts to perpetuate a lifelike appearance of the deceased by reconstructing the shape and contours of the body. Linen pads and bandages that had been soaked in a resinous substance were moulded around the body to recreate the face, torso and limbs. The arms, legs and fingers were carefully and individually wrapped, and details were painted on to the moulded face, genitalia and breasts. Inside, however, the body still decomposed, leaving only the skeletal form.

Arranged in the foetal position, the bodies were placed on a bed or in a house-shaped wooden coffin within the burial chamber. As a further precaution to preserve the owner's image, in case the wrapped body should be damaged or destroyed, royalty now also began to include an almost lifesize wooden figure amongst their burial goods.

The Royal Cemeteries

The location of the royal burials of the Archaic Period has been the subject of considerable debate. The city named This, the early capital of the Abydos area where the predynastic Naqada culture flourished, remained Egypt's most important religious centre even after the Unification, and the early dynastic kings, although they now ruled from Memphis, preserved their strong association with the Abydos area.

The royal necropolis area at Abydos, located at Umm el-Ga'ab ('Mother of Pots'), was first investigated by the French archaeologist Amélineau in 1895 ACE. Here, he uncovered a series of brick tombs that belonged to several early kings, but, at first, he wrongly identified them as the tombs of those who had ruled before the Unification. In 1899 ACE, the British archaeologist Petrie obtained the concession to re-work the site, and thirteen years later, Naville and Peet investigated parts of the site and discovered eight large Dynasty 1 and two Dynasty 2 tomb complexes, in addition to several small predynastic tombs.

Publication of the tombs, with their plans and contents which included inscribed stone vessels, stelae, jar sealings, and ivory and ebony tablets, enabled their date to be established as early dynastic rather than predynastic. Inscriptions on the objects provided the names of one queen and all the kings of Dynasty 1 and two kings of Dynasty 2. These names were subsequently identified with the early rulers listed by Manetho who were associated with This. No human remains were recovered from these tombs but this was explained in terms of plunder or marauding animals. Consequently, the Abydos monuments were assumed to be the burial places of the early dynastic rulers, who had been brought to the great religious centre of This for their final interment.

This assumption was not questioned until Emery[23] revealed large and impressive mastabas of the same period at Saqqara where he was carrying out excavations from 1938 ACE. Here, he uncovered a row of twelve brick mastabas with their subsidiary burials. These were much larger and more complex than the Abydos group, and objects found inside the tombs indicated that they dated to Dynasty 1. Emery found skeletal remains, but the ownership of the tombs remained uncertain because the associated inscriptional evidence only identified each tomb with a specific reign and not with an individual royal owner. There were no stelae to supply this definitive evidence, and it was subsequently suggested that the Saqqara tombs may have belonged to the courtiers of the period.

However, recent excavation[24] of cemeteries at Umm el-Ga'ab is revealing new information that may ultimately resolve the controversy over the two sets of royal monuments. One possible explanation is that both Abydos and Saqqara were royal funerary monuments, but that the bodies were interred at Saqqara, conveniently close to the royal residence at Memphis, while the Abydos group were regarded as cenotaphs. This would have emphasized the continuing dynastic association with

Abydos, and also reflected the king's status as ruler of both Upper and Lower Egypt.

At both sites, there were subsidiary burials of servants, artisans and pets who were intended to accompany their royal master into the next world. At Abydos, where there were more than 1,300 subsidiary burials, there was sufficient archaeological evidence to indicate that the burials were contemporary with the owner's death, since the tomb structure was erected over both the main burial and the subsidiary graves. Inscriptions on associated stelae, which give the individual tomb-owner's name, and sometimes the sex and other details, provide the information that these graves contained many women, and some war-captives, dwarfs and dogs.

At Saqqara, there were fewer burials, but the presence of tools in some of the subsidiary graves indicates that skilled craftsmen were buried there to provide a workforce to carry out the continuing repair and maintenance of the tomb. Wrapped in linen and buried in the contracted positions, these bodies had been placed inside wooden coffins and provided with food and toilet equipment for the next life.

From the forensic evidence provided by the bodies, it seems that, when they were buried, these servants were already dead, perhaps as the result of poisoning. This practice of live burials survived longer in the south, and reached its peak at Abydos in the reign of King Zer whose complex incorporated over 500 subsidiary burials. However, the custom did not continue beyond the Archaic Period, and model figurines of servants, acting as substitute workers, were found in the later tombs in place of these human sacrifices.

There were also boat-burials in the Abydos cemeteries. Twelve shallow boat-pits were discovered in 1991 ACE:[25] each contained a wooden hull, most of which rose above the ground surface, and the whole structure was enclosed within thick mudbrick, boat-shaped casings. These boats may date to Dynasty 1, but similar, smaller boat graves associated with the elite burials of the Early Dynastic Period have already been found at Saqqara and Helwan.

The purpose of these boat-burials remains uncertain: some may have played a part in the rulers' funerary cults in the earliest dynasties and have had a functional purpose, transporting the body of the deceased on his final journey, before they were buried within the funerary complex. However, in the Old Kingdom, boats found in association with pyramid complexes were possibly used as solar-, lunar- and stellar-barques to transport the king around the heavens and the underworld, and by this time may have fulfilled both functional and mythological purposes.

The existence of early dynastic boat-burials does not conclusively prove that there was already a solar cult and a belief that the great tomb-owners were expected to spend part of their eternity encircling the heavens in solar-barques, as well as continuing part of their existence in the tomb. Nevertheless, the early Abydos boat-burials do indicate that some funerary features were already emerging which later developed into major elements of the Old Kingdom pyramid complexes.

The Rise of the Sun-Cult

The Old Kingdom, *c*.2686 – *c*.2181 BCE

STRUCTURE OF THE SOCIETY

It was during the Archaic Period that the foundations of society became established, but in the Old Kingdom, Egypt developed into a highly organized and centralized theocracy. The great technical advances achieved in many areas were often first perfected in order to improve the king's burial place and funerary goods, and were then adapted to improve people's living conditions.

Society was itself organized in terms of a pyramid structure, with the king at the pinnacle and a broad base of peasantry at the bottom. The concept of divine kingship was essential to the Egyptian state, and was more clearly defined in the Old Kingdom than at any other period. Nevertheless, there has been considerable debate about the exact nature of this kingship.' The king was undeniably the prime son and image of the creator god, as well as the earthly representative of all the deities. However, unlike a cult-image or cult-animal, he did not usually receive a cult during his lifetime. The king acquired divinity through the rituals performed during his accession to the throne and the coronation when the insignia he received gave him special powers.

The king has been described as the 'incarnation' of the creator god and a token of his power on earth, but probably he was not regarded as a deity in his own right. His divine power was derived from his kingly office, and he was expected to execute the god's wishes. As the incarnation of Horus, the king did not actually become the god, but took on his attributes and enabled the god, through him, to become accessible to mankind. The king demonstrated human and divine attributes at different times, but whereas the gods were always immortal, the king had to achieve this status. The king was of great importance in the Old Kingdom; he was essential to the divine order, because without him neither the realm of the gods nor the world of mankind could function. The king was regarded both as a being and as the holder of an office, and divine kingship represented the amalgamation of these two facets. When the king was crowned, he acquired the powers of Horus who ascended to the throne of his father, Osiris, and the king transcended his mortality to become the divine ruler of the Two Lands. The Horus-name which the king acquired on his accession represented the divine aspect of kingship, while the other names in the titulary embodied his role as an earthly ruler.

The king's unique status created an impassable chasm between him and his subjects, which was most clearly demonstrated in the Old Kingdom pyramids and in the belief that only the king could experience an individual eternal life when, after death, he joined the gods to sail around the heavens. However, this status also gave him the power to mediate between gods and men, and royal divinity was expressed in many areas of society in the Old Kingdom. These included central and provincial administration, and the organization and administration of state institutions such as the royal residences, pyramid complexes, and sun-temples. His temporal duties, which had developed out of the role of the early tribal chieftain, embraced law and justice, politics, warfare, foreign policy, and social matters, as well as religion. In theory, the king owned the land, its resources and its people, but he was subject to Ma'at, the principle of balance in the universe which was personified as a goddess who ensured that justice and order prevailed on earth. He was constrained in his actions by this principle and by precedent; he was advised by royal counsellors and, increasingly, some of his extensive duties were delegated to royal officials.

The kings practised bigamy or polygamy, and there were often many descendants from the secondary or minor royal wives. This sometimes led to conflict over succession to the throne; the roles of the Great Royal Wife and Great Royal Daughter in relation to the succession will be considered later (*see* p. 305). To attempt to gain the loyalty of his closest relatives, the king appointed them to powerful political positions and provided them with finely equipped tombs. In the early Old Kingdom, the king rewarded loyal men with positions which they held for life; their tenure depended on the king, and this gave him control over them, even in distant provinces. However, when royal power waned in later dynasties, in order to gain favour, the kings made these positions hereditary, but the increasing independence of these governors eventually resulted in the establishment of their own family 'dynasties' and local power bases.

In addition, although key positions had been retained within the royal family in the early dynasties, later rulers sometimes chose to promote the careers of non-royal subjects. Also, to gain the support of the nobles, the king presented them with gifts of royal land and possessions, and even burial places which were close to his own pyramid; in addition, he provided them with estates to support the upkeep of these tombs and ensure the continuation of the funerary rituals. The ability of the nobility to survive after death was believed to rest entirely upon the king's personal approval and bounty.

An extensive hierarchy of minor officials and administrators supported the whole system; they operated in the main departments which were housed at Memphis and included the treasuries, the armoury, the granaries, and public works. Memphis functioned as Egypt's capital during the Old Kingdom, and accommodated not only the main administrative departments, but also the royal residence, the centres of religious organization which would have overseen the royal burial sites at Saqqara, Giza, Meydum and Dahshur, and also the residence city for the priests and other personnel who serviced these monuments.

The burials were often equipped with fine furniture, jewellery, toilette equipment, pottery, stone vessels and other articles of daily use. Wealthy clients also requested luxurious items for their own homes. The craftsmen who built, decorated and provided these goods lived at Memphis where they developed a distinctive classical style, which Egyptologists sometimes refer to as the 'Memphite' or 'Northern' school. This is distinguished by wall reliefs and statues which were executed according to a canon of proportions, so that there is a unity of representation in the figures. There was a high standard of craftsmanship, and the great technical advances and mastery of skills which are evident at this time were perhaps never again equalled or surpassed.

Most of the population, however, consisted of peasants or serfs who, although they cannot actually be termed as slaves because they were not owned by individual masters, nevertheless had little freedom of movement or action. They cultivated the land and produced food for the whole population, as well as supplies which were offered in the perpetual funerary rituals at the pyramids and tombs. For three months each year, the land was under water because of the Nile flood, and it is possible that, during this period, the state paid the peasants with food for themselves and their families in exchange for manual labour at the royal burial site. This would have ensured that they still received food even during the period when they could not work on the land, and prevented potential dissatisfaction and possible rebellion by a substantial group within society.

However, such a scheme would have involved considerable organizational problems in bringing workers many miles from the south to the pyramid sites in the north, and the labour force may have been raised more easily through corvée duty or perhaps by using only the peasants who lived relatively near to the building sites. Peasants were also conscripted to undertake military duties, as there was no standing professional army at this time, and were sent to Nubia to obtain the hard stone required for state building projects.

RELIGIOUS ORGANIZATION

This centralization of political organization was also reflected in religious developments. By the middle of the Old Kingdom, Upper Egypt was divided into twenty-two nomes, and later another twenty were established in Lower Egypt. Each nome was associated with its own local gods, but some provincial deities transcended their original limits to become nationally prominent. For example, the ibis-headed Thoth was supreme at Hermopolis, but also acquired a national role as god of writing. However, sometimes the process was reversed and some deities who had enjoyed widespread influence in earliest times found that they were reduced to a local significance. By the Old Kingdom, largely because of the process of syncretism, a confusing pantheon had emerged which contained a multiplicity of gods. Some cities had become major religious centres, associated with important gods or groups of gods, and their priests now developed and promoted distinctive theologies, which emphasized the supremacy of each city's god. Each priesthood claimed that its deity had created the universe, other gods, and mankind, and these cosmogonies ('Creation Myths') have survived in the literature.

THE CREATION MYTHS

Originally, Egyptologists explained the different accounts of creation by claiming that the various myths represented competing systems which each attempted to establish its own supremacy at the expense of the others. Now, however, the three greatest systems which emerged at Heliopolis, Memphis and Thebes are regarded as variant versions of a fairly uniform concept of the creation of the universe.[2] This concept proposed that all existence was derived from a single original source, and that the occasion of creation transformed the oneness of the creator god into multiple life forms throughout the world.

Before creation, there had been a state of non-existence that was characterized by total darkness and limitless waters. From this, there emerged a creator who established the universe; however, the act of creation did not obliterate the state of non-existence which remained outside the boundaries of the created world and also penetrated it in the form of sleep and death which represented a temporary return to the depths of the cosmos.[3] However, even death was not able to extinguish existence permanently; indeed, through the correct burial procedures, it could provide the means of attaining a better life in the next world. Non-existence, therefore, far from being a negative concept, was essential for renewal and rejuvenation.

There is no definitive text that summarizes the Egyptian concept of creation, although the most important creation myth (the Heliopolitan Cosmogony) emphasizes the role of Atum, claiming him as the deity from whose essence the whole universe had been created. However, most religious writings mention the nature of the universe and how it came into being. From this, it is possible to describe the main elements of the Egyptian universe. It contrasted strongly with the outer, 'non-existent' universe: the known world was finite, sunlit, and full of daily activity, whereas the outer region was limitless, dark and motionless. The known created world floated in the limitless ocean of dark and motionless water, from which it derived its own source of water.

The created world consisted of land below and sky above which were separated from each other by the atmosphere. The sky formed an interface between the land and the limitless ocean beyond. Within the created world, daily existence was ordered by the rising and setting of the sun, which sailed through the sky in the daytime and then disappeared inside the sky at night where it passed to another place, Duat, which was located within the body of the sky. The entrance to Duat lay somewhere below the visible horizon, at the intersection of the sky and earth. Inaccessible to the living, Duat was the abode of the gods and the dead who were governed by the sun during its passage through this realm. At sunset, the sun passed through the sky's mouth (the sky was conceptualized as a goddess, Nut) into Duat, and at dawn, re-emerged between Nut's legs. This daily drama of the sun's death and rebirth, disappearance and re-emergence, underpinned the Egyptian understanding of the human cycle of life, death and rebirth, and played a significant role in speculation about the origin of the universe. The Creation Myths reflect the Egyptian belief that the universe did not consist of physical components but was composed of individual deities who had distinctive personalities and wills. Thus, the sky was a goddess, while her consort, Geb, formed the earth. The Creation Myths do not explain creation in terms of the interaction of impersonal forces, but describe the process as the outcome of the wishes and actions of the gods.[4]

Although there is no one authoritative description of creation, and the various accounts provide different perspectives, they are consistent in their basic vision of how creation came into existence. The creator god was believed to have emerged from the primeval ocean and created his offspring from his own physical substance: the act of creation thus generated diverse, differentiated elements out of unity. Although the major creation texts were formed and developed over a period of some three thousand years, the earliest examples already contained all the major themes and were equal in complexity to those that came later.

A central feature of ancient Egyptian belief was the co-existence of stasis (the notion of creation as perfect and complete) and change (the idea that life was dynamic and recurrent). The created world was essentially complete and perfect at the moment of creation. An important aspect of this was the principle of Ma'at, which was immutable and underpinned every aspect of creation. Alongside this established creation, however, there were the dynamic forces that worked within it. These included the annual inundation of the Nile, the daily rising and setting of the sun, and mankind's birth and death. Whereas the first principle – stasis – has been described as the 'Eternal Sameness', which was a state of 'existing', the second was the 'Eternal Recurrence', in which the cycles of the sun and all living things changed and repeatedly developed. One scholar[5] has described this in terms of a dramatic play (representing Order and Eternal Sameness) in which the characters and script were established at the time of writing and remained invariable whereas the actors and settings (representing Life and Eternal Recurrence) changed when the play was acted out each day.

Major creation myths (Heliopolitan, Memphite and Hermopolitan) developed at the cities of Heliopolis, Memphis and Hermopolis during the Old Kingdom, while the cosmogony that placed the god Amun at the centre of creation was promoted at Thebes during the New Kingdom.

The Heliopolitan Cosmogony

The most important and influential creation myth evolved at Iwnw (a city later known as Heliopolis). This myth emphasized the role of Re (the sun-god) as creator, and his association with other deities. The main source for this myth are the Pyramid Texts, but texts from later periods are also important in defining the sun's pivotal role in creation. The 'Spell for Coming Forth by Day' (Spell 17 of the New Kingdom Book of the Dead) draws the parallel between the sun's passage from night to day, and the deceased's emergence from the tomb to the daylight. The sun embodied within itself the pattern of self-renewal, and its first rising was regarded as the concluding act of creation.

At Heliopolis, Re took over the cult and acquired the characteristics of Atum, an earlier god who had initiated the whole of creation. According to the Heliopolitan myth, Re-Atum was the creator who had emerged from the great primeval ocean (named Nun), and brought light into the dark state of non-existence. He took the form of a heron, known to the Egyptians as the Bennu-bird, who flew out of the darkness and alighted on a rock where it opened its beak and let out a cry that broke the silence of non-existence. This cry was part of the creative process and 'determined what is and what is not to be'. Thus, as the Bennu-bird, Re-Atum created a perch that, according to the Heliopolitan priests, became the site of their temple. In this temple at Heliopolis, a sacred fetish known as the Benben Stone was believed to be this actual rocky perch. It took the form of a pillar topped by a pyramidion (pyramid-shaped stone), which was probably covered in gold and reflected the sun's light at dawn. This Stone, the most sacred cult object of the sun-god, was regarded as the deity's locus, while the pyramidion or capstone of each pyramid was also considered to be a representation of the Benben which protected the royal burial in the pyramid chambers.

Much later, Herodotus[6] related the legend of the Bennu-bird (which the Greeks called a *phoenix*):

I have not seen a phoenix myself, except in paintings, for it is very rare and visits the country (so at least they say in Heliopolis) only at intervals of 500 years, on the occasion of the death of the parent bird . . . There is a story about the phoenix: it brings its parent in a lump of myrrh all the way from Arabia and buries the body in the Temple of the Sun. To perform this feat, the bird first shapes some myrrh into a sort of egg as big as it finds, by testing, that it can carry; then it hollows the lump out, puts its father inside and smears some more myrrh over the hole. The egg-shaped lump is then just of the same weight as it was originally. Finally, it is carried by the bird to the Temple of the Sun in Egypt. I give the story as it was told to me – but I do not believe it.

The Greeks enlarged on this story, and claimed that the phoenix was a mythical bird which was consumed by fire and then reborn from the ashes.

Re-Atum was believed to be self-creating and also to possess bisexual powers. One of the Pyramid Texts[7] provides an account of how he begot his children, Shu, god of the air, and Tefnut, goddess of moisture:

Atum became a creator by masturbating himself in Heliopolis. He took his penis in his hand so that he might obtain the pleasure of orgasm. A brother and sister were born – namely, Shu and Tefnut.

However, according to an alternative version, he created these gods by spitting out Shu and vomiting forth Tefnut. Their union in turn brought forth the earth-god Geb and the sky-goddess Nut, whose offspring – Osiris, Isis, Nephthys and Seth – played minor roles in this cosmogony, although they were key characters in another myth. Together, these gods formed the Great Ennead (nine gods); the Little or Lesser Ennead was closely associated with them and also formed part of the Heliopolitan mythology.

The Memphite Theology

The Heliopolitan cosmogony expressed a concept of self-development by which matter was transformed from a single source or primordial unity into multiple and diverse forms throughout the world. However, the most complete description of the second explanation of creation – that it began as a divine concept, given reality by being expressed through the spoken word – occurs in the Memphite Theology. Here, the two divine principles of 'perception' and 'creative speech' are the natural forces by which creation is achieved, when the creator god first perceives the world as a concept and then brings it into being through his first utterance. To achieve this, the creator uses the principle of magic, a force that, according to Egyptian belief, could transform a spoken command into reality.

The creator god at Memphis was Ptah who was regarded as an intellectual principle; he provided the earliest example of how the creator's mind and will functioned. Memphite theology described him as the supreme creator of the universe who made the world, the gods, their cult-centres, shrines and images, the cities, food, drink and all the physical requirements of life. As the Lord of Truth, he also created divine utterance and established ethics. His creative actions were carried out through his thoughts (expressed through his heart) and his will (spoken by means of his tongue).

The creative role of Ptah is described in a text known as the 'Memphite Theology' which is carved on a black granite stone (the Shabaka Stone – British Museum No 498), which was prepared to be set up in the Temple of Ptah at Memphis. It dates to the reign of King Shabaka (Dynasty 25, c.710 BCE), who ordered it to be carved because the original – written on papyrus or leather – was worm-eaten. Until the 1970s ACE, because of the archaic form of the language, Egyptologists considered that the original must have dated to the Old Kingdom, making it the oldest surviving example of a philosophical treatise. However, more recent research indicates that the earliest possible date for the original is the reign of Ramesses II (Dynasty 19, c.1250 BCE).[8]

The major part of the inscription provides a 'dramatic' text which describes the early division of Egypt into two kingdoms under Horus and Seth which are later brought together as one kingdom (the Unification) by Horus at Memphis. The mythology section (which comprises the final twelve columns of inscription) is mainly independent, although it is associated with the dramatic text. The text has posed many difficulties in translation, and there are conflicting interpretations. Some consider that the text, compiled from several different sources, introduced Ptah as a political ploy in order to emphasize the pre-eminence of the god and his city, whereas others regard it as an exposition both of Ptah's role as the intellectual principle of creation and of his presence in the multitude of created forms in the world. Where the text describes the primal role of Ptah as supreme god, it emphasizes that his actions in thinking and speaking, which set creation in action, preceded Atum's own acts:

There took shape in the heart, there took shape on the tongue the form of Atum. For the very great one is Ptah, who gave [life] to all the gods and their *kas* (spirits) through this heart and through this tongue, in which Horus has taken shape as Ptah, in which Thoth has taken shape as Ptah.[9]

The text conveys some advanced philosophical concepts which are not usually encountered in Egyptian mythology because the language was not rich and profound enough to express such ideas. From his own thoughts and commands, Ptah brought forth the forces and elements of creation; these reproduced the character and substance of the original primordial source, which had created both the static elements of existence and the dynamic principles of life and activity:

Sight, hearing, breathing – they report to the heart and it makes every concept come forth. As to the tongue, it repeats what the heart has thought. Thus all the gods were born and his (Ptah's) Ennead was completed. For every word of the god came about through what the heart thought and the tongue commanded.[10]

As well as embodying the intellectual principle or 'thought' of creation, Ptah was also the source of all matter from which that creation sprang. He was patron god of crafts and artisans (architects and craftsmen) who resided at Memphis in large numbers during the Old Kingdom. Their work involved transforming raw materials into the buildings or statues that they had already conceptualized, and Ptah personified this principle which enabled an idea to become a physical reality. The Memphite Theology is therefore primarily concerned with the creative functions of thought, utterance, and the transformation of concept into reality. Unlike the Heliopolitan cosmogony, it is not so much an account of the creator god's actions but an explanation of how he managed to transform his concept into reality.

Ptah always remained an abstract deity who was shown in fully human form, bandaged as a mummy. He was regarded as an intellectual force, but because he did not possess a mythology that was attractive to his followers, he achieved little widespread appeal and never enjoyed unrivalled supremacy. Consequently, he was never adopted as patron god by any dynasty of kings. In later times, through identification with Osiris and other funerary deities, he adopted some of their characteristics, and even acquired an animal form through his association with the Apis bull, which had an important cult at Memphis.

The Hermopolitan Cosmogony

The Hermopolitan myths represented several different, non-contradictory versions of creation, which were primarily concerned with emphasizing the importance of the city. Unlike other cosmogonies, creation at Hermopolis was not restricted to one supreme god. Indeed, the main myth centred around an Ogdoad (group of eight gods) which included four male gods and their female counterparts. These were Nun and Naunet (primeval waters), Huh and Hauhet (eternity), Kuk and Kauket (darkness) and Amun and Amaunet (air). These serpent-headed males and their frog-headed consorts were accredited with the creation of the world on the 'First Occasion'. Subsequently, they then ruled the world until they died and continued their existence in the underworld, where they ensured that the Nile flowed and the sun rose so that life could continue to flourish on earth. Unlike many other religious systems, that of the Egyptians did not regard the underworld as a place of darkness and misery. To them, it was the home of some of their gods – a place from which the deities could act to benefit mankind, and from the Middle Kingdom, it was the location of an ideal kingdom that everyone aspired to reach after death. This was a realm of eternal springtime – an idealized version of Egypt in fact, where there was no illness, danger or unhappiness.

According to another version of this myth, life had emerged from a Cosmic Egg which was laid on the Island of Creation either by a goose called the 'Great Cackler' or an ibis which represented Thoth, the chief god of Hermopolis; and in yet another account, the Ogdoad created a lotus which rose up from the Sacred Lake in the temple at Hermopolis, and opened its petals to reveal Re (either in the form of a child or a scarab-beetle which changed into a boy) who proceeded to create the world and mankind.

Therefore, although the cosmogonies presented different views of how creation had occurred, they shared several basic underlying concepts. Most stated that creation had taken place on a primordial mound or island (regarded as a place of great spiritual potency) that had emerged from the primeval ocean, and each temple was believed to be that Island of Creation where the king could approach the gods on behalf of mankind. The moment of creation achieved completion and perfection, but the dynamic principles of life and change continued to develop simultaneously alongside and within the static universe. At first, there was a golden age when the gods ruled on earth, providing mankind with all the elements for a stable, peaceful society, including law, ethics and religion. When they left the earth, their divine son and successor, the king of Egypt, inherited their rulership which he was expected to exercise according to the principles of order, equilibrium, truth and justice, personified by the goddess Ma'at. In order to uphold this standard, a constant battle had to be waged on many levels so that order was continually re-established, and the chaos or non-existence, which had prevailed before creation and still permeated the universe, could be vanquished.

Generally, these different texts represent concepts that are compatible and provide a uniform approach to questions that relate to the nature and creation of the universe. They do not appear to represent competing systems of thought and belief. However, once the Egyptians had developed an explanation of how the world had been created, they did not just limit themselves to one creation mythology but allowed and even encouraged a multiplicity of approaches. Later, in the New Kingdom, they identified the god Amun as the First Principle or Ultimate Cause of all creation who was beyond all human knowledge and whose nature and will were thus incomprehensible to mankind. This was the limit of their speculation about the origin of existence.

THE CULT OF RE

In the prime religious source of the Old Kingdom – the Pyramid Texts – the king is said to become a star amongst the 'imperishable stars', which perhaps reflects the existence of a prominent star-cult at this time.[11] In the Pyramid Texts, there are references to the king's relationship with the stars. For example, in Utterance 245,[12] the sky goddess addresses the king and identifies him with the Lone Star (Venus):

Make your seat in heaven,
Among the stars of heaven,
For you are the Lone Star, the comrade of Hu!

Relatively little evidence of the star-cults has survived, although one individual star, Sothis (the Egyptian name for Sirius, the Dog-star), was acclaimed as the goddess responsible for the Inundation and identified with two other goddesses, Isis and Satit. Also, the constellation Orion received worship through identification with the god Osiris.

Each king, however, proclaimed his allegiance to the sun-god (from Dynasty 4, he adopted the title 'Son of Re'), and it was this cult that came to dominate the religious beliefs and practices of the Old Kingdom. The construction of pyramids as royal burial places, a custom which reached its zenith in Dynasty 4, may be the most enduring expression of this cult, but it was in Dynasty 5, when the kings appear to have ruled subject to the god's will, that the worship of Re and the power of his priesthood reached their peak.

The sun was conceived as a sphere that, on occasions, might need wings or a beetle to propel it across the heavens. It was regarded as an eternal and self-renewing force that consistently appeared on earth at dawn and disappeared again at sunset. In the Egyptian universe, this daily cycle was the most important natural event, and the other elements of creation were only present as a setting for the culminating act of creation – the first rising of the sun. This prime act of creation had first occurred at Heliopolis, the cult-centre of Re.

The Egyptians believed that the sun-god sailed on a daily course around the circular ocean in which the earth was suspended. At dawn, he emerged at the intersection of the earth and sky, and used a day-barque to sail across the vault of heaven, lighting up the earth and bringing warmth and life. At sunset, he passed below the horizon into the underworld (where the lower half of the ocean flowed) and used the night-barque to traverse this region, leaving the earth in darkness. On his journey, he had to encounter and defeat many demons in order to continue his cyclical journey; the major obstacle was the serpent Apophis who threatened to devour the sun (symbolizing the clouds that intermittently swallowed the sun). The rich mythology relating to the sun's cult, which was preserved in various creation and funerary texts, provided a pattern for the king's own life, death and resurrection.

The sun, as the principal force involved in the struggle for existence, took various physical forms. At Iwnw, where he had taken over Atum's earlier cult-centre, he became Re-Atum and was worshipped as the creator of the world. As Khepri, he appeared as a dung-beetle, and was often shown propelling the sun in imitation of the way in which these beetles pushed dung-balls in front of themselves through the sand. As the symbol of renewal and self-regeneration, Khepri represented the daily rebirth of the sun, while Atum symbolized the sun as the source of all creation. As the mature sun, the god took the form of Re-Harakhte (Re in his horizon) while as Horus, he was king of gods and the predominant force in the world. Each of these different aspects of Re represented facets of the god's own character and functions, but they all contributed to the process of life, and manifested an aspect of the creative principle of the sun.

THE PYRAMID TEXTS

The idea that there was a close association between the king's passage from life to death and the cycle of the sun, demonstrated in the scenes and inscriptions of the New Kingdom royal tombs, was already present in the funerary texts of the Old Kingdom. The Pyramid Texts – the world's oldest extant substantial body of religious literature – provided an alternative method of attempting to secure the royal burials and ensure the king's ascent to heaven at a time when, because of economic, political and religious pressures, the pyramids of Dynasties 5 and 6 were reduced in size and quality.

Some of the texts may have been composed as early as Dynasty 4, but most date to Dynasty 5. The Pyramid Texts were primarily intended for royal persons, although a few may have been composed for commoners. During the Middle Kingdom, the texts evolved[13] and, with modifications and developments, came to be inscribed on the coffins of the nobility (see pp. 169–70). Thus, Egyptologists refer to them as 'Coffin Texts'. Eventually, by the New Kingdom, the texts became even more widely available as the basis for the compilation of the Theban funerary texts, particularly the Book of the Dead. Their main purpose was to supply the deceased (royal or non-royal) with spells that could ensure his safe passage into the next world.

The Pyramid Texts are inscribed on the walls of five pyramids at Saqqara which belong to the kings Unas, Teti, Pepy I, Merenre and Pepy II of Dynasties 5 and 6; they are also found in the pyramids of three queens of Pepy II, and that of King Ibi of Dynasty 7. The French archaeologist Gaston Maspero first discovered these texts in 1880 ACE, on the walls of the burial chamber in the pyramid of Pepy I. Subsequently, texts were found in the pyramids of Unas (these were the earliest, dating to Dynasty 5), Teti, Merenre, and Pepy II. In 1920 ACE and 1936 ACE, a Swiss Egyptologist, G. Jéquier, discovered the later texts which dated to Dynasty 7.

Maspero produced the first edition and translation of the Pyramid Texts, but a study by the German philologist K. Sethe became the earliest standard work. This was based on texts from the five Saqqara pyramids, although these were an incomplete record because large portions had been damaged or destroyed. Other major studies[14] have added considerably to current knowledge of the texts. Additional use has been made of more recently discovered material from other pyramids and later non-royal tombs and coffins, inscribed with derivative versions that sometimes provide exact parallels to the earlier spells. Translating the texts and interpreting their significance and meaning have posed considerable difficulties, but they remain a unique and unparalleled source for understanding the religious beliefs of the Old Kingdom.[15]

The texts, inscribed in hieroglyphs on the limestone walls inside the pyramids, were usually arranged in vertical columns on the walls of the antechamber, passageways, vestibule, ramp and burial chamber. This pattern of arrangement may reflect the order of part of the funerary service, and possibly follows the physical route taken by the priests when they brought the king's body to its final resting place in the sarcophagus in the burial chamber. The priests may have chanted these spells in the order in which they occur on the walls, or perhaps it was intended that they could be 'seen' and 'read' by the king as his body rested in the sarcophagus, thus providing him with spiritual strength to bring about his personal resurrection. The essential purpose of the texts was to enable the king to reach the sky and take his rightful place amongst the gods in the retinue of Re. They were primarily intended to ensure the immortality of the kings, although they were also placed in the pyramids of three queens.

Arranged as a set of 'utterances' or spells, most texts have been found in more than one pyramid although a few are repeated in all the pyramids. They appear to have been arranged in an arbitrary manner, with no attempt at systematic organization; there is no evidence that measures were taken to correct contradictory statements in the different versions. Compiled for the Saqqara pyramids by the priests of Re at Heliopolis in Dynasty 5, they retained and incorporated earlier concepts, although the main emphasis was placed upon the solar and celestial elements of the royal hereafter. The Egyptians believed that all magic was potent and, rather than excluding some elements, they tried to develop as diverse and inclusive a set of spells as possible so that this would enhance the overall efficacy of the texts and achieve the desired result. In order to ensure the dead king's resurrection and ascent to heaven, and to confirm his survival and immortality, the texts drew on a wealth of imagery. They refer to wings, steps and ramps in an attempt to provide the means by which the king could ascend to the sky. For example, Utterance 467 describes his journey to the sky:[16]

He that flies flies! He flies away from you, oh men.
He is no longer on earth, he is in the sky . . .
He rushes at the sky as a heron, he has kissed the sky as a hawk,
He has leapt skyward as a grasshopper.

In Utterance 267, it says:

A ramp to the sky is built for him, that he can go up to the sky on it.
He goes up upon the incense.
He flies as a bird, and he settles as a beetle on an empty seat that is in the ship
     of Re . . .

Sometimes, the spells request the assistance of the gods, although at other times, the king asserts his own strength. In an extreme measure, in the section known as the 'Cannibal Hymn', the king devours the gods in order to gain their powers for himself.[17] This is described in Utterances 273–274, from which the following passage is taken:[18]

It is he who devours their magic and swallows their lordliness. Their great ones are for his morning meal, their middle-sized ones for his evening meal, and their little ones for his night meal. Their old men and their old women are assigned for his fumigation.[19] The Great Ones who are in the north of the sky, they place for him the fire to the kettles, that which is under them being the thighs of their eldest ones.[20] The sky-dwellers serve him, and the cooking-pots are wiped out for him with the legs of their women.

Throughout the texts, there are allusions to several legends and myths which were probably regarded as metaphorical rather than true accounts of real events; there are also references to astronomy, cosmology, geography, 'historical' references, rituals, festivals, magic and morals. From this mass of material, three major strands have been identified which may reflect distinct but overlapping religious traditions. Some passages appear to indicate that the texts date back to a period before the unification of the Two Lands. These refer to aspects of ancient kingly ritual, hostilities that occurred during the Predynastic Period, and the Cannibal Hymn, which alludes to the practice of assembling the bones of the deceased, a custom that must have existed before the first attempts at mummification.

A second group of texts emphasizes the king's celestial afterlife. Two very ancient doctrines, which may have merged at an early date, appear to coexist here. Both emphasized the sky as the abode of the gods: in one, a sky-god reigned supreme and the deceased king was envisaged as a star, while in the other, the prominence of the sun-god Re and the king's close association with this cult is emphasized. It has been suggested that the sun-cult may have absorbed an earlier star-cult, a development that may be reflected in the architecture, when the true pyramids, perhaps symbols of the sun-cult, replaced the step pyramids which were possibly associated with a star-cult.[21] Later attempts in the Old Kingdom to break with the tradition of constructing the pyramid as a royal tomb (for example, when the mastaba tomb of Shepseskaf was built in Dynasty 4) may indicate that this particular king was attempting to break with the solar tradition.

The third element in the texts centres on the resurrection of Osiris, a god who, in the Old Kingdom, already played an important role in ensuring the king's eternity. By the Middle Kingdom, Osiris' cult virtually obliterated that of the former royal patron Re, and it offered a chance of individual resurrection and eternity to rich and poor alike. The cults of Osiris and Re shared the concept of survival after death – the daily rebirth of the sun after a night-time in the underworld, and the annual loss and subsequent renewal of vegetation after the inundation which was reflected in the death and resurrection of the god in the Osiris Myth. In both cases, the god's life, death and re-birth were reflected in the cycles of the natural world, a pattern that formed one of Egypt's most important religious concepts. In later times, however, the solar cult continued to symbolize the royal resurrection and afterlife whereas Osiris came to represent the immortality of ordinary people.

The inclusion of both Re and Osiris in the Pyramid Texts does not indicate an intrinsic rivalry between the cults during the Old Kingdom. Nor do the texts reflect a conflict between the sun-cult and the earlier role of the king as the incarnation of the sky-god Horus. As the cult of Re and his priesthood gained momentum at Heliopolis, the king may have wished to assert that he was not only the child of Re, which enabled him to accompany the sun-god through the sky and the underworld, but also the earthly embodiment of Horus, son of Osiris, and Horus, who became Osiris when he died. In this role, he ruled as god and judge of the underworld. The development of the sun-cult in Dynasty 5 could have threatened the position of the Horus-king, but the mythology of the Pyramid Texts combined all the traditions, and allowed the king to retain undisputed power on earth and in the underworld even while Re reigned supreme in heaven.

The Pyramid Texts integrated the three main gods and their mythologies, and allowed the Horus-kingship, the cult of Re, and the worship of Osiris to enhance the king's position. The king's strong association with the sun-god appears to have increased his divine role rather than diminished it. Predynastic traditions were probably handed down orally and then written on ostraca and papyrus before they were finally included in the Pyramid Texts. By incorporating them with later doctrines, the Egyptians sought to achieve their main aims of awakening the king from his deathly sleep in the pyramid, ensuring that he ascended to heaven, and confirming that the gods received him into their company. The latter aspiration was not always granted willingly, and spells had to be included which enabled the king to fight the gods and seize his rightful place in the heavens. Every effort had to be made to fulfil the king's supreme wish – to be reunited with the gods in heaven and avoid a continued existence in the underworld, which was the fate of his subjects.

THE PYRAMIDS

The pyramids, first built as royal burial places in the Old Kingdom, had the same two basic practical functions as other tombs – to house the body and accommodate funerary equipment for use in the next world. Although Egyptian archaeology has produced spectacular royal tomb treasures such as those of Tutankhamun and the less well-known material from Tanis, no burial has ever been discovered inside a pyramid. However, other archaeological and literary evidence indicates that the prime purpose of a pyramid was to accommodate a royal burial, although other, less acceptable theories abound, including suggestions that they may have had a cosmological significance and perhaps acted as observatories or repositories of hidden knowledge.

The first stone pyramid – the Step Pyramid at Saqqara – was originally designed as a mastaba tomb, but the architect changed the plan. A series of steps of decreasing size, each representing a mastaba, were piled on top of each other, indicating that the original idea of the pyramid was probably a development of earlier funerary architecture. The progression from the pit-grave, through to the mastaba tomb and then to the step and true pyramids, retained a characteristic feature – the site of the burial place was marked either by a mound of sand or stones for the pit-grave, by the superstructure of the mastaba, or by the respective stepped construction and the smooth-sided, sloping form of the stepped and true pyramids. One explanation of these markers, which all took the form of 'mounds', is that they represented the 'Island of Creation' where the first god had alighted and brought life into existence. As such, they would have acted as places of great magical potency, where the deceased tomb-owner could renew his life-force.

In the Step Pyramid at Saqqara, the burial chamber was situated underground, following the pattern of the mastaba tombs, but in the later pyramids, it was moved to the interior of the main pyramid structure. The step pyramid may simply have been a development of the early dynastic mastabas which had stepped, layered superstructures. Architects were always aware of the constant threat from tomb robbers, and possibly they intended that the size of a step pyramid would help to act as a deterrent. During the early Old Kingdom, step pyramids were transformed into true pyramids, which were characterized by their smooth, sloping sides.

The ancient Egyptian word for the pyramid was *Mer*. 'Pyramid' is derived from the Greek word *pyramis* which means 'wheaten cake', a term used by the Greeks to describe these buildings which they encountered many centuries later. *Mer* has traditionally been translated as 'Place of Ascension', and the pyramid may have been regarded as a means of access for the deceased king to reach heaven and also to return to his burial place where he could receive food offerings. The form of the true pyramid, with its smooth, sloping sides encased in white limestone, may have been an architectural attempt to re-create the sun's ray descending from heaven to earth, along which the king could travel.[22] The true pyramid appears to have had close connections with the sun-cult, and it may also have been regarded as a variation of the Benben Stone (*see* p. 84).

The Step Pyramid at Saqqara

The oldest known major stone building in the world is the Step Pyramid at Saqqara, built for King Djoser at the start of Dynasty 3 by his vizier and architect, Imhotep. This pyramid was an enhanced mastaba tomb which retained the main divisions of a superstructure and substructure: its superstructure consisted of six steps, while underground, there was a deep shaft that led to subterranean corridors and chambers where the burials of the king and members of his family had originally been housed.

However, this pyramid was only the central feature of an entire complex, planned as a complete unit, which was originally surrounded on four sides by an enclosure wall of white limestone that possibly imitated the wall around the king's palace at Memphis. This enclosure contained a range of religious buildings – a temple, shrines, altars, courts, subsidiary tombs, and storehouses. A southern mastaba was built against the southern enclosing wall, but its burial chamber is too small to have accommodated a body, and the use of the building has not yet been identified. Possibly the king's viscera, removed during mummification, were buried there, or it may have been a cenotaph so that the king – as ruler of the Two Lands – had two 'tombs' within this complex.

Many of the other buildings were arranged in pairs, probably so that rituals could be performed simultaneously for the king in his capacity as ruler of the Two Lands. An important feature of the complex was the area where the king's coronation could be re-enacted in his next life. During his reign, a king's coronation was commemorated by a series of jubilee festivals that were held at appropriate intervals. These were probably intended to restore the king's waning strength and powers by means of magic, and perhaps to replace earlier customs which may have included the ceremonial sacrifice of an ageing ruler so that he could be replaced by a younger and more vigorous king. The jubilee ceremony apparently included a ritual in which the king was required to run around an open court, in order to reaffirm his physical prowess. A court for this purpose was included as a feature of the Step Pyramid complex, so that the king could assert his right to rule in the next world.

Architecturally, the complex included many interesting and experimental features. The artisans were inexperienced in using large quantities of stone, and they tentatively translated older architectural forms, which had been built with wood, reed and mudbrick, into the new material. Stone fluted and ribbed columns now replaced the bundles of reeds and wooden pillars used as support structures in earlier buildings, but because they were uncertain of their ability to support the roof with free-standing columns, the architects and masons used engaged columns (two columns attached to each other) to provide additional stability. At this site, the dimensions of the stone blocks used to build the walls were the same as those used for the mudbricks, but later pyramid complexes were built of massive stone blocks, demonstrating a rapid development in the confident use of the new material.

The Step Pyramid complex has no known precedent, and the general design was never repeated. It has been suggested that such a complex may have been intended to create a royal residence for the king in the next world, which, once it was constructed in stone, could function throughout eternity. The various 'dummy' buildings and shrines within the complex would have been infused with life by means of magic, so that they could play their part in the rituals of the king's afterlife.

In an assessment of the royal cult complexes of the Old and Middle Kingdoms, Arnold[23] interprets the whole complex as a unification of the basic elements of the royal funerary architecture at Abydos with the traditions of Memphis. The jubilee court, he suggests, has its origin in the ancient tradition of assembling the statues of the gods of the Two Lands in the 'Fortress of the gods' (*see* pp. 69–70). In general, the complex was probably intended to provide the king with a residence for use in the next world. The two royal tombs in the complex – the main, northern one under the Step Pyramid and the southern mastaba adjacent to the enclosing wall – may exemplify, respectively, Memphite funerary architecture, and the royal Abydos tombs.

The Transitional Pyramids

The Saqqara Step Pyramid complex laid the foundations for the funerary structures of Dynasty 4, and some of the developmental stages from the Step Pyramid to the true pyramids are visible in the monuments built by

Djoser's immediate successors. The pyramid that was built at Meydum (probably early Dynasty 4) was conceived as a small stepped structure, but it was extended by the addition of seven or eight superimposed layers, which were then infilled with local stone. This became a true pyramid once the sides of the structure had been faced with white limestone. The axis of this complex was rotated so that it had an east–west rather than a north–south orientation – a realignment that may indicate that increased importance was now attached to the sun-cult. A small area probably intended as a ritual offering place was located in front of the east side of the pyramid. Arnold[24] emphasizes that this feature is important because it is the earliest known example of a cultic installation directly connected to a royal tomb.

There is a significant change in the meaning and form of the royal funerary complex when we move from the Step Pyramid to the Meydum complex. The Step Pyramid complex recreated buildings that, in the king's lifetime, were used for displaying royal power, whereas at Meydum, this concept was replaced by a symmetrical and centralized funerary complex which was dominated by the pyramid. Arnold suggests[25] that this may reflect a major change in the concept of the royal afterlife and perhaps even in the religion. The king was perhaps no longer regarded as merely a manifestation of Horus, but became identified with the sun-god. The pyramid was no longer just a burial place but enabled the king to be united with the sun-god, and to participate fully in his daily cycle of death and resurrection.

Some twenty-eight miles north of Meydum, at Dahshur, two other pyramids were built which are attributed to the reign of Sneferu, who may also have been responsible for part or all of the Meydum pyramid. It is possible that the relatively sharp angle of incline of the sides of the Meydum pyramid was responsible for the partial collapse of the building, and anxiety about this may have prompted a change in the design of the southernmost pyramid at Dahshur. Both pyramids at Dahshur were planned and executed as true pyramids, and their increased size indicates that they were regarded as important monuments. These complexes also include the earliest monumental funerary temples. However, in the southern pyramid, just beyond halfway up the height of the building, it was evidently decided that the angle of the incline of the sides should be sharply decreased. One explanation (not universally accepted) was that the architects were attempting to avoid the disaster that had occurred at Meydum. The change of design has given the monument a blunted appearance, and it is often referred to as the 'Bent' or 'Blunted' pyramid.

This complex contains the prototype of a royal statuary temple attached to a causeway, in which there are six statues of Sneferu, shown wearing the crowns of Upper and Lower Egypt and of the Two Lands. Wall reliefs show the king as the lord of the temple, accompanying the gods and performing ceremonies. Sneferu (c.2613–2589 BCE) inaugurated Dynasty 4 and ushered in a new era. Later generations remembered his importance and he was accorded the rare honour of receiving a personal cult (as opposed to the uniform worship offered to all legitimate previous royal rulers). This pyramid is the earliest example, which has survived above ground, of a royal funerary monument decorated with reliefs, but these are sufficiently sophisticated to indicate that there were earlier prototypes.

The northern monument at Dahshur – known as the 'Red Pyramid' – has two major features that are found later in Cheops' Great Pyramid complex at Giza. These are the pillared court and the statue sanctuary. Various theories have attempted to explain why the kings sometimes built more than one pyramid. According to one suggestion,[26] this was a political solution to an annual problem: during the months of the inundation, when the peasants could not work on the land, it may have been desirable to employ them on a major state building project which would not only feed them and their families, but also prevent them from becoming a potentially rebellious element in society. If one pyramid was finished, the workforce could then have been moved on to another, similar project. However, this practical explanation of the Egyptian rulers' motivation to build pyramids is not universally accepted. Another possibility is that some kings, who enjoyed long reigns and had sufficient resources, may have constructed more than one pyramid so that their double role as ruler of north and south could be reflected in the provision of two funerary monuments – a burial place and a 'cenotaph'.

The Giza Pyramids

The finest examples of pyramid complexes can be seen in the three monuments built at Giza by rulers of Dynasty 4 – Khufu, Khafre and Menkaure. Historical descriptions of Khufu (better known by his Graecized name of Cheops) present contrasting viewpoints of the man. Herodotus[27] relates that the Egyptians who lived in his reign hated and despised Cheops as a tyrant, because he closed the temples and forced his subjects to build his pyramid. The story also claimed that he used the proceeds from his daughter's prostitution to help to offset the cost of building this monument. Some Egyptian texts such as the Westcar Papyrus also present him as an autocrat, but others credited him with great sacred wisdom and knowledge, and he was obviously a pious son who reburied his mother's mortal remains in a tomb near his own pyramid after her original burial site was probably plundered. In truth, few verifiable facts about his character or reign have survived, although it is clear that, at this period, the kings enjoyed almost absolute control over the lives of their subjects and over the kingdom's resources and wealth which they could direct towards pyramid building. Indeed, these monuments became the focus of the whole society, and represented religious, economic, political and social interaction.

The Great Pyramid built at Giza for King Cheops is the largest and most famous of these monuments. Cheops chose the Giza plateau as his burial site first because it was near to the capital city of Memphis and to the limestone quarries at Tura, and secondly, because the slightly elevated site provided a setting that dominated the surrounding countryside but also extended far enough in distance to accommodate the subsidiary buildings required to serve the complex. The pyramid was the main feature of the typical Old Kingdom burial complex that reached its fullest and final form in the reign of his son Khafre (better known by his Graecized name of Chephren). Although many of the elements in his father's complex have wholly or partly disappeared, the remaining evidence shows that, in addition to Cheops' pyramid, there was a Valley Temple and a causeway which led to the pyramid temple situated on the east side of the pyramid. This temple originally contained a large pillared court and a broad room for the cult-statues. Cheops' pyramid complex was never completed, but Chephren's neighbouring, more completely preserved monument became the standard arrangement for later complexes.

Regarding Chephren's character, again Herodotus[28] records that he was hated by his subjects:

Chephren reigned for fifty-six years – so the Egyptians reckon a period of a hundred and six years, all told, during which the temples were never opened for worship and the country was reduced in every way to the greatest misery. The Egyptians can hardly bring themselves to mention the names of Cheops and Chephren, so great is their hatred of them . . .

However, it must be remembered that Herodotus lived and wrote his account over two thousand years after these kings reigned. As far as historical facts are concerned, Chephren remains a shadowy figure who can only be judged by his pyramid complex, a magnificent monument in which there are several distinct areas:

1 The Pyramid
This housed the burial and funerary goods, but by this reign, the burial chamber had moved from beneath the pyramid into the centre of the main structure. Uniquely, this pyramid retains some of its original limestone casing at its apex; the casing from other pyramids was removed as an easily accessible supply of reusable stone.

2 The Valley Building
Each pyramid was built on the edge of the desert, but was linked to the river's edge by a series of buildings. Initially, these facilitated the transport of heavy building materials from the river to the pyramid site during its construction, but subsequently, they also provided access for the funeral procession and the food provisions that continued to be offered in the pyramid temple after the king's burial.

The Valley Building, situated on the edge of the river, consisted of a transverse hall and a T-shaped interior pillared hall, and contained twenty-three seated statues of which the best-preserved example, now in the Cairo Museum, shows the king being transformed into a falcon.

The traditional explanation of this building was that it provided a landing stage where the king's body was first received into the complex, or that it accommodated the body during the mummification procedure. However, a more recent theory[29] has suggested that the Valley Building was in some way associated with the 'Fortress of the Gods' where the dead king met the gods.

The Abusir Papyri (discovered in 1893 ACE but not yet fully published)[30] come from the archive of the pyramid temples of Neferirkare and Neferefre of Dynasty 5. They do not refer to the burial of the king but provide details of the activities carried out after the funeral. There are lists of daily services, special festivals, inventories of temple furnishings and equipment, accounts, letters, and 'passports' for the temple staff. From this, it is evident that the temples were not used for the royal funerary procession, although we do not yet know which route this took. Similarly, the exact location where the funerary ceremonies were performed remains uncertain. The main purpose of the Valley Building was to house the celebration of religious ceremonies, particularly the king's meeting with the gods who arrived in boats and landed briefly at the Valley Temple.

3 The Causeway

The causeway provided a covered corridor that led from the Valley Building to the Pyramid Temple. It was roofed and enclosed to maintain the ritual and spiritual unity of the complex, and to ensure that evil could not enter this most sacred location.

4 The Pyramid Temple

The term 'mortuary temple' which was used by Egyptologists of the nineteenth century to describe the temples attached to pyramids of the Old and Middle Kingdoms is no longer considered acceptable (for discussion, *see* pp. 186–7). Instead, the term 'royal cult complex' is used, and although this provided a royal burial place, its prime function was to accommodate the rituals that would transform the mortal king into an immortal, divine being. The tomb was a particularly appropriate focus for these rites as it provided the king with a gateway to the next world. The pyramid temples provided a location for the king's statues and ceremonies that were associated with the daily presentation of offerings and the festivals when the gods visited the temples. Within the complex, the pyramid remained the key feature, but it was regarded not so much as an eternal resting place for the king's mummy but as a location where the king could be reborn, transformed and given access to heaven.

Therefore, according to this interpretation, the Valley Buildings and Pyramid Temples were never places where the burial rites were performed. They formed part of a complex which, through the rituals carried out there – such as the jubilee festivals at the Step Pyramid, and the rites performed before the royal statues – was essential in order to ensure the king's deification. The whole procedure has been described as an Ancestor Cult, in which the pyramid temples where the royal statues were housed, and the attached royal tomb, played their parts.[31]

Other Features of the Pyramid Complex

1 Subsidiary Pyramids

These satellite pyramids that form part of the complexes of Cheops and other kings were much smaller in size (often only one-fifth) than the main pyramid. They usually have no cult chapel and the burial chamber would have been too small for a full human burial. It is possible that they were used to house a statue of the king, or his viscera or, since no objects have ever been found in them, simply as a symbolic cenotaph or 'second tomb' for the king. Again, they may have played a part in the rituals associated with the pyramid temples.

2 Royal Boat Graves

The purpose of the boat burials found associated with Old Kingdom pyramids and with earlier tombs remains largely unresolved (see pp. 75–6). In the Old Kingdom, boat burials have been found near the pyramids of kings Cheops, Chephren, Djedefre and Unas, as well as some of Cheops' subsidiary pyramids and the tomb of Khentkaues who was possibly a queen of Shepseskaf. In the Cheops' complex, several boat-shaped rock-cut pits have been located outside the eastern enclosure wall of the pyramid. Three of these pits were found to be empty, and one remains unexcavated, but in one pit, parts of a wooden boat were discovered in the 1950s ACE. These were intended for assembly in the next world. The restoration of this boat took many years, but now the reassembled craft is magnificently displayed in the Boat Museum built at the site where it was discovered.

Various explanations have been advanced regarding the possible purpose and use of these boats.[32] It has been suggested that they may represent solar-, lunar- and stellar-barques which the king intended to use when he ascended to heaven and traversed the skies and the underworld. A possible association between these boats and the sun-cult is further supported by the discovery of large, brick-built reproductions of solar-barques near to some solar temples of Dynasty 5, although no actual boats have been discovered inside.

However, elsewhere, earlier boat-pits have been excavated in the vicinity of mastaba tombs where no direct link with the sun-cult can be established (see pp. 75–6), and they have also occurred near some of the Middle Kingdom pyramids. The remains of several working boats that had been deliberately disassembled were discovered near the pyramid of Senusret I at Lisht. In some cases, therefore, these boats may be the actual vessels (or models of them) which were used to convey the mummy in the funerary procession, and were subsequently buried near the tomb. In conclusion, boats buried near funerary monuments may have had different uses: some were possibly intended for transport, whereas others were for the king's use in his next life, or they may have combined both these functions. The discovery of boat graves in association with early dynastic burials probably indicates that there was a long tradition behind the boat pits and boat burials of the Old and Middle Kingdoms.

3 Queens' Tombs

Although some queens were buried in pyramids, there is no firm evidence that this was the custom at Giza. Some of Cheops' queens and many members of his family and court were buried in the fields of mastaba tombs, which were located in the areas to the east and west of his pyramid. These rows of tombs, arranged like streets of houses, accommodated the descendants of the king's wives and concubines, and favourite family members and courtiers, thus ensuring that they were close to the ruler in death as they had been in life. The contrast between these tombs and the pyramid is nevertheless stark, and emphasizes the gulf between the god-king and even his most esteemed subjects. In Chephren's reign, the policy changed and it was no longer customary to surround the pyramid complex with a family cemetery; instead, his queens and children were buried in rock-cut tombs to the east of the king's own pyramid.

4 Pyramid Cities

The funerary complexes of Cheops, Chephren and Mycerinus required constant attention and had to be provisioned with the food offerings that were presented to the dead. In front of the cemeteries, the king provided land for a Pyramid City to accommodate the priests who serviced the tombs and performed the royal rituals. The king provided them with endowments of agricultural land, and they enjoyed exemption from taxation. Ultimately, however, this system became a considerable burden, and the drain on the royal resources posed great problems towards the end of the Old Kingdom.

The peasant workforce who built the pyramids probably lived in settlements near the building site. A basalt wall belonging to one of these settlements has recently been discovered to the east of Cheops' pyramid, and to the south of the pyramid, the archaeologists have located a necropolis which housed the burials of the master builders and the officials once employed in the building yards. This discovery has provided important additional information about this special community.[33]

5 The Great Sphinx

The Great Sphinx is a unique feature of Chephren's complex. The original significance of this sculpture is unknown, although it was later regarded as the guardian of the area. When the architects encountered a large natural outcrop of rock in this position, they may simply have decided to create a sculpture instead of removing the stone. With the body of a crouching lion and a human head, which was perhaps carved to represent Chephren's own facial features, the Great Sphinx remains an unexplained but dramatic feature of the Giza plateau.[34]

Pyramids of the Later Old Kingdom

A third and final pyramid was built at Giza by Menkaure, the son of Chephren, who is better known by his Graecized name of Mycerinus. Herodotus' account[35] compared him favourably with his father and grandfather, commenting on his justice, piety, and beneficence as a ruler, but then he also related that the king's daughter committed suicide on account of his misdeeds. Herodotus stated that Mycerinus died prematurely, and another tale relates how the oracle at Buto (a town in the Delta) prophesied that he had only six years to live and so, in order to confound this prediction, he enjoyed life night and day, by the light of a candle, and thus gained another twelve years of pleasure. Perhaps as the result of his premature death, his pyramid was much smaller in scale than those of his predecessors, and was built of inferior materials. It was unfinished when Mycerinus died and had to be completed by his successor, Shepseskaf. However, even as early as the end of Dynasty 4, economic pressures appear to have played a part in restricting the size of pyramid that a king was able to construct.

The mortuary precinct of Shepseskaf demonstrates a dramatic change in policy. Built at Saqqara, it took the form of a large mastaba tomb with a funerary chapel attached to the east side. Known today as the 'Mastabat Fara'un', this probably represented an ancient palace surrounded by an enclosure wall, in which the dead king was thought to reside. By abandoning the tradition of pyramid-building, and adopting a tomb style which emphasized the king's mortality and need to receive food offerings, this monument probably reflected important religious changes which possibly included a different attitude towards the cult of the king.

The kings of Dynasty 5 revived the practice of pyramid building, and this tradition continued throughout Dynasty 6. As previously mentioned, these later monuments, built at Abusir and Saqqara, were considerably inferior in standard and in their method of construction, doubtless reflecting the reduction in the king's power and the contemporary political and economic pressures. King Userkaf, the first king of Dynasty 5, may have been a descendant of a secondary branch of Cheops' family. A folk-tale preserved in the Westcar Papyrus mentions that Userkaf was one of the triplets born to the wife of a priest of Re, who were all destined to exercise divine kingship in Egypt (see p. 111). Although the story gives an inaccurate description of his parentage and family, Userkaf undoubtedly inaugurated a dynasty that gave unprecedented power to the priesthood of Re (see pp. 111–12). He introduced a new type of monument – a sun temple – that emphasized the close association between this dynasty and the sun cult. This temple was built at Abu Gurob, but his pyramid complex was constructed at Saqqara and followed the layout of the Giza monuments of Cheops and Mycerinus. It had been used as a quarry in antiquity and was extensively damaged at the time of its discovery, but the remaining wall-reliefs in the court provided definite evidence that, at one time, the complex was decorated with finest quality scenes, which depicted hunting and fishing activities.

The later pyramids of Sahure, Neferirkare and Niuserre were built at Abusir, on the edge of the desert. Sahure, mentioned in the Westcar Papyrus as one of the triplets born to the wife of a priest of Re, was in fact the son and successor of Userkaf, who continued Userkaf's policy of promoting the sun cult (see pp. 111–12). Sahure's pyramid complex is the most completely preserved,[36] and became the prototype for the later examples of Dynasties 5 and 6 which, with minor variations, were all built on the same plan.

Architectural features included the replacement of the plain, rectangular columns found in earlier pyramid temples with columns representing papyrus stems bound together and palm-leaf capitals. The subject matter of the wall-reliefs (some of which are badly damaged) is wide ranging, and includes ritual scenes of the king hunting in the desert, baiting hippopotami, and campaigning against human enemies. In one scene, a sea-expedition to the Syrian coast is shown which probably represents a trading venture to Byblos to obtain cedar wood; on board the ships, sailors and Asiatics raise their arms in salutation to the Egyptian king. The representation of successful combat against human and animal foes would have been included to provide the complex with magical protection against evil forces.

In Niuserre's pyramid, this theme is continued with reliefs in the causeway corridor where the king is shown as a lion or griffin trampling his enemies underfoot. The quality of craftsmanship shown in the reliefs in the Dynasty 5 complexes indicates that standards of work were still high in some areas although the scale and levels of construction in these monuments had been reduced.

The last ruler of Dynasty 5, Unas, returned to Saqqara where he built a pyramid complex which, for the first time, incorporated the inscriptions known today as the Pyramid Texts; these decorated the walls of the vestibule and the burial chamber.[37] This complex also includes the best preserved example of a causeway;[38] on the inner walls of its corridor are fine quality wall-reliefs which depict hunting, labourers at work, possibly a trading expedition, and the 'Famine Relief' which shows emaciated people dying of hunger who, according to one explanation, may have been foreign famine victims in receipt of the king's bounty.

Rulers of Dynasty 6 – Teti,[39] Pepy I and Pepy II – also built pyramids at Saqqara. Scenes in the pyramid temple of Pepy II show the food and other offerings that the king would require throughout eternity, and outside the king's enclosure, a set of smaller pyramids were built for three queens. In general, the pyramid complexes of Dynasties 5 and 6 demonstrate an inferior level of construction. Instead of solid internal construction, the core of these pyramids was now made of small stones or rubble, bonded together with Nile mud; today, this core is exposed, because the original casing of Tura limestone has been removed, with the result these pyramids have the appearance of piles of rubble. Also, the pyramid itself was no longer placed at the centre of a family cemetery; instead, the tombs of courtiers and officials were more loosely arranged and were widely positioned across the whole burial area, perhaps symbolizing a lessening of the king's authority which was beginning to emerge at this time.

THE RISE OF THE SUN-CULT

The kings of Dynasty 5 patronized the sun-cult to an unprecedented level, and may have owed their accession to the priesthood of Re. Some of the historical facts that surrounded the beginning of Dynasty 5 may remain embedded in a folk-tale (often referred to as 'The Tale of King Cheops and the Magicians'), preserved in the Westcar Papyrus which perhaps dates to the Second Intermediate Period. In its original form, this tale may have been used as a form of propaganda to justify the rulership of the kings of Dynasty 5. Such stories would have been disseminated throughout the country, and handed down by generations of public story-tellers.[40]

The story attempts to establish the legitimacy of the divine origin of Dynasty 5, and to show that the sun-god was Egypt's supreme deity. The activities of a group of magicians are described, who are called to the palace of King Cheops to entertain him. One, with the gift of prophecy, tells the king that his dynastic line will be terminated by the birth of triplets to be borne by the wife of a priest of Re. These sons are in fact the offspring of Re himself, thus emphasizing the divine origin of the new line and Re's role in fathering a dynasty who would act as his earthly agents. The story confirms that these divine sons became good and pious rulers who built temples for the god and provisioned his altars. It also seeks to explain why the rulers of Dynasty 5 promoted the sun-cult. According to the tale, Cheops was much disturbed by this prophecy, although the magician assured him that his son, Chephren, and grandson, Mycerinus, would first rule Egypt before the new dynasty took control.

The story is inaccurate in certain respects – two other kings succeeded Mycerinus before Dynasty 5 came to power, and the three rulers of Dynasty 5, Userkaf, Sahure and Neferirkare (Kakai), were not triplets (see p. 109). Userkaf was the father of the other two men, and there is no supporting evidence that a priest's wife was the mother of any of these rulers. In fact, as previously stated, Userkaf, founder of Dynasty 5, was probably descended from a secondary branch of Cheops' family and married a daughter of Mycerinus to substantiate his claim to the throne. Nevertheless, the Westcar Papyrus probably accurately reflects the ideas that the kings of Dynasty 5 were attempting to promote about their own right to rule as Re's heirs.

THE SOLAR TEMPLES

Towards the end of the Old Kingdom, the Egyptians had already developed an established concept of a supreme being, the ruler and lord of all creation, who sustained all his creation. They did not, however, designate one god as this supreme deity, although Re appears to have embodied most of these qualities in Dynasty 5. In the later Old Kingdom, the king's power declined and more emphasis was placed on the cult of Re. The solar aspects of the king's deification had been important since Dynasty 4, as expressed in his title 'Son of Re', although this did not necessarily indicate a reduction in the royal status. It was, perhaps, more an association that linked the god with his earthly likeness, or a joint rulership that enabled the king to repeat on earth the deeds which the sun-god had performed at creation.

However, in Dynasty 5, it is apparent that the cult of Re became so prominent that special solar complexes, independent of the pyramid complexes, were required to accommodate ceremonies associated with the sun-cult. During this dynasty, solar temples were built, modelled on the original sun-temple at Heliopolis, which has never been discovered. Inscriptional evidence indicates that the first three kings and another three rulers of the dynasty built solar temples. However, only those of Userkaf[1] and Niuserre have been discovered and excavated on the edge of the desert at Abu Gurob, which lies south of Giza and not far from these kings' pyramids at Abusir.

Each temple consisted of a series of enclosures that led to a wide, paved, open-air court which accommodated a rectangular podium. This perhaps represented the Mound where creation was thought to have taken place. On top of the podium there stood a squat obelisk which was probably intended to replicate the Benben Stone, a key feature in the original temple at Heliopolis which was both the god's cult-symbol and perhaps a representation of a sun-ray (*see* p. 84). A low altar, with specially cut channels to drain away the sacrificial animal blood, stood in front of the podium. The roofless, open court enabled the sun-god to be present at the ceremonies. Elsewhere in the complex, there were magazines for storing offerings, and beyond the enclosure lay a brick-lined pit which may once have housed a wooden boat so that the sun could sail around the heavens.

Wall-reliefs found in the causeway and other areas of the temple of Niuserre (and subsequently removed to the Cairo and Berlin Museums) are particularly important. They depict the animals and birds created by the sun, and include scenes of religious ceremonies such as the foundation of the temple and the king's jubilee festival. They also show personifications of the three seasons (Akhet, Peret and Shemu) into which the Egyptian year was divided, the districts (nomes), and the Nile, Sea, Grain and Nourishment, who all present offerings to the sun-god.

NON-ROYAL (PRIVATE) TOMBS

During the Old Kingdom, only the kings and a few of the queens were buried in pyramids, but gradually, throughout this period, the nobles and officials became increasingly important, and their substantial tombs, provisioned with funerary goods, were either built at the foot of the king's pyramid or in the provinces where they held governorships. Two types of non-royal burial place were developed for the nobility which are known today as mastaba-tombs and rock-cut tombs. In Dynasty 4, the mastaba tomb predominated, although rock-cut tombs were more widely used towards the end of this period.

The concept of the mastaba tomb remained unchanged from earlier times; its main purpose was to house the body and the funerary equipment, and to provide an earthly location where food and other commodities could be offered to sustain the deceased owner's spirit. Rows of such tombs were built around the kings' pyramids at Giza, Dahshur, Saqqara, Meydum and Abusir, to represent in death the relationship that the king had once enjoyed with his court during his lifetime.

The tomb was regarded as a 'house' where the deceased continued to live after death. If a person survived and reached adulthood, he would begin to prepare for the transition to the next world. Death was not regarded as the end of individual existence, but merely as a means of access to the next world. In order to understand the Egyptian attitude to death, it is necessary to comprehend that the living and the dead were regarded as members of one community, and thus the dead continued to play an important part in influencing the daily events of the living. Provisioning a tomb was an essential duty, and the monument was used not only as a place of burial where offerings could be made but also as a showcase and memorial for the owner's life achievements.

Underground, the substructure contained the burial chamber, to which access was gained by a stairway or shaft. Sometimes, a second chamber, with its own shaft, was included for the owner's wife. Because the burial was vulnerable to tomb robbers, every attempt was made to protect this area: sometimes, a larger stairway or passage or a vertical pit was included so that the burial chamber could be positioned further into the ground, or the access shafts were blocked with gravel and rocks and the internal doors were filled in with stone or bricks after the burial.

Above ground, the superstructure marked the tomb's location and protected the burial, as well as providing an offering chapel where perpetual provisions could be presented to the deceased owner. In the earliest mastabas and at the start of Dynasty 4, the superstructure was built of mudbrick, but stone soon came to be used for these tombs as well as the pyramids. The brick cells found in the cores of earlier superstructures were now replaced either by a solid masonry structure or by rubble placed inside a bench-shaped wall. The mudbrick panelled façades of the earliest superstructures were now often replaced with smooth limestone facings.

With increased skill in stoneworking techniques and the ready availability of limestone from the nearby quarries, the craftsmen often used stone to build the offering chapel and to face some of the tomb chambers. This enabled these walls to be decorated with carved or painted reliefs, although in Dynasty 4 these were usually only placed in the outer rooms of the chapel and not in the offering chamber itself. These scenes represented aspects of the owner's earthly life and his possessions that he wished to magically perpetuate in the next world.

Two 'false doors' were set into the east wall of the superstructure. They provided a means of access for the owner's spirit to leave the burial chamber and to reach the food offerings that were left outside the tomb each day. The 'doors' were solid but decorated with relief sculpture so that they added to the appearance of the tomb as a house. Two inscribed stone blocks (stelae) associated with the false doors usually incorporated the name and titles of the owner, and an offering formula or 'menu'.

The offering chapel was regarded as an essential element of the tomb, because the provision of food and drink was considered vital to the owner's continued existence after death. At first, this offering area was attached to the east wall of the superstructure, but at the start of the Old Kingdom, it was incorporated within the superstructure to create a more secure monument. In addition, this area also came to house the *serdab*, a small enclosed room that held a statue of the deceased which could receive the offerings if the owner's mummified body had been destroyed. Generally, the tomb recreated elements of a contemporary domestic dwelling, because the dead were believed to have the same needs as the living. The tomb (known as the *House of the Ka*) provided a house for the deceased, the funerary goods supplied his possessions for eternity, and the mortuary ritual supplied perpetual food and drink. The offering chapel can be regarded as the equivalent of a reception area in a house, while the burial chamber provided the 'bedroom', and additional areas were included for storing possessions.

By Dynasty 5, royal relatives no longer exclusively occupied the senior government posts. Officials no longer expressed total loyalty to the king, and the appointments to governorships in the provinces were no longer held on a 'lifetime only' basis. Increasingly, they became hereditary and the governors became more independent of royal favour. This erosion of the king's authority became increasingly apparent in the funerary monuments. The pyramids of Dynasty 5 decreased in size and quality, but by the later years of this period, the non-royal tomb chapels became more complex and contained a larger number of rooms. The wall-scenes that depicted daily life now occurred in the offering chapel as well as the outer areas. Some tombs, such as those of the courtiers Ti and

Ptah-hotep who lived during Dynasty 5, and those of Kagemni and Mereruka, were built within the long-established necropolis at Saqqara. However, with the growing independence of the provincial governors, there was also a trend to abandon burial near to the king; instead, they constructed rock-cut tombs in their own districts. Cut high in the cliffs situated on the edge of the desert, these tombs also featured decorated offering chambers. They provided the prototype for a style of provincial funerary architecture, which continued throughout the First Intermediate Period and the early Middle Kingdom.

In Dynasty 6, there were further developments. On the one hand, mastaba tombs continued to be built near the royal pyramids at Saqqara, but these now incorporated large offering chapels within the superstructure which consisted of several rooms. Wall-reliefs, more extensive and elaborate than in the previous dynasty, were now also placed in the burial chamber. In the provincial rock-cut tombs, there is evidence of two art-styles in the wall scenes:[42] the finest tombs continued to be decorated in the classic style which had been developed at Memphis, but increasingly, in the less elaborate tombs, new and cruder forms emerged. Executed by provincial craftsmen, these scenes retained the essential subject matter of the classic wall decoration, but the figures were more angular in appearance. This style – which became increasingly divorced from the Memphite model – persisted throughout the First Intermediate Period.

THE CONCEPT OF THE PERSONALITY

The Egyptians believed that the human personality had many facets – a concept that was probably developed early in the Old Kingdom. In life, the person was a complete entity, but if he had led a virtuous life, he could also have access to a multiplicity of forms that could be used in the next world. In some instances, these forms could be employed to help those whom the deceased wished to support or, alternatively, to take revenge on his enemies.

The corpse or body was an essential link between the deceased and his former earthly existence because he was able to use it to receive the food and drink which would sustain his spirit. Mummification was developed first for royalty and then increasingly for the nobility and the middle classes. It attempted to preserve the body from decay and to ensure that a likeness of the deceased survived which his spirit would recognize. There was always the possibility that the mummy would perish, and so statues of the tomb-owner and magical spells were placed in the tomb to provide other means of sustaining the owner's spirit. The owner's name was also regarded as an integral part of his personality. This expressed or revealed his true nature or essence and was inscribed on his statue or mummy wrapping to identify him. Sometimes, a person's real name was concealed because knowledge of a name enabled people to direct evil as well as good against the owner. Another element of the personality was the owner's shadow, which emanated from a god and reflected the divine power; it was a silhouette of the body, and symbolized the god's presence within that person.

The most important element was the spirit (*ka*) which was essentially the vital force that enabled a person to continue to receive offerings in the next world. Originally, this life-force had been expressed through the creator-god, and it was passed across the successive generations, carrying the spiritual force of the first creation. Gods possessed *kas*, and these could reside temporarily in the god's statues or cult animals. This force was also present in the body of each king, empowering him to perform his duties. As the personification of the inherited life-force, the *ka* was not just specific to individuals, but also animated and sustained families and groups. However, sometimes, the *ka* could be regarded as the essential self of an individual, acting as his guide and protector. By incorporating the qualities and characteristics of each unique individual, the *ka* represented the personality and was also regarded as a person's 'double'. However, the *ka* only resided temporarily in the living body; at death, it became a separate entity that was non-corporeal and immortal. Nevertheless, it still provided the vital link with the earth and the person's body in the tomb, and was dependent on the tomb offerings for sustained sustenance. The *ka* was usually represented either as a human with upraised arms, or as a separate pair of upraised arms.

The *ba* is sometimes translated as 'soul'. Represented as a human-headed bird, the *ba* was closely linked to a particular body. Essentially, it was the 'spiritual body' of the deceased, and the *ba* and the corpse were believed to unite periodically after death. However, this force could also leave the body after death, and travel outside the tomb to visit places that the owner had favoured during life. Thus, essentially, it provided a person with the power to be free and function physically in the next world. Finally, both the living and the dead could draw on a supernatural power known as *akh*. As a spirit who could pass between this world and the next, the *akh* had the ability to intercede on behalf of the living or dead.

TOMB PROVISION AND EQUIPMENT

In order to ensure that the link was maintained between the living and the dead, so that the person's immortality was assured, all material needs had to be provided for the deceased, and the correct funerary rituals had to be performed. It was expected that a person's heir would bring the daily offerings to the tomb to sustain the owner's *ka*. This ritual was carried out in the offering chapel where, accompanied by prayers, the provisions were placed on a flat altar-table. It was believed that the owner's *ka* would enter the tomb through the false door, and take up residence in the mummy or the owner's statue (which was housed in the *serdab*), in order to absorb the sustaining essence of the food. However, after several generations, family members found that this regular attendance at an increasing number of tombs became a burden. The tombs became neglected, and it was feared that the *kas* would experience starvation, so other methods were adopted to ensure a continuous food supply.

Usually, a priest known as a '*Ka*-servant' was employed. The tomb-owner set aside a piece of land on his estate which supplied the food offerings and also paid the *Ka*-servant for placing the provisions at the tomb and performing the funerary rituals. The *Ka*-servant's descendants, who were expected to take on this obligation in perpetuity, were also paid from this source. However, the priests frequently neglected their duties, and other methods had to be adopted to ensure that the offerings continued. The most important was the provision of an Offering List inscribed on the walls. This included a formula known as the *Htp-di-nsw*.

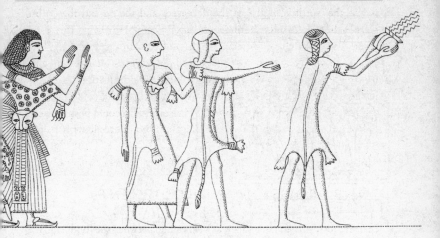

Sem-priests perform rites at a funeral, pouring out a libation (*right*) and presenting the funerary meal to the deceased owner.

This is generally translated as a 'Boon-which-the-king-gives', meaning that in theory the offerings were made to the dead person through the king's own beneficence and bounty. This gave the offerings added authority and lessened the owner's dependence on the food brought by the family or the *Ka*-servant. The Menu was often accompanied by a scene showing the owner in front of a table piled high with food and, once they had been magically activated, the scene and inscription were believed to supply eternal and abundant food.[43]

In addition to the Offering List, an Autobiography was included amongst the tomb inscriptions. This gave a summary of the life of the tomb-owner, emphasizing his virtues and worthiness, but omitting any reference to his failures or sins. It included his official rank and titles, and information about his family. The superficial purpose of such texts was to persuade visitors to enter the tomb and recite a prayer. They also asserted the status of the deceased, and justified his claim to hold high office in the next world. By asserting a person's ownership of the tomb, the inscriptions may have sought, although in vain, to prevent vandalism. The Autobiography also provides insight into the virtues and standards of behaviour that were deemed desirable at that period, such as kindness,

A tomb scene illustrates wine production: picking grapes (*right*), trampling fruit in the wine press (*left*), and collecting the extracted juice in jars (*centre*). Magic made the wine available to the tomb-owner.

courteousness, and the avoidance of envy, and amplifies the descriptions of good behaviour preserved in the contemporary Wisdom Texts (*see* pp. 130–33).

By Dynasty 5, the Offering List and the Autobiography had become essential features of the tomb, and by Dynasty 6, they occur in their most complete form. The concept continued throughout the troubled times of the First Intermediate Period, and reappeared in the form of the autobiographical stela. This was a stone block, often round-topped and decorated with a scene showing the deceased owner offering to gods, which was inscribed with an autobiography that recorded the owner's virtues and the major events of his life, as well as prayers which praised the king and the gods. Ordinary people often set up stelae as personal memorials and, because many were produced and stone is a durable material, a relatively large number of examples have survived.

* *

A tomb scene shows men eating various foods including cakes, bread, poultry, fish, fruit and vegetables. Food offerings to the dead were the same as the diet of the living.

To enable the mummy and the statue of the deceased to regain their life-force so that they could function and receive their offerings, a ritual known as the 'Ceremony of Opening the Mouth' was performed. This had early parallels in Mesopotamia, and studies have indicated that it may have had associations with customs surrounding childbirth.[44] In Egypt, although it was probably originally performed by the priests for the king in his pyramid temple, the ritual was gradually extended to the nobility and others who could afford it, and became a regular part of funerary rites. In its earliest form, the ceremony was carried out on the royal statues to enable the king's spirit to enter the inanimate statue and benefit from the food and incense offerings. Later, it was extended to all the sacred inanimate forms in the tomb, which included the mummy, statues, models and wall-scenes. The funerary priest used an adze (a carpenter's tool) to touch these on the mouth, hands and feet so that the life-force would be restored to them.

By the Old Kingdom, the nobles expected to continue their existence within the tomb, and the wall decoration and tomb contents were designed as a complete concept, to provide the deceased with all his requirements in the next world. There were wall scenes showing the production and provision of food, and statues and models of workers. Once these were activated by the Opening of the Mouth, they would guarantee an eternal food supply for the owner.

In some tombs at Giza and Saqqara, wall reliefs show a figure entitled 'Companion of the Tomb'. He is depicted near to the tomb-owner, so that he could share the offerings brought to the chapel. Studies of this person's role[45] indicate that he may have been a co-property-holder with the deceased even during the owner's lifetime, and that because he had received benefits from the deceased when he was alive, the Companion continued to be attached to him by this obligation after death. Another suggestion is that he acted as supervisor of the funerary endowment on behalf of the widow, thus guaranteeing her security and benefiting personally from the funerary offerings. Again, if there was no suitable next of kin, he may have taken on the administration of the funerary estate.

PRINCIPLES OF RELIGIOUS ART

In the nineteenth century ACE, it was customary to regard Egyptian art as immature and primitive, representing a stage in development that, through the works of the Greeks and Romans, ultimately culminated in 'Western art'. However, today, Egyptian art can be seen as a fully developed and sophisticated system that met the religious requirements of the contemporary society. Egyptian art, as we define it in the tombs and temples, consists mainly of horizontal wall registers that are filled with formalized scenes and figures. This style is only known to exist from c.2700 BCE; earlier art from the Predynastic and early Dynastic Periods took a much less structured form. This is evident on the slate palettes and 'Decorated Ware' pottery, and in a large wall scene found in a tomb of the Predynastic Period at Hieraconpolis which showed men, animals and boats arranged in small, scattered groups.

Once the traditions of classical Egyptian art had been established in the early Old Kingdom, there were relatively few major innovations or changes until the Graeco-Roman Period. As with other aspects of the civilization, foreign influences were largely absent during the period

A wall-scene in the Temple of Karnak shows priests carrying the Sacred Barque of Amen-Re during a procession.

when the art forms developed and reached maturity, and so in Egypt there is the rare opportunity to observe the development of an art style from its origin to its culmination some 4,000 years later. The only significant break with tradition, which occurred during the reign of Akhenaten in Dynasty 18, was underpinned by the king's religious revolution.

More evidence has survived of religious than secular art, partly because of the relative durability of the materials (stone and mudbrick) from which tombs and temples or domestic dwellings were built. Wall scenes in the temples provide evidence of the religious rites which were once performed there, while reliefs and paintings in the royal rock-cut tombs of the New Kingdom (which replaced the pyramids as places of royal burial) show scenes from the Funerary Books which were intended to ensure that the deceased king passed safely into the next world. By

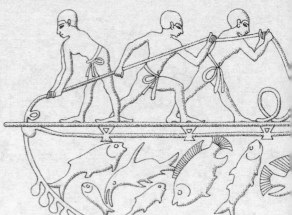

A tomb scene shows fishermen in papyrus skiffs and a sectional stretch of water. It is full of fish that can be 'brought to life' as a magic food source for the owner.

contrast, in the non-royal tombs of the wealthy at all periods, wall-scenes depicted the locations and activities of everyday life that the owner wanted to recreate in the next world.

None of the scenes were put in place simply to decorate the tomb or even to provide spiritual inspiration for the onlooker since, in many instances, these walls would no longer be visible to the outside world once the tomb had been sealed. The main purpose of the scenes was to recreate a world that the owner could continue to enjoy after death. By performing the Opening of the Mouth ritual on the contents of the scene, the figures would be activated and given the power to 'come to life' for eternity. The deceased tomb-owner could thus 'experience' these places, activities and possessions. The subject matter in these scenes reflects the contemporary world of the living, and provides information about the work and activities on the owner's estate, his pastimes, and various stages in the preparation of his funeral.

This art displays some features that puzzle the modern observer if he is unaware of the principles which probably underpinned these representations. The Egyptians have not left any record of the rules which may have governed their art, but a study in 1919 ACE by Heinrich Schäfer, who became Director of the Egyptian section at the Berlin Museum between 1914 and 1935 ACE, has greatly informed the modern

study of this subject.[46] From Schäfer's observations of a wide range of art, he concluded that there were two fundamental types.

He described one as 'conceptual' art, and this represents in a pictorial form what a person or an object *is*. It provides information about the essential character, features, or component parts of an object, depicting what the artist can see in front of him. On the other hand, 'perceptual' art demonstrates how a person or an object appears to an individual artist; to capture this realism, the artist includes perspective, the use of light and shade, and the representation of different textures. Conceptual art thus provides a kind of diagram of an object with details of all the individual parts, whereas perceptual art shows the scene or object from the artist's own viewpoint, although this may obscure or omit some of the features or parts of the whole.

Schäfer used the term 'pre-Greek' to describe all the art we now consider to be conceptual, but in fact it includes not only other ancient art and even early Greek art itself but also the work of modern 'primitive' artists and very young children. It is essentially all art that, regardless of its historical context, does not recognize or use the principles of perspective revealed by the Greeks in the fifth century BCE, which reached the height of scientific accuracy during the Renaissance. Conceptual art (sometimes known as 'Aspective' art) is expressed in its most

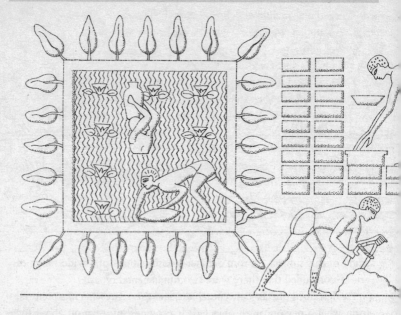

mature and sophisticated form in ancient Egypt, and far from being inferior to perceptual (or 'Perspective' art), it was introduced and retained because it met the Egyptians' religious and magical requirements. Schäfer showed that conceptual art is the natural method of choice adopted by all people to paint or draw people, animals and objects. It is only if they are taught or exposed to the laws of perspective that they will pursue a different approach.

From his observations, Schäfer provided a series of guidelines and principles that can be applied to Egyptian art in order to interpret each scene. Representations of figures and objects within the scenes provide diagrams of what the artist knew to exist, rather than his individual perception of them. By using this approach, as much information as possible was provided visually, so that all the details of the object could be 'brought to life' by means of magic. If any part or feature of the whole was not present in the scene, then it could not be activated in this way.

Certain conventions were strictly observed with regard to the human figure. Gods, royalty, or the tomb-owner and his family were always

A tomb scene showing mudbrick production. The pond (*left*) supplied water to mix with the alluvial mud; it is represented diagrammatically, in accordance with the principles of aspective art.

depicted as young adults with perfect bodies and indistinguishable 'idealized' faces which represented the contemporary concept of beauty. In order to identify these as individuals, their names were given in the accompanying inscriptions; here, also, conversational phrases attributed to these figures were included. The figures of men and women are shown in stiff, formal poses, with the head in profile so that only one eye is represented, the torso presented from a front view, and the legs and feet also depicted in profile. This physically impossible pose was used to ensure that the tomb-owner could utilize a maximum number of limbs and physical features in the next world, after they had been magically charged and transfused with the life-force.

However, if the Egyptians had applied the laws of perspective, then many of the body parts would have been flattened and foreshortened (such as the nose and feet), and much of the symbolic power would

A tomb scene illustrates the use of a bagpress to extract juice from grapes. A linen bag was stretched between two posts that were twisted hard to squeeze out the liquid.

have been lost. These principles can also be observed in some palaeolithic cave paintings in other parts of the world. Throughout the long period of art development in Egypt, there is little variation in the way in which the human figure is shown: this is because a canon was used which ensured that the individual parts of the human body were always shown in the correct proportion to each other.[47] In the Old Kingdom, this was achieved by using a simple series of guidelines that transversed the main points on the body, but by the Middle Kingdom, a more elaborate grid system was introduced.

There were also certain conventions regarding the representation of people's age. The tomb-owner and his wife were always shown as young adults and their children as infants who wore no clothes and had the hairstyle known as the 'Sidelock of Youth', which characterized children under the age of puberty. In reality, of course, the owner could have been middle-aged when he died, and his children may already have been young adults. The individual faces never express emotion, and although people are sometimes shown in groups, they never appear to interact with each other; their expressions remain calm and stereotyped, with no attempt to convey individual emotion or involvement. Again, crowds are not depicted; instead a group is indicated by the simple convention of placing three figures together. The size of the figures is also important in a scene. According to the laws of perspective, the largest figure would be the one positioned nearest to the artist. However, in conceptual art, the largest figure signifies the most important person who, in the context of the tomb, was the owner. His children are shown as smaller figures, and there is a further decrease in the size of the servants and menials.

The wall scenes are arranged in horizontal registers that progress from the top of the wall to the bottom, providing a corresponding sequence of action. There is no attempt to depict a background setting or scenery. An outdoors location is indicated by including a tree, or a stretch of water to represent the Nile or a garden pond that is often filled with plants and teeming fish. Indoor scenes are indicated by the inclusion of items of furniture. When dealing with buildings, lakes and gardens, the artist shows them in a diagrammatic form, providing maximum information about the layout and internal rooms, so that these individual characteristics can be 'activated'. They are shown as if turned through a 90-degree angle, so that both the façade and the interior of a building are visible, and the Nile or lake are never depicted as a thin blue line at ground level, but appear in section so that the fish can also be represented, thus enabling the owner to have an eternal supply of fish.

For the same reason, the contents of baskets and dishes are displayed in piles on top of their containers, to provide the owner with an abundant, eternal food supply. The information or 'set of instructions' provided in these diagrams was designed to enable the tomb-owner to possess at will a complete three-dimensional figure or object with all the powers of the original. Sometimes, however, the application of these rules produced anomalies, such as the inclusion of only one eye or breast on the human figure, although it was probably intended that this would bring about the reality of a pair of eyes or breasts when the three-dimensional figure was activated.

Although important individuals such as deities, royalty and tomb-owners were portrayed according to these strict conventions, less significant people – peasants, servants and attendants – could be shown more naturalistically. The artist had more freedom here to express his wit and humour, and to show some interaction between these figures. When birds and animals were depicted, the conventions were noticeably relaxed, and acute personal observations made by the artists are often evident in these studies. These depictions contrast sharply with the formal human stereotypes, and give a much better indication of the true ability of the Egyptian artist. In all its forms, however, religious art was not simply depictive; essentially, it was designed to convey a statement or to achieve a specific end.[48]

PERSONAL ETHICS AND WISDOM

Most of the literature from the Old Kingdom relates to mythology and the rituals performed for the king and the gods. However, one major source provides insight into the code of behaviour and moral and ethical values prevalent at this period. This major genre is often termed 'Wisdom Texts', although the Egyptians called them 'Instructions in Wisdom'. They believed that this code had been authorized by the gods, and although the actual manuscripts were written at a later date, some of them obviously preserve ideas that were current in the Old Kingdom, at a time when it was already recognized that a person's earthly deeds would have a profound influence on his ability to attain immortality.

The Instructions provided a set of rules for conducting personal relationships. They were a teaching code, which established the standards of behaviour that were acceptable for young people, and were used as models for successive generations of schoolboys to copy. Indeed, it is often the Schoolboy Exercises of later periods that have preserved these texts. They exemplified the values of the centralized hierarchy of the Old Kingdom, by emphasizing the importance of balance and order, and providing lessons in good manners and conduct as well as setting out a model for literary style and expression.[49]

The works usually consist of an address by a wise man (the king or vizier) to his son or pupils, who gives advice on how to advance in life, since it was believed that personal attainment would bring contentment. Most of the texts were composed in the Old and Middle Kingdoms, and provided a code of behaviour for training boys who would become officials. They present a picture of the 'ideal' courtier who was expected to exercise power with clemency and righteousness, and they emphasize the importance of kindness, moderation and good judgement. By the New Kingdom, however, the Wisdom Texts were more widely used for training middle-class boys, and it is their Schoolboy Exercises that have survived. Additionally, at this time, new texts were composed which included different ideas that were directed towards the middle classes, and authorship of the text was no longer attributed to the king or vizier but to a minor official addressing his own son.

Egyptian texts are usually anonymous, but these Instructions are attributed to particular authors, although this is probably a device to give them authority rather than any true reflection of the composer's actual identity. The earliest extant Instruction is attributed to Prince Hardedef, a famous wise man of the Old Kingdom, but the Instruction of Ptah-hotep is the most famous. Ptah-hotep, the vizier of King Isesi of Dynasty 5, was credited with its authorship, and such a man is known to have existed; also there is a well-known tomb of an official named Ptah-hotep at Saqqara. In another Instruction, the vizier is charged by King Huni of Dynasty 3 with the training and counselling of Prince Kagemni.[50]

The practical advice these texts offer covers subjects such as the correct behaviour towards superiors, peers and inferiors, and the need to be cautious in speech and prudent in friendship. The pupils were expected to behave well in houses they visited as guests, and to show the true qualities of leadership by treating kindly those people of lower status who would seek their help when they became officials. The young men are advised to marry young, to respect their wives, and to guard against unseemly friendships with women in other households. They are told how to rear their children:

If you are held in esteem, and have founded a household, and have a son who pleases god, if he does right and patterns himself on your model, and listens to your instruction, and his undertakings go well in your house, seek out everything for him that is good. (Instruction of Ptah-hotep)[51]

There are warnings against greediness and guidance on behaviour at meals:

> If you are a guest at a table of one who is greater than you,
> Take what he gives as it is set before you.
> Do not look at what is set before him
> But look at what lies before you . . .
> Cast down you countenance until he greet you,
> Speak only when he has greeted you.
> Laugh when he laughs.
> That will please his heart and what you do will be acceptable . . .
>
> (Instruction of Ptah-hotep)[52]

The most destructive and evil emotion is identified as covetousness:

> If you desire your conduct to be good, to set yourself free from all evil, then beware of covetousness which is an incurable disease. It is impossible to be intimate with it: it makes the good friend bitter, it alienates the trusted employee from his master, it makes bad both the father and the mother, together with the mother's brothers, and it divorces a man's wife . . .
>
> (Instruction of Ptah-hotep)[53]

The texts advise how covetousness should be avoided:

> Do not be not covetous regarding division, and do not be exacting with regard to what is due to you. Do not be covetous towards your family . . .
>
> (Instruction of Ptah-hotep)[54]

An Instruction which is rather different from the others is known either as the 'Satire on Trades', the 'Instruction of Duauf' or the 'Instruction of Khety'. Probably composed some time between the Old and Middle Kingdoms, the text is attributed to a humble man named Duauf, the son of Khety. Duauf provides good advice for his son, Pepy, who is fortunate to receive an education in the 'School of Books', amongst the magistrates' children. Duauf is concerned that his son should perform well at school and become a scribe (a 'learned man') so that he can avoid the hardships associated with the various trades. The text describes how Duauf, as he takes his son to school, enumerates the many difficulties encountered in the trades and compares them with the status and excellent conditions of the scribe's profession. To succeed as a scribe, the pupil must be hardworking, and the text praises schools and education generally. For this reason, it was a favourite model for later generations of students to copy out and learn.

The Wisdom Texts date back to at least 2400 BCE, and combined both didactic and contemplative concepts. The code of behaviour reflects the highest standards of the Old Kingdom, and enables us to view the personal attributes which were considered most desirable. These included kindness to petitioners, moderation in all dealings, self-control, wisdom, and the ability to exercise good judgement. In this way, the Egyptians sought to establish a high standard of behaviour for officials of the state.

DECLINE AND FALL OF THE OLD KINGDOM

The apparently well-ordered and stable society of the Old Kingdom did not survive. The seeds of its destruction, embedded in its political, economic, social and religious structures and policies from as early as Dynasty 4, led to disastrous consequences at the end of Dynasty 6. In political and economic spheres, the problems were associated with the status and role of the king. At the beginning of the Old Kingdom, the gulf between the divine ruler and his human subjects was emphasized: buried in a pyramid while his nobles were interred in mastaba tombs, the king alone could expect an individual eternity which he would spend in the heavens with the gods. On the other hand, everyone else could only hope to achieve immortality through the king's bounty: the nobles and officials received the gift of a tomb and land from the royal estate that would provision their burials; and the craftsmen and peasants gained eternal life because of their contribution to the construction and furbishment of the king's burial place. Royal power reached its zenith with the Giza pyramids in Dynasty 4, but from then onwards there was a gradual equalization of wealth. This was the result of several factors.

First, although the king theoretically owned all the land, people and resources, in practical terms the royal estates and wealth gradually passed into an ever-widening circle of inheritance and were increasingly divided into smaller units. Crown lands were given to nobles and officials so that they could provision their tombs and employ *Ka*-priests, and this property was also usually exempted from taxation, so that the kings gradually lost both their 'capital' and 'interest'. In addition, from Dynasty 4 onwards, royal decrees exempted the personnel and possessions belonging to the pyramid temples and pyramid cities from taxation and drafts of enforced labour. Concurrently, each king devoted massive resources to building a new pyramid complex for himself and maintaining the endowments and priesthoods associated with it, as well as repairing, maintaining and provisioning the burial places and priesthoods of his forebears. As time passed, this became an increasing burden.

Probably towards the end of Dynasty 4, the loss of the king's supreme economic power began to affect his overall status, while the position of the nobles and priesthoods showed a marked improvement. The king now took several actions in an attempt to restore his position and to re-establish the support of these two groups. First, there were policy changes in Dynasty 5 that enhanced the independence of the nobility. Originally, the highest administrative posts had been reserved for the king's relatives in order to preserve their loyalty and support. However, many men were now drawn from non-royal families. Again, posts had once been awarded on a temporary or lifetime basis, but now provincial governorships increasingly became hereditary. Any short-term support this gained for the king was offset by the increased independence it gave to the governors. They often ruled districts that were far away from the capital, and now the king could not control them either by direct force or by the withdrawal of their appointments. Gradually, these men became virtually independent rulers in their provinces, and this was underlined by the new custom of burial in their own districts. Whereas once they had been buried at the foot of the king's pyramid, thus indicating that they were dependent on the king's bounty to achieve immortality, now they clearly no longer considered this essential.

At the end of the Old Kingdom, this gradual decentralization of power led to a fragmentation of Egypt that reflected the conditions that had existed in Predynastic times. Now, instead of being united under a single ruler, these isolated governors once again attempted to form alliances so that they could fight each other. As his political and economic power declined, the king's divinity was undermined so that eventually he came to be regarded as simply another ruler among many. Smaller pyramids were built, and the quality of their construction declined, whereas the nobles' tombs became more elaborate.

In addition, because the sun-cult increased in significance, the king's own role and status underwent profound changes. For example, possibly because they were dependent for their power on the priesthood of Re, the kings of Dynasty 5 were willing to reduce the size and standard of their own burial places, and to build solar temples. Also, the tax exemptions, which had been made available to the royal funerary monuments and tombs of the nobility in previous centuries, were now extended to the solar temples, in order to increase their economic base.

Ultimately, however, all the actions taken by the kings to restore their power and gain support were futile. By Dynasty 6, internal weakness and dissolution of centralized government provided an opportunity for the Bedouin nomads on Egypt's north-eastern frontier to infiltrate and raid the country. The reign of Pepy II marked the final stage in disintegration: since he came to the throne as a young child and ruled for over ninety years, old age and his declining faculties ultimately provided an opportunity for other factions to take advantage of the situation. He was probably the king described in the 'Admonitions of a Prophet', a literary text which recalls how an aged and infirm ruler, living in his palace at Memphis, was unaware of the dangers that Egypt was facing.[55]

The collapse of the Old Kingdom profoundly affected the Egyptian psyche. The values, traditions and certainties of this period had seemed indestructible, and later generations clearly regarded it as a 'golden age' when the highest standards were achieved in many aspects of the civilization. The people never forgot the material and spiritual devastation of this collapse, which is probably described in the literature of the subsequent period. Profound social and religious changes can be observed in the First Intermediate Period and Middle Kingdom, when the Egyptians came to terms with the collapse of their society and many of their fondly held concepts about human life and continued existence after death were questioned and sometimes even discarded.

CHAPTER 4

Osiris, the People's God

The First Intermediate Period and the Middle Kingdom,
c.2181–1786 BCE

HISTORICAL BACKGROUND OF THE FIRST INTERMEDIATE PERIOD

The First Intermediate Period is the modern term used for the turbulent transitional years between the Old and Middle Kingdoms; it usually includes Dynasties 7 to 11 although some modern histories place Dynasty 11 in the Middle Kingdom. There are five distinct but overlapping stages in the First Intermediate Period.

The first stage was marked by the disintegration of the country at the end of Dynasty 6 and the subsequent decline in centralized government (Dynasties 7 and 8) when a series of ephemeral rulers continued to hold power at Memphis. Secondly, the collapse of the monarchy at Memphis in turn led to a period of chaos and anarchy when civil war broke out between the provincial governors. Famine, poverty and disease became widespread, and graves and monuments were ravaged and destroyed by tomb robbers. Such devastating conditions profoundly affected the physical and spiritual strength of the country, and the effect of these events upon the population at large and on individual belief is probably described in a collection of texts known as the Pessimistic Literature. Internal political and social collapse was probably exacerbated by continuing raids and incursions carried out by the Bedouin who lived on Egypt's north-eastern border.

In the third stage, the governors of Heracleopolis emerged as a new line of rulers who controlled Middle Egypt, between Memphis and Thebes (Dynasties 9 and 10). Akhtoy (Khety) was the local ruler who led his people to victory, and established Heracleopolis as the new capital. Warfare and anarchy were temporarily stopped, and in this period of comparative peace, local rulers in other centres were able to build themselves fine tombs at Beni Hasan, Akhmim and el-Bersha. However, another family – the Mentuhoteps – soon tried to seize power. Centred at the southern city of Thebes, these men gradually extended their influence northwards where they came into conflict with the Heracleopolitans. This was recorded in an inscription in the tomb of a man called Akhtoy at Assiut. Further information about this period is provided in a text known as 'The Instruction addressed to King Merikare', in which an elderly ruler (possibly one of the Akhtoys of Dynasty 9 or 10) addresses his son and successor. It follows the pattern of Wisdom Texts, which were probably composed in the Old Kingdom, but it has a different theme and purpose, representing a treatise on kingship and conveying the old king's wisdom and advice to Merikare.' Regarded by scholars as a genuine historical text, it was probably composed not by Akhtoy but in Merikare's own reign, with the purpose of setting out his policy. Here are some of the author's thoughts:

Do justice, then you will endure on earth;
Comfort the mourner, do not oppress the widow,
Do not expel a man from his father's property,
Do not reduce the possessions of the nobles.
Beware of punishing in a wrongful manner,
Do not kill, it does not serve you.
Punish with beatings, and with detention,
Then the land will be well-controlled . . .

In the fifth and final stage, the Mentuhoteps were able to seize overall control of the country and inaugurate Dynasty 11, thus restoring political and social order. It was their greatest ruler, Mentuhotep Nebhepetre, who overcame the Heracleopolitan rulers and brought civil war and anarchy to an end. He pacified the whole country, and created conditions of stability so that the provincial governors, although still preserving outward independence, owed him allegiance and were able to take advantage of this peace in order to build tombs in their own districts. He made Thebes the capital of the whole country, and fostered a revival in architecture and the arts. Memphis was no longer the home of the best artesans and craftsmen, and a new and vigorous art style that we term 'Theban' now replaced the classic Memphite style of the Old Kingdom. The wall reliefs and statuary at Thebes now displayed the characteristic strength and originality of this new style.

The most famous building of Dynasty 11 is the unique funerary monument that Mentuhotep Nebhepetre built for himself at Deir el-Bahri, Thebes. However, throughout the First Intermediate Period, provincial rulers who had gained their independence from centralized, royal control at the end of the Old Kingdom, continued to be buried near to their local towns, in rock-cut tombs hewn from the cliffs along the river's edge. These tombs, decorated with painted wall scenes and equipped with tomb goods made by local artists and craftsmen, demonstrate that there was a degree of lively provincial diversity from both the old Memphite and the new Theban styles of art. There was also some decentralization of political institutions, which moved away from Memphis throughout the First Intermediate Period; these were either re-established on a local basis in the provincial districts, or were centred at Thebes. However, despite its vigour and innovation, Dynasty 11 came to an abrupt end when its last king was probably assassinated by his vizier, Amenemhe, who seized the throne and became King Amenemhet I, the founder of Dynasty 12.

THE PESSIMISTIC LITERATURE

It is possible that the troubled conditions of the First Intermediate Period and the Egyptians' response to the ensuing social, political and religious upheaval may form the background to a group of texts which scholars currently term the 'Pessimistic Literature'. In some of these, the author questions the existing social and religious order against a historical background of troubled events, but in other texts, an individual crisis precipitated by social upheaval is explored, or the validity of a belief in the afterlife is questioned. The texts, which are preserved in later copies, may well have been composed at this time of historical upheaval; they certainly provide evidence of an attitude towards death and resurrection which is far less confident than that which we infer from the archaeological evidence provided by the tombs and funerary goods.

The first text – the 'Prophecy of Neferti' – describes how a sage Neferti is summoned to entertain King Sneferu (the first king of Dynasty 4) with his ability to prophesy. However, he presents a terrifying vision of future events that will befall Egypt, including internal strife and foreign infiltration:[2]

I will show you the land in lamentation and distress,
That which has never happened before has happened.
Men will take up weapons of warfare,
The land will live in uproar.
Men will fashion arrows of copper,
And beg for bread with blood,
And laugh aloud at distress.
Men will not weep because of death,
Men will not sleep hungry because of death.[3]
Each man's heart is for himself.

He then claims that the situation will be rectified by a great king, Ameny (Amenemhet I):

Then a king will come from the South,
Ameny, the justified, by name,
The son of a woman of Ta-seti,[4] born in Upper Egypt.
He will receive the White Crown,
He will wear the Red Crown;
He will unite the Two Powerful Ones,[5]
He will please the Two Lords[6] with what they wish . . .

In the second text, the 'Admonitions of a Prophet',[7] another sage named Ipuwer (who was possibly a treasury official from the Delta) arrives at the court of an aged and infirm king, possibly Pepy II. The old king has been protected from the truth by his sycophantic courtiers, and remains unaware of the dangers that threaten Egypt, but Ipuwer describes the terrible situation:

There is no remedy for it,
Ladies suffer like maidservants,
Singers are at the looms in the weaving-shops,
They sing dirges to the goddess . . .
Lo, all maidservants are rude in their speech,
When their mistresses speak, it irks the servants.

The world that Ipuwer describes represents a society collapsing from within: central government is overturned, the roles of rich and poor are reversed, and there is violence, robbery, murder, famine and disaster. Foreigners harass Egypt's borders, and the populace threaten the disintegrating administration. The irrigation and agricultural systems are collapsing, which results in famine and hunger and, because of this social collapse, thieves and murderers enjoy the freedom to terrorize their neighbours. Instead of hoping to perpetuate the joys of life, people now regard death as a welcome event and wish that they had never been born. However, even death cannot offer any release, because there are no longer the resources to build and equip the tombs that would have ensured a secure afterlife. Even when bodies and tombs are properly prepared, however, this does not provide a solution because they are frequently plundered and the contents destroyed:

Lo, great and small say 'I wish I were dead',
Little children say 'He should never have caused me to live!'
Lo, children of princes are dashed against walls,
Infants are put on the high ground.[8]

Ipuwer predicts future disasters and begs the court to take action and fight the king's enemies and restore the gods' traditions. However, his pleas are ignored, and the conditions continue to deteriorate so that eventually the vestiges of order are swept away. This probably resulted in the overthrow and removal of the king.

Although the events described in these texts appear to reflect conditions in the First Intermediate Period, there has been disagreement about their purpose – do they really describe historical events, or are they a literary device for discussing the theme of national distress, or the continuing conflict between order and chaos? They certainly address issues relating to the existence of evil as a cause for social unrest, the recognition that divine and human order could be overturned, and the need for constant vigilance to ensure that order prevailed over chaos. They affirm that harmony can only be guaranteed by the restoration of a powerful king and centralized authority, and they emphasize the role of Amenemhet I in restoring stability. In fact, they were probably composed either during his reign or shortly afterwards, thus providing a retrospective rather than a 'prophetic' view of events.

Another text ('The Dispute between a Man and his Soul' or 'The Dispute with his Soul of One-Who-is-Tired-of-Life')[9] is one of the most interesting examples of Egyptian religious writing, and is also regarded as a literary masterpiece of the ancient world. It addresses the predicament of a man whose life has been devastated by the collapse of his society, and probably tries to demonstrate the catastrophic effects of the First Intermediate Period on one individual, by exploring his self-doubts and fears. The man discusses his personal problems with his *ba* (soul), which is described as an independent entity; he longs for death and perhaps even contemplates suicide, but the Soul opposes his plan. Their argument is presented in the form of a dialogue, arranged in four poems. A selection is given here from three of the poems; in the first and second, the man describes the horrors of his current life, while in the third, as a contrast, he explains the joys that death would offer.

(From the First Poem)

Lo, my name reeks,
Lo, more than the stench of carrion
On summer days when the sky is hot.

Lo, my name reeks,
Lo, more than catching fish,
On the day of the catch, when the sky is hot . . .

(From the Second Poem)

To whom shall I speak today?
Brothers are evil,
The friends of today, they are not lovable.

To whom shall I speak today?
Men are covetous,
Everyone robs his neighbour's goods.

To whom shall I speak today?
There are none that are righteous,
The earth is given over to evildoers . . .

(From the Third Poem)

Death is before me today
As when a sick man recovers,
As when one goes outside after confinement.

Death is before me today
As the fragrance of myrrh,
As when one sits under sail on a breezy day.

Death is before me today,
As the fragrance of lotus flowers,
As when one sits on the shore of drunkenness.

Death is before me today,
As a well-trodden path,
As when a man comes home from warfare.

Death is before me today,
As the clearing of the sky,
As when a man discovers what he ignored.

Death is before me today,
As when a man longs to see his home
When he has spent many years in captivity.

Eventually, the Soul, who had the choice of remaining at the man's side or abandoning him to his fate, manages to persuade him to remain alive so that they can share their future and the afterlife together:

This is what my soul said to me: throw aside lamentation, my comrade, my brother . . . I will stay here if you reject the West.[10] But when you arrive in the West, and your body is united with the earth, then I will alight after you rest,[11] and then we shall dwell together.

Various interpretations of this text have been suggested. According to one, the man contemplates suicide but the Soul refuses to remain with him because of the hardships it will encounter if no tomb has been prepared. Instead, the Soul tries to persuade the man to stay alive by describing the dangers of death, but the man attempts to justify his decision by enumerating the evils he is encountering in life and emphasizing the comparative joy that death would bring. According to another interpretation, the man is looking forward to a natural death, but the text describes what might happen to him after death if his Soul deserts him: he might face personal annihilation rather than resurrection and immortality. The Soul tries to demonstrate that life is preferable to death, but the man recounts the horrors of life and the comparative delights of death. In the end, the Soul wins the argument, and persuades the man to continue his life. This text provides a real insight into individual self-doubts during a period of political and social upheaval, and shows that even oblivion in death was not regarded as a solution because people could no longer prepare adequately for the afterlife.

Another group of texts[12] preserves the hymns or songs that were performed at funerary services, to the accompaniment of harpists. Known as 'Songs at Banquets' or 'Harpers' Songs', they were usually inscribed on the tomb walls to revive the deceased owner, reassure him that he would experience eternal life, and provide instruction for the banquet guests about the inner meaning of the mortuary offering. They were probably recited or sung at the mortuary banquets which the relatives continued to celebrate at his tomb on feast days. Following an elaborate meal, the guests, adorned with flowers and perfume, would listen to these confident statements.

However, in the Middle Kingdom, a new concept was introduced: hymns such as the Song of Intef reflect a scepticism found in other pessimistic literature of this period. In this Song (which was apparently originally inscribed in King Intef's tomb), there is no praise of the joys of the afterlife; instead the listener is encouraged to enjoy life while he can, because the existence of an afterlife is uncertain and even a well-provisioned tomb cannot guarantee a person's survival. Earthly existence is acknowledged as transient, and there is no certainty about human life. Funerary preparations do not last and are therefore useless, and since the dead do not return to inform the living what they need, then all the provisioning of the tomb is futile. This contrasts markedly with the traditional view that a person could expect to attain a blessed afterlife, provided that he was morally and virtually prepared and had made the necessary arrangements for his funeral and mortuary maintenance.

Some scholars hold the view that this hymn was in fact composed in the Middle Kingdom but others have argued that the text could date to another period, since pessimistic attitudes probably existed at all times.[13] Fox's study claims that the hymn does not deny the existence of an afterlife, but simply emphasizes the opinion that the living do not have the ability to know about it, and are advised to enjoy earthly pleasures, not so much for their own sake but to divert the heart from the ultimate tragedy of life.

Lamentations were a part of the funerary rites intended to save the dead from the absolute death or 'second death' that was reserved for the wicked or those who had not made the necessary funerary preparations. Absolute death condemned the person to complete obliteration or to a form of semi-existence that punished the individual. However, this hymn states that lamentations are useless, because the gods do not listen to them. It also reflects the Egyptians' 'dualistic' concept of death by expressing their deepest fears, and at the same time, promoting those beliefs that were intended to assuage these doubts. It reversed the reassurance given in other hymns, but rather than expressing a gentle pessimism, it demonstrated pain and anger and a sense of betrayal.[14] The hymn does not attempt to present a solution to the problem, although it indicates that earthly pleasures could bring a kind of oblivion and lessen the awareness of ignorance of what lies beyond death:

The gods who were before rest in their tombs,
The blessed nobles too are buried in their tombs.
Those who built tombs,
Their places are no more,
What has become of them?

I have heard the words of Imhotep and Hardedef,
Whose sayings men repeat in their entirety.
What of their places now?
Their walls have crumbled,
Their places are no more,
As though they had never been.

None comes from there,
To tell us how they fare,
To tell us what they need,
To set our hearts at rest,
Until we also go where they have gone.

Therefore, be glad,
It is good to forget,
Follow your heart as long as you live!
Put myrrh on your head,
Dress in fine linen,
Anoint yourself with the genuine marvels that belong to a god.'[5]

(Refrain):
Spend the day happily!
Do not weary of it!
Lo, none is allowed to take his goods with him,
Lo, none who has departed can come back again!

However, by the New Kingdom, there was an attempt to counteract this scepticism, and to reassure the deceased of the reality and joys of the afterlife. The Intef Song continued to be sung, but new hymns were composed to offset its effect. In a tomb at Thebes which dates to the reign of Horemheb (c.1325 BCE), the owner Neferhotep was supplied with three songs which encompassed a range of responses.[16] The so-called 'Second Song' attempted to reject the earlier scepticism, and to reassure the dead and the gods of the necropolis of the deceased's continuing belief in immortality:

I have heard those songs that are in tombs of old,
What they say in praise of life on earth,
Belittling the land of the dead.
Why is this done to the land of eternity?
. . .
No one may linger in the land of Egypt,
There is none who does not arrive in it (i.e. the West).
Regarding the time of deeds on earth,
It is the length of a dream;
One says: 'Welcome, safe and sound,'
To him who reaches the West.

Thus, the Song tried to reassert traditional beliefs and to present a convincing picture of the afterlife, but it is still essentially a pessimistic poem in which formalities are used to hide continuing doubts. It claims that merrymaking should be a complement rather than a substitute for ritual and ethical preparations for death. In the Ramesside Period (1320–1085 BCE), the pessimistic approach is still evident in songs in four tombs, indicating that these questions remained unresolved for the Egyptians.

This literature provides a unique insight into the Egyptians' response to national upheaval and personal doubts and fears. At a time when the arts and crafts were in decline and there was great political and economic uncertainty, they produced literary compositions that demonstrated an unprecedented maturity of expression, possibly reaching a standard that was never again achieved. The Pessimistic Literature has been compared with the much later description of a man's moods of despair found in the Old Testament Book of Job. Again, this explores acute personal distress and Job's reaction to the misfortunes he encountered. Both provide early accounts of individual response to disaster, but the Egyptian texts also present a view that was clearly at variance with the funerary preparations, which are so clearly emphasized by the archaeological evidence.

THE MIDDLE KINGDOM:
THE HISTORICAL CONTEXT

The Middle Kingdom, which consists of Dynasty 12, was inaugurated by Amenemhet I (Ameny) who probably seized the throne at the end of Dynasty 11.[17] He and his successors established a kingdom that flourished and prospered, and came to represent the second great period of Egypt's history. However, Amenemhet I had no royal blood and no legitimate claim to rule Egypt; his father Senusret had held the priestly title of 'god's father' and his mother came from the southernmost district of Upper Egypt whose capital was situated at Elephantine. Nevertheless, with the help of a series of shrewd political measures, he was able not only to establish the dynasty, but also to create a stable and peaceful kingdom that could be handed on to his son, Senusret I, although Amenemhet was probably the victim of assassination.

As a key move in his domestic policy, the king moved the capital city from Thebes to a new site at It-towy, some distance south of Memphis, from which the whole country could be more easily governed.[18] On the west Bank near to It-towy, he started a new royal burial site (known today as el-Lisht) where he revived the typical pyramid complex of the Old Kingdom; around the base of this complex, the nobles' once again built their tombs, although many officials still chose rock-cut tombs in their own districts. As well as the new capital, this king and his successors continued to develop Thebes as a great religious centre, where they maintained the royal temples and provided cemeteries for the priests and officials who worked or were buried there. They also enhanced the cult of the Theban god Amun.

Amenemhet I tried to counteract any attempt to place a rival claimant on the throne after his death, by introducing the system of co-regency. Thus, he and his successors took their chosen heirs as co-rulers so that the succession would pass smoothly when the older man died. The power of the provincial nobility had contributed to the downfall of the king at the end of the Old Kingdom, and this new dynasty faced the same threat. In order to gain the support of the provincial governors, Amenemhet I restored many of their favours and created new appointments. Once again, they held hereditary tenure of their governorships, supervised their local courts, raised troops locally, and established the levels of taxation for their subjects.

However, the king recognized that, at any time, they might pose a threat to his own supremacy and the stability of the country, and a later ruler, Senusret III (1878–1843 BCE), seems to have taken decisive action to suppress the nobles. After his reign, there is no evidence of the continuation of the governorships, and from the reign of Amenemhet III (1842–1797 BCE), the great provincial tombs were no longer built. The king may have taken action in several ways in order to undermine the governors' powers. In one case, it is known that the son of a provincial governor of Beni Hasan was educated at the royal court, and that, ultimately, unlike his father who was buried in his own district, he chose to be buried near the king's pyramid at Dahshur. This may indicate that education at the royal court was a factor in ensuring allegiance to the king; such a system was perhaps used widely and effectively to absorb powerful provincial families into the main administration, which in turn contributed to the eventual decline in nobles' wealth and independence.[19]

The kings of this dynasty also pursued an active building programme: in addition to founding the new capital of It-towy and enhancing Thebes, they developed local temples and refurbished important cult centres. The Chief Treasurer Ikhernofret oversaw major works at the Temple of Osiris at Abydos, and Senusret I built a magnificent temple at Heliopolis. His jubilee chapel (now reassembled and reconstructed) has been placed in the Open Air Museum at Karnak. Its combination of simplicity of shape, finest quality limestone, and exquisitely carved reliefs, which demonstrate a high quality of craftsmanship, make it one of the most memorable monuments in Egypt.

The Fayoum – an area of great natural beauty which lies south-west of Cairo, outside the Nile Valley – was a focus of activity during this dynasty. Some kings chose to be buried there at Hawara and Lahun, and there is a relatively well-preserved temple at Medinet Maadi. Amenemhet III also built a temple to the crocodile-god Sobek, and undertook construction works at the great lake that lies at the centre of this area. He and a predecessor, Senusret II, were also probably responsible for a programme of extensive land reclamation around the lake.

The theory of kingship underwent a profound change during the Middle Kingdom. The concept of inheritance through divine birth and royal blood had been severely undermined by the events at the end of the Old Kingdom and, although these kings of Dynasty 12 now once again controlled a unified country, they chose to emphasize their personal qualities as rulers, rather than the concept of absolute and supreme royal power that had characterized the Old Kingdom kings. In the First Intermediate Period, for the first time, the gods were held responsible for political events, and in the Middle Kingdom, the king accepted the precedence of divine authority: he was elected by the gods, acted according to their commands, and accredited them with his victories. However, although the human qualities and abilities of the king were now paramount, and he duly acknowledged the gods' supreme role, the myth still continued throughout this period that he was the son of the gods, and ruled Egypt with divine authority.

Important literary sources which provide insight into the revised concept of kingship include the 'Instruction addressed to King Merikare' (see pp. 138–9). This not only presents the god Re as a hidden, omniscient, provident and just creator-god, but also describes King Akhtoy as a pious and humble ruler whose standing in relation to the god had been diminished by events in earlier times. In the Instruction of King Amenemhet I,[20] the ruler is depicted as a cynical and world-weary ruler, reflecting the attitude found in the Pessimistic Literature; this text emphasizes the general theme that only a strong ruler could restore the country's stability. Couched in terms of a Wisdom Text in which Amenemhet I gives advice to his son, Senusret I, it is propagandist in glorifying the actions of the king, and it also deals with the theme of regicide. The king warns his son of the dangers of royal office, and particularly of the treachery of subjects. It appears that, despite his many beneficent deeds, the king had only reaped ingratitude, and had finally been assassinated by his traitorous subjects. He warns his son not to befriend any of his own followers.

The text was probably composed in the reign of Senusret I, to serve as royal propaganda and justify his own rulership (in the account, Amenemhet designates him as his heir), but it is unique because it acknowledges that a divine and immortal ruler can be assassinated. This text has been described as a testament rather than an instruction, in which the king assigns his inheritance to his legitimate heir, and gives him some final advice. The instruction, read by members of the royal court, would have added support to Senusret's claim to be the rightful successor.[21]

The rulers of Dynasty 12 not only pursued an active domestic policy, but they also renewed interest in foreign trading and military activities. Their relationships with different areas varied considerably. For example, when they revived contact with Nubia, they pursued an outright policy of force. Nubia straddled the area that now forms the southernmost and northernmost parts of the modern states of Egypt and the Sudan, and it had been important to the Egyptians since earliest times because of its good supply of hard stone. Expeditions had been sent there in the Old Kingdom to maintain access, but this relationship disappeared after the Old Kingdom collapsed.

The kings of Dynasty 12 now sought to re-establish this relationship. However, in the meantime, a more aggressive people had entered Nubia, and in facing this new threat to their ambitions, the Egyptians were driven to pursue a more forceful policy. This included the construction of a string of large brick fortresses along the river between the cataracts. Manned by Egyptian soldiers and non-military personnel, they were intended to impress the local inhabitants with Egypt's might and also to control the surrounding land so that access for goods to be brought from Nubia to Egypt could be guaranteed. Amenemhet I may have reached Kerma (just south of the Third Cataract) where he established a fortress, but it was Senusret III who made such an impression on the area that his personal cult was still practised there hundreds of years later (*see* p. 155).

Egypt's relationships with other areas were quite different. In order to obtain incense for religious rituals, expeditions were sent to Punt, which was probably located somewhere near the Red Sea coast, perhaps in the region of modern Somalia or part of the Sudan. In addition, they obtained raw materials from the turquoise and copper mines in Sinai which were once again in production. In dealings with their northern neighbours during this period, the Egyptians also seem to have concentrated on developing trading and diplomatic relations, rather than conquest or colonization. In Syria/Palestine, they encountered many small tribes or communities, each led by its own ruler or prince; these had their own degree of independence and would not have been as readily colonized as the Nubians, who were closely linked to Egypt through geographical proximity and because there had been contact between the two peoples since earliest times. Therefore, although the Egyptians built fortifications along the north-eastern border to repel the attacks of the Bedouin (the so-called 'Asiatics' of the texts), and there is some evidence that prisoners of war were captured and brought back to Egypt to work on building sites, for the most part, relations between the two areas were built on diplomacy and trade which in particular flourished between the Egyptians and Byblos, a city on the Syrian coast.

There were also contacts between Egypt and the Aegean Islands, and although these relationships present a confusing picture at this time, there is evidence of increased contact and an interchange of ideas and products between Minoan Crete and Egypt in Dynasty 12.[22] One of the most important examples of this contact, the Minoan pottery found at various sites in Egypt, is known today as 'Kamares Ware'; some of these vessels were genuine imports, although others were evidently of Egyptian manufacture. There is less evidence of Egyptian influence on Crete at this period. Later, in the New Kingdom, there may have been direct Minoan influence on Egyptian tomb-art at Thebes and on the palace decoration at Malkata and Amarna.[23] In these tomb-scenes, people identified in the accompanying inscriptions as 'Keftians' are shown bringing tribute to the Egyptian Treasury. However, it is unclear if they were envoys from Crete or elsewhere. Also, if they were Cretans, were they sent to Egypt in the Middle Kingdom as well as the New Kingdom?

Whether Aegean influence on Egypt – demonstrated most clearly in the art and pottery styles – came about through trade or immigration remains uncertain. However, even if some Aegean islanders did settle there during these periods, their presence would not have had any major impact on the Egyptians' lives or beliefs. As with other groups of foreigners who became resident in Egypt, they would have been allowed to continue to worship their own deities, but their religious beliefs and practices would have exerted little or no influence on Egyptian customs. Nevertheless, despite the limitations in interpreting the evidence, the Middle Kingdom artifacts do demonstrate that the countries around the Mediterranean were in contact with Egypt by this time, and this interaction laid the foundation for the cosmopolitan society of the New Kingdom.

RELIGIOUS DEVELOPMENTS IN THE FIRST INTERMEDIATE PERIOD AND MIDDLE KINGDOM

With the collapse of the Old Kingdom, the Memphite kings and their patron god Re were no longer credible protectors of the land and its people. New divine cults were promoted, but the god Osiris attracted the most widespread support not only because he was associated with the divine rituals and rites performed at the king's accession and coronation, but because he could also offer immortality to ordinary people. Whereas during the Old Kingdom, only the king could expect to enjoy an individual immortality, in Dynasties 11 and 12, this was replaced with a democratization of beliefs. Although the kings of Dynasty 12 restored the custom of pyramid-building, most great provincial governors continued to be buried in their own districts. They now attempted to gain eternal life by means of some of the religious and magical devices that had protected the rulers of the Old Kingdom and secured their safe passage to the next world. Non-royal people now made lavish preparation for death, which included the provision of fine tombs and funerary goods. These beliefs and customs gradually permeated down to the middle classes, but the cult of Osiris promised eternity to all, not only to those who could afford to prepare elaborate burials. A virtuous life, correct performance of the funerary rites, and worship of the god were now the only essentials required to obtain a blessed hereafter.

The rulers of Dynasty 11 elevated their local deity, the falcon-headed god of war named Montu, to become royal patron and supreme state-god. The Egyptian pantheon consisted of state gods, local gods, and 'household' gods. State gods were the most important deities, and some retained their status throughout Egyptian history; their significance and powers were such that they were always guaranteed a place in the top league. They had temples in the major cities, where they received divine worship in the form of rituals. Below them were the local gods; these deities were important within certain towns or districts, where they received cults in the local temples. In some cases, however, as with

Montu, a local god could be elevated to the status of state god and could even become a royal patron, if the throne were seized by a line of rulers who already worshipped the god. The gods revered in the temples, however, had little direct contact with ordinary people, and so there were also household gods to whom people prayed and made offerings at domestic shrines in their homes.

In Dynasty 12, Montu was replaced as the supreme state god by a Theban deity, Amun.[24] For the first time, the Temple of Amun at Karnak became a national shrine, foreshadowing its role as the country's greatest religious complex in the New Kingdom. Amenemhet I promoted the cult of Amun. Cults of other gods were also supported, and the Middle Kingdom rulers inaugurated building works at the cult-centres of Ptah at Memphis, Hathor at Denderah, Re-Atum at Heliopolis, Min at Koptos, Sobek in the Fayoum, and Osiris at Abydos. In addition, some of the kings of this dynasty were worshipped as gods. Senusret II received a cult during his lifetime which was continued in the New Kingdom, and the cult of Senusret III was still practised in Nubia hundreds of years later (see p. 152). Such individual royal cults were rare, and distinct from the general deification of all dead kings as 'Royal Ancestors', but they involved the usual form of temple worship, namely a regular ritual which made food and other offerings available to the person, who was represented in the temple or shrine in the form of his statue. By the performance of this ritual, it was believed that the person's spirit derived benefit from the spiritual sustenance provided by the offerings.

By the Middle Kingdom, there were royal cult complexes which included temples for the king's funerary cult, and also modest, stone-built temples (divine cult centres) such as those at Tod, Medinet Maadi and Medamud, where the gods were worshipped with rituals in which food and other offerings were presented to them. These would have been very similar to the rites performed in the later temples of the New Kingdom (see pp. 186–96). Possibly, the national cults were only located in these complexes from Dynasty 11 onwards but earlier, in the Old Kingdom, they may have been accommodated in the royal cult complexes.[25] One inscription on a pink granite slab, reused in c.1250 BCE in the pedestal of a colossal statue in the Temple of Ptah at Memphis, describes events at the court of Amenemhet II, which was probably situated at el-Lisht. As the most detailed extant example of the annual accounts that described 'historical events', it records the expeditions sent to destroy foreign cities and return with booty, and the donations decreed to the sanctuaries of local gods. Originally, it may have been written on papyrus as part of a 'day-book' and then inscribed on a temple wall.[26]

The god Osiris played a uniquely important role in the democratization of religious beliefs, and became the most significant deity of the Middle Kingdom. One of the Egyptians' most important myths, which recounts the major events in the life, death and rebirth of this god, is preserved in its fullest version in the writings of the Classical author Plutarch (50–120 ACE).[27] This account, written in Greek, is entitled *De Iside et Osiride*.[28] Although it is of a much later date, this version possibly reflects actual historical events which may have taken place in either the Predynastic Period or in Dynasty 2, and may embody details of an actual conflict which occurred at an early date between the followers of the two gods, Horus and Seth. The god Seth (identified in the Myth as the murderer of his own brother Osiris and as the enemy of Osiris' son, Horus) was certainly important in early times and had a cult centre at the predynastic town of Nubt. If the Myth does describe a real historical event, in which the followers of Horus eventually triumphed over the supporters of Seth, then this would perhaps explain why Horus was described as the winner who receives the reward of the kingship, while Seth, as the loser, became the symbol of evil and was subsequently cast out of the pantheon.

Apart from Plutarch's account, there are many references in the Egyptian texts to Osiris; however, no other extant account of his myth has survived, although it may have been handed down as an oral tradition. The two main Egyptian sources in which reference to Osiris occurs are the Pyramid Texts and the inscriptions found in New Kingdom or Graeco-Roman Period temples that relate to the annual temple festivals of Osiris. In brief, the myth describes Osiris as an early human king who introduced agriculture and civilization to Egypt. Osiris was murdered by his brother Seth, and his body was dismembered and scattered throughout Egypt. His sister/wife Isis, who was a skilled magician, gathered together his limbs and reunited them; she then posthumously conceived a child, Horus, by Osiris, and reared him in the marshes where Seth could not find him. When Horus grew to adulthood, he sought out Seth in order to fight him and avenge his father's death, but in the ensuing conflict, the two gods inflicted physical damage on each other. The dispute was then brought before the divine tribunal whose judgement favoured Horus and Osiris. As a result of this, Osiris was resurrected from the dead, and then continued his existence in the underworld where he became king and judge of the dead, while Horus, with whom every living king was identified, became ruler of the living on earth. Seth, the loser, was characterized as the 'Evil One' and became an outcast.

Originally, however, Osiris was regarded as a vegetation god who personified the annual rebirth of the trees and plants after the inundation. The god's life, death and rebirth were believed to coincide with the yearly cycle of the seasons. He personified the annual renewal of the vegetation, and was regarded as a life-giver and source of fertility for the whole country. The annual Festival of Khoiakh, which celebrated his death and resurrection, was performed in major towns throughout Egypt; it also marked his installation as king of the dead, and was closely associated with the living king's accession, coronation and jubilee. Temple scenes such as those in the Osiris Complex in the Temple of Sethos I at Abydos (*c.*1300 BCE) provide important information about these rituals.

In an inscription on the Stela of Ikhernofret (*see* p. 196), Ikhernofret describes how he participated in the Mystery Plays which enacted stages in the life and death of Osiris. They were part of the Festival of Khoiakh, held in the last month of inundation, but unlike most of the sacred rites performed inside the temple, these plays were enacted outside. They gave ordinary pilgrims (who had travelled many miles to take part in the god's festival at Abydos) an unusual, firsthand opportunity to follow some of the god's mysteries. The Festival celebrated the Nile inundation and the renewal of the vegetation, and also confirmed the accession of the living king as the embodiment of Horus and the triumphal resurrection of the dead king as Osiris. The rites were expected to ensure a successful inundation, growth of the vegetation, and a plentiful harvest.

Although originally associated with fertility and rejuvenation, Osiris was equally famous as the ruler of the underworld and divine judge. In earlier times, the jackal-headed god Anubis had been ruler of the underworld and performed the embalming of the dead king, but as Osiris gradually replaced him in this role, Anubis ultimately retained only his function as the god of mummification. As a vegetation god, Osiris symbolized his annual personal triumph over death; he had also successfully faced trial before the divine judges. The murder of Osiris showed that gods could be mortal, but he also personified victory over evil and the conquest of death, and through his own experiences, he could promise eternal life to his followers who had lived blameless lives. When he became ruler of the dead and the underworld, his son Horus became king of the living. Because he could offer immortality to his followers, Osiris gained widespread popularity in the Middle Kingdom, and this became an important element in the democratization of religious beliefs.

The concept of a Day of Judgement had now become widespread, and entry into Osiris's kingdom was dependent not only on the correct burial procedure but also on a satisfactory outcome of this divine trial. According to Egyptian belief, every person was judged by a tribunal of forty-two divine judges. The depictions of this event, which are found on papyri and coffins, show the deceased in the presence of the gods, defended by Thoth, the ibis-headed god of writing and knowledge. As he addresses each of the judges in turn, the deceased recites the 'Negative Confession', declaring that he has committed no serious crime or offence. At this stage, he could use magic or spells to try to deceive the gods, but these would not help him in the second part of the interrogation.

Two of the state gods – Ma'at, goddess of truth, and Anubis, god of embalming – also appeared in the scene, as well as a large balance that held a feather (symbol of Truth) in one pan, and the deceased's heart (symbol of his intellect and emotions) in the other. The goddesses of fate and destiny (Meskhenet and Renenutet) provided testimonies regarding the deceased's character and, if he were found to be innocent, the heart and feather would 'balance' each other. Thoth would then record the verdict and declare the deceased to be 'true of voice' or 'vindicated' (from Dynasty 11, it was customary to add this phrase after the deceased's name in the funerary inscriptions). Once accepted by the divine judges, this verdict enabled the deceased to be reunited with his *ba* (soul) so that they could enter into the kingdom of Osiris together (*see* pp. 144–5).

A successful outcome of the judgement ensured that each person became an 'Osiris', and the title 'Osiris' was placed in front of his own name. This did not imply that the deceased was actually identified with Osiris; it meant that the deceased, through his own efforts, had taken on the role of victor over death that Osiris had originally experienced. In practice, when the word 'Osiris' was included in an inscription, it was simply read as 'the deceased, NAME', thus indicating that the person was dead. If found guilty, the deceased's heart was cast to the 'Devourer', a composite, mythical animal shown crouching at the side of the balance. As a result of this, the owner would lose any hope of an immortal life.

Moral fitness and worship of Osiris were now more important factors than wealth in ensuring an individual's access to eternity. This became one of the most significant beliefs of the Middle Kingdom. The afterlife was no longer limited to royalty: an exemplary life, and knowledge of the correct responses and actions to be taken when facing the gods and demigods in the underworld – these qualifications made immortality accessible even to the humblest worshipper.

The sacred texts – the Coffin Texts and Book of the Dead, which provided guidelines concerning correct behaviour – were a vital element in this quest.

Osiris also came to be regarded as a corn-god (whose rebirth was represented by the sprouting grain), and he took on features of an earlier corn-deity, Neper. In another manifestation, he was a moon-god. However, union with the sun-god Re must be regarded as his most important role which was enacted daily, when Osiris was absorbed into Re and became the night sun which awakened the underworld from the sleep of death. At dawn, the union was dissolved when Re (the sun) appeared on the horizon. Thus, the dead king, identified with the sun, fought and triumphed over the forces of evil throughout the twelve hours of the night, and was reborn at sunrise. The cycle of day and night was a constant and potent reminder of the regular triumphs of life over death and good over evil.

The identification of personalities and events in the Osiris Myth with historical realities has been the subject of a considerable but largely unresolved debate. One theory has suggested that Osiris may have been a historical ruler who, in predynastic times, led tribes into the Delta from another area and, after settling at Busiris, introduced civilization to the Egyptians. This idea is closely associated with the now largely discredited theory of a 'Dynastic Race', because it explains the success of Osiris and Horus and the defeat of Seth in terms of the outcome of a conflict between the immigrants (as worshippers of Osiris and Horus) and the indigenous population (whose chief god was Seth) (*see* pp. 42–4). Alternatively, as discussed above (*see* p. 55), the mythical conflict between Horus and Seth may recall events in the Early Dynastic Period, when rival religious groups collided and the worshippers of Horus gained the final victory.

By the Old Kingdom, solar and Osirian elements existed side by side in literature and religious practice. It was believed that the king became an Osiris at death, and spells in the Pyramid Texts attempted to ensure the king's resurrection. The solar and Osirian beliefs had much in common: Osiris and Re were both nature deities, reborn either on a daily (Re) or annual (Osiris) basis; they reflected the cycle of life, death and rebirth in nature, and through their cults, this regenerative ability was transmitted to the king and eventually to all believers. A major difference between Osiris and Re was the fact that Osiris, as king of the underworld, did not directly rival any gods of the living, whereas Re, at least during the Old Kingdom, was supreme deity on earth. Osiris' funerary nature thus enabled him to be worshipped alongside other gods and probably helped him to develop a widespread popularity, whereas Re's supremacy was often challenged and even overturned by other gods who were chosen as patrons and protectors by various dynastic rulers.

The underworld kingdom of Osiris was believed to be a place of lush vegetation, with eternal springtime, unfailing harvests, and no pain or suffering. Sometimes called the 'Fields of Reeds', it was envisaged as a 'mirror image' of the cultivated area in Egypt where rich and poor alike were provided with plots of land on which they were expected to grow crops. The location of this kingdom was fixed either below the western horizon or on a group of islands in the west. By the Middle Kingdom, three main concepts of the afterlife had begun to emerge: the poor could expect to cultivate their plots of land in the kingdom of Osiris; the wealthy commoners (who did not wish to undertake these labours) prepared lavish tombs where they could enjoy at least part of the hereafter; and the kings still joined the gods to sail around the heavens. These ideas, which overlapped and were partly interchangeable, largely reflected the social divisions and aspirations of the period.

As a dead, deified ruler, Osiris was always shown as a mummiform king, wearing a long white cloak, Upper Egyptian crown, and carrying the royal insignia of a crook and flail. Sometimes, his face is coloured black or green to symbolize his ability to regenerate himself. Osiris had two major cult-centres.[29] Busiris in the Delta is mentioned as his birthplace. Here, his most famous cult-symbol originated; the *djed*-pillar or Busirite Symbol represented the god's resurrection, and was used as an amulet to provide its owner with strength, permanence and stability. It was a prehistoric fetish of uncertain origin, which may have come to be regarded either as a lopped tree (perhaps associated with Osiris' role as a vegetation god) or as a stylized representation of the god's backbone, which symbolized the resurrection of his body from the supine position of death.

Abydos, however, was the god's greatest religious centre. There was no trace of the god at Abydos in the Archaic Period, but it was probably the fact that many of the kings may have been buried here which gave the site its initial importance. It is not known how Osiris first came to be associated with Abydos, but this probably took place in the Middle Kingdom. By Dynasty 13, the kings certainly showed considerable interest in the site and the god's cult.[30] At Abydos, Osiris assimilated the characteristics of an earlier necropolis god, the 'First of the Westerners', and also took over another cult image known as the 'Abydene Symbol'. Again, the original meaning of this symbol remains obscure, although it may represent a stylized head and wig – a locus in which the god's spirit could reside.

Abydos became the main centre of pilgrimage during the Middle Kingdom; the early royal cemeteries and the cult of Osiris emphasized its role as a place of spiritual potency where an individual's chances of eternal life could be enhanced. As the presumed burial place of Osiris, it was thought that personal contact with Abydos would benefit the worshipper, and thus many people visited the place as pilgrims. In death, some wealthy believers made arrangements to be buried at Abydos or to have their mummies taken there before burial in their own districts; others set up stelae there, or included model boats in their tombs in which they hoped to reach the sacred city after death.

Royal Burial Places

During the troubled period of Dynasties 7 and 8, the Memphite rulers would not have been able to sustain the pyramid construction programme of the Old Kingdom. In Dynasty 11, however, the renowned ruler Mentuhotep Nebhepetre designed a unique funerary monument which incorporated a burial area and temple dedicated to Montu-Re.[31] Following the earlier family tradition, Mentuhotep was buried at Thebes, on the west bank of the Nile at Deir el-Bahri, where the cliffs form an imposing background for this and the later funerary monument of Queen Hatshepsut. The Mentuhotep monument was the first true royal cult complex of the Middle Kingdom.

It was excavated by the archaeologists Naville and Hall[32] for the Egypt Exploration Society in 1893–6 ACE and 1903–6 ACE, and subsequently by Winlock for the Metropolitan Museum, New York. Their discoveries included the tombs and shrines of the contemporary royal women and a mass grave of young soldiers who had probably died while fighting in Mentuhotep's civil wars. The monument consists of a central structure, surrounded on three sides by a pillared ambulatory; the complex apparently underwent several changes of plan and, although it was not similar to Old Kingdom monuments, it retained some Old Kingdom decorative features alongside new concepts.

The structure, which once stood on top of the high rectangular podium at the centre, has been the subject of continuing discussion. Naville decided that it was a pyramid (a conclusion accepted by Winlock), although Petrie disagreed with this. Re-examination of the monument by Arnold for the German Archaeological Institute in Cairo (1966–71 ACE) has led to the suggestion that it was a mastaba-type construction.[33] As Edwards explains,[34] this confirms that the monument cannot be regarded as a link '. . . in the long chain of pyramid history'. It emphasizes the difference between the ideas of the afterlife that were held by these kings and by their Memphite predecessors: the wish to perpetuate in the afterlife the dominant position enjoyed by the king in this world was replaced by the king 'leading his afterlife in company with the gods whose cults were celebrated in this temple'. The actual burial chamber was situated elsewhere in the complex and the monument also apparently included a 'second tomb' or cenotaph. The complex provided a family burial place not only for the king but also for several female relatives. It is the first example of a temple attached to a royal burial place which was not a 'mortuary' but provided the location for a cult in which the king and the god were jointly worshipped, through the presentation of offerings, within the same statue.[35]

In Dynasty 12, the new rulers largely reverted to using the Old Kingdom pyramid complex style of Dynasty 6. Amenemhet I built a pyramid complex at el-Lisht which incorporated earlier features as well as some innovations from Thebes. It included a pyramid built completely from stone, a temple, and reintroduced the idea of an adjacent necropolis for some of the officials and courtiers. Another complex was built at el-Lisht by Amenemhet's successor, Senusret I. Excavated first by the French in 1882 and 1894 ACE, further work was then undertaken (1906–34 ACE) for the Metropolitan Museum, New York. In the 1980s ACE, Arnold resumed this work and produced an important structural analysis of the pyramid complex.[36]

Other kings of this dynasty chose Dahshur, the southernmost area of the Memphis necropolis, for their burials. Amenemhet II built the 'White Pyramid' and nearby, to the west, treasure belonging to two princesses was discovered in royal burials. Jewellery of the royal princesses Sithathor and Mereret was also found in a tomb near the pyramid of Senusret III (*see* p. 177). This king was the first ruler since Dynasty 2 to build a large cult complex at Abydos which incorporated a Valley Building and funerary enclosure with a vast underground rock tomb. He was probably buried at Abydos,[37] since his pyramid at Dahshur seems to have remained unused. Amenemhet III also built a complex at Dahshur (the 'Black Pyramid') which was excavated by early archaeologists and, from 1976 ACE, by Arnold.[38]

Amenemhet III constructed a second pyramid at Hawara,[39] perhaps because of the subsidence which Arnold discovered in the monument at Dahshur. It is possible that the king was buried at Hawara, while the less stable pyramid was used for the burial of his queens. The Hawara pyramid, originally excavated in the nineteenth century ACE, formed an addition to a building known as the 'Labyrinth' which Petrie excavated in 1889 ACE.[40] The Labyrinth was described as a legendary building by the Classical writers Herodotus and Strabo, who recorded that it was as important a monument as the pyramids. Little survives today, but originally, it incorporated the temple associated with Amenemhet III's pyramid, a causeway, a Valley Building, administrative quarters and possibly a royal residence. There were halls to represent each of the administrative districts, and the temple served as an assembly place for the gods.[41]

As mentioned previously (*see* p. 150), it was because the rulers of this dynasty were particularly drawn to the beauty and fertile landscape of the Fayoum that they chose to move their capital to nearby Lisht. Consequently, it became essential that they also selected sites in the same area for their pyramids. One of these kings – Senusret II – decided to build his burial place at Lahun, which lies on the desert edge that fringes the Fayoum.[42] For this pyramid, his architect used an existing natural knoll of rock as the core to support the building, which was constructed of layers of mudbrick and then cased with blocks of limestone. As with other examples, this original casing has long since been removed, so that the mudbrick inner structure is now revealed. Petrie excavated the pyramid in 1889 ACE, and in 1914 ACE, when he and Brunton explored four shaft tombs to the south of the pyramid, they discovered that the easternmost shaft contained the treasure of Princess Sit-Hathor-Iunit (*c.*1860 BCE) (*see* p. 177). This find was similar to the treasure uncovered at Dahshur.[43]

Non-Royal Tombs

A major development in the First Intermediate Period and Middle Kingdom were the changes that occurred in the construction and location of private (non-royal) tombs. At Thebes, the predecessors of

Mentuhotep Nebhepetre had built freestanding structures, known today as 'saff' tombs, which were arranged in rows,[44] but rock-cut tombs were the most characteristic of this whole transitional period. They can be traced back to the latter part of the Old Kingdom when provincial rulers chose burial in their own districts rather than in a cemetery adjacent to the royal burial site. Although, to some extent, the kings of Dynasty 12 reversed this trend, the provincial tombs remained an important feature for much of the Middle Kingdom.

Located in the cliffs which descend steeply to the edges of the river in parts of middle and southern Egypt, each rock-cut tomb included a columned portico or terraced courtyard which led into a columned hall. The walls in the hall were painted with scenes. The hall led into a small chapel or niche where the tomb-owner's funerary statue was placed to receive food offerings. In many instances, the burial chamber, which lay beyond, could be reached through an opening cut into the floor of the columned hall. Tombs of this type, which are found at many sites, vary only in the detail of their design and decoration.

Some of the most famous rock-cut tombs which occur at Beni Hasan in Middle Egypt[45] date from Dynasty 6. The most important, however, occurred from the end of Dynasty 11. They belonged to the great provincial rulers of the 16th nome of Upper Egypt, and were excavated in 1902–4 ACE. These men lived at the town of Monet-Khufu, which flourished from the end of Dynasty 11 until provincial power ebbed away in Dynasty 12. The wall-scenes in these tombs, which have been recorded and studied by various scholars, depict daily activities such as food and textile production. However, although their general content and purpose follow earlier patterns, they also include unusual and sometimes unique representations. For example, there are scenes showing spinning and weaving, and a whole series of wrestling positions and holds which appear to have played a part in military training; other scenes depict youngsters playing ball-games and a version of leap-frog.

A similar set of tombs exists at Deir el-Bersha, in a desert ravine called Wadi el-Nakhla.[46] The most important of these date to Dynasty 12, and belonged to the provincial rulers of the 15th Upper Egyptian nome whose capital was at Khnumu. Other tombs can be found near to the modern town of Assiut. In antiquity, this was the capital of the 13th nome of Upper Egypt and the cult-centre of the god Wepwawet. The town had considerable commercial importance as it lay at the beginning of the caravan route to the oases in the western desert. Here, the great provincial governors of the First Intermediate Period and the Middle Kingdom built fine tombs; on the walls, there are biographical inscriptions recording the governors' support for the Heracleopolitan rulers of Dynasties 9 and 10 which provide one of the few sources of information about the Heracleopolitan and Theban conflict of Dynasty 11.[47]

Another important centre emerged in the First Intermediate Period at Akhmim in Middle Egypt. Officials and priests were buried here, in an extensive provincial cemetery in the mountainside (known today as el-Hawawish). Early archaeological investigations at this site have been brought up to date by a systematic programme of excavation and recording undertaken since 1979 by Macquarie University, Sydney. In addition to recording the tomb-plans and wall-decoration and translating the inscriptions, the archaeologists have discovered some previously undisturbed burials, complete with mummies and funerary goods, which have enabled studies to be undertaken of familial relationships and burial customs.[48] In one particular tomb, inscriptions have indicated that the six bodies belonged to members of the same family; in parallel scientific studies, it has been possible to obtain DNA from four of the mummies and, in three cases, to demonstrate that they were related to each other.

Far to the south, the Egyptians established the ancient town of Yebu as the capital of the 1st Upper Egyptian nome. This garrison town was a great trading centre from which expeditions set out to Nubia and the south. It lay just north of the First Cataract and, as the gateway to Nubia, was always an important centre. Just north of the modern city of Aswan, on the west bank of the Nile at Qubhet el-Hawa, tombs were built for local dignitaries from the time of the Old Kingdom through to the New Kingdom.[49] They include the burials of some expedition leaders of the Old Kingdom, and provide unique inscriptional evidence about these early ventures, as well as showing how provincial tombs of Dynasty 6 were built and decorated.

Another type of funerary arrangement existed at Saqqara where offering niches which formed part of a private family cenotaph of the First Intermediate Period have been discovered, to the north of the

Dynasty 5 pyramid of Teti.[50] This family was associated with the cult of the pyramid. Their cenotaph, probably erected long after the death of those whom it commemorates, was not discovered in association with any burial place. It is possible that the area was consecrated for the dedication of such cenotaphs. A similar but more extensive area was established in the Middle Kingdom at Abydos, where the monuments were furnished with stelae, offering tables and statuettes. The person who established the cenotaph sought to associate his family and himself with the local gods and to share in the offerings made to the gods. Thus, in the First Intermediate Period, there appear to have been two main centres for such cenotaphs, at Abydos and Saqqara, but, as the cult of Osiris developed, Abydos became the pre-eminent site. Nevertheless, the establishment of this particular cenotaph at Saqqara in the First Intermediate Period may indicate that the role of this family in serving the Teti Pyramid had not died out by that time, and that some governmental order and control survived in this area even in the troubled years after the end of the Old Kingdom.

TOMB ART AND EQUIPMENT

With the decline of Memphis as a religious centre and a focus for craftsmanship, the general trend in the First Intermediate Period was towards a decentralization of the religious art forms. Local artisans were now employed to decorate and equip provincial tombs, and to some extent, a geographical variation in style emerged, although the basic content of Old Kingdom tomb design and decoration was still retained. A new art style now developed at the Dynasty 11 capital of Thebes (Egyptologists sometimes refer to this as the 'Theban School' or 'southern style'). It was distinguished from the northern or 'Memphite School' in several ways: for example, in tomb wall-scenes, there was now a combination of high and low relief, or in some cases, the scenes were simply painted directly on the plaster. In addition, the human figures were differently proportioned, and they can be recognized by their small heads and tall, slender bodies. In Dynasty 12, when the kings restored several Old Kingdom customs, some of the classic Memphite

A tomb scene shows a treasury official weighing gold rings in a balance. A set of weights in the shape of animal heads can be seen (*bottom right*).

traditions returned, although the new Theban realism was retained. In fact, the art of these periods was never entirely northern or southern in terms of influence, but incorporated the local styles of many provincial sites; sometimes roughly executed, the work was nevertheless often vigorous and vibrant.

Religious democratization ensured that the range and quantity of funerary goods were greatly expanded. The coffins clearly show that there were pronounced regional differences, but such variations became increasingly less obvious from the First Intermediate Period to the later Middle Kingdom.[51] There were also changes in the type of funerary equipment provided, such as the introduction of the *ushabti* figure (*see* pp. 172–3) as a new type of statuary.

A nest of two or three coffins was usually included amongst the tomb goods in which an outer, rectangular coffin contained the body-shaped (anthropoid) inner coffins.[52] Royalty and the great nobles sometimes had stone rectangular coffins but wood was most frequently employed for others. Coffins were locally produced and kept as part of the undertaker's stock. Many of the outer coffins, probably regarded as a 'house' for the deceased, had flat lids although some were vaulted, and they were decorated with horizontal lines of inscription and brightly painted geometric designs which incorporated painted panels, representing the stylized façade of a house or palace. Some paintings also depicted the food offerings that the deceased would need in the next world.

The body coffin represented a mummy. It had probably developed from the cartonnage masks that were placed over the head of the mummy in the Old Kingdom, to act as a protection and a substitute for the mummy if it was destroyed. Cartonnage (a mixture of gum and papyrus) continued to be used for body coffins throughout the First Intermediate Period, but wood replaced it in the Middle Kingdom. The exterior of the coffin was decorated with paintings of the items of equipment that had been placed on the mummy inside: a bead collar, other jewellery, a girdle and bandages. The face on the body coffin was always stylized, and showed the deceased as an 'Osiris' with a false beard and an uraeus (snake) on the forehead. The coffin was personally identified with its owner by inscribing his or her name in the coffin inscriptions. The body was placed inside the body coffin so that it faced the left side; in turn, this body coffin was positioned inside the outer coffin so that the deceased could 'look out' through a pair of eyes that were painted on the outer coffin's external surface. This enabled the owner to 'see' the food offerings set out inside the tomb.

Texts inscribed on the surfaces of the coffins (known today as the 'Coffin Texts') provide the most important funerary literature for this period.[53] These texts included not only edited versions of earlier spells, but also original compositions.[54] Although they were based on the Pyramid Texts in that they sought to protect the dead person when he passed through the dangers of the underworld, the Coffin Texts probably did not attempt to duplicate the texts found in specific pyramids. It is likely that they represented an evolution in the development of funerary spells rather than a direct reflection of the Pyramid Texts.[55] By the First

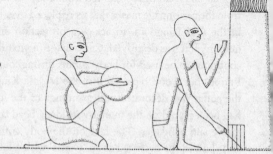

A tomb scene illustrates various stages in the production of pots. Tomb art is a major source of information about contemporary, everyday activities.

Intermediate Period, the Coffin Texts had become available to wealthy commoners who could afford a coffin, tomb and funerary equipment, and their use became increasingly widespread throughout the Middle Kingdom. They were briefly revived during Dynasty 26.

Generally, the texts sought to ensure that the tomb-owner would experience an individual eternity, quite separate from the king's own immortality, but whereas the Pyramid Texts asserted the king's divine rights, the Coffin Texts addressed the owner's fear of death and deprivation. By providing spells to enable the deceased to reach heaven and be reunited with his family, and by including a 'menu' of food and drink to sustain him after death, the Coffin Texts were an attempt to secure a safe and blessed eternity for the owner. Originally written on papyrus (although such examples are rare), the spells were later inscribed in ink or paint on the panels of the coffin.

Tomb equipment also included a wooden canopic chest, which con-

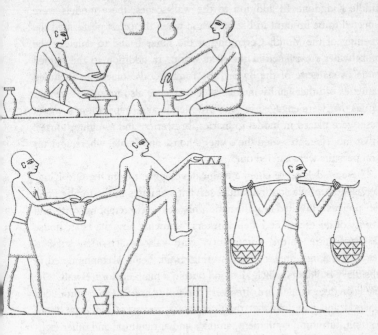

tained four canopic jars.[56] This square, lidded box was a smaller version of the rectangular coffin, with its exterior painted decoration which included inscriptions, false doors and a pair of eyes. The jars were used to store the viscera (abdominal and chest organs), removed from the body during the mummification process and subsequently dehydrated with natron (*see* previous discussion, p. 21). Since the owner would require his viscera to be magically reunited with his body after death, it was necessary that the painted features on the canopic chest could allow the owner's spirit to enter the box and gain access to the viscera. In Dynasty 12, the canopic chest was usually placed in a niche in the east wall of the burial chamber so that it was within sight of the deceased in his coffin. This enabled the deceased to make contact with the viscera. Four goddesses – Isis, Nephthys, Neith and Serket – protected the organs, assisted by their helpers, the demi-gods known as the 'Four Sons of Horus'.

* *

A large and varied selection of tomb models was also introduced in the Middle Kingdom. In addition to the wall-scenes, these models were expected to be brought to life by magic when the priest performed the Opening of the Mouth Ceremony at the funeral, and to enhance the tomb-owner's existence in the next world. In addition to the named statue or statuette of the owner, the tomb goods sometimes included statuettes of other family members. There were also groups of servant statues that were engaged in food production and preparation; some of these were placed in model granaries, breweries, and slaughterhouses. Other models represented the owner's house and estate, where agricultural pursuits were carried out.

These models represented a major development from the Old Kingdom custom of placing individual servant statuettes in the tomb. They also preserve invaluable information about the contemporary life and activity of the estates and their workers,[57] showing how the estate house was the centre of this community, with various activities, such as weaving, baking, brewing, and storing grain, being accommodated in subsidiary buildings which all stood within a main enclosure wall. The details on these models are often very carefully observed and reproduced in wood and paint, so that they provide a wealth of evidence about clothing, furniture, equipment, animals and agricultural and other technologies.

There were also the servant models that Egyptologists describe as *shabtis* or *ushabtis* (*see* p. 168). A set of ushabtis, placed in the tomb, incorporated hundreds of figurines that, according to one explanation, supplied the owner with one agricultural worker for each day of the year, plus an additional group of 'overseer' figures. Ushabtis first appeared in Dynasties 9 and 10, and continued to be included in burials until the end of Egyptian history. They were intended to relieve the owner of his arduous agricultural labours in the realm of Osiris and enable him to spend his eternity enjoying the leisure activities of the day, such as fishing, hunting, and attending banquets and parties.

These mummiform figures were represented with agricultural equipment, which was either carved or painted on to the body; they were inscribed with the owner's name and titles, and with a formulaic text which asserted that they would undertake the necessary duties for the owner. The overseer figures, required to control the workers, were shown wearing stiffened kilts and carrying whips. The basic shape and form of all these statuettes remained the same, although there was some variation in their size, inscription and material. At first, wood was used, but examples in painted pottery occur in the New Kingdom, and faience eventually became the most popular material.

The soul-house, another distinctive tomb model introduced in the Middle Kingdom, was a pottery model house with the open courtyard at the front which was used as an offering tray or slab for the presentation of food. These developed from the circular stone offering-tables or rectangular slabs placed in front of the funerary stelae in Old Kingdom tombs. The soul-houses show some individual variation in design, but they usually incorporate a two-storeyed portico, a flat roof approached by a staircase, and a cooking area within the front courtyard. Apart from their religious function as an offering tray, they provide us with an insight into the contemporary domestic architecture of the Middle Kingdom, on which they were based.

Other models included troops of soldiers, armed with weapons to protect the owner during troubled times, and different types of model boats. In addition to providing 'magical' transport for the owner to visit the sacred city of Abydos, these were intended to enable the deceased to be transported across the Nile to his tomb on the west bank, to travel long distances, or to catch fish that would augment his eternal food supply.

A wide variety of human and animal figurines have also been found. These probably had different functions: for example, toys were included in children's burials while other figures had magico-religious purposes associated with fertility, animal cults or rebirth. Some animal models may have been part of the food supply, or were intended to provide the owner with magical powers, whereas others portrayed domestic pets who would accompany the deceased into the next world. In Dynasty 11, 'paddle-dolls' were also introduced into the tomb equipment. This term is used by Egyptologists to describe flat figures which resemble paddles: each body is shown with a long, narrow upper part, but below this the 'paddle' provides space to depict detailed and accentuated genital features. These 'dolls', and the 'concubine-figures' of later times, may have been included to provide 'companions' for the tomb-owner or they may have been linked to female fertility and rebirth. Similarly, models of dwarfs and musicians were probably included to entertain the deceased owner.

To protect the king or non-royal tomb-owners against their enemies, the Egyptians resorted to magic. They either represented the danger as a bound captive, or described it in an inscription on small clay or stone tablets, or small pottery bowls. These inscriptions, known as the 'Execration Texts', identified various royal or non-royal enemies. Some, such as foreign enemies, were specific, whereas others represented more general threats. These evils could be destroyed by smashing the inscribed bowls and burying the fragments near to the tomb.

Thus, within the burial context, the Egyptians attempted to anticipate all the owner's needs in the next world. In addition to the food offerings, specific models, and protection devices, the burial goods included furniture, clothing, cosmetics and perfumes, toilette equipment, games, and domestic pottery and utensils. One particularly important funerary provision was jewellery, which provided the owner with both adornment and protection. Important groups of royal jewellery belonging to the queens and princesses of Dynasty 12 and objects found in non-royal tombs provide evidence of the highest quality craftsmanship ever produced in ancient Egypt. They also supply information about the magico-religious significance of jewellery.

The Egyptians adorned themselves with jewellery in life and in death.[58] Its prime function was to enhance the owner's well-being, and thus it was worn by all classes, both sexes, and by adults and children. For the gods, jewellery also provided magical protection and increased their divine powers. In the temple rituals, the god's statue was presented with insignia and jewellery, and the various crowns and collars were believed to possess special powers, such as vigour and control, which the gods could acquire and use.

Humans also wore jewellery to indicate status and wealth. Sometimes, the king presented his courtiers and officials with jewellery to mark outstanding service or bravery; commoners were only permitted to wear

This early twentieth-century photograph shows the Great Sphinx at Giza (c.2570 BCE) which formed part of Chephren's pyramid complex, with the Great Pyramid, built by his father Cheops, in the background (c.2500 BCE).

A wall relief (Temple of Amun, Karnak) shows priests wearing animal masks who carry the god's statue in the sacred barque. The king (*far left*) burns incense to purify the processional route.

The rock-cut Great Temple at Abu Simbel, built by Ramesses II (*c.*1290 BCE). The façade shows colossal figures of the king and smaller ones of his family.

The finely carved façade of the Temple of Denderah (*c.*300 BCE) showing the Hathor-headed capitals of the columns. This early photograph illustrates the extent of sand encroachment on the monuments.

A wall scene from the tomb of Sennedjem at Deir el-Medina, Thebes (*c.*1200 BCE), showing a *sem*-priest performing funerary rites for the seated tomb-owner and his wife.

An aerial view of the West Bank, Thebes, shows tombs built for courtiers and officials of the New Kingdom (*c.*1567–1085 BCE)

The *Djed*-pillar or Busirite Symbol shown on a frieze at the Step Pyramid complex at Saqqara (*c.*2650 BCE). This symbolized resurrection and probably represented the backbone of the god Osiris.

A wall scene from a tomb (*c.*second century ACE) at Kom es Shuqafa, Alexandria, shows a mummy on a bier. It illustrates the characteristic Alexandrian fusion of Egyptian and Graeco-Roman art styles.

Above left: The hypostyle hall of the Temple of Sethos I at Abydos (*c*.1300 BCE). The columns symbolized the plant growth on the original Island of Creation; here, the capitals represent lotus buds.

Above right: The Bubastite Column, Temple of Karnak.

Right: A detail of a wall scene (Tomb of Petosiris, Tuna-el-Gebel, *c*.300 BCE) shows a hybrid art style: the scene content and inscriptions are Egyptian but the figures wear Greek clothes and hairstyles.

Part of the hypostyle hall in the Temple of Hathor at Denderah (*c*.300 BCE). This shows massive columns and Hathor-headed capitals which have human facial features and cow ears.

The Valley Temple of Chephren at Giza (*c*.2550 BCE); at his funeral, this was the place where the king's body first entered the pyramid complex.

An early twentieth-century photograph shows the temples of Philae, partly covered by the annual floodwaters. The rescued temples have now been moved to a neighbouring island.

A 'Queen's pyramid' at Giza (c.2570 BCE); the exact function of such pyramids remains uncertain. The pyramid of Chephren is visible in the distance.

A diorite bowl incised with a king's name placed inside the *serekh* (palace façade) (*c*.2900 BCE).

Right: An incense stand of beaten bronze, used in offering rituals. It carries a Carian inscription. Found in the Hawk Gallery, North Saqqara (*c*.350 BCE).

A gold pendant in the form of a bivalve shell; the name of King Senusret III is shown in the cartouche (*centre*), flanked by two *uraei*. From Riqqeh (*c*.1850 BCE).

A plaited rush sandal, fibre brush and rush basket used to carry a workman's chisels and hatchet to the pyramid site. From Kahun (c.1890 BCE).

A wooden mudbrick mould (*top*), plasterer's float (*bottom right*) with remains of plaster, and two wooden butterfly clamps used to hold stones together. From Kahun (c.1890 BCE).

A wooden figurine of the divine magician Beset, wearing a mask and holding two copper serpents. Found with a group of magic objects and papryi in a priest's tomb near the Ramesseum, Thebes (c.1900 BCE).

A copper mirror with a wooden handle carved to represent Hathor, goddess of love and beauty. Found in a house at Kahun (c.1890 BCE).

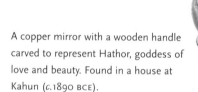

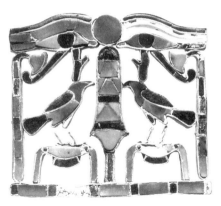

A pectoral found in place on a mummy in a tomb at Riqqeh (*c.*1850 BCE). This fine example of cloisonné-work is made of gold, inlaid with turquoise, lapis lazuli and carnelian.

A mask belonging to a dancer or magician. Made of three layers of canvas, it probably represents the goddess Beset. Found in a house at Kahun (*c.*1890 BCE).

A stone offering stand found in a house at Kahun (*c.*1890 BCE); probably used to support a dish containing food offered to the household gods.

A woollen border (perhaps part of a tapestry hanging). The subject – a female mask and floral garlands – was common in mosaics, but this is the only known textile example (late third century ACE).

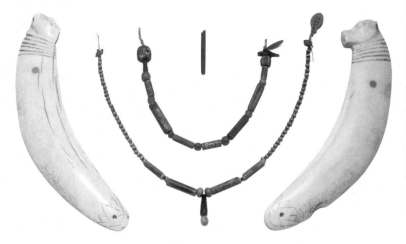

A selection of beads, and a pair of ivory clappers from a house at Kahun (c.1890 BCE). The clappers, a mask, and other items were used by a local practitioner of magic.

A painted limestone group statue of Amenhotep IV (Akhenaten) and Nefertiti
(*c.*1370 BCE). The Louvre, Paris.

A colossal sculpture of Amenhotep IV (Akhenaten), (c.1370 BCE) shows some characteristics of the unique style of Amarna art. The Egyptian Museum, Cairo.

Opposite: Ivory throwsticks, used for playing games; three are carved to represent jackal heads. From a tomb, provenance unknown (c.1450 BCE).

A terracotta figure (*c.* second century ACE) of the bow-legged deity Bes, wearing his traditional feathered headdress. His influence continued into the Roman period; here, he is shown as a Roman soldier.

A detail of a marble bust of Serapis, the god introduced by Ptolemy I to unite his Greek and Egyptian subjects (*c.*300 BCE). The Egyptian Museum, Cairo.

very rich displays as 'favours of the king', which emphasized their social importance. Royal occasions were also marked by the presentation of jewellery such as the king's gift to his queen on the occasion of their marriage, or the donations made by courtiers to the king and queen to celebrate their jubilee festival.

However, the essential meaning of jewellery was to provide the wearer with magical protection in life and in death, particularly against hostile forces such as wild animals, disease, and natural disasters.[59] By the principles of sympathetic magic, jewellery became a focus which could attract benign forces to help the wearer, a belief derived from the Egyptian principle that inanimate objects could be activated by magic to influence the well-being of both the living and the dead.

This power was intrinsic in the design of the item of jewellery and in the materials used in its manufacture.[60] Pieces were often designed to incorporate popular symbols which were thought to bring health and good luck to the wearer. One very important feature of Egyptian jewellery – the amulet – might be an intrinsic feature of a piece of jewellery or it could be worn alone. We use the word 'amulet' for body adornments that are believed to have special powers to bring good luck or assistance to the wearer. The word comes from the Arabic *hamulet* which means 'something which is worn or carried'. Some Egyptian amulets were regarded as universally potent, such as the Sacred Eye of Horus (*wedjat*), which was linked to the Myth of Osiris and rebirth; the *ankh*-sign, which symbolized life; and the *djed*-pillar, which was associated with the death and resurrection of Osiris.

One of the best-known amulets is the scarab, which represents the dung-beetle; usually made of stone or faience, these occur in a range of sizes. The flat underside is often inscribed either with the name or title of a god, king, or the owner, or with a motto, figures of gods, humans or animals, or a geometric pattern. Originally used as personal seals, they soon took on a second role as good-luck charms. The life cycle of the dung beetle inspired the idea that the creature was symbolic of regeneration and rebirth: when the beetle has laid its eggs, well hidden in the sand, the newly hatched beetles emerge as if from nowhere, inspiring the myth that they were the result of constant self-generation. Other amulets of a more personal nature were intended to help their individual owners to overcome particular problems. Some of these, resembling a limb or body part, were designed either to attract powerful magical forces to cure a weakness or disability in the owner's body, or to provide a 'double' to which the physical defect could be transferred, so that the owner's body could be restored and become whole again.

The materials used in the manufacture of jewellery and amulets were also important because they had their own magical properties. Colours were particularly significant: for some amulets, stones that resembled the appearance and colour of the original object or part were chosen, so that they could confer special benefits on the owner. The Egyptians made excellent use of gemstones, selecting them primarily because of the symbolism of their colours, but there was no attempt to choose precious stones on account of their brilliance or refraction of light. Colour was regarded as an integral element of all art representations, including wall-scenes, statuary, tomb goods and jewellery, and the magical qualities of a specific colour were believed to become an integral part of any object to which it was added.

A favourite material, gold, was chosen because it reflected the sun and symbolized durability. Stone, whether used for building or for jewellery inlays, was a symbol of timeless endurance which far exceeded the human lifespan; by contrast, ephemeral materials such as flowers and leaves were symbolic of beauty and were therefore used for wreaths and collars. Some jewellery, manufactured for wear in the owner's lifetime, was subsequently taken into the tomb as a favourite possession, whereas other pieces were made specially for the burial. These can generally be identified because they are heavier and more traditional in design, usually incorporating symbols of rebirth, life, protection and resurrection, such as the winged scarab, *ankh*-sign, and *djed*-pillar.

As well as gold, the Egyptians used 'electrum' (a combination of gold and silver), and silver (they regarded this as 'white gold') which was mainly imported from Asia Minor. Copper was also widely used. Favourite semi-precious stones included carnelian, turquoise and lapis lazuli; there are also many examples in which garnets, jasper, green feldspar, amethyst, rock crystal, obsidian and calcite are used. In the Graeco-Roman Period, some other stones were introduced. Sometimes, gemstones were replaced with artificial substances such as rock crystal backed with coloured cements, faience (which was originally blue to imitate lapis lazuli, although it was later produced in a much wider colour range), and glass which started to be produced commercially in Egypt during the New Kingdom. Other materials found in jewellery include shells, pebbles, seeds, bone, teeth, plant remains, and the vast quantities of beads that were manufactured in Egypt.

Some of the finest designs can be seen in the eight royal treasures belonging to the royal women of Dynasty 12 (see p. 163). These include crowns, pectorals, collars, bracelets and girdles, and feature a range of semi-precious stones including amethyst, carnelian, feldspar and lapis lazuli, all set in silver and gold. These groups were discovered in the precincts of Amenemhet II's pyramid at Dahshur, in the enclosure of Senusret III's pyramid at Dahshur, and in a royal tomb near the pyramid of Senusret II at Lahun. Pieces in the Dahshur treasure of Princess Khnumet display design features and techniques which may not be Egyptian in origin: possibly the jewellery was a gift from a foreign ruler, or perhaps the pieces were modelled on Asiatic or Aegean designs which may have been manufactured either by Egyptian jewellers or by foreign craftsmen who were resident in Egypt. Contemporary non-royal pieces also display a high quality of craftsmanship and may have been produced by the royal jewellers for favoured courtiers. A good example is the Riqqeh Pectoral, which was found in Tomb 124 at Riqqeh, together with a gold shell bearing the name of Senusret III and a second broken pectoral which incorporates the name of Senusret II.

CHAPTER 5

Religion and Empire

Transition from the Second Intermediate Period to
the Early New Kingdom, 1786 – c.1400 BCE

THE SECOND INTERMEDIATE PERIOD

Dynasty 12 ended with the reign of Queen Sobeknefru and was followed
by the so-called Second Intermediate Period, which included Dynasties
13 to 17 (c.1786 – c.1575 BCE). This was a time of confusion and conflict,
but there appears to have been no major political upheaval in the
changeover from Dynasty 12 to 13, and the kings of Dynasty 13 may
have been related to the earlier rulers. According to Manetho, this
dynasty consisted of a series of brief but numerous reigns when there
may have been 'puppet' kings dominated by a line of powerful viziers.
In Dynasty 13, there was more emphasis on the office of kingship than
on the individual power of the king. The kings ruled from Memphis,
but retained the Fayoum town of It-towy as a royal residence.[1] The
pyramids of this dynasty were never finished, and emphasize the general
diminution of royal power and divinity.[2] However, there was intense
royal interest in Abydos during this period: images occur on stelae,
showing kings of late Dynasty 13 worshipping gods. Formal royal

contributions were also made to the Osiris cult, and there was greater personal involvement by the rulers in the Osiris festival.[3] At Abydos, evidence of personal piety is also expressed in inscriptions on stelae set up by local residents, officials on commission, and pilgrims.[4]

Towards the end of Dynasty 13, however, the king's position had evidently weakened: the dynasty no longer controlled the whole country, and probably Dynasty 14 (and possibly other lines of rulers) ran concurrently with Dynasty 13. These years have been compared with the First Intermediate Period, since they were both times of internal collapse when the country was ruled by a succession of native kings who failed to hold Egypt together. Now, these conditions allowed a group of foreign dynasts, the Hyksos, to seize power and rule the country for many years throughout Dynasties 15 and 16. However, unlike the minor intrusions on Egypt's borders in the First Intermediate Period, these people were regarded as foreign conquerors.

Originally, historians described the Hyksos as a military force who represented a new ethnic group, but this 'invasion' is now viewed as a gradual and progressive infiltration, which probably represented just a change of rulers rather than as a massive influx of people.[5] However, the original homeland of these people has been a matter of much discussion. In his account *Against Apion*, Josephus (who has been followed by some modern scholars) implied that the Hyksos were a race of invaders who first conquered Syria and Palestine and then pushed their way into Egypt. Another ancient writer, Manetho (preserved in Josephus' writings), said that they were Arabians and Phoenicians. Manetho suggested that the word 'Hyksos' meant 'Shepherd Kings', being derived from 'hyk' (meaning 'king' in the 'sacred language') and 'sos' (meaning 'shepherd' in the vulgar tongue). However, Josephus provided another possible interpretation of the word 'Hyksos', stating that it may have meant 'captive-shepherds' from the Egyptian word 'hyk' for a 'captive'. He believed that this interpretation could be tied in with his idea (which most modern scholars do not support) that the Hyksos' descent into Egypt, occupation of the country, and final expulsion were the basis for the Biblical account of the Exodus. Today, it is generally accepted that the name 'Hyksos' is actually derived from the two Egyptian words *hk3w h3swt*, meaning 'rulers of foreign lands'. This phrase had been used earlier in the Middle Kingdom with reference to the leaders of the Bedouin tribes who had always lived on Egypt's north-eastern border. Now, it meant the new foreign rulers of Egypt, but not a special race who invaded the country. Modern scholarship has suggested that the Hyksos may have originated in Asia Minor and that Syria/Palestine was perhaps merely one stage on their journey where they were joined by Semitic peoples who then accompanied them when they infiltrated Egypt. Again, it has been argued (but without conclusive evidence) that they may have included numbers of Hurrians (people from the Caspian region) who swept down from the north, gathering up some Semitic peoples on their way as they passed through Syria/Palestine.

Josephus – claiming to quote the words of Manetho – provides a damning report of the Hyksos. According to his version, they ravaged the land, burnt the cities, destroyed the temples and dealt harshly with the population. However, this account was probably first written down in the early years following the Egyptians' expulsion of the Hyksos, when such propagandist techniques would have been adopted to justify this action. In fact, the Hyksos appear to have adopted the bureaucracy and customs of the native kings, and they supported the arts, crafts and literary composition.[6] In religion, also, they promoted Egyptian traditions: they initiated programmes of temple building, supported the worship of Re, and chose an Egyptian god, Seth, as their state god. His cult-centre was established at Avaris, the rebuilt and massively fortified city on the east of the Bubastite branch of the Nile, but he was probably a variation of one of their own gods rather than the despised combatant in the Osiris Myth. There have also been detailed studies of the Hyksos burial customs.[7]

Since 1989, excavations have almost certainly identified the site of Tell el-Dab'a as Avaris, the capital established in Egypt by the Hyksos rulers. Evidence found there demonstrates that both Asiatics and Minoans were present in Egypt, and that Minoan art was a favoured style at this time, thus substantially changing our perception of the Second Intermediate Period.[8] At Tell el-Dab'a, archaeologists have discovered an Egyptian palace and gardens, established in Dynasty 13, which was apparently run by Asiatics; their nearby tombs represent a hybrid of native and Egyptian traditions, and this settlement developed and expanded during the Hyksos Period.[9] From this palace, numerous fragments of wall plaster with traces of painting have survived, which probably date to the late Hyksos Period. These display designs are well known from the Minoan world, including floral motifs, bull leapers and acrobats, and leopards and lions.[10] Minoan artists were probably brought to Egypt to decorate the palace of the ruler or high officials, and continued to live there. Elsewhere, Minoan-style paintings have been discovered at Tell Kabri in northern Israel and at Allalakh (Tell Atchana in Turkey), perhaps indicating close links between several ruling families, and also between the Hyksos and the Minoans.

Generally, wall-paintings in Egypt and the Aegean were different in context and function, since they are found mainly in the tombs in Egypt, whereas in Crete they usually occur in palaces.[11] The discovery of paintings in a palace at Tell el-Dab'a is therefore unusual; in the context of its original homeland, Minoan art was primarily ritual, and Bietak[12] has suggested that this was also its main function at Tell el-Dab'a. These paintings have raised many questions; for example, why have no traces of Minoan daily life been found in the palace complex, if Minoans were settled at Tell el-Dab'a, and are the frescoes in fact entirely Minoan in origin? Another possible explanation of the remains at Tell el-Dab'a is that a Hyksos ruler married a Minoan and built a palace for her that was decorated in the Minoan style by Minoan artists. It is evident that further work at this site may reveal new information about relations between Egypt, the Near East, and the Aegean, and the period of transition from the Middle to New Kingdoms.[13]

THE EGYPTIAN EMPIRE

The palace at Tell el-Dab'a appears to have been destroyed in the reign of Amosis I, the founder of Dynasty 18 who completed the task of driving the Hyksos rulers out of Egypt. Three princes of Dynasty 17, who ruled an area around the southern city of Thebes – Seqenenre, Kamose and Amosis I – carried out this expulsion, and Amosis subsequently established the New Kingdom which was to become the great period of Egypt's empire. The Hyksos interlude marked a turning point in the country's history: the national character was profoundly changed, and the people no longer remained isolated from their foreign neighbours. In order to ensure access to resources found only abroad, and also to prevent any other attempt to seize their land, the Egyptians now adopted an aggressive foreign policy. By using new skills and war techniques that they had adopted from the Hyksos, and by establishing a professional army, the Theban rulers were able to lay the foundations of Egypt's empire.

The first great military ruler of Dynasty 18, Tuthmosis I, launched this new policy. He campaigned in Nubia, where he greatly extended Egyptian control, pushing it to its furthermost limit beyond the Fourth Cataract. New fortresses were built to control this territory. However, it was in relationships with her northern neighbours that Egypt's new policy was most evident. By the beginning of Dynasty 18 (c.1567 BCE), ethnic movements in the Near East had created a power vacuum, and a new kingdom, Mitanni, had established itself in the land between the Tigris and Euphrates. This kingdom consisted of a population known as the Hurrians (who had branched out from their original homeland south of the Caspian Sea from c.2300 BCE) and a ruling aristocracy of Indo-Aryan descent. The Mitannians provided a threat to Egypt's ambitions to set its northern boundary at the Euphrates, and when the Mitannians attempted to push southwards, the two powers were drawn into conflict in northern Syria. The collection of petty princedoms and city-states that occupied Palestine and the remainder of Syria were no threat to Egypt or Mitanni, but they were drawn into the power struggles of the two great kingdoms who each tried to make them vassal states.

Tuthmosis I was the first Egyptian king to launch a major offensive in Syria, leading an expedition across the Euphrates into the Mitannian heartland. During his reign, Egypt's empire stretched from the River Euphrates in the north towards the Fifth Cataract on the Nile in Nubia. Under his grandson, Tuthmosis III, who restored possessions in Syria/Palestine that had been lost during the intervening reigns, Egypt became the greatest military power in the ancient world. However, towards the middle of Dynasty 18, it was tacitly acknowledged that neither Egypt nor Mitanni could gain complete supremacy in the region, and they finally made a peaceful alliance. Diplomacy replaced warfare, and the new order was marked by a series of marriages between Egyptian kings and Mitannian princesses. However, a new northern enemy soon emerged, when a king of the Hittites attacked Mitanni and precipitated its downfall. The Hittites came to replace Mitanni as the prime threat to the Egyptians during the late Dynasty 18 and Dynasty 19. Egyptian rulers again campaigned against them in Syria/Palestine, but finally, it was again acknowledged that neither side could achieve a sustainable victory, and the Egyptians and Hittites declared a truce and signed a treaty; their alliance was marked by the marriage of Ramesses II to a Hittite princess (1256 BCE).

An important result of Egypt's successful campaigns in Syria/ Palestine was the country's enhanced wealth in terms of booty and prisoners of war which were brought back. In gratitude to their patron god, Amun, who had helped them to expel the Hyksos, found their dynasty, and establish an empire, the early rulers of Dynasty 18 (c.1567–c.1400 BCE) made lavish donations to the god's temple and priesthood at Karnak. They created large estates to support the temple and its personnel, and donated raw materials and prisoners of war to ensure that the god was well served. However, towards the end of Dynasty 18, the disastrous results of this policy became evident. Royal generosity to the state's chief god created an imbalance of power whereby the priesthood came to rival the king's own wealth and power. In particular, since the god was the king's divine father, his priests had great authority in the selection and support of a candidate for the kingship. They could express or withhold their approval of any particular heir to the throne, and whenever controversy arose over the succession, the priests could ensure that their candidate was successful.

Amun was the local god who had been worshipped at Thebes since Dynasty 12. He had been brought to Thebes at some time during the First Intermediate Period, but in the Old Kingdom, Amun was worshipped as one of the Hermopolitan Ogdoad. He also had close associations with Min, the ithyphallic fertility god of Koptos and Akhmim. He was given unequalled status by the rulers of Dynasty 18, when he had no rivals, a position which was justified in his title 'King of Gods'. However, to ensure that no effective divine competition would emerge or develop, the Theban rulers now united Amun with the Heliopolitan god Re, creating the all-encompassing deity Amen-Re. Amun thus absorbed the characteristics of the sun-god, and to acquire even greater powers, he adopted Re's mythology and his role as royal patron. Originally, Amun had been regarded as a god of air, but now it was his solar characteristics that were emphasized.

In the early years of the dynasty, when the empire was being established, Amen-Re was promoted as a great god of war, but later, in order to give him supreme power over all the peoples whom Egypt had conquered and amalgamated into the empire, it was necessary that he was accorded the role of universal creator and ruler. The priesthood of Amun at Thebes promoted his temple at Karnak as the original site of creation, and a Theban cosmogony emerged which claimed that all gods had been created by Amen-Re. This now became more significant than the earlier great creation myths of Heliopolis, Memphis and Hermopolis. The Theban mythology emphasized the primary significance of Amen-Re, and stated that Thebes was the place where the Island of Creation had first emerged from the primeval waters.

In the New Kingdom, Amun was believed to be both immanent in the cycle of life (which was governed by the pattern of existence that the god had created in the beginning and thereafter maintained in continual action) and also to be transcendent and above this cycle.[14] The god's name, Amun, has been translated as 'Self-concealing' or 'To be hidden', which implied that he was transcendent and could not be perceived by mankind.[15] As a universal ruler, Amen-Re was associated with the sun as a creative principle, and manifested his powers through the sun; it was in this capacity that he was worshipped at Karnak.[16] His three main aspects were as a primordial god who had existed before creation at Hermopolis and later at Thebes; as the creative principle, expressed through the sun; and as the ruler of existence. All the gods within the pantheon were believed to be expressions of the sum total and image of Amun as creator, and even the creation process was considered to be a manifestation of the god himself.

Amun had existed before and apart from the created world, and was therefore transcendent, but he was also immanent because he was present, and could be comprehended, in that which he had created.[7] However, he was not confined to the created universe but, as a truly transcendent god, was beyond the limits of human experience. The god's true nature could not therefore be perceived or known; it was only through the immanent elements of the god, present in the pattern of existence, that mankind could gain some idea of his being. This concept is expressed in the Great Hymn to Amun:[8]

'You are the Sole One, who made all that exists . . . He who made pasture for the cattle and the fruit-tree for men. He who made the food for fish in the river and the birds which live in the sky. He who gives breath to the living creature in the egg, and sustains the son of the worm . . . Praise to you, who made all this! Sole One and Only One with many hands, who passes the night in wakefulness, when all men sleep, seeking the best for his cattle. Amun, who abides in all things!'

The Theban cosmogony explored Amun's role as a creator. This creation myth went back at least to the Middle Kingdom and possibly to the Pyramid Texts, but reached its most developed form in the New Kingdom. Through this myth, the Egyptians reached their limits in speculating about the cause and origin of existence.[9] Amun represented the Ultimate Cause or First Principle of creation who, as a transcendental creator, had existed before and was independent of his creation. However, the question of ultimate causality – where the intellectual principle came from – remained unanswered. It was considered that this ultimate principle, Amun, lay outside creation; he was therefore hidden, and beyond human knowledge or experience.

Although Amun was the ultimate god from whom all other deities were thought to be derived, he was not the only god. As his creation, all other gods derived their being from Amun and therefore formed part of him, but they also retained their individual identities and were not cancelled out by his omnipotence. As the single ultimate cause of all creation, Amun was unique and supreme, but creation was expressed and manifested through the forms of many gods. Allen[20] explains this concept in terms of 'gods are many but deity is one'. The three major gods – Amun, Ptah and Re – were separate deities who each represented a different principle that determined existence, but they were all regarded as aspects of a concept of divinity.

The date at which Amun came to be recognized as a single transcendent creator cannot be identified with certainty, but his interpretation as the Ultimate Cause did not fully develop until the New Kingdom. However, even when the Theban cosmogony became pre-eminent, this did not undermine the earlier myths, since the Egyptians believed that all interpretations were facets that encouraged a fuller understanding of the origin and nature of the universe. Another aspect of Amun is the role that he played in the divine triad of Thebes. Triads were an important part of Egyptian religion, appearing either as one god expressed as three separate aspects (for example, the three forms of the sun-god associated with different times of the day), or as three distinct deities associated in a family group." Amun formed a trinity with Re and Ptah, and was also joined by his consort Mut and their son, Khonsu, in a family triad at Thebes.

THE EGYPTIAN TEMPLE

Historical Background

As the cult-centre of Amen-Re, Thebes was now the unchallenged religious capital of Egypt; it was also the political capital of a great empire, the main royal residence, and the site of the kings' burials. The temple at Karnak was enlarged and enhanced many times from Dynasty 18 onwards by rulers who attempted to surpass their predecessors' contributions. Amun's priesthood adopted the titles of other important gods such as Re and Ptah, and brought the cults of other deities under its own supervision. In political and economic matters, as well as religious affairs, the priests acquired unprecedented power.

However, the Temple of Karnak was only the greatest version of a special type of temple which flourished and developed throughout Egypt during the New Kingdom. These are currently described as divine cult complexes. Traditionally, Egyptologists of the nineteenth century divided temples into (a) 'divine' or 'cultus' (where the resident deity was worshipped through regular rituals carried out by the king or priest) and (b) 'mortuary' (where the king or priest performed rituals for a resident deity plus the dead, deified ruler who had built the temple, together with all the previous legitimate rulers who were known as the 'Royal Ancestors').

However, Arnold[22] has indicated that this division is misleading because it infers that each type of temple was limited to the cult of either a god or the king; it suggests that the recipient of the mortuary rituals was not divine; and it indicates that the Egyptians themselves made a clear distinction between 'divine' and 'mortuary' temples.[23] It has been argued that temples should not be divided in this simplistic way, because their functions were too varied and interwoven. Alternatively, it has been proposed that the term 'cult complex' should be used for all cultic enclosures and structures, but if it is necessary to be more specific, then 'royal cult complex' should replace the term 'mortuary temple' and 'divine cult complex' should stand instead of 'divine' or 'cultus' temple.[24] In the divine cult complex, therefore, the worship of the gods, and sometimes of a (usually) living divine king, was performed, whereas the royal cult complexes maintained the cult of a divine king (usually deceased), sometimes accompanied by the worship of another god.

The Egyptians began to build stone divine cult complexes in the Middle Kingdom, but these were relatively modest in scale, as exemplified by the temples at Tod, Medinet Maadi and Medamud. It was not until the New Kingdom that these complexes became elaborate constructions, magnificently represented by the Temples of Karnak and Luxor. However, the royal cult complexes were built of stone at a much earlier date: the pyramid temples of the Old Kingdom, which fall into this category (*see* p. 104), were possibly the only centres for national cults up until Dynasty 11. In the Dynasty 11 temple, which formed part of the mortuary complex of Mentuhotep at Thebes, we find the first evidence of a cult performed jointly for the king and the god Amen-Re.[25] This dual cultic use of a temple became standard in the New Kingdom royal cult complexes (previously termed 'mortuary temples') on the west bank at Thebes. The true purpose of the royal cult complex, however, was not funerary: it was to provide a place where the life of the deceased ruler could continue to be sustained in the hereafter, and where the god would give the king eternal life in exchange for ritual offerings.

Assmann[26] claims that religion and politics were 'aspects or dimensions of one single, indivisible theopolitical unity'. The temples were an integral part of Egyptian political, economic and social structures which, as well as providing residences for the gods, were also vital elements of the state, kingship, the economy, and the continuation of life after death. They reunited the concepts of heaven, earth and the underworld that had been separated at Creation, and through their architecture and rituals, provided barriers against chaos which always threatened the established order.

The temple had developed from the reed shrines found in the Predynastic villages. Most of our information about temple architecture and ritual comes from the well-preserved temples of the New Kingdom and Graeco-Roman Period, but even though they were built thousands of years later, they retain the main elements that were present in the reed shrines. They probably represent a different tradition from the solar temples of Dynasty 5 and the Amarna Period, which do not appear to have the same direct derivation from the reed shrines.

Mythology

Built of stone to last for eternity, the divine cult complexes all had similar basic features that were determined by their underlying mythology and ritual requirements. In the Temple of Horus at Edfu, a series of wall inscriptions known as the 'Building Texts' provides a history of the temple and gives details of the names and uses of the halls and chambers within the building. The texts also include a full account of the mythology of the Egyptian temple. This claimed that every temple was in effect the mythical 'Island of Creation' where the first deity, in the form of a bird, had alighted on the highest point of the island. Walls of reed were later constructed around this perch, and it became the sanctuary and place of shelter for the god. As the location where the universe and mankind were believed to have been created on the 'First Occasion', the island was regarded as a place of great magical and religious potency.

The Egyptians did not regard their world as a constantly evolving and changing concept; all the elements of a stable society, such as the principles of law, ethics, religion and kingship, had been established on the 'First Occasion', and in order to gain access to this wisdom and power, it was necessary to recreate the physical features of the Island of Creation. Thus, the layout and architecture of each temple were designed to represent the conditions on the 'island'; the temples did not differ substantially from each other and, because it was unnecessary and even undesirable to change the main characteristics of the 'island', no major innovations were introduced.

As a development of this original mythological concept, the temple became the god's residence where he could receive shelter, protection, food and worship. The temple was called the 'Mansion of the God' (*hwt ntr*) and provided a house for the deity in the way that a tomb was the residence for the deceased owner's spirit. Tombs and temples reflected contemporary domestic dwellings in that they provided the equivalents of a bedroom, reception area and storerooms; however, the temple building was modified and elongated to include a central processional route and to accommodate the rituals. Gods and the dead were believed to have the same requirements as the living – food, washing, dressing, rest and recreation – and these were supplied for them by the divine and funerary rites carried out in the temples and the tombs.

Finally, in later times, the Egyptians explained the temple in cosmo-logical terms. They saw the building either as a microcosm of the universe, or as a reflection of the heavens, or a great sarcophagus in which the miracle of the sun-god's rebirth occurred each day. The temple was the locus for the performance of state magic, where the rites performed within the building could be relied upon to bring about events and actions throughout the universe.

Rituals

In the New Kingdom temples, there were three main areas which each had a different degree of sanctity. A mudbrick enclosure wall surrounded the temple precinct and the temple itself, and access to this whole complex was gained through a great stone gateway (pylon) that was set in the wall. In the precinct there was a courtyard, which contained the priests' houses, shrines, work places, storage areas, slaughter yards for the preparation of meat, which would be offered to the god's statue within the temple, the locations for processing other offerings, and a Sacred Lake where the priests and cult utensils underwent ritual lustrations. This whole area was not considered to be especially sacred, since none of the rituals for the gods were carried out here, and so it was possible for lay persons to be admitted. In the construction of the mudbrick enclosure wall, the bricks were arranged in alternating concave and convex sections so that they formed a wavy line pattern; in this way, the whole wall represented the waves of the ocean from which the Island of Creation (the temple) had emerged. This wall also protected the temple from the view of the inhabitants of the surrounding town, emphasizing that the temple was primarily the god's private house and not a centre of community worship or activity.

The temple (rectangular in design) was divided into two main areas: the front courts were open to the sky and the more sacred rear chambers were roofed. At the front of the temple, another pylon, situated on the main axis, gave access to one or two unroofed courts. In this area, which was less sacred than the interior, wall scenes show the king as a great warrior and the son and heir of the gods. These courts contained the statues of people whom the king allowed to receive benefits from the temple offerings, and ordinary people could come here to pour water libations, offer prayers, and watch the god's festival procession. This area had evolved from the open enclosure that once stood in front of the reed shrine.

Behind this stood the sacred, roofed area of the temple, which contained the hypostyle halls and the sanctuary. The priests entered through the central doorway on the main axis of the temple and passed into one or two hypostyle halls. Roofed and dark, these were lit by clerestory lighting (stone grids inserted between the top of the walls and the ceiling, which filtered sunlight into the hall), and by flares carried by the priests. In these halls, which formed the reception area in front of the god's sanctuary, there were heavy stone columns arranged in rows; these had palmiform, lotiform or papyriform capitals, and represented the abundance of plant life on the Island of Creation. It was believed that these columns recreated the original lush environment that, through the agency of magic, could ensure the fertility of the landscape of Egypt.

This symbolic function of the columns was as important as their role in supporting the roof, and indeed, more columns were included here than was necessary for architectural support, simply because they represented the fertile abundance of the environment. Other architectural features also recreated features of the Island – the ceiling was decorated to depict the sky,[27] and plants were carved on the bases of the walls to represent vegetation growing out of the soil. Today, in these halls, something of the original power and mystery still remains: it is easy to imagine the procession of shaven-headed, white-robed priests, wafting incense and performing their sonorous chants as they moved forward through the central aisle of the temple, dwarfed by the overwhelming size and magnificence of the walls and columns, on which the bright colours of the scenes were dimly illuminated by shafts of filtered light.

At the rear of the temple stood the sanctuary; the floor level gradually inclined towards it from the temple entrance. Representing the highest point of the Island where the bird-god had first alighted, this small, dark chamber echoed the shape and dimensions of the early reed shrine. The god's cult-statue was kept here in a small box-shrine where it received the most sacred rites, which were performed by the king or high-priest. The statue was the image of the god, the locus into which the divine spirit could enter, but the god was not limited or confined by this image because he also existed in other forms and dimensions. In some temples, there were also cults for subsidiary deities, whose sanctuaries were adjacent to that of the chief god, which always stood on the main axis of the temple.

Subsidiary rooms, sometimes placed near the sanctuary but often in other parts of the temple, were used to store the god's clothing, jewellery, insignia and sacred utensils that featured in the rituals. Occasionally, butchering and food preparation were carried out in the temple proper, although these were more often confined to the external courtyard. Some temples also had special areas that were devoted to particular aspects of the god's cult.

Each temple was decorated with wall scenes. Those on the interior walls either commemorated historical events or provided a summarized version of the various rituals which had regularly taken place inside the temple.[28] The scenes, arranged in two or three horizontal registers, were 'brought to life' by means of magic when the ceremony of 'Opening the Mouth' was performed (*see* p. 124) as each new temple was handed over to its resident god at the Consecration Ceremony. In this way, the vital energy of the temple was charged, and it was assumed that the building would acquire all the potent forces of the original island. The wall-scenes became perpetually effective, ensuring that the rituals would continue even if the priests ceased to function.[29]

In some areas, the scenes depicted historical events such as the king's success in battle,[30] his coronation,[31] or the foundation and consecration of the temple. The foundation ceremonies were carried out over a period of one or two weeks, during which time the king or high priest would perform a series of rites. First, they delineated the boundary of the temple, by staking out the ground with four boundary poles and a length of rope. Next, the land on the four sides of the site was hacked up with a hoe to form trenches that would hold the foundation blocks of the building, and pits were excavated in the foundation trench at the points required for the blocks. Then, the ditch was filled with a mixture of sand and sherds, because sand would protect the building against the infiltration of water. The next step involved placing foundation deposits containing small models of tools and implements at various points under the walls, and depositing four bricks at the four corners of the temple. Finally, the king 'whitewashed' the foundation trench with *bsn*, which was probably chalk; in later times, this rite represented a purification of the building. As well as staking out the site, the Foundation Ceremony also consecrated the land, and reinforced the process of creation. Once the temple had been completed, it was handed over to the resident deity during the Consecration Ceremony, with a series of rituals, including the Opening of the Mouth Ceremony, that made each area cultically operational. These culminated with the installation of the god's statue in the sanctuary, and when all the necessary purifications had been completed, the king handed over the temple to the god to whom the temple had been dedicated. This process of consecration and delivery of the temple to the god was renewed each New Year's Day.

In other areas, the scenes depict the rituals that were once performed there. These rites, carried out daily on a regular basis, were the same in all temples throughout Egypt. The most important – the Daily Temple

Ritual – was performed in all New Kingdom temples, and dramatized and ritualized the mundane events of everyday existence. Before sunrise, the king or high priest would wash and dress in his ceremonial garments. He would perform his ablutions by entering the Sacred Lake in the temple precinct, where the water was believed to possess healing and revivifying properties that would enable the king or his delegate to experience a daily 'rebirth' and to be cleansed and purified so that he could enter the god's presence. The king then consecrated the divine offerings, which were either paid as 'taxes' to the state, or donated by royal or private persons, or produced by the royal or temple estates and industries. At sunrise, the officiant would then proceed to the sanctuary to present the offerings. These replenished the god's life-force, and prevented the cosmos from returning to chaos. They included wine, vegetables, fruit, different kinds of bread and cakes, and cuts of meat from the sacred cattle that belonged to the temple. These animals had previously been slaughtered in the temple precinct, according to strict ritual procedures; it was probably considered that, by eating certain joints of meat, the officiant would absorb the animal's strength and power. As symbols of life and order, these offerings provided an essential link between the gods and mankind; through their spiritual power and nourishment, the king was able to achieve rebirth and sustain his immortality, as well as ensuring that order prevailed throughout Egypt.

Next, the god's statue was removed from the box-shrine, and the clothing and cosmetics worn on the previous day were removed. It was then fumigated with incense and presented with different kinds of natron which could be chewed to cleanse the mouth. Natron is a naturally occurring compound which is found in desert valleys and was used for mummification and cleansing or purification. The statue was given fresh clothing and facial cosmetics, and adorned with jewellery and insignia before it was presented with the morning meal. The officiant then withdrew backwards from the sanctuary. The same ritual and food offerings were presented at midday and in the evening, when the statue was finally returned to the box-shrine. In reality, the food remained intact and was subsequently recirculated; it was regularly presented as payment to the priests, or offered to the royal and private statues which had been set up in the temple.[32]

In the New Kingdom royal cult complexes on the west bank at Thebes, a secondary ritual was enacted at the conclusion of the Daily Temple Ritual. This is known as the 'Ritual of the Royal Ancestors' or the 'Ritual of Amenhotep I'[33] and was performed for the dead, deified king and for the Royal Ancestors who were worshipped collectively in these temples. The Ancestors were the legitimate rulers of Egypt from King Menes in Dynasty 1 down to the builder of any particular temple. It was believed that each king joined them when he died, and in his lifetime, it was essential that they accepted him as rightful ruler and supported his reign. The ritual in these temples thus benefited the Ancestors and the king whose name it perpetuated, ensuring him an eternal food supply. The king was expected to honour the cult of the divine Ancestors in the same way that a private person was obliged to bury his parents, perform their burial rites, and maintain their mortuary cult.

In these temples, at the conclusion of the Daily Temple Ritual, the food offerings were taken from the god's sanctuary to another area of the temple where the Ritual of the Royal Ancestors was performed. After some preliminary rites, the food was offered to the Ancestors who were usually represented in the form of a 'King List' inscribed on a temple wall, which included the names of all legitimate previous rulers. At the conclusion of this ritual, the food was removed and divided up amongst the priests, or presented to the royal and private statues and their attendants.

The Daily Temple Ritual reaffirmed the god's daily rebirth, and combined Osirian and solar elements to renew the god's strength. In return for the provision of a residence, food and other offerings, the Egyptians expected the gods to give the king power, fame, eternal life and success in battle, and to make Egypt secure and prosperous. Effective rituals performed at the tombs and in the temples were intended to ensure that the Egyptian state would remain stable and cohesive. The Ritual of the Royal Ancestors established the role of kingship and enabled the dead rulers to receive perpetual sustenance.

In the temple scenes, the king is always shown performing the rituals for the gods, although the High-priest would usually have played this role. The king may have attended the consecration of each temple, and perhaps officiated at the main temple of the chief state god but elsewhere, his duties were delegated to the High-priest. However, it was essential that only he was represented as the officiant in the wall-scenes because, as the god's son and heir, he alone, as the personification of Egypt, could present the offerings on behalf of all his people. This role had developed from the functions of the predynastic local chieftains who made offerings to the god in his reed shrine.

Festivals

A second group of rituals – the festivals – celebrated the major events in a god's life, and were closely integrated into the god's mythology. They varied in content and meaning from one temple to another, and were held on different dates. At each festival, the most sacred rites would be performed within a special area of the temple, but usually they also involved a procession in which the portable divine statue was carried outside the temple in a sacred barque, to be shown to the crowds. This gave the people the chance to view the deity on an occasion that attracted many pilgrims who welcomed this infrequent opportunity to have contact with the temple god.

Some festivals were held monthly but others occurred on an irregular pattern, based on local astronomical sightings or calendars. Some were held in two or more temples, where they enacted a celebration, such as a divine marriage, between the resident deities, but most were held annually at a single temple. Famous examples included natural events such as the festival of the New Year's Day in the first month of the inundation season: legend maintains that in the summer months, when the Nile began to rise, a young virgin was thrown into the river in order to celebrate the inundation and to request the gods to bestow an adequate flood and to grant prosperity to the land and its people. Later, following the Moslem conquest of Egypt in the seventh century ACE, this custom was abolished, although a substitute 'bride' was constructed every year in the form of an earthen pillar which, when it was eventually swallowed by the rising Nile waters, became an 'offering' to the river.

The mystical union of the god and king was celebrated in the Festival of Opet at Thebes: this involved a procession, led by the king, in which the statue of Amun was carried in a barque through the city from the

Temple of Karnak to the Temple of Luxor. Elsewhere, at Abydos, the annual Osiris Festival celebrated the main events in the life, death and resurrection of the god. Some rites were performed within the most sacred areas of the temple, such as the 'Raising of the *Djed*-pillar' when the priests lifted the supine pillar (which represented Osiris) into the upright position, thus signifying his resurrection. Other stages in the Osiris Mysteries, however, were performed out of doors: the statue of the god was moved in procession between his temple and his 'tomb', accompanied by scenes of combat, enacted to re-create events in the god's kingship, death and resurrection. This enabled the lay people who had travelled to Abydos as pilgrims to participate directly in the celebration. The Stela of Ikhernofret provides details of how a high official who served King Senusret III was sent to organize the annual festival of Osiris:[34]

I furnished his great barque, the eternal, everlasting one. I made for him the portable shrine that carries the beauty of the Foremost-of-the-Westerners . . . The gods who attend him were fashioned, their shrines were made anew. I made the hour-priests [diligent] at their tasks; I made them know the ritual of every day and of the feasts of the beginnings of the seasons . . .

During the Festival of Sokar,[35] this god of the necropolis was taken across to the shrines and temples on the west bank at Thebes, while other occasions celebrated the conjugal visits of gods, when the statue of one deity would be carried in a barque, by land or river, to the temple of his consort so that they could spend time together. One of the most famous was the Festival of the Sacred Marriage, celebrated between Hathor, goddess of love and beauty, who resided at Denderah, and her husband, Horus, the god of Edfu. As well as these great national festivals, there were also important local celebrations for some deified, deceased rulers such as Mentuhotep, Senusret II and Amenhotep I.

Again, in theory, the king led all the festivals, but in practice, he usually delegated this duty to the high-priest. The celebrations were colourful events, in which the god's statue, carried on a barque or sledge, was often taken to special shrines on the rooftop of the temple, so that it could come into direct contact with the sun, and was then paraded outside. There were stations inside and outside the temple where the priests rested the barque and performed special rites. On many occasions, when the procession moved outside the temple precinct, the barque was accompanied by an entourage of priests, dancers, musicians and singers who performed sacred songs and dances and burnt incense. These processions gave the ordinary people a rare chance to have contact with the deity, and even to approach the barque and present oracular questions to the god's statue, hidden inside its portable shrine.

The Economy of the Temples

The temples were not only centres of religious power; they also exerted considerable economic, educational and social influence on the country. The Egyptian economy was a mixture of private exchanges, state redistribution, and a small private sector that functioned at a local and regional level. Peasants depended mainly on subsistence agriculture and personal barter and trade, whereas officials and soldiers received payment from the state (which was derived from the agricultural produce paid as taxation to the state) and food grown on government estates. The temples formed part of this system. Each temple owned estates with livestock, crops, vineyards and gardens. The peasants employed in these areas produced food for the temple priests, workers, and themselves, as well as for the personnel employed in the necropolis. They also provided the offerings for the temple deities, most of which were eventually redistributed to the priests and their families. The offerings prepared for the celebration of feasts were often abundant enough to feed some of the local populace as well.

Temple income was assured by presentation of the booty that the king brought back from his military campaigns, and by revenue collected from districts throughout the country that was paid in kind, and included grain, oil, wine, beer, metals and other materials. In addition, some individuals donated land, offerings or services to the temple, which in turn supplied and maintained their mortuary rites. Some temples also owned mines that produced the materials used in the temple workshops to make the god's equipment and possessions. Requisition lists indicate that metals, garments, cattle, vegetables and other commodities were paid in taxes by the temples to the state.[36] Essentially, the temple was 'the repository for the revenues of the empire'[37] where the revenue was received, recorded, and kept in the temple storehouses before it was redistributed as payment amongst the temple employees. Some temples, such as Karnak, possessed their own fleets of ships that were used for tax collection. The temples in turn paid out some form of tax to the state, but royal decrees gave them certain tax exemptions and privileges, and protected them from the worst extortions of the state agents.

The temples retained considerable autonomy, and were also major employers: in addition to the priests, large numbers of people were required to perform the secular tasks associated with running these extensive estates. The Temple of Amun at Karnak was treated as a department of the royal administration that was directly responsible to the king, but regular supervision and organization of the temple and its staff were undertaken by senior government officials. At Karnak and other leading temples, the chief priests exerted great political influence on the country.

The Priesthood

In theory, the king was the sole priest in every temple throughout Egypt, but in reality, this responsibility was delegated to the priests whose prime duty was to minister to the god's needs.[38] The term *ḥm-nṯr* ('servant of the god') aptly describes the priest's main duties. He controlled the entrance to the temple, had access to the sanctuary, and prepared the offerings and performed the rituals. The priest was expected to understand the liturgy and teach his specialization within the temple, but the priesthood was never regarded as a special sect set apart because they had received divine revelation.

The temples were houses of the gods and not places of congregational worship; the priests had no pastoral duties and were not expected to preach or give guidance to the populace. Essentially a wealthy and privileged class, they were functionaries who performed the rituals, and although they were probably dedicated officials who generally followed the ethical standards set out in the Instructions in Wisdom, there was no concept of vocation and personal spirituality was not a prerequisite for the priesthood. The career of a priest offered wealth, power and prestige and, because of this, it attracted able and ambitious people who wanted to succeed in the society.

The earliest 'priests' were the community leaders of the Predynastic villages who offered food regularly to the local deity in his reed shrine, in order to ensure the community's well-being. In the Old Kingdom, local government officials were sometimes requested to administer local temples where the cults were performed for the gods. However, in some of the temples dedicated to the royal cults, there were already companies of priests who served in the temple in rotation, and in their off-duty periods, administered the temple estates or worked in the state bureaucracy.[39] At this time, many women from leading families participated in the divine cults, particularly those of the goddesses Neith and Hathor, although they could also serve male gods. There appears to be no consistent pattern of hereditary status in the titles associated with the cult of Hathor, but the role seems to have carried social and possibly political significance.[40] The duties of these female 'servants' included music-making, dancing and singing, and the head of the group was in charge of musical training and practice.

The priesthood was usually held by men as a secondary profession. In many cases, it was hereditary, with the son following his father's profession, and some priesthoods continued in the same families for up to seventeen generations. In theory, the king retained the right to confirm all priestly appointments, but in reality, he only selected candidates for significant posts in major centres such as Memphis, Thebes and Heliopolis, although sometimes he also promoted a priest who had shown that he was particularly deserving, or he presented priesthoods to people whom he wished to reward. He rarely refused an appointment, although he could adjust the balance of power by introducing a high-priest from another priesthood, or a man from the royal court, or an army general, rather than promoting an internal candidate.

In other instances, candidates could be selected and appointed by a collegium of priests; even if a son inherited a priesthood, it was probably necessary to obtain approval from such a committee as a formality. As early as the Middle Kingdom, it was also possible to purchase some offices by bartering for them, a custom which became widespread in the Graeco-Roman Period.

In the Old and Middle Kingdoms, almost all prominent men acted as lay-priests. They performed their temple duties for several months each year, and served elsewhere in the state structure for the rest of the time. Doctors, lawyers and scribes, for example, held priesthoods associated with those professions, so that doctors became priests of Sekhmet, the goddess of disease and epidemics, lawyers became priests of Ma'at, the goddess of truth and justice, and scribes served Thoth, the god of writing. This system ensured that religion and the state were completely interwoven. The priests worked for the king and state in civil positions for most of the time, and were employed in the temples on a part-time basis, so that the temples had little real opportunity to act independently of the state.

By the New Kingdom, however, a permanent class of priests was established in the larger temples, although most positions were still part-time and few priests received any formal training as ritual specialists. Generally, each temple had four groups (*phyles*) of lay-priests who performed the rituals for the god. Each group consisted of the same number of people who performed the same functions; they each served for three months in a year on a rotational basis, and each group's term of duty lasted for one month.[41] In the off-duty periods, they pursued their main professions within the community. They could marry and, although they were expected to reside within the temple precinct during their term of duty, at other times they lived outside with their families.

The novice priest was probably initiated into religious ceremonies and daily rituals during his first term of duty in the temple. He may have been formally installed and presented, possibly receiving a ritual baptism and purification before he was allowed into the god's presence within the sanctuary area. At some stage during this initiation ceremony, the secret knowledge of the god's cult was probably revealed to the priest. He also doubtless took vows that committed him to maintain integrity and ritual purity, and to obey the ethical principles and cultic regulations associated with the post.

Herodotus[42] provides details of the purification requirements for priests. Certain taboos had to be observed: the priest was obliged to bathe in cold water twice daily and twice nightly, in the temple's Sacred Lake; he cleansed his mouth with natron and shaved his head and body all over every day. Not all Egyptian males were circumcised, although the custom seems to have been quite widespread, and priests probably underwent this ceremony when they entered the profession. Although they were allowed to marry, priests were expected to observe sexual abstinence during their periods of temple duty and were required not to have physical contact with women for several days beforehand. This was to ensure that they were ritually cleansed so that they could enter the god's presence: possibly contact with menstrual blood or body fluids was considered to be a form of contamination which would destroy this purified status.

In terms of their clothing, they were forbidden to use materials (wool or leather) that came from living animals. It was apparently believed that such clothes would contaminate the purity of the god's sanctuary, although the reason for this is unclear. Possibly, since they worshipped many gods in animal forms, it was thought unacceptable that they should come before the gods wearing clothes made from the skins or hair of animals who, in some instances, provided the locus for the god's spirit. Therefore, they wore only linen garments and shoes made from vegetable fibres. The style of the priest's garments changed little from the Old Kingdom: only the details on the garment indicated the owner's rank or function, as in the case of the high-priests and special category officiants who wore distinctive clothes. There were also restrictions on the food that the priest could eat, although these varied from area to area, from post to post, and from the service of one god to another. Herodotus states that fish and beans were prohibited, but other sources include pork, lamb, pigeon and garlic. Sometimes, priests of one district would be prohibited from eating the flesh of their own cult animal or the sacred plant associated with their particular god, but this taboo would not apply elsewhere. The physical purity of the priest was therefore defined by abstinence from certain physical conditions that, for various reasons, would have made his presence unacceptable to the god. However, it was also essential that the utensils and vessels used in the rituals were appropriately cleansed, and they were regularly washed in the Sacred Lake where the water was believed to possess special purificatory properties.

Many details of the organization of the temple staff and their duties and functions are still obscure, but some information is preserved in the names and lists of titles of priests that have survived.[43] The Temple of Amun at Karnak employed thousands of people, and by the New Kingdom had a larger staff than the king himself. In Papyrus Harris, it is recorded that, in the reign of Ramesses III, the temple employed more than 80,000 people and owned more than 2,000 square kilometres of land. Staff performed 125 different functions within the temple, which included both liturgical and ritual duties, as well as tasks which maintained the fabric of the building and ensured that its organization ran smoothly.

The priesthood of Amun wielded unprecedented power. The most important post – the high-priest of Amun whose title was the 'First Prophet of Amun' – had extensive powers. He owned a great house and estates, and was a trusted official. The 'Fathers of the God' (who included the Second, Third and Fourth Prophets of Amun) were next in rank, and then there were the 'Servants'. In other temples these formed the category of senior priests who usually came into contact with the divine cult-statue during the daily rituals. Some were specialists, employed in the House of Life; this was an institution, probably attached to all major temples, where the sacred wisdom of the cult was preserved and continued by means of the composition and copying of texts on papyri and on the temple walls. In Greek sources, these scribes are called *Hierogrammatists*, and they included both priests and lay specialists in fields such as medicine, geography, history of the kings, use of plants, astronomy and astrology. They also probably instructed students in a wide range of subjects.

The second group of temple personnel included the minor priests who probably assisted in religious activities such as carrying the sacred barque during festival processions, and supervising employees who were engaged to decorate and renovate the temple. This category, however, did not enter the god's sanctuary, although they assisted with the lesser tasks associated with maintaining the temple and the rituals. However, since they handled the ritual and cultic objects, they also had to be ritually 'pure' and were given the title of *W'b*, which meant 'the purified one'.

The third group were lay personnel who included architects, stewards, clerks, police, overseers of the granaries and estates, and estate workers. There were also confectioners, bakers, brewers and cooks who prepared the divine food offerings; textile workers and craftsmen who produced the god's clothes, insignia, jewellery, vessels and statues; and florists who delivered the floral offerings presented to the deity. In addition, there were people who cleaned, repaired and maintained the temples.

Some special categories of priests are also known. As early as Dynasty 2, there were lector-priests (*hry-hb*) who carried the ritual book and recited the formulae while the rituals were being performed, and presided at oracles and divinations. In earliest times, this important post was held by members of the royal family or the highest nobility. There were also mortuary priests who were associated with the rituals performed at tombs rather than temples. They carried out rites connected with mourning, the preparation and burial of the corpse, and the cult which the living heirs continued to perform for the deceased. The most important mortuary officiant was known as a *sem*-priest. The royal heir acted as a *sem*-priest for the dead king but, as early as Dynasty 1, there were professional *sem*-priests who performed the burial rites for non-royal individuals, acting on behalf of the deceased's son and heir who was responsible for ensuring that the correct burial procedure was followed. These *sem*-priests can be distinguished in the scenes in tombs and on papyri by a hairstyle known as the 'Sidelock of Youth' and by a panther skin worn across one shoulder.

MORTUARY CUSTOMS IN THE NEW KINGDOM

The pyramids of earlier dynasties had been continuously plundered, and this was perhaps one of the main reasons why the rulers of Dynasty 18 selected a less ostentatious burial site. However, it was essential that it was also close to Thebes. Thus, early in the dynasty, they began to bury their dead in the bleak and desolate hills on the west bank of the river, opposite Thebes. The natural shape and colour of these hills resemble the appearance of a pyramid, which may also have influenced this choice, and the Egyptians referred to the highest point as 'The Peak'. Sometimes, they personified and worshipped elements of the natural world as deities, and in this instance, 'The Peak' was designated as the divine protectress of the dead buried in the valleys below. Here, in this desolate area, the Egyptians selected a barren, narrow valley (known today as 'Biban el-Moluk' or the 'Valley of the Kings') for the burial of the kings who were placed in deep, rock-cut tombs that descended for many feet into the mountainside. This area became the nucleus of a vast necropolis that housed the tombs of royalty and officials of the New Kingdom. Since Napoleon's Egyptian expedition, many archaeological missions have worked in the area, but systematic records were not usually kept before the mid nineteenth century ACE when a system of government concessions to excavate was introduced. Thus, in many cases, the locations of tombs and knowledge of the objects found in them have been lost.[44]

On the west bank at Thebes, several areas were used for royal tombs dating to different periods. For example, the rulers of Dynasty 11 built *saff* or 'row' tombs at El-Tarif, in the northernmost part of the necropolis, while the rulers of Dynasty 17 used the northern necropolis at Dra'abu el-Naga'. Details of their location and ownership are preserved in a record of inspection undertaken in antiquity (Papyrus Abbott). These royal tombs may have incorporated small brick pyramids, and important discoveries have included objects from the burials of Kamose and Queen Ah-hotpe, which include weapons, a toilet box and jewellery. A long-term project was launched in 1990 by the German Institute of Archaeology in Cairo, with the aim of excavating, documenting and publishing this royal and private cemetery of the Second Intermediate Period and early New Kingdom.[45] This study is providing evidence about the funerary architecture and burial practices of the lower and middle classes during the early New Kingdom; previously, it was not known where most of the inhabitants of Thebes were buried at this period. It is estimated that some 17,000 ordinary people were interred in this cemetery, and it was probably also the burial place of Amenhotep I,

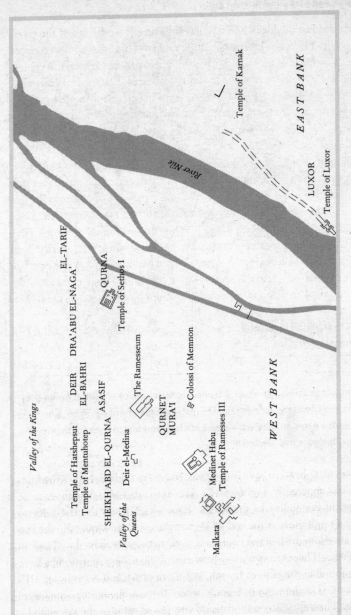

Map of Thebes

EAST BANK

Temple of Karnak

River Nile

LUXOR
Temple of Luxor

EL-TARIF

DRA'ABU EL-NAGA'

QURNA
Temple of Sethos I

DEIR
EL-BAHRI

ASASIF

Valley of the Kings

Temple of Hatshepsut
Temple of Mentuhotep

SHEIKH ABD EL-QURNA

Deir el-Medina

The Ramesseum

QURNET
MURA'I

Valley of the
Queens

Colossi of Memnon

Medinet Habu
Temple of Ramesses III

WEST BANK

Malkata

A tomb scene shows Ramesses II (*seated*) in the presence of deities: Amun (*left*), Thoth, god of writing (*far right*), and Seshat, goddess of writing (*right*), who inscribe his name on the Persea tree. Each leaf represented a year of the king's life that the gods had allotted him.

whose cult appears to have been practised here in the later New Kingdom.

It was apparently Tuthmosis I (1525–1510 BCE) who first chose to be buried in the Valley of the Kings. Ramesses XI was the last ruler to build a tomb there at the end of Dynasty 20, and subsequently, the site was abandoned when the court and royal necropolis moved to Tanis in the Delta. There are two main branches of the valley; most tombs have been found in the eastern branch, but those of Ay and Amenhotep III[46] are located in the western branch, where there is much scope for future work. The valley accommodated the tombs of most of the rulers and a few non-royals throughout Dynasties 18 to 20. Altogether, archaeologists have uncovered over sixty tombs,[47] but the only virtually intact royal burial which has been found is that of Tutankhamun.[48]

The tombs followed a basic plan, and were designed to defeat the tomb-robbers. The entrance was cut into the rock, and a stairway and corridor then descend to the burial chamber. En route, the corridor is interrupted by one or more pillared halls. The burial chamber (also featuring pillars cut from the rock) accommodated the royal burial in a sarcophagus (large stone coffin), mounted on an alabaster base, which was located at the innermost end of the chamber. The four storerooms that lead off the burial chamber once housed the tomb goods. This plan remained virtually unchanged except that, until the end of Dynasty 18, the descending corridor turned either right or left, usually at a right angle, but in the later dynasties, the corridor ran straight to the burial hall.

Even the tomb of Tutankhamun was entered in antiquity, but it escaped severe plundering, and the treasure discovered there still provides our only evidence of a virtually intact New Kingdom royal burial. The treasure is magnificent, but Tutankhamun was a minor, short-lived king and his tomb was apparently hastily prepared and scantily decorated. Other royal tombs were much larger and often have elaborate wall-scenes, indicating the quality and quantity of the treasure that must have accompanied the original burials. Sadly, these tomb goods were extensively plundered in antiquity, and even the mummies were badly damaged when the plunderers stripped them of their funerary jewellery.

In the royal tombs, the subject matter of the wall and ceiling decorations concentrates on the passage of the king into the next world. In this respect, these scenes are quite different from those in the non-royal tombs which illustrate the everyday activities that the owner wished to perpetuate in the hereafter. Recent studies[49] have assembled information about the decipherment, translation and interpretation of these royal wall scenes and inscriptions. Taken from the various funerary papyri (the so-called 'Books'), the scenes were placed as guides in the king's tomb to help him overcome the dangers as he passed from the world of the living to the land of the dead. Today, scholars recognize the religious significance of this wall decoration, and have revised their earlier opinion that royal tomb-art was banal and unsophisticated.

The most famous of these texts, the Book of the Dead,[50] which the Egyptians called the 'Book of Coming Forth by Day', emphasized the daily death and rebirth of the sun, and continued the idea of the Pyramid and Coffin Texts as providing a series of spells to ensure the resurrection of the deceased and his safety in the next world. The Book of Amduat (the Netherworld) was particularly important because it illustrates the journey of the sun-god through the underworld where he fought against demons and evils for twelve hours of the night. The rebirth of the sun each morning symbolized the renewal of creation and the emergence of the whole world from the chaos of night.

In a nearby area known today as the 'Valley of the Queens', tombs were built for some queens of Dynasties 19 and 20 but also for other royal members, particularly some of the princes of the Ramesside Period. In fact, in Dynasty 18, there was no specific area reserved for the queens' burials and their tombs were scattered across the whole necropolis. Many of the tombs in the Valley of the Queens were unfinished and undecorated, but in those scenes and inscriptions that have survived, the main theme is the relationship between the deceased and the gods and the successful completion of the final journey to the realm of the dead. Over seventy tombs have been discovered and excavated here, the most famous one belonging to Nefertari, the favourite queen of Ramesses II. This contains scenes that are amongst the finest examples of Egyptian tomb art, and recent restoration now enables visitors to see something of the tomb's original beauty and magnificence.

The non-royal tombs of many courtiers and officials of the New

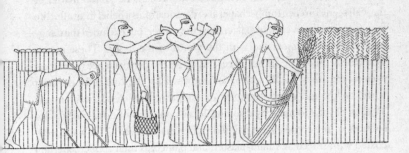

Most tombs contained wall scenes depicting food production (as here) to ensure a perpetual food supply for the deceased owner.

Kingdom have also been found in this area. They are scattered across several sites and represent the period from Dynasty 6 to the Graeco-Roman Period, although about five hundred date to the New Kingdom.[51] Although there is a considerable variation in the plan and layout of these tombs over this timespan, a basic plan had already emerged in the New Kingdom. The typical Theban private tomb of Dynasty 18 consisted of an open rectangular forecourt behind which lay an inverted T-shaped chapel, cut into the hillside. At the rear of the chapel, or in a corner of the forecourt, a hidden shaft descended to one or more subterranean chambers where the burial and tomb goods were placed. Sometimes, these walls were decorated with inscriptions from the funerary books, but usually scenes occurred only on the walls of the offering chapel.

The chapel, where the family or priest presented offerings to the deceased, was an innovation introduced early in Dynasty 18, but it was a development of the arrangement found in the Middle Kingdom portico tombs. It consists of a transverse hall, and a passage that runs longitudinally from the centre of this hall back into the mountainside.[52] A small sanctuary is located at the far end of this passage, which contains a niche where, in antiquity, statues of the owner and his wife were placed. Sometimes, there is also a 'false-door' through which the owner's spirit could pass to gain access to the food offerings.

Far from presenting a world of darkness, the Egyptian tombs delight the visitor with paintings in which the colours are often almost as bright and clear as when they were first put on the walls. The subject matter of the wall scenes in each tomb-chapel also demonstrates a belief in an afterlife that mirrored the everyday existence of the owner, but excluded the dangers and illnesses associated with the world of the living. These scenes would be activated at the burial ceremony by the performance of magical rites so that they could act for and be used by the owner in the next world. Although some examples of sculptured relief do occur in the Theban royal and non-royal tombs, local stone was of poor quality and so most of the scenes were painted rather than carved. The walls were coated with stucco and mud-plaster, and paint was then applied. Certain scenes occur in particular locations within the tomb. Some illustrate daily activities, the owner's profession or occupation, his devotion to the gods, sports and recreation, family, and social activities, whereas others record the preparations undertaken for his funeral, and the burial ceremony itself. Therefore, these scenes continued the general themes found in the Old and Middle Kingdom tombs, but they also often reflected the cosmopolitan influences of the New Kingdom, showing, for example, foreign envoys from Syria and the Aegean Islands bringing tribute to Egypt. Although many of these tombs remain unstudied, a series of modern copyists including Burton, Hay, Wilkinson, Carter and Norman and Nina de Garis Davies have recorded these scenes, often preserving information which has subsequently been damaged or destroyed.[53]

The burial goods found in New Kingdom tombs show that some of the Middle Kingdom categories still continued: these include canopic jars, statues of the owner and his wife, models of boats and servants, and ushabtis. The New Kingdom burials also had a lavish array of clothing, jewellery, perfumes and cosmetics, games, furniture, pottery and other articles of daily use. With the wall-scenes, these objects provide an insight into the affluent lifestyle of a wealthy and sophisticated society. The funeral and burial of the dead, depicted in the wall-scenes, can also be reconstructed. After the body was mummified at the embalmer's workshop, the family transported it from the east bank, where most people lived, to the necropolis on the west bank. The procession then made its way to the tomb: the funerary goods were carried by bearers, and female professional mourners accompanied the group. Hired specifically for this duty, they are shown with torn dresses and dishevelled hair, rubbing dirt on to their foreheads and bewailing the deceased. When the procession arrived at the tomb, the mummy was placed upright at the entrance, and the *sem*-priest performed the 'Opening of the Mouth' ceremony on the body and on all the inanimate figures in the tomb, to bring them to life for the deceased owner's use. Once the mummy had been placed in the tomb, this 'homecoming' was celebrated by a burial service which included the recitation of hymns and songs, often accompanied by a harpist. Finally, the family shared a funerary meal at the tomb in which the deceased was thought to participate. On subsequent occasions, people would visit the tombs and share commemorative meals with their dead relatives, a custom which has continued in modern times.[54]

CHAPTER 6

The Amarna Heresy

The New Kingdom, *c.*1400 – *c.*1320 BCE

THE EARLY YEARS OF AMENHOTEP IV
(AKHENATEN)

By the reign of Amenhotep III (1417–1379 BCE), Egypt had reached the height of its power and wealth. Earlier military expeditions had laid the foundations of the empire, and Amenhotep III's court reflected Egypt's international status. Peace replaced earlier conflicts, and diplomatic ties were established with other countries. There were now close family bonds between the royal courts of Egypt and Mitanni – formerly Egypt's main enemy – and Gilukhepa and Tadukhipa, daughters of two Mitannian kings, became wives of Amenhotep III.

These settled conditions at home enabled the king to build extensively. He enhanced the Temple of Karnak, made major contributions to the nearby Temple of Luxor, and built a substantial mortuary temple on the west bank at Thebes, of which only the Colossi of Memnon, a pair of massive statues which once flanked the entrance, now survive. He also built an extensive palace complex at Malkata on the west bank, to the south-east of where the temples of Medinet Habu still stand. Originally called the 'House of Joy', this site is now known by the modern Arabic name of Malkata. Every king customarily built a new palace that included both private royal apartments and administrative quarters. This palace covered an area over 80 acres, and accommodated the king's state apartments, a residence for his chief wife, Queen Tiye, quarters for his other wives and courtiers, workshops and administrative areas, a temple to the principal god Amun, dwellings for people of various social classes, a hall for the celebration of the king's second jubilee festival, and a large artificial lake or harbour on the east.

Excavated by the New York Metropolitan Museum of Art's expedition between 1910 and 1920 ACE, and subsequently by the University of Pennsylvania Museum, the buildings reflect the cosmopolitan atmosphere of the period. The palace was built of mudbrick, and had plastered walls that, in some chambers, were decorated with painted scenes of plants, animals and motifs, indicating that some artisans may have come from Mediterranean lands. Malkata was also supplied with goods from other parts of Africa and the eastern Mediterranean,' again emphasizing Egypt's international standing.

It was here that Amenhotep IV, the son of Amenhotep III and Tiye, grew up; then, following the premature death of his elder brother, Prince Thutmose, Amenhotep IV became royal heir and spent the early years of his reign at Malkata. He married Nefertiti, whose art representations – particularly the heads discovered in workshops at Tell el-Amarna in 1914 ACE, which are now in museums in Cairo and Berlin – indicate that she was a woman of great beauty. However, there is little information about her origins: she never claimed the titles of 'King's Daughter' or 'King's Sister' and was probably not related by family ties to her husband. Nevertheless, she became his chief wife (his other wives included Kiya and two of his own daughters), and apparently played an important political and religious role, being appointed as her husband's adviser at the beginning of his reign.

Amenhotep IV followed the example of his father and grandfather, Tuthmosis IV, in breaking the tradition that each king should marry within the royal family. According to some scholarly interpretations (although this is not accepted by everyone, *see* pp. 305–6), royal inheritance and succession passed through the person of the principal queen (known as the 'Great Royal Wife'), who was usually the 'Great Royal Daughter' (the eldest daughter) of the previous king and queen. The fiction was maintained that each king was the offspring of the divine union between the country's chief state-god and the ruling king's principal wife. The Great Royal Wife was therefore regarded as the divine consort and mother of the next heir apparent, and she also conferred on her husband the right to rule Egypt. According to this tradition, the royal male heir had to marry the Great Royal Daughter (although she was often his full or half-sister), in order to substantiate his claim to rule Egypt and to ensure that his son was accepted as the legitimate successor to the throne. Sometimes, however, an ambitious 'upstart' male claimant to the throne would succeed in marrying the Great Royal Daughter so that he could inherit the kingship.

For various reasons (for example, in some reigns, there was not a royal daughter available for marriage), this system was not practised universally throughout Egyptian history. Nevertheless, in early Dynasty 18, the custom was usually observed. However, by the reign of Tuthmosis IV (1425–1417 BCE), the kings no longer followed this tradition: Tuthmosis IV probably took a foreign wife as his chief queen (see below), and the Great Royal Wife of his son, Amenhotep III, was Tiye, the daughter of commoners. Her father, Yuya, was Prophet of Min and Overseer of Cattle at Akhmim, and her mother, Thuya, held the title 'Chief Lady of Amun's harem'. On the occasion of his marriage, Amenhotep III issued commemorative scarabs that emphasized the non-royal origin of Yuya and Thuya, who ultimately enjoyed a commoner's rare privilege of a tomb in the Valley of the Kings.

Amenhotep III was the son of Tuthmosis IV and a Mitannian princess, Mutemweya. It is possible that, by rejecting the traditional royal marriage, all these kings were attempting to curb the power of the priests of Amen-Re, because the priests' support was traditionally required in the selection of a royal heir and, as part of this process, they had customarily approved the person who was married to the Great Royal Daughter. Also, the possibility of a co-regency between Amenhotep III and Amenhotep IV has been extensively debated;[2] there is insufficient evidence to prove that any one theory is correct, but various suggestions have indicated that they may have shared the throne for twelve years, or a few months, or that the younger king only succeeded at his father's death. However, if there was a period of joint rule, the kings probably spent it at Malkata.[3]

HISTORY OF THE ATEN

In Year 4 of his reign, Amenhotep IV replaced Amun with the Aten as the supreme god of the pantheon and embarked on a course of action which has been variously interpreted as a 'religious revolution' or an 'evolution'.[4] The Aten (*Itn*) was a hitherto unimportant god who was symbolized by the disc of the sun. References to the deity occur as early as the Middle Kingdom, but it is not clear when the Aten began to receive a separate and distinctive cult. However, during the reign of Tuthmosis IV, the Aten was already identified as a separate solar god and not just a variant of the sun-god Re. Its significance increased greatly in the reign of Amenhotep III: there were more references to the god, and the king promoted a distinctive cult of the Aten which may have been intended to rival the previously unfettered powers of Amen-Re's priesthood. The Aten's universality was now promoted, again perhaps to threaten the role of Amen-Re as 'King of Gods'.

However, Amenhotep III avoided any direct clash with Amen-Re; there was no attempt to make the Aten an exclusive god, or to curtail the traditional cults. Indeed, the king respected Amen-Re's popularity and power, and Queen Tiye's brother, Anen, held a high office in the god's priesthood. During his lifetime, Amenhotep III also emphasized and promoted his own divine kingship, representing his divine birth in a chamber in the Temple of Luxor. However, royal divinity and the worship of the Aten were developed in unprecedented ways by his son, Amenhotep IV.

When evidence for this unique period of history was first uncovered, historians regarded Amenhotep IV as the creator of the Aten and the instigator of a 'religious revolution'. Today, however, it is acknowledged that, although he took a series of progressive steps to introduce innovations, in fact his actions had been foreshadowed by events in the reigns of his father and grandfather. His own contribution was nevertheless unique in that, for the first time, a ruler attempted to impose a form of solar monotheism on Egypt. No other king ever claimed that one god was exclusive or tried to exterminate all other cults. At other periods, a dynasty had sometimes promoted the worship of one deity as the supreme god of the pantheon, but this had existed alongside many other, equally valid cults. At times, the sun-god Re had become predominant, but never to the exclusion of all other gods. Now, however, the cult of the Aten centred around the worship of the life-force and energy which emanated from the sun, rather than its actual material form.

The cult of the Aten, as developed by Amenhotep IV, may reflect an attempt to revive the power of the king and to restore his pivotal importance, which had been under threat since Dynasty 5. During Amenhotep IV's reign, the Aten was represented as a sun's disc from which descending rays, each ending in a hand, bestowed bounty on the royal family in return for their devotion to the god. Three aspects of the god were differentiated: the creative energy of the sun, the sun disc as the god's symbol, and the king as the god's earthly agent. The god and the king were now regarded as two equal aspects and, both in concept and titles, they became virtually interchangeable. The king became a god instead of 'god's son', and he acted as the sole representative of the Aten on earth. Therefore, although the Aten originated as an aspect of Re, under Amenhotep IV it changed to become a separate and unique deity.

Contemporary literature emphasizes the god's distinctive nature, as the creator of mankind and all creatures and plants. The Aten was the beneficent, universal force that emanated from the sun, and brought life to Egypt and the lands beyond. Since Egypt now possessed an empire, of which Amen-Re had previously been regarded as the supreme god, it now became necessary to endow the Aten with the powers of a universal creator-god in order to establish him as a convincing rival to Amen-Re. There has been speculation that the inspiration for Amenhotep IV's reforms may have originated in the beliefs of his father and in the influence of the cosmopolitan court at Malkata, where queens and their attendants had come from other homelands. However, in fact, the

Aten was firmly rooted in Egyptian history, and there is probably no good reason to search for a foreign origin for Amenhotep IV's innovations.

The king spent the first part of his reign at Thebes, but the significance these years played in the development of the Aten cult was not fully appreciated until evidence of Aten temples was discovered there. It is now apparent that, during this period, the king began to support and promote the Aten while also tolerating the existence of the traditional gods. Many thousands of stone blocks, decorated with reliefs and inscriptions, were discovered at Karnak and Luxor.[5] These have provided unprecedented information about religious events early in the reign, proving that the king constructed several buildings, which included temples for the Aten cult. The most important was located behind and outside the main precinct of the Temple of Amun at Karnak. Later rulers dismantled these buildings and used the blocks as infill for the pylons (large stone gateways) they constructed in the Temples of Luxor and Karnak. When these pylons were dismantled in the course of restoration in modern times, the existence of the blocks was revealed. A study, the 'Akhenaten Temple Project', used a computer to assist in the evaluation of the information on these blocks.[6] The content of some of the wall-scenes and inscriptions has provided unique information about these buildings and the development of the cult.

The Aten temples at Thebes celebrated the identification of the king with his god.[7] In these buildings, there was no sanctuary or cult-statue and no divine barque. The king was the sole earthly image of the god, but instead of the daily temple rituals which were traditionally offered to the gods and ruling king in the temples, the king was now attended in his palace, and received worship in household shrines, where ordinary people approached the Aten through prayers on stelae and statuettes dedicated to the king. In effect, the Aten and the king had become one, and the king was now the only means by which ordinary worshippers could reach the god.

For the first time, the Aten blocks revealed the significance of these early years at Thebes in terms of the development of the cult. They also suggested that Nefertiti played a role of unprecedented importance for a queen, holding equal status with the king. Growth of the Aten's cult at Thebes undoubtedly led to increased problems with the priesthood of Amen-Re, and the king soon took a series of unprecedented moves. In Year 5, he pronounced that the Aten would no longer tolerate the existence of any other gods. He disbanded the priesthoods of all other gods and diverted the income from their temples to support the Aten. He also renounced his formal association with Amen-Re by changing his name from Amenhotep ('Amun-is-satisfied') to Akhenaten (probably the 'Servant of the Aten'). Nefertiti took the additional name of Neferneferuaten ('Fair is the goddess of the Aten'). These actions undoubtedly precipitated the king's next move – to relocate his residence and religious capital to a new site that was untainted by any association with the traditional gods.

THE MOVE TO AMARNA

Akhenaten chose a virgin site for his new capital, roughly equidistant from Thebes and Lower Egypt. The selection of this location was apparently made in accordance with the god's instruction, and the city was duly named Akhetaten ('Horizon of the Aten'). Today, it is often referred to as 'Amarna' or 'Tell el-Amarna', and the terms 'Amarna Period', 'Amarna Literature' and 'Amarna Art' are frequently used in association with this site.

The city was situated in the Hermopolitan nome, and extended for over eight miles on both banks of the river. Fourteen large boundary stelae, inscribed with the king's conditions for establishing the city, delineated the boundaries. These conditions included the king's directive that his body should be brought back to Akhetaten for burial if he should die elsewhere (this also applied to other family members), and the declaration that he would never extend the city beyond its original limits. Although the reason for this is not stated, he may have considered that, since the location and perimeter of the city had been divinely authorized, these sacred instructions should not be altered by additional building.

The layout of the city generally ignored the traditional religious conventions. Whereas, customarily, the west bank had been reserved for burial sites, at Akhetaten, the cultivated land on the west was probably used to supply food for the city, while the east bank was occupied with the main urban buildings and the cemeteries. Here, the city, built between the river and the encircling eastern mountains, comprised three key districts.[8] The main building in the North City was the Northern Palace; the Maruaten (the Summer Palace, which incorporated a group of buildings decorated with painted scenes and pavements) was located in the South City, and also featured a lake, an island with a kiosk (a type of pavilion or summerhouse), and flower gardens; and the Central City accommodated the Great Temple and Smaller Temple to the Aten, as well as the Great Palace. As usual, the Palace served several functions, and included the king's official head-quarters, state apartments, servants' quarters, and a coronation hall. A bridge ran across the city's main road to join the Great Palace to the king's private residence. To the north and south, there were houses, workshops and sculptors' studios where many sculptures and plaster masks of the royal family and others were discovered by the archaeologists.

Major excavations were carried out at the site in the early twentieth century ACE,[9] and in 1977 ACE, the Egypt Exploration Society resumed work there. Its three major projects have included a survey of the site to produce detailed maps on which all the ground plans of the buildings could be seen, together with topographic details of the extensive unexcavated areas; excavation of the Workmen's Village; and re-excavation and investigation of the North City which had been worked in the 1920s and 1930s ACE but was not fully recorded.[10] The North City included royal and government buildings and houses; the recent excavations have revealed the presence of an aristocratic estate and a major royal building that was possibly a principal royal residence.

The Workmen's Village had been partially cleared in 1921 ACE. It was a square, walled unit, with a regimental arrangement of houses, and there were also some adjacent chapels. Its location and architectural features had always indicated that the village was very similar to the royal necropolis workers' town of Deir el-Medina at Thebes, and recent excavations have confirmed that the village at Amarna accommodated those engaged in constructing the royal tomb and courtiers' tombs.

The recent excavations (1979–86 ACE)[11] have produced a wide range of evidence about the life and economic basis of the village. The structures appear to have been built with two types of bricks, the state perhaps providing proper mudbricks for the enclosure wall and foundation courses of the houses, while the families then obtained other bricks to complete their homes.[12] Faunal analysis[13] has indicated that pigs were the most common mammalian food species kept at the site. This is at variance with other evidence that suggests that there was a religious proscription in Egypt against eating pork, but possibly this was a localized practice which diverged from the general custom. Mudbrick chapels associated with the site are decorated with painted scenes of men and women making offerings; the accompanying texts provide their names and titles, and brief prayers. The exact nature of the ritual use of these buildings remains obscure, but evidently they accommodated the presentation of food; other debris indicated that, in addition to worship, the chapels were used for eating meals, spinning, and carving wood.

In general, a variety of religious practices seem to have been observed in the village, but there is very little evidence of the Aten cult here, and only a single potsherd depicting the Aten and its rays in ink has been found. Inscribed ring bezels found in the village indicate that the highest level of occupancy occurred mainly in the later Amarna Period, and the site was apparently abandoned during Tutankhamun's reign, perhaps when the court returned to Memphis.

The community was similar to, but not identical with, that at Deir el-Medina. Most of the work at Amarna would have involved cutting the tomb-chapels and burial chambers in the nobles' tombs. The occupants of the village were probably labourers rather than artists, and it may also have accommodated unskilled workers and a policing unit, but the role and function of the residents cannot be definitively established from the available evidence.

Research has also expanded our knowledge of other aspects of architecture at Amarna. Religious and ceremonial buildings at the site provide important source material relating to the rituals and symbolism of Atenism. Re-examination of sculptured and inscribed pieces, excavated between 1891 and the 1930s ACE and now held in museum collections, has provided information about a distinctive architectural feature of the Aten temples and shrines.[14] This feature incorporated ramps and steps, flanked by balustrades, which led to altars surrounded by parapets. Of the surviving balustrades and parapets from Amarna, all have the same scene of the king, queen and a princess, under the rays of the Aten, processing towards the altars or cult-stands. Evidence to date shows that Aten temple architecture consisted of a series of interlinked elements which each contributed to the overall theme and was designed to facilitate the royal enactment of the temple ceremonies. The cult was performed in open courtyards and unroofed sanctuaries, so that the sun could be present in the temple; this was in contrast to the traditional roofed building with a sanctuary and cult-statue. Therefore, in order to enhance these temples, an innovative style of architecture was required.

The original sun-cult, which had been performed at Heliopolis during the Old Kingdom in an unroofed building with a series of courts, undoubtedly had a profound influence upon the development of the Aten temples.[15] Akhenaten himself dedicated a temple to the Aten at Heliopolis, but only a few traces of this have been discovered. It is probable that the Aten temples at Amarna, and presumably those at Thebes, all followed a predetermined pattern, in which pylons and a series of courts led towards the rear of the temple. However, instead of including a sanctuary and a cult-statue in these temples, the god was considered to be present in the form of the sun, to which food, flowers and other offerings were presented by the king and members of the royal family. These gifts were placed on rows of small altars set out inside the temple courts. Full details of the ritual use of these temples are not known,[16] but the rites would have emphasized the king's unique identification with the god. It is evident that the Aten temples were not confined to Amarna; in addition to those at Thebes and Heliopolis, there was the temple of Gem-Aten in Nubia, and indeed, there may have been many more of these buildings than Egyptologists previously envisaged.

Other evidence for worship of the Aten at Amarna occurs in the chapels and kiosks found in some of the gardens of the Amarna villas.[17] Found in association with forty-six buildings in the city, these include simple shrines, bipartite shrines, small temples, and altars. The simple shrines were often separated from the main house and surrounded by trees; they consisted of a staircase that led to a platform, on which there was a walled room which often contained an altar. The bipartite shrine was similar, but the small temples were much more complex; these buildings resembled proper cult temples but were contained within private house enclosures. Finally, the most basic form was an altar that consisted of a raised platform approached by steps; no evidence of a superstructure has been found associated with these altars.

These garden shrines are similar to some of the altars found in the central rooms in Amarna houses, which also occur at Deir el-Medina. The house altar consisted of a small brick platform with a low wall, which was approached by a set of steps; the shrine probably contained a statue of the king. Stelae from the shrines show the royal family in the presence of the Aten within a chapel or temple. The garden shrines occur only in the house enclosures of the wealthy, and probably demonstrate the owner's attempt to show his loyalty to Akhenaten. The shrines were dedicated either to the Aten or to the king or both. They were probably built to enable their owners to worship the royal family as the human manifestation of the Aten, thus allowing them to make contact with the god. Such domestic shrines were unique because they made this possible – an opportunity which was not available for ordinary people within the Aten temples where access for worship remained the exclusive prerogative of the royal family and their delegates. Here, even favoured courtiers were only allowed into the exterior courts to pray to the king's statues.

Funerary architecture at Amarna provides extensive information about the Aten cult. The Royal Tomb, built for the royal family but probably never used, is located several miles away from the city. Situated at the end of one of the *wadis* in the eastern cliffs, it broke with the established Theban tradition of burial in the west. The Royal Tomb has been re-examined in recent years,[18] and the architecture and remaining inscriptions and decoration have been studied, but the burial chamber appears to have been desecrated in antiquity.

The tombs of the courtiers and officials were cut into the eastern cliffs, which encircled the city.[19] Arranged in two main groups, situated in the north and south, they followed the pattern of tombs built in the earlier Dynasty 18; each has a forecourt that leads through a doorway into a long hall, which in turn provides access to a broad hall. In some cases, both these halls have columns, and in the broad hall, there is a statue niche.

These tombs provide unique information about the Aten cult. The wall-scenes and inscriptions are badly damaged, but clearly indicate that there was a break with traditional funerary art. The king, rather than the customary gods of the underworld, is represented as the agent by which people could attain personal immortality, reflecting the early Old Kingdom belief that individual survival after death was dependent on the king's bounty. The scenes show the tomb-owner in relation to the king and the Aten; they also provide information about the layout of the Aten temples at Amarna, and the royal cultic activities within the city. Today, the wall inscriptions remain our main source of knowledge about the doctrine of Atenism, which is set out in the hymns to the Aten found here. Many of these tomb-owners were courtiers who had been elevated to positions of importance by Akhenaten, and in return, they gave at least superficial devotion to Akhenaten and the Aten. However, with the desertion of Akhetaten when the site was abandoned after the Amarna Period, many of the tomb-owners doubtless returned to Thebes, and their tombs at Amarna were left unfinished or unused, while they prepared other burial places elsewhere.

Akhetaten was never reoccupied. The buildings were desecrated by those who eventually obliterated the religious 'revolution', and the stones were removed to other sites, including nearby el-Ashmunein. However, because there were no subsequent layers of occupation at Akhetaten, it has provided archaeologists with an almost unique opportunity to determine the layout of an Egyptian city. It is one of the few domestic sites that has been extensively excavated and studied, initially by the British archaeologist Petrie, then by Borchadt for the Berlin Museum, and subsequently by the Egypt Exploration Fund which, now known as the Egypt Exploration Society, has continued to work there over the past couple of decades.

THE AMARNA LITERATURE

Literary sources relating to the historical, political and religious aspects of the period include tomb and other inscriptions from Amarna, and the Amarna Letters.[20]

The Amarna Letters[21]

These form the archive of correspondence between members of the Egyptian royal family and various rulers of other states.[22] They were originally stored in the Records Office at Amarna. A few months after the archaeologist Petrie briefly visited the site in 1886 ACE, a peasant woman discovered several inscribed clay tablets when she was digging in the mudbrick remains at the site for soil (*sebakh*) to fertilize the fields. These tablets were sold on through a chain of agents and dealers and eventually, in 1887 ACE, some were viewed by the Keeper at the British Museum who decided that they were genuine. When another group were brought to him in Luxor, he purchased them for the Museum's collection.

When Petrie began to excavate at Amarna, he found another eighteen fragments of similar tablets in rubbish holes under the floor of a room which he named the Foreign Office. Thus, he was able to identify the original source of the tablets found earlier. Today, these tablets are housed in museums in Cairo, Berlin, London, Paris, Oxford, Brussels, New York and Chicago, as well as in private collections. Inscribed in cuneiform, they formed part of the official correspondence between Egyptian kings of this period – Amenhotep III, Akhenaten, and Tutankhamun (1361–1352 BCE) – and the rulers of states in Palestine, Syria, Mesopotamia and Asia Minor, as well as other members of their families.

They provide a unique insight into contemporary foreign policy, indicating the fact that Egypt's military aid to her vassals in Syria/Palestine was less prompt and reliable than in previous years. At one time, historians regarded this as evidence that Akhenaten pursued pacifist policies, allowing Egypt's empire to disintegrate while he continued his religious revolution at Amarna. However, now it is simply perceived as a continuation of his father's policy to replace major military expeditions with international diplomacy and subsidies of gold. In fact, Akhenaten is depicted as a warrior king in scenes at Amarna, and there are soldiers prominently represented at court in some of the reliefs.

The Hymns to the Aten

There is no single document or inscription which preserves details of the Aten doctrine (Atenism), but information can be gleaned from the king's own statements on the city's boundary stelae, and in the hymns and prayers inscribed on the walls of the officials' tombs at Amarna. The most extensive of these occur on the walls of the tomb of Ay, a courtier who eventually succeeded Tutankhamun as king. Although he was ultimately buried as a king at Thebes, Ay had earlier prepared a tomb for himself at Amarna, where several short hymns and prayers and the Great Hymn to the Aten are inscribed on the walls. Short hymns and prayers also occur in other courtiers' tombs at Amarna. Addressed jointly to the king and the Aten, or to the Aten alone, these are clearly all derived from a common source compiled by the royal scribes.

The main tenets of Atenism are set out in the Great Hymn to the Aten[23] and the Shorter Hymn[24]. Three basic concepts can be identified. First, the god's supremacy and role as a creator is emphasized: the Aten was regarded as the 'Sole God', supreme in heaven and earth, who rose and set each day. His presence in the sky enabled him to nurture his creation, and the deity's beneficent power is emphasized, as the creator of mankind, animals, birds and plants:

How manifold are your deeds!
They are hidden from sight,
O Sole God, like whom there is no other!
You made the earth as you desired, you alone.

All people, herds and flocks,
All that is on earth that walks on legs,
All that soars above, that flies on wings,
The lands of Khor (Syria) and Kush (Nubia)
And the land of Egypt.   (The Great Hymn to the Aten)

Secondly, the god is promoted as the creator of all mankind, including Egyptians and foreigners. This universal nature was essential to the Aten's role as god of Egypt and its empire, and the texts indicate that he provided light, heat and water to sustain all peoples:

You set every man in his place,
You supply their needs,
Each one has provision,
His lifetime is reckoned.

Their tongues are diverse in speech,
And their characters likewise;
Their skins are distinct,
For you have distinguished the peoples.

You made the Nile in the netherworld,
You bring it when you so desire,
To sustain the people,
Even as you have given them life.　　　　　(The Great Hymn to the Aten)

Thirdly, the significance of the god's transcendent nature is underlined: unlike earlier gods who were worshipped in a material form (for example, Re in the form of the sun in the sky), Aten was not believed to be immanent in a physical body, except as the king on earth:

The earth comes into being as the result of your hand,
For you have created them.
When you have arisen, they live,
When you set, they die.
You yourself are lifetime and men live in you.

(The Great Hymn to the Aten)

In order to function in these roles, the Aten possessed three almost interchangeable forms: (i) the sun-disc, the deity's representative symbol, enabled him to give forth warmth and light; (ii) his all-pervading life-force was present everywhere and manifest itself in all creation; (iii) the king was the god's human form on earth. There appears to have been an almost complete identification between the god and the king: their names and titles were virtually interchangeable and the king became the sole representative of the god on earth, preventing the development of a powerful priesthood that could come between the god and his son. The formal representation of this concept occurs in scenes which show the Aten as the sun's disc from which rays descend and confer bounty on Akhenaten and his family, which usually included Nefertiti and one or more of their daughters.

When these texts were first translated, the concepts attributed to Atenism appeared to be unique and original. Now, however, it is recognized that most of these ideas were present in earlier hymns to the sun and in the Great Hymn to Amun, where the god's universal creative powers and transcendent nature were already foreshadowed.[25] When Amun rose to power at the start of Dynasty 18, in order to become an all-powerful and all-embracing creator-god, he absorbed the mythology, property, and many of the forms and titles of the sun-god Re. Thus, important aspects of Re's attributes and cult are preserved in the texts relating to Amun (Amen-Re) and the Aten. For example, in hymns dedicated to Re by two brothers, Suti and Hor, inscribed on a stela dating to the reign of Amenhotep III, the Aten appears as a manifestation of the sun-god Re. Also, hundreds of sun-hymns were written in Dynasties 18 and 19, and either inscribed on the walls of Theban tombs or included in the Book of the Dead, which was written on a papyrus and placed in the tomb. One, addressed to the evening sun, reads as follows:[26]

Adoration of Re-Harakhte,
When he sets in the western horizon of heaven.
Praise to you, O Re, when you set,
Atum, Harakhte!
Divine god, who created himself,
Primeval god, who existed at the beginning . . .

These hymns are especially important because they can be closely dated and identified with particular localities and social groups. Generally, they are concerned with personal piety, and indicate that there was a continuing quest to understand the nature of divinity even after the Amarna Period.[27]

The Great Hymn to Amun provides the most important precedent to the Amarna literature. Together with the Great Hymn to the Aten, it is the most famous example of a genre of hymns dedicated to a solar creator that was developed in the New Kingdom. It explored the themes of the solar sequence of creation from the primeval ocean through to the sun's daytime and night-time journeys, and the attributes of the god as creator of the universe. These were apparently non-liturgical hymns, but expressed individual thoughts and beliefs rather than being composed for temple cults.[28]

The Amun Hymn contains several concepts that occur later in the Aten hymns and prayers, including the role of the god as universal creator, his title of 'Sole God', and his transcendent nature. Generally, therefore, most of the ideas found in the Aten texts are not original and do not form a complete break with tradition; rather, they represent an evolution of earlier concepts. The only true innovation introduced by Akhenaten was the belief that the Aten was the *only* god and that the existence of all other deities should be denied.

Another interesting aspect of the Amarna texts is the similarity that we can observe between ideas found in the Great Hymn to the Aten and Psalm 104 in the Bible. This may be an example of either direct or indirect borrowing between the two sources, or possibly it indicates that there was a common tradition from which both texts drew their concepts. Here is a selection of passages that show a particularly close association of ideas:

He causeth the grass to grow for the cattle, and herb for the service of man: that he may bring forth food out of the earth.

(Psalm 104:14)

Your rays give sustenance to all fields: when you shine forth, they live and grow for you. You make the seasons to nurture all you have made.

(Hymn to the Aten)

Thou makest darkness, and it is night: wherein all the beasts of the forest do creep forth. The young lions roar after their prey, and seek their meat from God.
(Psalm 104:20–21)

Every lion comes forth from its den, and all the serpents bite. The darkness hovers, and the earth is silent while their creator rests in his horizon.
(Hymn to the Aten)

The sun ariseth, they gather themselves together, and lay them down in their dens. Man goeth forth unto his work and to his labour until the evening.
(Psalm 104:22–23)

The earth grows bright when you arise in the horizon . . . the Two Lands make festival. Awakened, they stand on their feet, for you have raised them up . . . The entire land goes about its work.
(Hymn to the Aten)

So is this great and wide sea, wherein are things creeping innumerable, both small and great. There go the ships: there is that leviathan, whom Thou hast made to play therein.
(Psalm 104:25, 26)

Ships fare north and also fare south. Every route is opened when you appear. The fish in the river leap before your face, your rays are in the midst of the sea.
(Hymn to the Aten)

THE ATEN AND MONOTHEISM

The monotheistic nature of Atenism has been identified as the one original and revolutionary aspect of the cult. This is the first record in history when 'the divine had become one, henotheism was transferred into monotheism'.[29] In this cult, the worshippers could no longer turn to sacred animals, cult-statues or deified dead men for assistance in approaching the god; the only intermediary was the king, who taught the doctrine to his people. In the earlier years of his reign, Akhenaten had chosen the Aten as supreme god, but still retained other solar deities

– Re, Harakhte and Shu – alongside his god; in one example, Harakhte and the Aten were even combined to form a hawk-headed deity, Re-Harakhte-Aten. At first, therefore, he limited the pantheon to include only solar gods, but eventually even these were removed to promote the exclusive worship of the Aten. Popular traditional funerary deities were also discarded, which marked a fundamentally different and unprecedented approach. These developments were short lived and came to an end when Akhenaten's reign finished. Even though the reinstatement of the traditional pantheon probably occurred over a span of several reigns and the Aten continued as supreme god for several years, Akhenaten's demise marked the end of this unique experiment.

Early studies in religion proposed that monotheism had developed out of polytheism, and it was argued that titles such as 'Lord of All', which were applied to Amun, were indicative of a trend towards monotheism even before the Amarna Period. However, more recently, it has been argued that this title does not describe the god's transcendent nature but instead indicates that he was lord of the whole temporal and spatial world. Also, the terms applied to Amun as 'King of Gods' are no longer regarded as evidence of a progression from polytheism to monotheism. The Egyptologist Hornung[30] has described how Egyptian logic may have approached the problem of divinity in a different way from Western thought processes. They may have adopted a dualistic approach in which 'One and Many' may have been complementary concepts which 'contributed together to the whole truth'. It was perhaps envisaged that 'god is a unity in worship and revelation, and multiple in nature and manifestation'.

Hornung has argued that, because traditionally the Egyptians could not conceive of an exclusive unity or oneness of god, monotheism was an impossible progression for them. Therefore, although they took steps along the way to monotheism, such as reorganization of the pantheon and the promotion of a 'King of gods', this was never developed further within their traditional system. Hornung has emphasized that monotheism is not the logical outcome of polytheism, arrived at through the slow process of accumulating 'monotheistic tendencies'. The introduction of monotheism in fact involves a fundamental change of logic, involving the complete denial of a multiplicity of gods. By taking this step, Akhenaten profoundly transformed the traditional beliefs and it was this that made his innovations truly revolutionary.

Hornung claimed that the Aten was the only truly unique god in ancient Egyptian religion, defined as such by the fact that the deity did not tolerate the existence of any other gods. Where other gods were described as 'unique god, without equal', this did not imply monotheism but meant 'unequalled' in the sense that each god was different from all others. Each retained a separate nature that, despite the multiplicity of deities and the practice of syncretism, ensured that the gods did not merge indiscriminately into each other.

Again, Hornung discusses the term 'Great God' which he proposes should be translated as the 'greatest god'. Junker[31] however argued that this term implied a supreme deity who was the universal and original god of the earth and sky. However, he later suggested[32] that, although this term was used for the creator-god Atum, it did not imply that Atum was a deity above and beyond all other gods.

In a discussion of the transcendent nature of the gods, Morenz[33] suggested that Egyptian religion expressed the great and single reality of God through many forms and manifestations and that, in the later periods, there is clear evidence of a transcendent deity. However, Hornung[34] has argued that every god in the pantheon was transcendent in that his divine nature was superior to human nature and because the deity had power beyond this world. Nevertheless, he claims that no traditional deity had the capability to rise above time, space and fate, and to exist in the realms of the absolute and limitless. Therefore, given the limited traditional concept of divinity in Egypt, Akhenaten's interpretation of the nature and powers of the Aten marks an unprecedented and unparalleled departure in religious thought. Against this background, it becomes essential to ask what, in fact, were his motives. This question will be addressed later (see pp. 243–5).

THE ROYAL FAMILY AT AMARNA

There has been speculation that Akhenaten's cult grew out of his father's own policy of identification with the sun's disc and his personal deification; in fact, the cult may have represented the culmination of Amenhotep III's own ideas. He was deified and worshipped as a god while still alive, and reliefs in his temple at Soleb in Nubia represent him performing the cult to his own deified self. It has also been argued that there is convincing circumstantial evidence that Amenhotep III spent his final years at Amarna, perhaps providing theological motivation for Akhenaten's own actions.[35]

Akhenaten and Nefertiti lived at Amarna with their six daughters but the marriage apparently produced no sons. Their second daughter, Maketaten, died shortly after Year 12 of the reign, and soon after this, Nefertiti no longer features in the Amarna inscriptions. Death or banishment (perhaps because her opinions about the course of the religious revolution may have differed from those of her husband) have been suggested as explanations for her disappearance. However, between Years 13 and 15 of the reign, the eldest daughter Meritaten apparently replaced Nefertiti as her father's consort. The custom of the king marrying his own daughter was not unique to Akhenaten, although it was far less common than the union between the royal heir and the Great Royal Daughter. Akhenaten may have entered into this relationship to ensure that no other external claimant attempted to marry the royal heiress (there was probably no royal brother to wed her), but it is most likely that his main aim was to try to beget a male heir with a new wife. However, the young queen apparently only gave birth to a daughter, Meritaten-tasherit, who survived briefly.

Meritaten's name was subsequently associated with that of the royal relative whom Akhenaten appears to have taken as his co-regent in Year 13 of his reign. Details of Smenkhkare's origins and life remain obscure. Apart from a suggestion that Smenkhkare was in fact a re-named Nefertiti[36] (Smenkhkare was given one of the names of Nefertiti, and also the title 'Beloved of Akhenaten'), it is generally assumed that both Smenkhkare and Tutankhaten were closely related royal princes. They may have been Akhenaten's sons by a secondary wife, but it is perhaps more probable that their father was Amenhotep III, and their mother was either Queen Tiye (unlikely because of her age), or Sitamun (the daughter of Amenhotep III and Tiye who became her father's wife),[37] or another secondary wife. Marriage to Meritaten would have consolidated Smenkhkare's claim to the throne, but she probably died before him and may have been buried at Thebes, although her tomb has never been found. When Meritaten became Smenkhkare's wife, it is possible that Akhenaten married his third daughter, Ankhesenpaaten, and fathered another short-lived daughter, Ankhesenpaaten-Sherit. Eventually, Ankhesenpaaten became the wife of Tutankhaten (Tutankhamun) when he ascended the throne.

Only one known date of Smenkhkare's reign survives, in a hieratic graffito in the Theban tomb of the official Pere. This gives a regnal date of Year 3, and indicates that Amun's cult was already being reinstated. According to one interpretation,[38] there may have been a struggle between two parties within the royal family following Akhenaten's death, with Smenkhkare (supported by the courtier Ay) leading one, while Nefertiti headed the other. With Ay's control of the military faction, Smenkhkare was successful. However, this reconstruction of events is not universally accepted, and Hornung[39] has suggested that the persecution of Atenism in fact began long after Akhenaten's death.

Once Smenkhkare succeeded as an independent ruler after Akhenaten's death, he may have tried to compromise with orthodoxy, although apparently this was not official policy until Year 3 of his reign, and Amarna appears to have continued to be used as Smenkhkare's capital.[40] An alternative interpretation of the facts is that Akhenaten, recognizing that his Aten revolution was failing, sent Smenkhkare to Thebes as his co-regent, in order to restore the royal relationship with the supporters of Amun. According to yet another theory, the two kings may have disagreed fundamentally over the course of the religious revolution, with the result that Smenkhkare chose to return to traditional beliefs.

Akhenaten appears to have died during or after Year 17 (the highest recorded date of his reign), and Smenkhkare may then have ruled alone for a short time. Meritaten probably predeceased Smenkhkare who then possibly married Akhenaten's daughter-widow, Ankhesenpaaten, in order to consolidate his claim to the throne. However, he apparently left no living heirs, because the throne passed to his relative Tutankhaten, who in turn married the royal heiress and widow, Ankhesenpaaten. Akhenaten's body has never been discovered, and there has been speculation that it was torn to pieces in a post-Atenist persecution. However, Hornung[41] rejects this, and suggests that Akhenaten ordered a tomb and a royal cult temple at Thebes.[42] Smenkhkare apparently intended to be buried at Thebes, where he constructed a royal cult temple, and there is substantial evidence that the mummified body discovered in Tomb 55 belonged to him.[43]

Tomb 55 in the Valley of the Kings at Thebes was discovered by the Theodore M. Davis expedition in 1907; its contents indicate that it was associated with at least two members of the Amarna royal family, but it contained only one mummy. Studies of the tomb have resulted in contradictory and controversial theories, and its ownership remains uncertain.[44] The tomb contained funerary equipment and a badly deteriorated body, which was examined on various occasions by different experts. Initially, Davis concluded that the tomb and the mummy belonged to Queen Tiye,[45] but subsequently, the body was examined by Elliot Smith, Professor of Anatomy in Cairo, and declared to be that of a man, aged about twenty-five at death and with a distortion of the skull characteristically associated with hydrocephalus. It was suggested that this was the body of Akhenaten (art representations show him with a distorted skull, see below pp. 236–7), brought back to Thebes from Amarna when his revolution failed. Later, when Derry (Elliot Smith's successor in Cairo) re-examined the body, another opinion prevailed: that this was a young man of twenty-three, and that there was no evidence of hydrocephalus.[46] Since Akhenaten's reign lasted at least seventeen years, it was argued that this could not be his body; a review of the texts on the coffin led to the suggestion that it had belonged to Smenkhkare.

During the 1960s ACE, further anatomical and serological studies were carried out by Harrison and his colleagues.[47] These indicated that the mummy had belonged to a man in his early twenties, and that it possessed an unusual but not abnormal platycephalic skull similar to that of Tutankhaten. The physical evidence suggested that he was a close relative (probably a full brother or half-brother) of Tutankhaten, and that Amenhotep III was probably their father. The team concluded that this was likely to be the body of Smenkhkare.

However, a subsequent suggestion[48] – that Smenkhkare was not a separate person but that Nefertiti herself took this name, perhaps to mark a major event in her reign with Akhenaten – provoked further speculation. If this interpretation is true, then another explanation would have to be found for the body in Tomb 55 – perhaps it belonged to another as yet unidentified member of the royal family. The tomb equipment only adds to the confusion: the coffin and the associated canopic jars were apparently originally prepared for Meritaten and later adapted for Smenkhkare. This may indicate that Smenkhkare died unexpectedly and his wife's remains were then immediately moved elsewhere so that the king could be given her coffin and jars for a hastily prepared burial in an unfinished tomb. Alternatively, the equipment could have been prepared for Meritaten before marriage to Smenkhkare, but never used for her burial. When Smenkhkare died, her coffin and jars were perhaps brought out of storage and adapted for his burial.

The role of the royal women at Amarna[49] has also been the subject of much speculation. A recent study[50] considers whether Nefertiti was a living goddess worshipped in her own right, or the personification of the female aspects of the Aten. Or was it her marriage to the king that conferred religious status and power on her? Since evidence of Kiya, a secondary wife of Akhenaten, was first noted in print,[51] other studies have concentrated on her role and status.[52] She was important at Akhenaten's court during the middle years of his reign (before Year 9 to at least Year 11), and she bore the king at least one daughter and perhaps was also the mother of Tutankhaten.[53] She had a unique and favoured status at court, although the basis for this is never explicitly stated, but she eventually fell from favour: her monuments were taken over and adapted for others and some of her art representations were maliciously damaged.

ART OF THE AMARNA PERIOD

The distinctive art that developed and flourished during the Amarna Period represents the only known break with traditional forms throughout the whole of the Pharaonic Period. This came about because the artists at Amarna were briefly released from the religious conventions of earlier periods, although these were re-established in the post-Amarna Period. In line with the new concepts associated with Atenism, the artists were required to emphasize the joy and beauty of nature.

There had been some attempt in the reign of Amenhotep III (particularly in the wall decoration of the palace at Malkata) to introduce realism and naturalism, but once the court moved to Amarna, a radically new art form soon developed. Some artists may have continued to function at Thebes, but Akhenaten probably employed new men at Amarna, instructing them to explore fresh ideas. At its best, Amarna art expressed the joy in all living things, which was a significant tenet of the faith.[54] Indeed, the artists' workshops appear to have become an important element in the Atenist propaganda, with temple and tomb sculptures and reliefs placing unprecedented emphasis on the relationship between the Aten and the royal family. The new loyalty is proclaimed without hesitation, and art is used to serve religious propaganda as never before.[55]

Recent studies of wall-paintings and painted pavements associated with the Great Palace[56] show that the designs incorporated birds, animals, and plants which represented the land's abundance, and bound human captives which symbolized the king's dominion over his foreign enemies. The similarity with the palace decoration at Malkata, and also with later Dynasty 19 palaces at Memphis and Qantir, shows that this was a continuing tradition. Painted pavement scenes probably adorned the Throne Room of the Great Palace at Amarna, and tiles and inlays, which decorated other architectural features, appear to have repeated the subject matter found in the floor scenes, creating a magnificent and vibrant setting.

Representations of the royal family were either sculpted or painted, and although intended for a variety of locations, they invariably depict the royal couple and their children in informal poses. The most notable diversion from traditional art, however, is the emphasis that was placed on the apparently abnormal physique of the king (in traditional art, royalty and even the upper classes were always shown with an idealized perfection).[57] However, statues and representations of Akhenaten now showed him with a long, narrow face and slanting eyes; his head was elongated and his malformed body featured an excessively thin neck, broad hips and thighs, and pronounced breasts. These characteristics only appeared during the middle and later years of Akhenaten's reign; earlier on, he was portrayed in a more conventional, stylized way, but ultimately, his physical characteristics were exaggerated almost to the point of caricature. This soon became the accepted norm, not only for representations of the king but also for members of the royal family and even for courtiers and personnel who were not related to him.

There has been much speculation about this art form. Since the bodies of the king and of most members of his family have never been discovered, it is impossible to tell if these features indicate that he suffered from a medical condition such as a disorder of the endocrine glands (possibly Fröhlich's Syndrome), or if they simply express his role as the god's earthly agent, symbolizing both male and female creative characteristics. Where the bodies of members of the Amarna royal family have survived (Tutankhaten and the body in Tomb 55), they do not confirm that these abnormalities were physical realities. Nevertheless, the one deity retained alongside the Aten was Ma'at, goddess of truth and righteousness. Akhenaten described himself as 'Living in Truth', and these art representations may indeed have been an attempt to show the reality of the king's physical abnormalities instead of attempting to present him in the traditional manner, with an idealized and perfect form.

THE COUNTER-REVOLUTION

Akhenaten apparently had no son to continue his reforms and embrace his ideas, and the cult of the Aten did not survive long enough to become rooted in the Egyptian psyche.[58] In fact, it was probably mainly confined to the royal family and their courtiers and officials, and made little impact on the masses. It had little to offer the ordinary worshipper, since it provided no moral philosophy (as the cult of Osiris did, with its emphasis on judgement after death, according to a person's good or evil deeds in life). The Aten generally remained remote from people's lives: there was no mythology that explained the god to his worshippers, and the cult offered no alternative, comforting beliefs to replace the funerary gods who had been banished.

Later generations regarded Akhenaten as a heretic. His name was obliterated from the monuments, and his buildings at Amarna and Thebes were destroyed. This attitude towards him probably did not develop for at least two generations,[59] and it may have been partly generated by the propaganda of the reinstated priesthoods and the counter-revolutionary forces. His experiment was destined to fail, and the royal family and courtiers eventually decided to restore the traditional gods.

His religious reforms must have also profoundly affected the economy and prosperity of Egypt. Closure of the old temples would have deprived many people of work, since the relationship between the temples and the populace had always been economic as well as religious: the temples employed the country's largest workforce which included secular posts as well as the priests. The construction of the new city of Akhetaten would have placed an additional burden on the economy and resources. Akhenaten's programmes may have been facilitated by greatly increased taxation, which was perhaps enforced by the military class who had an important status at Amarna.[60] However, there is no evidence that economic burdens or a decline in prestige abroad precipitated any popular uprising in Egypt. The counter-revolution appears to have been initiated by the royal relatives and courtiers who had once supported Akhenaten but perhaps came to recognize that the experiment was doomed to failure.

With the demise of Smenkhkare, the throne passed to Tutankhaten, who was then a child of eight or nine years. To consolidate his claim to the throne, he married the royal widow, Ankhesenpaaten. The chief advisers of his reign were the vizier Ay, a courtier of long-standing loyalty to Akhenaten, and Horemheb, who had been Akhenaten's army general and now rose to become King's Deputy. Outwardly, these men had always supported the Atenist reforms, but now they apparently acted together to restore the old values and traditions. Tutankhaten's immaturity at accession would have made it impossible for him to continue Akhenaten's reforms, even if he had wished to do so, and now he became the figurehead of the counter-revolution.

It is uncertain how long Tutankhaten and his queen remained at Amarna. They may have continued to rule from there for most of the reign, ensuring that the Aten cult was only gradually replaced. Some furniture found in the king's tomb at Thebes has scenes which show the couple expressing the same informal poses and gestures that can be observed in the Amarna art. On his gilded coronation throne, the king is shown being anointed by his wife, in the presence of the Aten whose rays bestow bounty on the royal couple. This surely indicates that any break with Atenism did not occur early in the reign.

However, other evidence suggests that there was now a definite attempt on behalf of royalty to become acceptable again to the traditional gods, particularly Amun,[61] and at some point, the royal couple took up residence in their new capital of Memphis. They changed their names from Tutankhaten and Ankhesenpaaten to Tutankhamun and Ankhesenamun, to indicate their restored allegiance to Amun. From Memphis, the king issued the directives that are preserved on his Restoration Stela, which was set up in the Temple of Karnak at Thebes. This text described the chaos that had prevailed throughout the country, and gave details of the measures which the king took to restore the old order and to reinstate the traditional gods, particularly Amun.

Since no priests could be found (presumably either Akhenaten had eliminated them or they had died out naturally during the course of the Amarna Period), a new priesthood was brought together which included worthy persons from the major towns. Practical measures included new building and restoration programmes carried out at the temples of the traditional gods, and at Luxor, a great hall was decorated with wall scenes that depicted the king's great festival of Amun.

However, Tutankhamun met an untimely death before the age of twenty.[62] Examination of his mummy has not revealed conclusive evidence of the cause of death, although various theories have been proposed. The king was buried in a tomb in the Valley of the Kings at

Thebes which was originally prepared for another unidentified person.[63] The tomb was discovered on 4 November 1922 ACE by Howard Carter and subsequently opened on 26 November. As a rare example of an almost complete royal burial – in fact, the only one discovered in the Valley of the Kings – the tomb and its contents have become legendary, although Tutankhamun was only a minor, short-lived ruler. After the burial, the tomb entrance was later covered over by the debris which had resulted from the excavation of the nearby tomb of Ramesses VI, and although Tutankhamun's tomb was robbed twice in antiquity (presumably before this debris concealed its entrance), the treasure remained substantially intact.

The tomb contains four small chambers; funerary goods included three golden anthropoid coffins and a gold face mask, as well as the king's mummified body,[64] together with two mummified female foetuses (who may have been the offspring of Tutankhamun and his queen), each contained within a set of miniature gold coffins.[65] The tomb contents provide a unique opportunity to study the funerary art and ritual of the New Kingdom. Today, the treasure is kept at the Egyptian Museum in Cairo, although the king's body and one of the golden coffins remain inside the tomb.

The tomb goods also included some of the king's possessions, which he would have used when alive, as well as some specially prepared funerary pieces.[66] In addition to the gilded shrines,[67] sarcophagus, and anthropoid coffins in the Burial Chamber, the Treasury beyond housed the canopic jars, items of everyday use, and funerary goods for the next world. In the chamber known as the Annex, the archaeologists found a scene of great upheaval: this was the result of the robberies carried out in antiquity. The plunderers' main targets – jewellery and perfumed oils and unguents – had been stored in this chamber.

The treasure provided a wealth of unparalleled material: chests, headrests, gaming boards, royal insignia and jewellery, writing utensils, lamps, ostrich feather fans, model boats, and clothing were just some of the items recovered. However, this apparently magnificent treasure may have represented only a modest burial compared with the lost funerary goods of great rulers such as Sethos I or Ramesses II, although an alternative explanation is that Tutankhamun's burial was especially splendid because he was credited with the restoration of the traditional gods.

Since there was no direct heir to the throne, Tutankhamun's death apparently prompted an internal conflict in Egypt. A cuneiform text quotes a letter that was sent by an Egyptian royal widow (probably Ankhesenamun) to Suppiluliumas, the king of Egypt's new enemy, the Hittites.[68] The queen stated that she had no son, and begged the king to send one of his sons to marry her, promising that he would become the ruler of Egypt. The Hittite king, understandably suspicious, sent an official to investigate, but finally, he dispatched a prince, Zennanza. However, he was murdered en route to Egypt, presumably by agents of a rival faction in Egypt, and this death ultimately precipitated war between Egypt and the Hittites. The queen's motives are obscure, and although her stated reason was that she did not wish to marry one of her subjects, it is possible that one of the rival factions in Egypt considered this marriage expedient since the Hittites, who had recently overthrown the Mitannians, had become the new power in the region.

With the failure of this plan, Ankhesenamun now married Ay who had been the vizier and senior courtier to Tutankhamun.[69] Since he apparently had no royal blood, this marriage would have enabled Ay to inherit the throne (in the wall-scenes in Tutankhamun's tomb, he is depicted performing the burial rites for the young king in the tradition of a royal heir), but Ankhesenamun subsequently disappears from the records. Ay had begun to construct a tomb at Amarna early in Akhenaten's reign, but it was never finished or occupied, and he was ultimately buried as a king at Thebes.[70] His reign lasted for only four years, and during this period, he continued the gradual but inevitable return to traditionalism.

It was under his successor, Horemheb, that the systematic destruction of Atenism was probably pursued. It is impossible to determine if Horemheb had originally used the Amarna heresy to advance his own position at Akhenaten's court (he apparently came from humble origins), and waited for the opportunity to seize power, or whether he genuinely supported the reforms at first but later became disillusioned. He held senior posts in the army in the reigns of Akhenaten and Tutankhamun, and initially prepared a fine tomb at Saqqara,[71] although he was ultimately buried in the Valley of the Kings at Thebes.

The transition from Ay to Horemheb was apparently achieved peacefully, since Horemheb had probably been selected as Ay's co-regent. He subsequently ruled Egypt for twenty-seven years, supported by the priesthood of Amun at Thebes and the army, and he was able to provide a period of much-needed unity and stability. He probably established his capital at Memphis, and undertook a major reorganization of the country, establishing a strong aggressive army and a powerful priesthood who supported the multiplicity of the traditional pantheon, and owed their appointment to Horemheb. The details of his reforms are preserved in his Edict, a badly preserved copy of which has survived on a stela at Karnak.[72] His actions included reorganization of the army; elimination of abuses in central and local government; the reinstatement of local law-courts and the appointment of judges from amongst the temple priests and town mayors, who were directly responsible to the king; widespread rehabilitation of the temples which reversed the neglect of the Amarna Period; the restoration of temple property; and the appointment of priests drawn from the army rather than the old nobility.

Alongside this determined attempt to restore the traditional beliefs and values, there was probably also a systematic policy of destroying all traces of Akhenaten and the Aten cult. Under Horemheb and his successors, the city of Amarna was dismantled and the blocks removed for building projects elsewhere; the tombs including the Royal Tomb were desecrated; the Great Temple was razed to the ground, and its sacred contents were smashed and destroyed. At Thebes, the Aten temples were dismantled and the blocks used as infill for pylons in the Temple of Karnak. Wherever possible, the name of Akhenaten was erased from inscriptions and traces of his cult were obliterated. It is uncertain if these actions were mainly taken in the reign of Horemheb or if his Ramesside successors perpetrated most of the damage. The end result, however, ensured that this religious interlude was obliterated from the official records; it was only finally revealed by the chance discovery of Amarna thousands of years later.

AKHENATEN'S MOTIVES

It is crucial to attempt to understand the motives that lay behind Akhenaten's 'heresy' in order to fathom the events of this period (*see* p. 231). The Amarna revolution failed because it did not promote a god who could receive widespread acceptance. Lack of a cult-statue which could be paraded on festivals, and of a mythology which would have given the god human appeal and interest, were important factors, but Akhenaten's radical actions in discontinuing the funerary customs, particularly the Osirian concept of the afterlife with its moral teachings and promise of immortality, must have deprived the cult of an important ethical dimension.

Profound changes occurred in the funerary customs. The wall-scenes in courtiers' tombs at Amarna no longer showed the traditional aspects of everyday life; instead, they emphasized the dependence of the dead on the god-king rather than on the traditional funerary gods, depicting the royal family's unique role in the various temple rituals associated with Atenism. It is unclear if the peasants continued to be buried in shallow graves in the sand, as in earlier times. Indeed, apart from the Royal Tomb and the courtiers' tombs at Amarna, we have little information about funerary beliefs and burial practices during this period. Mummification probably continued for the wealthy: large scarabs have been found which presumably were still inserted between the bandages, as in earlier and later mummies, but these were no longer inscribed with the spell from the Book of the Dead which linked the scarab and the mummy to Osiris and the Day of Judgement. Also, with less emphasis on the cult of the dead, there was no longer the need for a funerary priesthood. Instead, the king revived the concept of divine kingship and the associated belief (prevalent in the Old Kingdom) that ordinary people could only aspire to individual immortality through the king. Presumably, the royal officials would have ensured that, as part of the new state religion, these ideas were put into practice throughout the country. However, it is difficult to assess the extent to which ordinary people accepted these beliefs; in the Amarna Workmen's Village, for example, there is evidence that traditional domestic religious practices continued (*see* p. 220), with people worshipping the old household gods, but we do not know how the population (apart from the Amarna courtiers and officials) reacted to the general changes in funerary customs.

Now, we return to Akhenaten's personal motives in overturning the age-old beliefs and customs. There has been much discussion about his actions – were his motives 'political' or 'religious'? Early studies presented him as a 'failed Messiah' whose solar monotheism was a revealed truth and whose reforms were curtailed by an untimely death. These descriptions, however, are based on a Western, Christian assessment rather than considering his actions in terms of Egyptian religion. More recent studies[73] have tried to show that Akhenaten was a political opportunist who used the Aten cult to destroy the power of Amen-Re and the priesthood and to restore the supremacy of the kingship. In this way, his actions can be seen as carrying to a logical conclusion the moves started by Tuthmosis IV and Amenhotep III in an attempt to curtail the power of Amen-Re.

Akhenaten certainly claimed a unique relationship with the Aten. Because the god has no cult images, and appeared only in heaven, represented by the symbol of the sun-disc, the deity was not visible to everyone on earth; thus, it was necessary for him to make contact with mankind through an intermediary – the king.[74] In assessing whether Akhenaten was pursuing a personal religious commitment, or his own political ambitions, or whether he was mentally disturbed, we must consider his course of action. In fact, he appears to have adopted a well-ordered approach, pursuing a carefully planned scheme that involved moving the capital to Amarna, closing all other temples and changing his name and allegiance to honour the Aten. There is no real evidence that he was simply developing his own religious beliefs and putting them into effect, regardless of any political implications.

However, he placed unprecedented emphasis on the divinity of the Pharaoh, and he took a unique stance in making the god and king equal. Both were now creator-gods, but only Akhenaten was accessible to mankind who therefore had no choice but to approach the deity through the king. Another new feature of the cult was a lack of the strong contrasts which had always been such a feature of traditional beliefs:

there was now no symbolic conflict between the cosmic forces of order and chaos,[75] nor any struggle between life and death, or good and evil. For the Egyptians, the traditional concepts of good and evil were encapsulated in the Negative Confession, which the deceased was requested to recite at his Day of Judgement. In many respects, these were similar to the Biblical Ten Commandments, categorizing murder, theft and adultery as some of the 'evils' of their society. Also, in the Wisdom Texts, we can gain further insight into the Egyptian idea of what constituted a 'good' or an 'evil' person: coveting another person's possessions, losing one's temper, and speaking ill of other people were all regarded as undesirable character traits.

Atenism denied the very existence of darkness and evil, and by emphasizing the immortality and indestructibility of the king and by dispensing with the customary funerary beliefs, gods and mortuary cult, it even attempted to obliterate the reality of death and did not even try to address the fears which are common to all mankind. It only emphasized life, order and goodness. Akhenaten successfully removed the middle tier of religion – the multiplicity of gods[76] – so that there was no rival to the Aten or the new faith, but the old beliefs were 'replaced with an almost simplistic faith in the positive'.[77] However, people still clearly felt the need for the comfort previously offered by the traditional gods and, even in the houses at Amarna, the centre of Atenism, people kept amulets of these deities to provide magical protection for their family members, and divine statuettes as a focus for their prayers.

Perhaps Akhenaten's motives cannot be separated and categorized as either 'religious' or 'political'; these are modern terms that we try to impose on an ancient civilization which did not differentiate between the sacred and the secular. The king was probably prompted by both political and religious considerations, and he may have combined his personal inspiration with political pragmatism. Ultimately, however, the cult was destined to fail because it did not address people's most basic fears and uncertainties, which are common to all mankind; by denying the very existence of evil and death, Atenism could not hope to provide either comfort or inspiration for the Egyptians.

CHAPTER 7

The Return to Orthodoxy

Later New Kingdom, c.1320–1085 BCE

RESTORATION OF THE TRADITIONAL RELIGION

When Horemheb died, the throne passed to his old comrade Pa-Ramesses, a man who had also come from humble origins and followed a career as a soldier. As Ramesses I, he ruled only briefly, but his reign introduced Dynasty 19, when his descendants continued to reinstate the traditional beliefs and to restore Egypt's internal stability and military successes abroad. However, although the Ramesside rulers managed to successfully obliterate the official worship of the Aten, traces of its influence still remained. Some of the doctrinal issues raised by Akhenaten continued to exert an influence, particularly relating to divine creation, and it is evident that doubts that had been raised by the Aten were not completely reversed in the immediate post-Amarna period. The kings abandoned the idea of a single god and now developed a special relationship with the principal traditional deities.' Thus, although

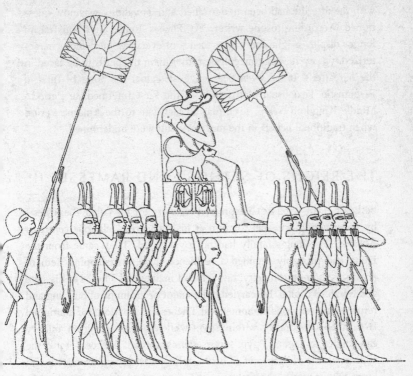

King Horemheb, carried here in procession by his soldiers, used his powers as head of the army to take over the kingship and restore the traditional religion.

Amun's cult was restored, he was no longer pre-eminent, but shared power with Re and Ptah; Seth (no longer envisaged as the embodiment of evil but as a patron god of these Dynasty 19 kings whose family had originated in the Delta) was also added to this group. Together, the four deities symbolized totality or completeness, developing a concept based on the triads of gods who were established in the early New Kingdom.

The effects of the Amarna art-style, with its fluidity of form, can be observed in the art of the Ramesside Period, and changes are also evident in the mortuary beliefs. Although the funerary cult was restored after the Amarna Period, the security that was traditionally associated with the afterlife had been undermined and its validity was now questioned. According to one writer, 'At Thebes, tombs after Amarna no longer display bright and happy scenes of everyday life which characterize Dynasty 18, but concentrate rather upon the perils to be faced in the hereafter'.[2] It has even been suggested[3] that the Song of Intef, a Pessimistic Text usually attributed to the First Intermediate Period/ Middle Kingdom (*see* p. 145), may in fact date to the Amarna Period when traditional beliefs in the mortuary cult were undermined.

THE REIGNS OF SETHOS I AND RAMESSES II[4]

Sethos I (1318–1304 BCE) expressed his piety for his father Ramesses I by constructing a chapel for him at his own great religious centre at Abydos. The king's family had no royal blood. They came from the Delta and probably retained a residence there, worshipping Seth of Avaris as their patron deity, but Sethos I maintained Thebes as his state and religious capital. He carried out a major programme of building and refurbishing religious monuments at Thebes and Abydos, and continued Horemheb's restoration within Egypt while also embarking on military campaigns to regain Egypt's possessions abroad. Sethos I took the additional title of 'Repeater of Births' which was always associated with kings who regarded themselves as the inaugurator of a new era.

His military successes are recorded in scenes on the north and east walls in the Hypostyle Hall of the Temple of Karnak.[5] He engaged in conflict against the Libyans in the western Delta, but his main offensives lay in Palestine/Syria. By progressing along the Phoenician coast and taking control of the towns there, he was able to launch an attack into central and northern Syria. He took the town of Kadesh which brought him into conflict with the Hittites, but under the terms of a treaty, the Egyptians allowed Kadesh and the land of Amurru to revert to Hittite control in return for Hittite respect for Egyptian interests, particularly the Phoenician coastal towns.

At home, Sethos I authorized major construction work and decoration of the Great Hypostyle Hall at Karnak, and there were additional projects at the temples of Re at Heliopolis and Ptah at Memphis. He built a royal cult temple at Qurna on the west bank at Thebes, and a magnificent temple at Abydos, the cult-centre of Osiris. His tomb – the finest in the Valley of the Kings – descends over three hundred feet into the rock; it is decorated with finely carved and painted scenes taken from the Funerary Books. When Belzoni discovered this tomb in 1817 ACE, he copied the wall-scenes in preparation for a tomb model which was constructed and exhibited in London in 1821 ACE. The king's alabaster sarcophagus, decorated with scenes from the Book of Gates, also featured in this display. It was intended for the British Museum, but because of a dispute with the Trustees it was sold instead to Sir John Soane in whose London home (now a museum) it is currently displayed.

The achievements of Sethos I were considerable, and he restored Egypt's stability at home and military prestige abroad.[6] His son, Ramesses II, continued his policies and sought to gain even greater glory. He is probably the best-known Egyptian ruler although this is perhaps due to his ability to perpetuate his own memory through the size and quantity of his monuments rather than his qualities as a great king. In his Great Dedicatory Inscription in the Temple of Sethos I at Abydos (a building which Ramesses II completed), he attempted to establish his father's approval of his reign, and to ensure his acceptance by the gods, in order to justify his own rulership. According to this text, Ramesses became co-regent with his father at a very early age.

His military career was already established when he came to the throne: he had accompanied a Libyan expedition in his early teens, and had campaigned with his father in Syria against the Hittites. In Year 4 of his own reign, he began a series of military expeditions to Syria, and ultimately repossessed from the Hittites the town of Kadesh on the River Orontes.[7] An account of the battle is preserved in an epic poem in eight inscriptions in the temples of Karnak, Luxor, Abydos and the Ramesseum; a shorter version, known as the 'Report' or 'Bulletin', can also be seen in all these temples except Karnak, and it occurs in Ramesses' temple at Abu Simbel. These accounts claim that the king routed the Hittites in a single-handed victory, and the Hittite ruler is reported to have sent a letter to Ramesses, praising his personal bravery. However, official records discovered at Boghazkoy (the Hittite capital) provide a different version of events; according to these, the Egyptians returned home after a strategic defeat. In reality, the king probably did demonstrate considerable skill and bravery, but it was the timely arrival of his young troops to attack the Hittite army from the rear which probably saved the day.

Despite their conflicts and relative successes, the Egyptians and the Hittites soon realized that neither side really gained from this state of war, and in Year 21 of his reign, Ramesses II signed a Peace Treaty with the Hittite king.[8] The Egyptian version is inscribed in hieroglyphs on a stela in the Temple of Karnak, while the Hittite one is preserved on two clay tablets inscribed in Babylonian cuneiform. According to this treaty, the Egyptians and Hittites were equal partners in a pact of perpetual peace and brotherhood which included reciprocal agreements on non-aggression, recognition of a mutual frontier, and a joint defensive policy against other aggressors. The gods of both countries were called upon to witness the treaty, and subsequent friendship developed between the two royal households, leading to the marriage of Ramesses II and a Hittite princess.

Ramesses II had at least six major queens and many concubines, and his children, who numbered over a hundred, are represented on the walls of his temples. One of his favourite queens, Nefertari, was granted the finest tomb in the Valley of the Queens at Thebes and the smaller temple at Abu Simbel was dedicated to her. As part of his domestic policy, Ramesses pursued an extensive building programme. In addition to constructional work at the Temple of Ptah at Memphis and the Temple of Re at Heliopolis, he built a royal cult temple (the Ramesseum) at Thebes and another temple at Abydos. At all these temples, the traditional rituals, which had been performed before the Amarna Period, where once again carried out by the priests.

However, his most celebrated monuments were the two rock-cut temples at Abu Simbel in Nubia, built to impress the local population with the might and divinity of their Egyptian overlord. Thebes remained the main state and religious capital, but Memphis now became the most important administrative centre. Ramesses II also built a residence in the Delta, named Pi-Ramesse ('House of Ramesses'), which has been tentatively identified with the city of Ramses built by the Hebrews which is mentioned in the Bible. When his reign ended, Ramesses II was buried in the Valley of the Kings at Thebes, and his mummy has been the subject of an intensive scientific study.[9]

He was responsible for more major monuments than any other ruler, but the quality of the architecture and decoration of these buildings already indicates a decline in standards. However, in later times, he was regarded as a great king and ideal ruler, and was emulated by others who succeeded him in the Ramesside Period. He successfully completed the ambitious schemes of his father and grandfather, and reinstated Egypt's empire, after the turmoil of the Amarna Period. In many ways, it must have seemed as if the Amarna experiment had never occurred; instead, political and religious traditions were restored, and a new empire was established.

However, Ramesses II was clearly aware of the mistakes of earlier rulers, and he limited the power of Amun by promoting the cults of other gods. Also, he emphasized the role and divinity of the king: there was a formal royal cult in his reign, and colossal temple statuary represented him equal in size to the gods; this helped to check the ambitions of the priesthood. The importance of the king was also promoted in some literary texts which, although they outwardly presented a conservative reaction against monotheism and a return to polytheism, nevertheless enhanced the king's status by mocking the foolishness of the gods.[10] Behind a façade of conventional traditionalism and polytheism, Ramesses II achieved at least some of the goals that Akhenaten had unsuccessfully pursued. Nevertheless, the reign probably marked the watershed between Egypt's great past and the slow but inevitable decline of the next thousand years when this once-vigorous civilization gradually disintegrated.

SOME MAJOR TEMPLES OF THE LATER NEW KINGDOM

The Temple of Sethos I at Abydos"

This temple, started by Sethos I and completed by Ramesses II,[12] was designed both as a national shrine to win popularity and support for the king, and as a temple to honour the dead, deified Sethos. It included seven chapels in the sanctuary area, dedicated to six major gods and to the deified king himself, and thus accommodated both the rituals to the gods and the king's own mortuary cult. The temple also included a set of special chambers where the Osirian Mysteries were performed annually to ensure the rebirth of Osiris.

At the rear of the temple, there is a unique building known as the Osireion which probably represented the burial place of Osiris in the form of a primeval island.[13] It may have had spiritual links with the temple in the way that the Theban royal cult temples were associated with the royal tombs. As the Cenotaph of Sethos as the dead god Osiris, it was probably designed to function together with the temple so that the rituals performed within the temple would bring about the god-king's resurrection.

The Osiris Mysteries were associated with the death and resurrection of Osiris, the identification of Osiris with King Sethos, and the consequent rebirth of Sethos as ruler of the dead. It may seem strange that, as a ruler who went to great lengths to promote the cult of Osiris at Abydos, Sethos bore a name that associated him with Seth, the arch-enemy of Osiris. However, Seth had always possessed two sides to his nature: he was regarded as both an evil and a beneficial force. The Egyptians feared his wicked aspect but also admired his strength, and in some historical periods, he became a pre-eminent deity, either because of the political climate or because the rulers chose to worship him. For example, in the Hyksos Period (see pp. 178–81), when the kings established their capital at Avaris in the Delta – a region where Seth had long been worshipped – they adopted him as their dynastic god. They identified him with their own deity Baal, and called him Sutekh.

Now, in Dynasty 19, the first king, Ramesses I, came from a family who lived in the Delta and worshipped Seth of Avaris, and thus he named his son, Sethos I, after this god.

The Osiris Mysteries were probably only performed once a year in the temple, as part of the Festival of Osiris. Secret rites inside the temple would have complemented the dramatic enactments of the events in the life, death and resurrection of Osiris which took place outside the precinct, and which the pilgrims could experience at first hand. In the scenes in the Osiris Complex, the culmination of the ritual is depicted: the *djed*-pillar, the symbol of Osiris, is raised into the upright position, thus renewing the god's vigour and strength and ensuring his resurrection.

In the sanctuary area of the temple, the priests performed the Daily Temple Ritual in six shrines which were all dedicated to gods – the two triads of imperial Ramesside gods (Amun, Re-Harakhte and Ptah) and the Osirian family of Osiris, Isis and Horus.[14] Abydos was a national shrine, and this wide range of gods was probably included here to emphasize the return to traditionalism after the Amarna Period. The scenes and inscriptions in this area provide the most complete extant texts of the Daily Temple Ritual. After this ritual was completed, the second part of the daily worship followed. This served the needs of the Royal Ancestors (former dead kings) and established the kingship of Sethos I after his death; it also confirmed his consequent ability to receive the offerings as a dead ruler in his temple so that his personal resurrection would be ensured. This ritual started in the seventh shrine of the sanctuary, which was dedicated to the dead, deified Sethos, and the offerings which had been presented at the conclusion of the Daily Temple Ritual were now placed before the king.

Subsequently, they were taken into adjoining rooms in the Nefertem-Ptah-Sokar Complex, which was dedicated to the Memphite funerary gods. Here, the initial stages of the Ritual of the Royal Ancestors took place, before the food was finally offered to the Royal Ancestors in the adjacent Gallery of the Lists. The Ancestors were present in the form of a list of kings' names inscribed along one wall of the Gallery. This presentation is known as the 'First Reversion of Offerings' (the food had reverted from the god's altar to the Ancestors). This sacred food, which carried with it all the power of an offering which had been presented to the gods, was believed to provide spiritual nourishment for the Ancestors, and thus enable them to continue in the afterlife. Subsequently, in the nearby Hall of Barques, the food was divided up to be given to the priests as their daily payment. This was known as the 'Second Reversion of Offerings', when the food passed from the Ancestors to the priests. Again, the food was thought to provide them with spiritual as well as physical sustenance, which it had acquired from the altars of the god and the Ancestors. Finally, the offerings were taken out of the temple through a side exit so that they could be distributed to the priests.

The Temple of Sethos at Abydos displays some of the finest examples of Egyptian temple art; executed during the king's own reign, they provide a marked contrast to the heavy, incised reliefs which were carried out in the building under his successor, Ramesses II. Although the scenes of the Sethos' period represent a return to orthodoxy, the influence of Amarna art can still be perceived in the form and elegance of these reliefs.

Essentially, this building was the same as all other traditional temples in terms of its design, mythology and ritual, but because of the L-shaped plan of the building, the inclusion of seven sanctuaries instead of one, and the presence of the Osiris Complex, it represents a unique concept. Its dual ritual function – to ensure the resurrection of Osiris, and to make provision for the worship of gods, Ancestors and the deified king – is also unparalleled. The quantity and quality of its wall-scenes and inscriptions provide an unrivalled opportunity to study the temple rituals which are described above.'[5]

The Temples at Abu Simbel

Ramesses II built two magnificent temples at Abu Simbel which, in recent years, have played an important part in a UNESCO project to save the monuments of Egypt. The Great Temple was dedicated to Ptah, Amen-Re, Re-Harakhte and Ramesses II who was deified during his own lifetime. Apart from its size and the grandeur of its natural setting, the temple has important historical scenes and inscriptions, which relate the king's military successes at the Battle of Kadesh, and in his Syrian, Libyan and Nubian campaigns, and commemorate his marriage to a Hittite princess, which marked the end of the conflict between the Egyptians and Hittites. Nearby is the second rock-cut temple, also built by Ramesses II, which honoured his queen Nefertari; this was dedicated to Hathor, goddess of love and beauty.

Both these monuments were moved between 1964 ACE and 1968 ACE to a new location slightly further away from the river, at a higher level, so that they would not be submerged by the rising waters of Lake Nasser, created by the construction of the High Dam at Aswan. The project involved the building of a cofferdam to hold back the waters of the lake; the temples were cut into blocks and dismantled, and the façades and the interior walls were then rebuilt in the new location. Concrete, dome-shaped structures were constructed to support the two temples and act as replacements for the mountain into which the original monuments had been cut.[16]

The Mortuary Temple of Ramesses III at Medinet Habu[17]

Ramesses III, the last great warrior king of Egypt, conducted a series of successful, defensive campaigns against a coalition of potential invaders known as the Sea-peoples who, with others, threatened to overwhelm the Egyptian Delta. The Sea-peoples were a confederation of peoples or tribes who may have come from a number of different homelands. They seem to have been driven southwards by hunger and possibly displacement: after the turn of the thirteenth century BCE, they attacked the Hittites, Cyprus and the coastal cities of Syria, before flooding down through Palestine and joining with the Libyan tribes, to attack Egypt from the west. They brought their families and domestic possessions with them in ox-drawn carts, and obviously intended to invade and settle in Palestine and the Egyptian Delta.

Repulsed by Ramesses III, they eventually settled in Palestine and probably also in areas of the Mediterranean; indeed, they are of great historical interest because the names of some of their tribes are very similar to later racial groups who lived in some of the Mediterranean countries and islands. In Ramesses III's temple at Medinet Habu on the west bank at Thebes, there is a substantial record of the engagement between the Egyptians and the Sea-peoples, preserved in wall-scenes and inscriptions.[18] This site was also an important centre during the earlier New Kingdom (when a temple had been built there by Hatshepsut and Tuthmosis III), but in Ramesside times, Ramesses III constructed a second great temple which was dedicated to Amun and also provided accommodation for the cult associated with Ramesses III's tomb in the Valley of the Kings.

Ramesses III greatly admired his illustrious ancestor, Ramesses II, and his temple at Medinet Habu was based on the design of Ramesses II's own west bank temple, the Ramesseum. As well as the temple, the Medinet Habu enclosure also contained workshops, magazines, priests' houses and offices inside a large mudbrick wall. In the Ramesside Period, Medinet Habu became the administrative centre of Thebes.

In addition to famous historical records, temple scenes in the Second Court depict the Festival of Sokar, which was one of the great Theban festivals (*see* p. 195). There is also an astronomical ceiling inside the temple; examples of such ceilings also occurred in royal and private tombs. The significance of the astronomical ceiling in the temple context was to show the passage of time, in terms of years, months, days and hours, which was regulated by the gods in order that this continuous process could be sustained and made eternally effective. Astronomical ceilings were an important feature of the temple that helped to maintain the order of the universe.[19] To the south of the First Court of this temple, there was a palace where Ramesses III stayed when he was engaged in performing the rituals and religious ceremonies in the temple.

THE RAMESSIDE TOMBS

Thebes remained the royal burial place throughout the New Kingdom (Dynasties 18–20). The last ruler to be buried in the Valley of the Kings was Ramesses XI, who died at the end of Dynasty 20. The tombs follow a general plan in which a rock-cut corridor, interrupted by one or more pillared halls, descends to the burial chamber. The wall and ceiling decoration, representing the king's journey from this world to the next, depicts subject matter from various funerary papyri, including scenes and inscriptions from the Books of the Dead, the Netherworld, Gates, Caverns and the Litany of Re.

The tomb of Ramesses III displays an exceptional variety of scenes, including those from the funerary books and also one depicting a harper singing to the gods. The text of the songs is inscribed on the walls. The tomb of Ramesses VI, originally prepared for Ramesses V, also provides a wealth of information. As the result of a photographic survey undertaken in 1948–51 ACE, this was the first royal tomb in the Valley to have been completely published; the study includes an inventory, description and translation of each part of every scene.[20]

Some recent studies have been undertaken in the Valley by the Institute of Theban Egyptology of the Louvre Museum, which is involved in a Franco-Egyptian mission to systematically clear and study the tomb of Ramesses II.[21] It has been possible to determine that this tomb has two axes, returning to the pattern of royal tomb architecture which was in existence before the Amarna Period (other royal tombs after Akhenaten have a single axis), but the reason for this change is unclear.

Other excavations, undertaken by the American archaeologist K. Weeks, are in the process of clearing Tomb KV5, with the ultimate goal of recording and conserving the monument.[22] Already, it has been possible to show that at least two and perhaps as many as eleven of Ramesses II's eldest sons were buried here.[23] This tomb may be the one referred to as the 'tomb of the royal children' in the Turin Papyrus, which deals with the tomb robberies in the later reign of Ramesses III.

The tomb was located in 1987–8 ACE by the Theban Mapping Project, an American study established in 1978 ACE to prepare a survey of the entire Theban necropolis.[24] Current studies have indicated that the tomb had not been entered since 1150 BCE, except by two nineteenth-century explorers and the workmen of the archaeologist Howard Carter (the discoverer of Tutankhamun's tomb) who partially cleared and subsequently reburied the entrance to KV5 early in the twentieth century. Situated about 40 metres (131 feet) to the north-east of Ramesses II's own tomb, KV5 is one of the largest burial places ever found in the Valley of the Kings.

Originally, all the walls were decorated with fine relief carvings and texts, but considerable damage has been caused to the interior by flash floods, the heavy tourist bus traffic (now discontinued) that used the nearby asphalt-paved parking area, and a sewer pipe that had been laid some years ago from the Valley of the Kings rest-house (which has now been relocated). Nevertheless, careful study of the tomb, involving the production of detailed drawings, plans and photographs of the interior chambers, has revealed that some carvings and wall paintings have survived, and is providing valuable evidence about contemporary funerary practices.

Ramesses II did not commission the tomb; he usurped an existing burial place which may have been prepared originally in Dynasty 18 for someone of importance, but the current excavation will perhaps ultimately reveal the identity of this original owner. The sons of Ramesses II were buried here as they died; of his first twelve sons, only Prince Khaemweset is thought to have been buried elsewhere. It appears that several sons were interred at the same time, perhaps as the result of an accident, military action, a conspiracy, or even disease. The human mummified remains that have so far been discovered are significant because of their potential for biomedical studies and for DNA identifications relating to the royal family. Ultimately, it may be possible to identify from inscriptional and other evidence which of the princes were buried here, and to determine the physical extent of the tomb. However, the main aim of the programme is to clear, clean and chemically treat the walls and, where necessary, to rebond them to the stone.

In the nearby Valley of the Queens, the tombs (which mainly date to Dynasties 19 and 20) belong to some of the queens and princes of the Ramesside Period. Most of these tombs were discovered and excavated by the Italian Archaeological Mission between 1903 and 1920 ACE and 1926 and 1927 ACE. Although some tombs were never finished and remain undecorated, in others, the wall-scenes are of a very high standard. The subject matter concentrates on the owner's relationship with the gods and the passage to the next world.

The tomb of Nefertari, a major queen of Ramesses II, is the finest and most famous. The superb wall paintings show the queen in the company of the gods, indicating that queens as well as kings could expect to spend their eternity in divine company in the heavens, once they had successfully overcome the dangers which attended their passage from this world to the next. An international project has recently undertaken a unique restoration programme here, with the aim of restoring the wall-paintings and attempting to prevent further deterioration.[25] Other important tombs in this area belonged to Princes Khaemweset and Amenhirkhopshef.

In addition to the Theban necropolis, there was also considerable activity at Saqqara in the later New Kingdom. When Tutankhamun returned from Amarna and established his political capital at Memphis, Saqqara was selected as the main cemetery for non-royal burials and continued in use until the reign of Ramesses II.[26] These tombs were plundered or inadequately excavated, and some had been dismantled, with the result that their stone blocks, decorated with scenes and inscriptions, were ultimately removed to museum collections.

An important group of tombs has recently been uncovered here by the Anglo-Dutch expedition of the Egypt Exploration Society and the National Museum of Antiquities in Leiden. Their discoveries have included the tombs of Horemheb, Tia and Tia, Maya, and Iurudef. The studies carried out on these tombs have provided evidence about the daily life, administration, and religious beliefs in the period from the reign of Tutankhamun to the early Ramessides. Although evidence from Thebes is well documented in the temples and in the royal and private tombs, and has been extensively studied, very little information is forthcoming about contemporary conditions at Memphis, so these excavations are particularly important.

In his extensive survey of standing monuments in Egypt and Nubia, the German Egyptologist Lepsius recorded parts of several New Kingdom tombs at Saqqara, including the tomb of Maya, and marked the position of these tombs on a map of the area which was subsequently drawn up by his surveyor. The recent expedition, searching for the tomb of Maya in 1975 ACE, used Lepsius' map as a guide but instead, because of a slight inaccuracy in the map, they discovered the long-lost tomb of Horemheb. When Horemheb became king, he was ultimately buried in the Valley of the Kings, but this northern tomb had been prepared while he was still a high-ranking commoner and Commander of Tutankhamun's army. Much of the tomb's superstructure is preserved, and it has some of the finest wall-reliefs which depict aspects of society and life in the New Kingdom.

Following this discovery, the expedition then explored further, in the hope that they had found the nucleus of a group of officials' tombs. The tomb of Maya, Overseer of the Treasury under the kings Tutankhamun, Ay and Horemheb, was last seen in 1843 ACE by Lepsius, but as early as the 1820s, three statues of Maya and his wife Meryt had entered the museum collection in Leiden. The tomb of Maya was finally rediscovered in 1986 ACE,[27] while the team was clearing the substructure of a neighbouring tomb. The expedition then continued to complete excavation of the superstructure, and to investigate the substructure. It was evident that the tomb, once richly furbished, had been plundered and reused for later burials but nevertheless, skeletal fragments of Maya and possibly Meryt were recovered.

A later, important tomb belonged to Tia and Tia, the sister and brother-in-law of Ramesses II.[28] It is perhaps surprising that such close royal relatives were buried at Saqqara rather than at Thebes. This is the first large tomb of the Ramesside Period at Saqqara which has been revealed, excavated and planned in its entirety. It had space to accommodate several burials, and was probably used for the whole family of Tia and Tia. The wall scenes show the tomb-owners and the royal family making offerings and worshipping the gods.

Situated in the south-west corner of the first court of this funerary monument, there is the tomb-chapel of Iurudef who was a Scribe of the Treasury and an employee of Tia.[29] This tomb was originally used for the burial of the owner and members of his family, but appears to have been usurped at a later date (perhaps in the Third Intermediate Period) to accommodate an extensive multiple burial. There was much evidence of skeletal material, and many coffins, papyrus coffers and reed mat burials were discovered. In all, seventy-five burials, including many children, were uncovered. These, and other skeletal remains found in the tombs, provide the basis for anthropological studies which will contribute to future population biology studies of ancient Memphis.[30]

Other research being carried out on the inscriptions and scenes found in the tombs, the extensive collection of pottery, and the coffins, will also provide new information about the residents of Saqqara during this period.

NEW KINGDOM TEXTS

The Funerary Books

At this period, an important addition to the funerary preparations were the 'books' of spells which assisted the passage of the deceased.[3] Compilation of the most famous, the Book of the Dead, was started in the early New Kingdom but the finalized sequence of spells was established much later in Dynasty 26.

Essentially, the Book of the Dead provided spells to ensure the resurrection of the deceased and his safety in the next world, but the spells also represented the ritual acts performed at the burial and in the subsequent mortuary cult, and they also related to the Day of Judgement. The texts provided the deceased with a guide to facilitate entry into the underworld, and details of what he would encounter there. The spells were first found in the form of vignettes (small scenes that accompanied inscriptions) on some Dynasty 11 coffins, but by the early Dynasty 18, the texts were being written on papyrus scrolls.

Arranged in chapters, the spells continued to be accompanied by vignettes which, by Dynasty 19, had expanded to occupy most of the papyrus, with a corresponding reduction in the text. Regarded as a work of divine authorship, the Book of the Dead was attributed to Thoth, god of writing. These mass-produced, ready-made scrolls were widely available, and there were either custom-made or ready-made versions to which the buyer's name and titles were added. The inscription was written in cursive hieroglyphs on the scroll which provided a more affordable option than a painted coffin. It was placed with the burial, either inside the coffin on the mummy, or in a niche in the tomb wall, or in a special hollowed-out wooden figure of Osiris or Ptah-Sokar-Osiris.

The Book of the Dead provided the deceased with the means to challenge death; it promoted the need to possess the high moral values which are listed in the Negative Confession, but if an individual lacked these, other spells supplied magical alternatives. However, it is unclear if the option of magic was regarded as a truly effective method if the owner did not meet the required moral standards. Other funerary books with a similar purpose were derived from the Book of the Dead.

Traditional methods of dating the New Kingdom funerary papyri have included comparisons of the vignettes with scenes found in the Theban tombs, using an analysis of the hairstyles and garments on the figures. However, the details shown in the vignettes may not represent contemporary fashion, and a new search for all-embracing dating criteria has attempted to incorporate historical, linguistic and iconographic elements.[32]

Ethical and Moral Teaching

The Egyptian system of education is not clearly defined in any of the inscriptions, but the Wisdom Literature and other texts provide some information about the moral and ethical content of school instruction.

The Wisdom Literature

The Instructions in Wisdom, first composed in the Old and Middle Kingdoms, continued to play an important role in education. Although these early texts were still copied out by schoolboys, new compositions were also introduced. However, whereas the early examples had been used to instruct the sons of the aristocracy (who would eventually take up high-level government posts) how they should behave in their dealings with people over whom they would have authority, these New Kingdom additions were intended for the sons of the expanded middle classes.

One important new text – the Instruction of Any – was almost certainly composed in the New Kingdom.[33] It retained the traditional concept of an older man (here, the scribe Any, employed at the palace of Queen Nefertari) giving advice to a younger person. However, the tradition in earlier texts where a king or vizier instructs the country's future leaders is now replaced by a situation in which a minor official addresses his own son. Thus, rather than aristocratic values, it is middle-class values such as honesty and humility which are now promoted.

Another Wisdom Text – the Instruction of Amenemope – was probably composed in the Ramesside Period.[34] It is of great interest for several reasons. First, it emphasizes a new attitude – although material success was still the expected outcome of a righteous life, now the ideal person is not necessarily one who holds a powerful position but one who is humble in his relationship with gods and men. Honesty, rather than wealth and status, is highly regarded, and whereas correct social behaviour was once necessary to bring about personal advancement, individual qualities such as endurance, self-control and kindliness are now to be encouraged. The most significant new concept, however, was the belief that only god is perfect, a state which no human could hope to emulate, and because of this chasm between gods and men, human beings were expected to show humility before the gods. This text, closer in style and content to Hebrew literature than to any other Egyptian writings, has been compared especially to Chapters 22 and 23 in the Biblical Book of Proverbs. During the Ramesside Period (the suggested date of the composition of this Wisdom Text), Egyptian influence on the Hebrews probably reached its peak, and the Egyptian writings may have directly or indirectly contributed to parts of Proverbs. A few examples from Amenemope and Proverbs will demonstrate the similarity of these texts:

Make no friendship with an angry man, and with a furious man thou shalt not go: Lest thou learn his ways, and get a snare to thy soul.

(Proverbs 22, verses 24–5)

Do not force yourself to greet the heated man,
For then you injure your own heart;
Do not say 'greetings' to him falsely,
While there is terror in your belly.[35]   (Amenemope, ch.10)

A good name is rather to be chosen than great riches, and loving favour rather than silver and gold.   (Proverbs 22, verse 1)

Poverty is better in the hand of the god
Than wealth in the storehouse;
Bread is better with a happy heart
Than wealth with vexation.[36]

(Amenemope, ch.6)

Remove not the old landmark; enter not into the fields of the fatherless.

(Proverbs 23, verse 10)

Do not move the markers on the borders of the fields,
Nor shift the position of the measuring-cord.
Do not be greedy for a cubit of land,
Nor encroach on the boundaries of a widow.[37]

(Amenemope, ch.6)

Schoolboy Letters

Another important genre which appears in the later New Kingdom are the so-called 'Schoolboy Letters' which have survived on numerous Ramesside papyri and ostraca.[38] These arose from the school system: composed by teachers, they include three main themes in which (i) the teacher gives the pupil good advice and encourages him to work hard and reject excessive pleasure; (ii) the scribal profession is praised and extolled above all others; and (iii) the student praises his teacher and thanks him for his advice, wishing him wealth and happiness.

These schoolboy exercises provide ample evidence that there was an educational system which existed to teach and train the professional classes. Scribes were regarded as a separate and privileged group in society whose knowledge of reading and writing gave them superiority. The training of the professional classes was carried out at two levels. After an elementary education at school, where the boy learnt to read and write and to understand and appreciate literature, he was attached to a centre of administration where he continued his training as a junior official, receiving personal supervision and tuition from a senior scribe.

An important part of this education was the pupil's duty to copy out various compositions such as the Wisdom Texts and the so-called Model Letters. This not only enabled the pupil to acquire skills in reading, writing, and understanding grammar, composition and vocabulary, but

A tomb scene shows scribes writing on papyrus. They have pushed spare pens behind their ears.

also provided instruction in the moral and ethical values that were regarded as desirable.

Only boys intended for the priesthood and its associated professions, or the civil service, seem to have received an academic education. This was provided in a variety of schools: palace schools where chosen children were taught alongside the often numerous royal offspring; government schools which specialized in training future officials for particular departments; and temple schools where, in some instances, medical training may have been undertaken.

Archaeological evidence has indicated that a temple school once existed in the precinct of the Ramesseum at Thebes where, in the rubbish heaps, large numbers of inscribed sherds have been discovered. Thrown there by the pupils once they had completed their writing exercises, these sherds carry inscriptions which indicate that the boys repeatedly copied out the same passages. These may express moral sentiments which the teachers particularly wanted the children to study and remember.

THE EXODUS[39]

It has been suggested that the Ramesside Period was the time when events associated with the Biblical Exodus may have occurred. In fact, in the Egyptian records, there is no extant reference either to the sojourn of the Hebrews in Egypt or to the Exodus, but the subject has excited considerable debate and controversy.

In the Biblical account,[40] Joseph, the son of Jacob, was sold into slavery by his jealous half-brothers. Sent down to Egypt, he entered the house of a wealthy Egyptian, Potiphar, who came to respect him and made him overseer of his household. However, because of lies told by Potiphar's wife, Joseph fell from favour and was cast into prison. Nevertheless, his ability to interpret dreams came to the king's attention, and he was finally released to unravel Pharaoh's dream.

Ultimately, he gained great wealth and prestige and even became vizier; he was able to bring his family (the tribe of Israel) to Egypt where their descendants remained for some four hundred and thirty years until a later king forced them to work as labourers, making bricks for the cities of Pithom and Ramses. According to the Bible,[41] as the child of Hebrew slaves living in Egypt at that time, Moses was rescued from the edge of the Nile by an Egyptian princess, and brought up in the palace as an Egyptian prince. Eventually, he led the Hebrews out of Egypt. They probably lived near the building sites in the Delta where they worked, and their Exodus route would have departed from this area. Despite the king's unsuccessful attempt to recapture them, they were able to escape and pass into Sinai, where Moses received the Ten Commandments, before finally reaching their destination in the Holy Land.

Attempts to uncover any contemporary literary or archaeological evidence of the Exodus in Egypt have so far failed. This is perhaps not surprising since a minor uprising on the part of their workforce would not have been of great significance to the Egyptians; also, their historical records are almost invariably propagandist and record only their successes. Nevertheless, there have been various attempts by scholars to fix the date of the Exodus within Egyptian chronology, and to identify the pharaoh who was engaged in this conflict.

According to the early historian Josephus, the Hyksos were identified as the 'tribe of Israel' (*see* p. 179); he stated that their conquest of Egypt in the Second Intermediate Period was the event that coincided with the arrival of Joseph's family. He also claimed that the Exodus should be equated with the expulsion of the Hyksos rulers by the Thebans of Dynasty 17 (*c.*1550 BCE), but this seems a most unlikely interpretation since, whereas the Hyksos were driven out of the country, the Hebrews made every effort to leave.

It is possible that Joseph and his kinsmen entered Egypt at some time between the Old Kingdom (*c.*2340 BCE) and the Hyksos Period (*c.*1650 BCE), amongst the groups of Semitic peoples who were arriving and settling in the eastern Delta and Upper Egypt; there is evidence in Egyptian literature that many of these probably became servants in Egyptian households. By the New Kingdom (*c.*1450 BCE), other foreigners entered Egypt, either as prisoners of war (some of whom became employees on temple estates and state building projects), or as merchants and envoys to the royal court.

There have also been attempts to identify Joseph with Yuya, the father-in-law of Amenhotep III, and to place the Exodus at the end of the Amarna Period.[42] However, the description of events given in the Bible appears to fit most closely with the conditions known to have existed in the Ramesside Period. The Hebrews may have formed part of a group of itinerant labourers called 'Apiru (*Habiru* in the cuneiform texts) who had lived in the Delta for many years but were now obliged to undertake forced labour at the building sites.

By Ramesside times, the numbers of the 'tribe of Israel' would have greatly increased since their first arrival in Egypt, and the Egyptian rulers may have come to perceive them as a threat. In addition to forcing them to produce mudbricks for the royal Delta cities, the pharaoh issued a royal decree that demanded the slaughter of all their newborn males, and it was in order to escape this fate for their son that the parents of Moses hid him in the bulrushes.

According to the Bible, when Moses grew to adulthood, he witnessed the mistreatment of a Hebrew labourer by an Egyptian overseer, and murdered him. Subsequently, he was forced to flee into exile in the desert where he had his first encounter with God who spoke to him

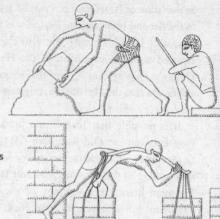

A tomb scene illustrates some stages in the production of mudbricks. An overseer is shown (*right*), carrying a whip.

from a burning bush, telling him that he had been chosen to return to Egypt and lead his people out of bondage to their promised homeland.

Pharaoh's refusal to countenance the Hebrews' departure resulted in a series of disasters (a Nile flood, devastation of the crops, disease and plague, and finally the death of the Egyptian firstborn), and so eventually he agreed to let them leave. Moses then led his people away, probably taking the route that passed south and then east to Succoth, before moving north again to the Bitter Lakes.[43] However, at this point, the king changed his mind again and sent a chariot force to round them up and force them to return to the Delta. At the Biblical 'Red Sea' (which was probably the 'Sea of Reeds'), a strong wind parted the waters and allowed the Hebrews to pass through, but afterwards the waters rushed back, catching and drowning the Egyptian troops who were in pursuit.

Many of the Biblical details coincide with information about the Ramesside Period which has been derived from other sources. Many foreigners held high positions at court at this time, and Moses would have been readily accepted in the highest levels of society. His education as an Egyptian prince would have prepared him well for his later role as leader and law-giver. The labourers' working conditions mentioned in the Bible are reminiscent of conditions (known from other sources)

at other New Kingdom sites, and the Biblical names of the cities they were constructing – Ramses and Pithom – are strongly indicative of the Ramesside Period. Other sources also record that the Ramesside rulers of Dynasty 19 introduced stern measures against people who lived on the borders of Egypt.

However, some scholars have suggested a later Saite/Persian date for the Exodus,[44] or have agreed that the Exodus did not occur at all as a historical event, but was perhaps a Canaanite folk-memory of the expulsion,[45] or even that the Biblical account may be a compilation of several historical events which perhaps occurred over a considerable length of time.

In his erudite study of Moses and monotheism, Assmann has explored the significance of Moses as a figure of memory rather than history. The same work also examines the theory that Moses was actually an Egyptian priest who led a group of followers out of his country, and revealed to them the hidden truth of his own Egyptian religion: that there was a single supreme source of all things. This great knowledge may have only been handed down to initiates in the Egyptian priesthood after a long period of instruction and preparation, but never before had it been made available to the masses because the state needed to retain control over them by ensuring that their belief continued both in polytheism (including the king's own divinity) and in an afterlife dependent upon correct behaviour in this world. However, according to this possible reconstruction of events, the Egyptian premises of monotheism were first revealed to a group of the uninitiated when Moses addressed his followers in the Sinai desert.

Even if one accepts that the Exodus did occur in Dynasty 19, the identity of the pharaoh remains uncertain. Originally, it was proposed that the persecutions may have occurred under Ramesses II and Merneptah and that the latter was the pharaoh of the Exodus, but evidence discovered in 1896 ACE has cast considerable doubt on this theory. A stela (now known as the Israel Stela), usurped by Merneptah from Amenhotep III and erected in his royal cult temple at Thebes, was inscribed with an account of Merneptah's Libyan War. This provides the only extant reference to Israel in Egyptian texts, and proves that Israel was already an established geographical entity and homeland by the middle of Merneptah's reign. If Merneptah was indeed the pharaoh associated with the story of the Exodus, then Israel could not have been already established, so the persecutions and the Exodus seem most likely to have occurred in the reign of his predecessor, Ramesses II. However, only further excavation can reveal more conclusive evidence about these events.

POPULAR RELIGION

Apart from its funerary aspects, evidence for practical religion and piety is scanty before the New Kingdom.[46] The scenes that occur in private tombs of the Old, Middle and New Kingdoms represent an idealized world but, although these representations did not set out to falsify reality, they had a specific function which was to ensure that the owner enjoyed a perfect life in the next world. The content of such scenes did not attempt to address the problems encountered by ordinary people in their daily lives.

Most 'official' religion, which was concerned with the stability of the universe and the status of gods, kings and the elite, did not have a widespread appeal, but all humans, whether rich or poor, also required a means of comprehending, accepting and responding to the loss and suffering that they encountered in their lives. Therefore, alongside the temples and the funerary cult, there existed a variety of approaches which sought to deal with individual problems and uncertainties. Sometimes, these avenues overlapped with 'official' religious and secular systems such as law and medicine.

These approaches included the use of oracles and magic, letters to the dead, dreams and other forms of divination, ancestor cults, and the worship of special gods. It was believed that society consisted of four groups – gods, the king, the blessed dead and humanity – who shared certain moral obligations and a duty to interact in order to maintain world order.[47] The existence of this order, and the assumption that it was constantly under threat, was a basic premise of Egyptian belief.

In every individual's life, the ordered pattern consisted of several rites of transition – birth, puberty, marriage, parenthood and death. These were accompanied by rituals that had varying degrees of significance. Certain rites surrounded the dangerous time of childbirth and a successful outcome was celebrated fourteen days after birth. At puberty, many boys were circumcised, relinquished the childhood hairstyle known as the 'Sidelock of Youth', and began to wear clothes in public. There is no surviving evidence of any religious rites or observances that were associated with marriage, which was a secular, legal contract, but the rituals linked to death and burial are the most fully documented, presumably because they represented the most important features of an individual's passage through this world. However, it was accepted that life was pursued within the context of a dangerous cosmos,[48] and that this orderly pattern was frequently disturbed by disasters which included illness, sudden or premature death, and natural dangers. Personal faith was needed to respond to life's tragedies, but affliction was not regarded as an overwhelmingly bad experience, because the sufferer could gain strength and spiritual sustenance from his loss.

Most extant evidence of personal religion dates to the later New Kingdom, but the reason for this is unclear. One theory is that piety ('direct contact with the gods and personal experience of them')[49] did not exist until that period and that it then emerged as a result of

Akhenaten's earlier reforms. However, some inscriptions appear to indicate that piety had existed in earlier periods.[50] In fact, it is most likely that this imbalance in the evidence of personal religion in the different periods is due to other factors. These include an increased literacy amongst the populace in the later New Kingdom which, for the first time, enabled them to record their beliefs and feelings; and the discovery of the royal workmen's town of Deir el-Medina, Thebes, where much of the evidence for practical religion and piety has been found.

Gods and Rituals

However, earlier royal workmen's towns have been excavated which also provide information about popular religion.[51] The Workmen's Village at Amarna has already been discussed (see pp. 219–20), but a Middle Kingdom pyramid workmen's town, Kahun, can also be considered here. This townsite, excavated by William Flinders Petrie in 1888–9 ACE,[52] was built by Senusret II in Dynasty 12, to house the officials, workmen and their families engaged in the construction of the king's nearby pyramid at Lahun. Known in antiquity as 'Hetep-Senusret' ('Senusret-is-satisfied'), the site was important because, for the first time, excavation revealed a virtually complete plan of an Egyptian town.

Objects belonging to the inhabitants which were left behind in the houses provide an opportunity to study unique material evidence which has come from a domestic site rather than a tomb. A collection of papyri also found at Kahun has provided a written record of their civil and domestic life, including legal and medical practices.[53] The evidence about popular religion is particularly important. The official religion was centred on the pyramid temple of Senusret II, where his mortuary cult was performed, and the Kahun papyri provide details about the temple administration and its rituals and festivals. However, artifacts from the town show that people also pursued their own modes of worship. As at Deir el-Medina, offerings of food were made to 'household gods' in the homes, where bread and other items were probably presented to the deities as part of a daily ritual. At Kahun, distinctive stone offering stands were found which supported offering dishes; some of these took the form of a simple column whereas others incorporated primitive human figures.

Evidence of the gods at Kahun indicates that 'state gods' such as Hathor were worshipped alongside 'domestic deities' such as Bes and Tauert. Hathor, the cow-goddess, had been worshipped in Egypt since earliest times. She had many attributes and functions, but was particularly concerned with royal births and with suckling and nursing the king. Also, she was the goddess of love and beauty, and patron deity of the Theban necropolis. At Kahun, inscriptions indicate that some of the residents may have been of foreign origin (perhaps coming from Syria/ Palestine), and so Hathor was possibly worshipped there in her role as goddess of foreign lands. Bes, originally mentioned in the Pyramid Texts of the Old Kingdom, was a very ancient god who possibly came to Egypt from Ethiopia or Asia.

He was usually represented as a dwarf with a lion's mane and tail, and wore a hideous mask, to scare away the demons; he is often shown playing a drum or other musical instrument. He was the god of love, marriage and jollification who made people laugh; as the guardian of Horus, he was also a protective deity, who chased away snakes, and used music, singing and dancing to defeat the forces of evil. He comforted and supported women during childbirth, and befriended children and the weak.[54] He was also present at the circumcision ceremony which marked a boy's passage from childhood to adult status. Tauert was his wife: shown in the form of a pregnant hippopotamus, she was a symbol of fecundity, and assisted all women in labour. Some of the evidence for popular religion found at Kahun is unusual, including the shapes and styles of some of the offering stands, and the occurrence of baby burials under the houses. Such burials do not fit into the pattern of Egyptian funerary customs which required that the dead were interred on the edges of the desert, but they are known from other Near Eastern sites. However, because so few domestic sites such as Kahun have been discovered, it is difficult to determine if such customs were indeed due to foreign influence or if they were commonplace features of indigenous Egyptian popular religion which are only rarely revealed. Today, the baby burials that the excavators uncovered cannot be identified in any museum collections — they may have been re-interred in the ground —

so it is impossible to examine the babies in order to confirm whether they died from natural or more sinister causes.

The town of the royal necropolis workmen at Deir el-Medina was built on the west bank at Thebes, near to the Valley of the Kings.[55] It housed the workmen (and their families) who were engaged in the construction and decoration of the kings' tombs. The royal gang was probably assembled during the reign of Amenhotep I, but the town appears to have been built by his successor Tuthmosis I. It was occupied for some 450 years, from Dynasty 18 to Dynasty 20, during the period when the Valley of the Kings continued to be used for royal burials. It was continuously occupied (although it was downgraded during the Amarna Period, when the royal court moved from Thebes), and enjoyed its greatest prosperity in the reign of Ramesses II.

A wealth of information has been recovered from the houses and nearby tombs and, although artifacts such as those found at Kahun were not present here, there is a unique inscriptional record at Deir el-Medina, drawn from the papyri, ostraca and stelae. This provides information about the community's working conditions, legal arrangements, and religious and funerary beliefs and customs.

The workmen's main project was to prepare the king's tomb, but once this was completed, they could be dispatched to decorate the tombs of favoured queens, princes and officials. They also prepared elegant tombs for themselves which incorporated a burial chamber and funerary chapel, surmounted by a miniature pyramid. These tombs were lavishly decorated and equipped.

The religious practices of the workmen and their families are a subject of considerable interest. There were several temples and chapels, dedicated to various gods, which contained stelae, statues and offering tables, and in the chapels and houses, there were stelae and offering tables for the performance of rites to honour deceased relatives. Ancestral busts placed in the chapels and houses were the focus of devotions.[56] At first, the archaeologists thought that these were a main element in household worship, but it is most likely that, since many were originally placed in the temples or at other parts of the site, they had a ceremonial function as the recipients of food offerings, and were associated with the stelae and offering tables. In the domestic context, these busts probably

A tomb scene shows the transportation of a colossal statue, probably to a temple location. A man pours milk in front of the sledge to lubricate the runners.

represented the blessed dead who were feared and worshipped because they could have an impact on the fortunes of the living. The busts provided the inhabitants of the house with a means of protection against evil forces and with the facility to present petitions to request favours.

The men in this community spent their working time away from the town, living in huts near to the Valley of the Kings; they returned regularly to the village for rest on the ninth and tenth days and on special holidays. While they were absent, the town was largely organized and run by the women, and the local gods were mainly female protectors such as Isis, and those seen at Kahun – Bes, Tauert, and Hathor.[57] At Deir el-Medina, Hathor was worshipped as a local deity, and more generally on the west

Thebes, she was particularly revered as a cow-goddess and had ... ne in Hatshepsut's temple at Deir el-Bahri. Other goddesses ...ntified with Hathor at Deir el-Medina include Renenutet, and Mertet-seger, the serpent-goddess of the necropolis who was also associated with the 'Peak-of-the-West', a goddess who personified the mountain peak that towered over the Theban necropolis area. Other deities worshipped at Deir el-Medina included Anubis, jackal-headed god of embalming and cemeteries; Thoth, god of writing, architects and builders; Ptah, patron of craftsmen; Sobek, the crocodile-god; and Osiris and Isis.

Some deities found at Deir el-Medina – the ram-headed god Khnum and the goddesses Anukit and Satit – all originated in the region of Elephantine, at the First Cataract. Khnum was worshipped in the form of a ram or ram-headed man, and he was believed to model men and women on his potter's turntable, giving each an allotted lifespan. He was also closely connected with the inundation which was thought to start in a sacred pool on Elephantine Island. Anukit, usually shown wearing a feathered headdress, was a concubine of Khnum; she was the goddess of the cataract on Egypt's southern border, and had her chief shrine on the nearby island of Seheil. Satit, the daughter of Khnum and Anukit, was another ancient deity who may have originated in the Sudan. She married her father, Khnum, and was also worshipped on the island of Seheil as a goddess of hunting and the inundation.

By the New Kingdom, foreign gods also came to feature in the Egyptian pantheon, reflecting Egypt's increasingly cosmopolitan population. With the influx of Asiatic merchants and workmen in Dynasty 18, the range of these deities increased, and although some retained their distinctive foreign origins and features, others became identified with indigenous gods. Their presence amongst the Egyptian gods allowed their adherents to continue to worship them without compromising their loyalty to the state gods of their new homeland. The titles and attributes of these deities indicate where they originated: for example, Baal, a god of war, Resheph, a deity of thunder and war, and Anath and Astarte, both goddesses of war, came from Ugarit and Canaan.

Qudshu, Anat, Astarte and Resheph were all known at Deir el-Medina, but evidence of foreign deities also occurs elsewhere. For example, in a pre-Saite tomb at Nebesheh, five statuettes have been discovered which include three Egyptian deities, plus Beset who was the wife of Bes, and an Asiatic deity.[58] People had the freedom either to worship their own gods, or to approach other deities who possessed special powers. For example, Amenhotep II regarded Resheph as a deity who was especially beneficial in warfare (the god's name is first incorporated in people's names in Egypt during his reign), and thereafter, he became a god of the ordinary people who 'heard prayers'.[59]

In general, the temples and shrines at Deir el-Medina were used by the villagers even if some were built by the rulers. Deities worshipped there included 'state gods' and lesser deities; these co-existed in harmony, and an important conclusion that can be drawn from the Deir el-Medina evidence is that there was an apparent lack of rivalry between state and popular religion.[60] Also, it is evident that a god could be worshipped at a number of different levels: in one location, he could receive a temple cult but elsewhere could play a role in popular religion. At Deir el-Medina, the supreme state god Amen-Re was worshipped as a personal god, and the very special relationship that had originally existed between the Thebans and Amun as their local god was continued here. Amun received the personal prayers and devotion of the workmen and their families, and was regarded as protector of the weak and poor, and the arbiter of divine justice. Most of the stelae in the town and at a local temple were dedicated to him.

Another important cult honoured the deified king, Amenhotep I, and his mother, Ahmose-Nefertari. Amenhotep I, who had probably established the royal workforce, was depicted on many stelae and tomb walls; additionally, there was a local temple dedicated to his cult at Deir el-Medina. Although it was customary in the New Kingdom to deify and worship the living king, a few kings were so popular that they received separate and special worship as intercessors between the populace and other gods. Amenhotep I seems to have enjoyed this status, and he was consulted by means of an oracle with regard to legal decisions, and prayers were frequently addressed to him.

Occasionally, private individuals were also deified and worshipped; examples include Imhotep, the architect of the Step Pyramid at Saqqara, me a god of medicine; the nomarch Heqaib whose chapel at ...ntine was built in the Middle Kingdom for his cult both during ...fetime and after death; and an official in the reign of Amenhotep ..., known as Amenhotep, son of Hapu, was worshipped at Thebes shortly after his death, because of his wisdom and medical skills. Other humans who were deified and received cults included the Old Kingdom sages, Hardedef, Ptahhotep and Kagemni, to whom some of the Wisdom Texts were attributed. These wise men and the fictional royal authors of the wisdom literature thus became powerful proponents of ethical values.

Many popular deities featured in the local festivals when their statues were carried in procession through Deir el-Medina by the workmen who acted as their priests, performing duties on behalf of the gods. These were occasions of great rejoicing and also meditation. There were nine feast days associated with the cult of Amenhotep I, and on the ninth day, his image was carried to the Valley of the Kings. The people also probably participated in some of the great Theban state festivals when Amun's statue was brought from Karnak to visit the temples on the west bank. Generally, the villagers approached their gods through different avenues, but their main aim was to derive help and comfort from a personal relationship with these deities.

Sin and Salvation

One particularly interesting example of personal piety occurs at Deir el-Medina in inscriptions found on memorial stelae which the workmen set up in the chapels.[61] Some of these prayers, which appealed to various gods, expressed humility and gratitude for recovery from an illness or affliction brought about by the workman's own sins (these are not specified but may have involved blasphemy). This concept of confession and salvation (the translation from one state in which a person had incurred the god's wrath because he had committed a sin, to another in which the sinner received the god's forgiveness) was apparently rare in Egypt, although in the Middle Kingdom Story of Sinuhe, the return of Sinuhe to Egypt after his period of self-exile and his reintegration into society may represent a kind of secular salvation.[62]

However, the idea of religious salvation found in these texts may have been new. It is possible that this concept had always been part of popular faith, but was expressed here in writing because the community was literate; alternatively, it may represent a new idea introduced to Egypt at this time by Asiatic immigrants. However, such sentiments do not appear to have been unique to this community, as similar hymns and prayers have been found elsewhere.

Some of the prayers occur in documents and others are on memorial stones. One example, on a stela found in a small brick temple dedicated to Amun, was inscribed by a local draughtsman, Nebre, and his son, Kha'y. It thanks Amun for the return to health of Kha'y's brother. On another, Nebre, son of Pay, begs the god Haroeris to 'Let mine eyes behold the way to go', and in a further example, Nekhtamun, a scribe of the necropolis, says to the goddess of the Peak, 'Thou causest me to see darkness by day.'

The frequent references to blindness in these texts may either indicate a widespread physical problem amongst these men who were engaged in decorating badly lit tombs, or the condition may describe spiritual rather than physical blindness, perhaps indicating a form of emotional depression. Whatever its true nature, 'blindness' appears to have been regarded as a special punishment for any personal sin which aroused divine wrath. The exact form of transgression is not clear, but the petitioners would have regarded impiety and swearing falsely by a god's name to be sufficiently serious to be punished by illness. Nevertheless, they evidently believed that sometimes, prayers and contrition could placate the god and result in a cure for the petitioner or his relatives.

Oracles

The use of the oracle is well attested both at Deir el-Medina, and within the wider context of Egyptian religion and law.[63] Oracles were used as a form of divination or a means of obtaining a decision and were mainly employed within the context of the temple, although deified individuals such as Amenhotep I could also be consulted, and in the later periods there is evidence that animals were used as intermediaries.[64] It is recorded that kings consulted oracles from the New Kingdom onwards, and even earlier, in the Middle Kingdom, there are statements that they received divine commands which may have been delivered in the form of an oracle. In fact, oracles were probably in use at all periods, although earlier evidence is lacking.[65]

At Deir el-Medina, the oracle was worked through the priests who acted as the god's intermediary. Here, the community enjoyed an amazing degree of autonomy in both religious and legal matters, and the workmen themselves organized rotas in which they sat as magistrates in their own local law-court, and acted as priests for their community cults and oracle. They obtained results from the oracle by holding the god's statue in front of the petitioner and moving it from side to side or up and down so that it could give a 'response' to the petitioner's question.

Oracle petitions from other sites provide further information about the system. Two examples from El-Hiba, which date to Dynasty 20/21,[66] indicate that some gods may have played a special role in delivering oracles. Documentation associated with oracles includes the petition to the god, the decision made by the god through an oracular decree, and a letter of thanks from the petitioner. Sometimes, the oracle-questions were presented verbally, but often they were made in writing. As the procession of the god approached, it was customary for the intermediary to approach the deity and request permission to act on behalf of the petitioner. The deity could not be directly addressed, and would not give his decision personally to the petitioner. Two petitions were drawn up, providing two responses, and the god was asked to make his decision by indicating, through the intermediary, which answer he had selected.[67]

Some oracles were also used to assure the living of their personal safety:[68] on one occasion at Deir el-Medina, the oracle was asked for a statement and reassurance that the community's senior scribe, who was accompanying a military expedition to Nubia, would return safely.[69] Consultation with an oracle could also be used to authenticate amuletic rolls of spells which were produced to protect children against a variety of dangers.[70] These consisted of texts written on papyrus or metal, often worn around the neck, and sometimes enclosed in hollow cylindrical pendants. Couched in terms of decrees that had been issued by the oracle of one or more gods, they provided comprehensive protection for the wearer.[71]

Oracles were just one method of seeking divine intervention in human lives, but they covered a wide variety of subject matter, ranging from the king's request for divine approval for a military campaign to questions posed by people about their everyday choices and problems. They were regarded as the most practical method of obtaining answers about the future, but they had their own limitations, and other means of divination were also sought.

Seers and Dreams

In the Deir el-Medina texts, there are references to 'wise-women' and the role they played in predicting future events and their causation. It has been suggested that such seers may have been a regular aspect of practical religion in the New Kingdom and possibly even in earlier times.[72]

Sometimes dreams could give access to otherwise hidden agencies such as the dead or the gods, who might be available to offer help or advice. Dreams which gave advance notice of auspicious or inauspicious events would require further interpretation by specialists in this subject. The most important compilation of dreams from ancient Egypt is accredited to Hor of Sebennytos.[73] Extant texts provide evidence of attempts to send dreams or to prevent their outcome; there are also books written in hieratic and demotic (the cursive scripts developed from hieroglyphs) which provided the basis of dream interpretation.

Some temples were renowned as centres of dream incubation where the petitioner could pass the night in a special building, and communicate with the gods or deceased relatives in order to gain insight into the future. The most famous example is the Sanatorium attached to the Temple of Hathor at Denderah, but other centres existed in much earlier times such as the one attested in a Ramesside copy of a Middle Kingdom Dream Book which was owned by a man called Qenherkhepshef. The institutionalized type of organization which existed at Denerah may have provided a method of dream interpretation which was only common in the later periods, and earlier practices may have been less formal.

Generally, the dream state was believed to convey the sleeper into the next world, the realm of the gods. However, 'dreams' were not regarded simply as night-time events; the term also included daytime 'visions' in which the god was revealed and took action in relation to the human 'visionary'.

Letters to the Dead

An important means of contact with those who had passed into the next world was provided by the so-called 'Letters to the Dead'. People who considered that they had suffered injustice could write a letter to the dead, asking them to intercede on the writer's behalf. If a living person with problems had no powerful patron in this world, he could seek the help of the dead. However, relatively few of these letters have survived (less than twenty from a period of about a thousand years),[74] although it is possible that these are drawn only from the small section of society that was literate. There may have been a much wider oral tradition to convey the same sentiments verbally to the dead.[75]

The letters were placed in the tomb-chapel, at the side of the offering table where the deceased's spirit would find them when it came to partake of food. Requests found in the letters are varied: some sought help against dead or living enemies, particularly in family disputes; others asked for legal assistance in support of a petitioner who had to appear before the divine tribunal at the Day of Judgement; and some pleaded for special blessings or benefits.[76]

Therefore, popular religion was expressed in a variety of ways which might include the presentation of offerings to the gods, intercession, pleas for help, and methods of divination. However, whereas a wealth of evidence relating to state religion has survived, relatively little information is available for the study of popular beliefs and practices. For example, whereas many aspects of the organization of the temple priesthood can be reconstructed, it is more difficult to determine how the shrines and chapels of the popular gods were manned. However, evidence at Deir el-Medina indicates that religious fraternities, consisting of lay officials, probably organized themselves to oversee and maintain these small buildings.[77]

Again, although it is known that votive offerings (personal gifts) were made to the gods in the hope of securing their favours, evidence about this practice is sparse. As well as these divine offerings, on special occasions such as a child's birthday or a religious festival, it was the custom for people at Deir el-Medina to present each other with small quantities of food and gifts of everyday use.[78] The role played by religion in motivating gift-giving amongst the populace, and the major impact the temple economy had upon society, are subjects worthy of further study.

The evidence for popular religion is therefore sparse and historically uneven, but it has been shown[79] that this form of worship was not restricted to the poor. The highest-ranking officials as well as the peasantry used the same 'mechanisms' to approach and gain responses from their personal gods. As always, the Egyptians welcomed a diversified approach, and made use of all available means of attaining their religious goals.

THE ROLE OF MAGIC

Funerary magic, ritual magic performed in the temples, and everyday magic enacted to help individual petitioners were all interelated and widely practised in ancient Egypt. According to Egyptian belief, the divine creative word and magical energy could be used to turn concepts into reality. It was magic that had made creation possible and allowed the universe to be maintained.[80] The continued struggle against chaos, waged by the gods in the sky and the underworld and the king on earth, was always successful because magic could be used to fight all enemies. Magic was actually only available to the gods, but as divine agent on earth, the king had this force at his disposal, and by means of rituals, he could impose his will on distant situations and events. Temples, through their rituals, were the centres where the state magic was performed.

According to the Instruction to Merikare, magic had been given by the gods to mankind as a means of self-defence,[81] and this could be exercised by the king or by magicians who effectively took on the role of the gods. The Egyptian word *heka*, which we translate as 'magic', was one of the forces which the creator-god had used in order to bring the world into existence. Creation was a development of the spoken word, and magic was the principle through which a spoken command was turned into reality, but magic could be achieved through acts and gestures as well as speech.[82]

Magic was a potent force – it has been described as the 'nuclear energy of early civilizations'[83] – but it could also be exploited by mankind to produce evil results. For example, men could use it to threaten the gods, as in the Pyramid Texts, and they had the power to act independently of the gods, or even against the divine will. However, ultimately, the divine will would prevail because it alone could achieve lasting results. Although magic was such a powerful force which had precedence and influence over other forces of nature and all created forms, it was itself subordinate to the creator deity who brought magic into existence with his first utterance. Nevertheless, in human hands, magic could sometimes be perverted and used for evil purposes which were the antithesis of the divine will.

Because of the relative quantity of available source material, there is a tendency to identify the Ramesside and later periods as the time when magic was most widely used. However, the evidence actually indicates that magic continued for some four and a half thousand years: for example, amulets can be dated as early as the fourth millennium BCE and magical texts existed from the late third millennium BCE down to the fifth century ACE.[84] There is ample evidence that magic played an important and integral part in Egyptian belief from earliest times, and that the later periods did not represent a decline into superstitious practices after an era of 'rational' belief and worship.

Two particularly interesting Middle Kingdom examples which relate to the practice of magic were discovered by Flinders Petrie. Excavation of the precinct of the Ramesseum at Thebes revealed a very important tomb-group which probably once belonged to a lector-priest of Dynasty 12.[85] Lector-priests, literate members of the upper classes, were regarded as the principal magicians of ancient Egypt.

In this tomb shaft, as part of the initial burial (the main contents of the tomb were robbed in antiquity, and the tomb was re-used in Dynasty 22), Petrie found a set of papyri inside a wooden box, and a collection of magical objects. These fragile papyri were inscribed in hieratic with Instruction Texts, hymns, royal rituals, and magical and medical texts.

They were probably the priest's own books, interred with him for use in the next world.

Other items[86] included a bundle of pens; parts of four ivory magical clappers inscribed with mythical creatures; a bronze snake wand; green-glazed figurines of baboons and a cat; a selection of beads including amethyst, agate, hematite, and carnelian; four fertility figurines in wood and stone; palm seeds; a blue glaze cup; an ivory handle with two lions engraved on it; and various ivory and other fragments whose use cannot be determined. However, the most impressive item was a wooden statuette of a woman in a Bes-mask, holding a bronze serpent in each hand. It has been suggested[87] that the magic wand, baboon and lion figurines, and ivory clappers represent the protective spirits that the magician would invoke, and that the fertility figurines symbolized either the religious dancers who assisted in this rite or the women who sought protection. The owner of this equipment was probably a man who may have been associated with the House of Nurses at a palace, or headed a dancing troupe of Hathor.[88]

The Ramesseum statuette is similar to another example discovered in a house at Kahun, in a hole in the floor of one of the rooms. This formed part of a group of magical implements which also included a pair of ivory clappers. Stolen in 1892 ACE, the figurine represented a dancer wearing a mask and a costume with a tail.[89] In the next room in the same house, Petrie discovered a full-sized canvas mask, made of three layers of canvas, and covered with stucco; it was painted black, and the nostrils and eyes were pierced to enable the wearer to breathe and see. The mask, which represented the deities Bes or Beset, had obvious signs of frequent wear and had been repaired in antiquity.

This group of magical items was probably used by a woman of lower status, to imitate the deity in protective rites which were carried out on behalf of ordinary women. A similar mask of Bes in moulded clay was also found at Deir el-Medina. Evidence to explain the role of these female magicians is sparse, but widespread magical protection of women and children of all classes probably existed, which attempted to combat the dangers which constantly surrounded childbirth and produced a high rate of infant mortality.

* *

From the late New Kingdom, the wealthy sometimes used magic indirectly to attempt to obtain immortality and personal prestige: as benefactors, they placed magical texts, in addition to or in place of biographical texts, on statues which were probably set up in the outer areas of temples.[90] These statues became integrated into the temple cult, and priests and visitors poured libations over them to ensure magical protection for the owner.[91]

Magic was thus widely used at all periods and at all levels of society: ordinary people wore amulets to ward off evil and they visited magicians to obtain the benefits of protective rites, while in the temples the priests employed their extensive knowledge of magic and special techniques to provide themselves with exclusive powers. In Egypt, the magician had great authority because he could declare that he would destroy the world if the result he desired did not come to pass. Thus, he was able to acquire an almost divine status.

MEDICAL AND LEGAL PRACTICE

Generally, people turned to magic when the more rational approaches and straightforward procedures were ineffective. This can be observed particularly in relation to medical practice[92] and the legal system.

Medical practice combined measures which were either objective and scientific (based on observation of the patient, knowledge of anatomy, and general experience of disease) or which relied on the use of magic. These processes often overlapped and were considered to be equally efficacious in healing the patient. Every disease was attributed to a specific cause. This might be an outward, visible cause where 'rational' remedies could be applied, or a hidden, inward cause (such as the ill wishes of the dead or an enemy, or the displeasure of the gods) where spells and incantations could be used to draw the 'devil' out of the patient. The healer would sometimes accompany these incantations with a ritual which involved carrying out a series of acts and gestures upon the patient or a substitute figurine.

Religious factors played an important part in the treatment of the sick and in diet and hygiene.[93] There were a number of deities who had responsibility for different aspects of disease and its treatment. One of the most important, the lioness Sekhmet, who was believed to bring epidemics and disease, was also worshipped to try to placate and persuade her to remove these terrors. She was the patron deity of doctors. Thoth, god of writing, was credited with the invention of the healing formulae; Isis, who had reassembled the scattered limbs of her murdered husband Osiris, was patroness of magicians; Amun and Horus presided over eye diseases; and Tauert protected women in childbirth. Imhotep, the architect of the Step Pyramid at Saqqara, was probably also the royal physician. As the Egyptians believed that he had great healing powers and was the founder of medical science, they deified him as a god of medicine. His cult survived for centuries in Egypt and the Greeks ultimately identified him with their own god of medicine, Aesculapius.

The Egyptian temple also played a major role in medicine. The earliest local chieftains who acted as community priests were believed to possess special powers; when the most powerful of these leaders eventually became king, the holder of this position was also credited with this ability, and he in turn delegated it to certain groups of priests. For part of each year, these men carried out their ritual and liturgical duties in the temple where they also headed the medical hierarchy and perhaps attended patients and trained students; for the remainder of the year, they pursued their medical profession in the community.

Egyptian doctors had high ethical standards and treated the sick in an enlightened and considerate manner: no patient was considered untouchable, whatever his disease, and doctors were prohibited from divulging patients' confidences. Some temples acquired reputations for medical healing: in Ptolemaic times, these included Denderah, Memphis and Deir el-Bahri,[94] but the role of the temple in healing probably goes back to early times. The 'House of Life' within the temple was a scriptorium where the sacred texts were composed and copied, but some may also have functioned as places where students received training and patients were examined.

The ten major medical papyri[95] are our most important source for information about symptoms, diagnosis and the treatment of a wide range of illnesses. In these documents, many of the prescriptions were given authority either by asserting the antiquity of the text or by attributing its authorship to gods, kings, High-priests or officials. Most extant papyri date from the Hyksos Period onwards, but many are probably copies of earlier works. Some seem to have been handbooks for doctors' daily use, some were perhaps outlines for medical lectures, while others were probably the lecture notes and clinical notebooks kept by students. Many other papyri may still await discovery, but the existing copies reveal that the structure of medicine in the Pharaonic Period was very complex, and that the proportion of 'rational' and 'magical' treatments varies considerably from one document to another.

In the legal system also, it is evident that the organization was governed by religious principles, although in comparison with some other ancient societies, Egyptian law has yielded relatively little evidence of its institutions. Law was believed to have been handed down from the gods to mankind at the time of creation, and the gods were responsible for maintaining the concept of law. Personified as Ma'at, the goddess of truth, justice, righteousness and the correct order and balance of the universe, the law stood above all humans.

Even the king, an absolute monarch who upheld the law and was theoretically the sole legislator with the power of life and death over his people, was also subject to the law. In reality, his freedom of choice in legal matters was very limited and was largely determined by established precedent. The king was the chief official of the judicial system; as his delegate, the vizier was the High-priest of Ma'at and head of the courts of justice, while legal practitioners held priesthoods of Ma'at.

Although the king theoretically controlled the life, death, labour and property of his subjects, there was a fully operational system of private law under which property could be the subject of private transactions. The earliest extant written references to such transactions occur in tomb and stelae inscriptions of Dynasty 3 and on papyri that date to Dynasty 6, but the legal system was clearly operational before this time, and may have originated in the first settlements of the Predynastic Period.

Because of the emphasis placed on funerary customs, many legal transactions are concerned with situations relating to funerary property. Special arrangements were made to ensure that the upkeep and pro-visioning of the tomb continued in perpetuity. These arrangements, known as 'ka-settlements', involved the appointment of a special priest, a 'ka-servant', who would undertake this duty in return for an income from the dead person's estate. In turn, this obligation and remuneration would pass to the ka-priest's descendants.

The legal system operated through the law courts, although some settlements were reached out of court. There were the local courts (Kenbet) where dignitaries sat under the chairmanship of an official and were permitted to deal with most cases; and the High Court which, in the New Kingdom, sat at Thebes under the presidency of the vizier, and exercised judgement over serious crimes, particularly those which involved capital punishment. The courts admitted and considered all kinds of evidence, which was weighed by the judges.

From the later New Kingdom (c.1250 BCE), a change was introduced which involved the use of an oracle.[96] The statue of a god became the judge, and his decision was ascertained through ceremonies performed in front of the statue. The enquirer (the professional scribe who looked after the administration in local courts) stood in front of the statue and read out the list of named suspects, and would then interpret the god's answer. This practice was clearly open to corruption and abuse, and marked a deterioration in the system.

Through acting as members of special courts associated with the temples, temple personnel played an important role in secular affairs, and considered cases relating to temple employees.[97] 'Curses' or 'imprecations', another aspect of legislation and jurisdiction,[98] were issued by tomb-owners against those who desecrated their tombs. This could be regarded as a form of 'sacred law' which employed 'metaphysical agents' rather than earthly punishments to ensure that the violator suffered for his crime.[99] Generally, punishments for all crimes were severe, supposedly designed to act as deterrents in an essentially law-abiding society.

Much of the documentary evidence that has survived relates to civil law – marriage, property and inheritance.[100] There have been studies of the ancient Egyptian attitude towards theft, corruption and sexuality and the information they provide about the moral codes of ancient Egypt;[101] sometimes, personal difficulties were attributed to the vengeance of gods who had been offended.[102]

TOMB ROBBERIES

A number of documents reveal interesting evidence about important trials in the later New Kingdom. The Conspiracy Papyri are the state records of trials relating to the reign of Ramesses III,[103] which perhaps were originally housed in the library of the temple of Medinet Habu. These trials were concerned with the attempted assassination of Ramesses III and a plot to place the son of a secondary wife on the throne. This conspiracy was supported by the women and some of the officials of an itinerant royal harem which accompanied the king as he travelled around the country. To achieve their end, the plotters apparently used magical spells and made waxen images which they intended to smuggle into the harem so that they could carry out magic rites on these images to bring about the king's demise. However, the plot was uncovered and the accused were brought to trial.

In the later years of Dynasty 20, there was a great deal of social unrest; this was marked by corruption, failing food supplies, industrial action by the royal workforce, and tomb robberies.[104] Several well-preserved documents (particularly the Amherst, Abbott and Mayer A papyri) provide details of the arrests and trials begun in Year 16 of Ramesses IX's reign, which continued for many years. Tomb robbery had always afflicted ancient Egypt, but it seems to have reached unprecedented levels at this time. Active measures were taken to bring the culprits to court, and the king himself inaugurated the state trials at which high officials were appointed as judges. The evidence revealed that, in a major robbery of royal and nobles' tombs which occurred in Ramesses IX's reign, the employees of various temples were implicated, as well as some of the royal necropolis workmen. A house-to-house search at Deir el-Medina enabled the authorities to recover goods stolen from the tombs. Although they may not have initiated the robberies, the royal workmen took a share of the treasure once the tombs were opened, and they may have advised the robbers about the well-concealed locations of the tombs.

No deterrent action was ever truly successful, however, because the tomb treasure would always provide a readily available resource which was increasingly tempting in times of great hardship and hunger. The temples were vulnerable as well as the tombs, as revealed by a papyrus of Year 19 of the reign of Ramesses IX which refers to thefts in the Temple of Amun at Karnak.[105] Generally, the late New Kingdom witnessed conditions which led to an accelerated decline in respect for religious and funerary property.

Kings and Priests: The Final Conflict

The Third Intermediate and Late Periods, 1085–332 BCE

THE THIRD INTERMEDIATE PERIOD: TANITES AND THEBANS (1085–668 BCE)

The 'Third Intermediate Period' is a term that is now applied to the timespan which includes Dynasty 21 to the end of Dynasty 25.' This transitional stage from the final glories of the New Kingdom to the end of pharaonic history was a time of gradual decline and disintegration, which to some extent reflects the First and Second Intermediate Periods. In the reign of Ramesses XI, the last ruler of Dynasty 20, the north and south areas of the country were divided, and the rivalry that had existed between the king and the priesthood of Amun since Dynasty 18 now became a political reality. In the earlier reign of Ramesses IX, Amen-hotep, High-priest of Amun at Thebes, acquired great personal power by gaining control of the god's wealth and estates; in two temple wall-scenes, he emphasized his status by ensuring that his figure was the same size as that of the king. Finally, his position became hereditary, thus confirming that, at Thebes, the power of the High-priests of Amun now equalled royal status in all but name.

In the reign of Ramesses XI, this arrangement was formalized when Herihor (originally an army general who, when he was also appointed as High-priest of Amun and Viceroy of Nubia, became the first commoner to combine great religious and military power) assumed unrivalled control at Thebes. He still owed nominal allegiance to his king who now resided in the north, where Smendes (a man of unknown origin) was appointed as the king's supreme executive, with a status parallel to that of Herihor. This political arrangement, whereby the country was effectively divided into two great provinces (with the boundary fixed at el-Hibeh) which were separately governed but still owed nominal allegiance to the king, remained in place for three hundred years.

When Ramesses XI died, his throne was inherited by Nesbenebded (Smendes), the governor of the northern province, who became the first king of Dynasty 21 and ruled the country from the new northern capital of Tanis. At the same time, Herihor's descendants formed a hereditary 'dynasty' of High-priests of Amun at Thebes, where they continued to rule the south, subject to the nominal kingship exercised in the north. They inherited the considerable political powers which Herihor had established. However, the two groups appear to have remained on good terms.

Pinudjem I, a High-priest at Thebes during the reign of Smendes, formalized an agreement with the king by which he recognized Smendes as the pharaoh, and Smendes accepted Pinudjem as the effective ruler of the south; they both agreed to mutual rights of succession at Tanis and Thebes. From this time onwards, marriage between the royal princesses and the Theban High-priests established that, through their mothers, all the High-priests of Amun were also descendants of the Tanite kings. This ensured that the fictional claim that the Theban High-priests were ruling the south subject to the royal line at Tanis did in fact become a dynastic reality. Towards the end of Dynasty 21, a son of the Theban High-priest Pinudjem II inherited the throne as King Psusennes II. He moved north to Tanis, and became ruler of the entire country, thus finally reuniting the concurrent lines of kings and

High-priests of Amun, and bringing the Theban theocracy to an end. As Psusennes II had no heir, the country then passed to his son-in-law, Shoshenk, the founder of Dynasty 22.

The City of Tanis

Ramesses XI was probably the last king to be buried in the Valley of the Kings at Thebes. His successors moved to a new city at Tanis in the Delta, which became the country's capital and main royal residence, although Memphis probably remained the administrative centre. Tanis has posed some interesting archaeological puzzles; it is also the site where the magnificent royal tombs and treasure, which rivalled the contents of Tutankhamun's burial, were uncovered by the French archaeologist Pierre Montet.[2] Tanis is the later Greek name for this site which the pharaohs of Dynasties 21 and 22 chose as their residence and place of burial; its ancient Egyptian name was Dja'net, and today it is known as Tell San el-Hagar.

Situated on the eastern bank of a subsidiary branch of the Nile, in the north-eastern part of the Delta, about 130 km north of Cairo, it still preserves its isolation – a factor which probably contributed to the security of its royal burials. Today, the main and most visible feature of the site is a large, rectangular mudbrick enclosure; inside this is another enclosure where the main Temple of Amun was discovered. This building was decorated with blocks, columns, obelisks and statues that represent a wide range of dates; some are inscribed with the names of rulers of the Old and Middle Kingdoms, although most carry texts associated with the reign of Ramesses II. Archaeologists who have worked at the site have included Mariette, Petrie[3] and Montet.

Tanis began to decline during the Roman Period, but the most important historical questions relate to the city's origin. Since so many of the inscribed objects in the temple area are associated with Ramesses II, Egyptologists have speculated that Tanis may have been the site of Pi-Ramesse, an important Ramesside city. However, it has also been proposed that perhaps Tanis was the earlier Hyksos capital of Avaris,[4] but it is now generally accepted that Tanis was probably established as a new city in Dynasty 20, and had no direct connection with either

Pi-Ramesse or Avaris. The Ramesside and earlier pieces found there were probably examples of re-used material that had been removed from other sites. This was a common practice, and the masons would either incorporate the blocks in the new construction or use particularly fine pieces to adorn the buildings as 'works of art'.

As well as the main temple to Amun (the chief god of the Tanite rulers), there were other temples and chapels built at different periods. An important temple precinct to Amun's consort, Anta (Mut), also occupied the central area. Indeed, to date, most excavation has focussed on this district, which once accommodated the major temples, but most of this extensive city (which represents two thousand years of urban occupation) still awaits rediscovery.

The Tanis Treasure[5]

The royal tombs of Dynasties 21 and 22 were also located within this central area. Situated inside the inner enclosure wall, near the southwest corner of the great temple, they were first revealed by Montet in 1939 ACE when he was exploring this area. Instead of building the royal cemetery away from the city in the usual manner, it was evidently the custom at Tanis to locate the burials centrally, in order to provide them with additional protection. Over a period of several years, Montet discovered six tombs here that contained royal and non-royal burials. Constructed underground, each tomb consisted of several chambers built of limestone, granite or mudbrick, and in some, there were reliefs and inscriptions on the walls. No superstructures, where the dead rulers would have received their cults, have been discovered (the tombs have to be entered down shafts), although these may have originally existed but were later dismantled and removed.

The necropolis occupied a very limited area and some tombs were used for more than one burial. These royal burials are the only examples (apart from Tutankhamun's tomb) that have been found intact, and their magnificent treasure, which includes silver coffins, gold face masks, fine jewellery, vases and vessels, demonstrates the standards of wealth and excellence of craftsmanship which existed even in this period of decline. Egyptologists have speculated[6] that, as a result of the division of the country between kings and priests of Amun during Dynasty 21, the divinity of the kingship reached its lowest ebb at this time, but the contents of the Tanis tombs indicate that these kings still commanded great wealth and respect.

In these burials, it is the climatic and environmental conditions of the Delta, rather than tomb robbers, that have depleted the funerary goods. Although objects in stone, faience and metal have survived, organic materials such as wood, cloth, leather, and foodstuffs have disappeared as a result of high humidity levels. In addition, by the time the tombs were excavated, the mummies had deteriorated into a skeletal state, and could not be preserved. However, the existing treasure includes precious vessels and vases, used for cultic and other purposes; articles originally placed on the bodies; canopic jars and magnificent coffins; and the exquisite jewellery found on the decomposed mummies.

Although made for the burials by contemporary jewellers in Egypt, some of these pieces include precious items such as beads, which had either belonged to earlier kings or, in some cases, had been brought to Egypt from Mesopotamia. These were probably intended to emphasize the Tanite rulers' legitimacy as heirs of a long royal tradition and to boost the status of this dynasty which, since it had only recently been established, was politically insecure. A key feature of the treasure was the series of four funerary masks which belonged to three kings and an army general; these are unequalled, and compare favourably in terms of design and craftsmanship with the earlier, single example found on Tutankhamun's mummy.

The Royal Mummies

During Dynasty 21, the High-priests of Amun at Thebes undertook a programme of rescue and reburial of some of the royal mummies that had been buried at Thebes from Dynasty 17 to Dynasty 20.[7] Tomb robbers had plundered and desecrated the original burials and so, by removing and reinterring the mummies and coffins, the priests now hoped to provide the owners with another chance of eternity. Two caches of royal mummies have been discovered to date. The first was uncovered in 1881 ACE by Ahmed Abd er-Rasul from the nearby village of Qurna, who stumbled across this find while searching for a goat. These mummies had been placed in a tomb belonging to Queen Inha'pi which lay to the south of the Deir el-Bahri temples on the Theban west bank, and later, necropolis officials added mummies of priests and other royal members to this group.

This discovery provided Abd er-Rasul's family with a ready supply of funerary artifacts which they could sell to the dealers and tourists who now flocked to nearby Luxor. However, the royal inscriptions on these objects soon captured the attention of Gaston Maspero, Director of the Egyptian Antiquities Service, who investigated the matter further and ultimately removed the mummies to the Cairo Museum. Subsequently, in 1898 ACE, a second royal cache was discovered by the archaeologist Loret. These mummies, which had been reburied in the tomb of Amenhotep II in the Valley of the Kings at Thebes, were also taken to the Cairo Museum in 1901 ACE.

In addition to the royal mummies, important priests' burials were also found. In 1891 ACE, the Qurna villagers who had revealed the first royal cache now identified another tomb, to the north of the temple at Deir el-Bahri. Here, Daressy, who excavated the site for the Antiquities Service, discovered funerary goods − coffins, statuettes, *ushabtis* and other items − which had once belonged to the family of the High-priest Menkheperre and the priests of Amun. The inscribed material and the human remains from these burials have provided invaluable information about the history of this period, and the process of mummification during the New Kingdom.

Although the royal mummies represent only one social class who lived during a specific historical period, they nevertheless provide the basis for our knowledge of mummification and supply ample evidence about funerary customs. In addition to this, such mummies have become an invaluable resource for studying diet and disease patterns. The royal mummies were systematically unwrapped and partly autopsied in Cairo by the Australian anatomist and anthropologist, Grafton Elliot Smith, who was Professor of Anatomy in the Cairo School of Medicine (1900−1909 ACE).[8] During his time in Egypt, he had the opportunity to examine human skeletal and mummified remains from many sites, including a survey he undertook with F. Wood Jones of the bodies

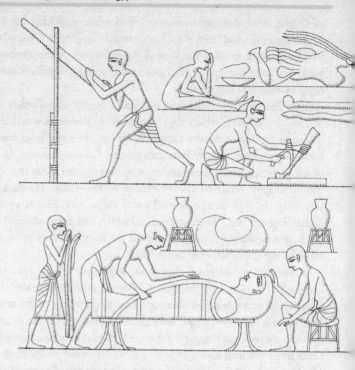

discovered during the Archaeological Survey of Nubia.[9] This general background of experience and knowledge, together with his detailed examination of the royal mummies, enabled him to produce a definitive account of the techniques used in mummification.[10]

Mummification

Today, the term 'mummy' is used to describe a naturally or artificially preserved body in which desiccation of the tissues has enabled it to resist putrefaction. Examples occur in a number of countries worldwide. Originally, however, the word 'mummy' (which is derived from the Persian or Arabic word *mumia* which means 'pitch' or 'bitumen') was used only to describe the artificially preserved bodies of the ancient Egyptians.

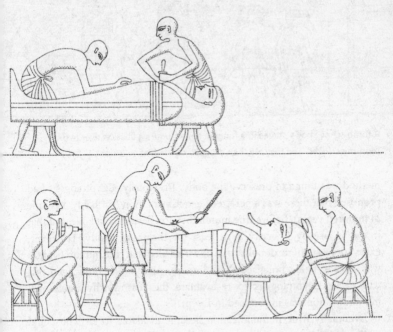

A tomb scene shows a workshop where men bandage mummies and make coffins.

In the Predynastic Period, the bodies were naturally or unintentionally preserved because the heat and dryness of the environment in the shallow pit-graves in the sand had the effect of desiccating the body. When the mastaba-tombs were introduced in *c*.3400 BCE for the ruling class, the body was placed in a brick-lined burial chamber where it rapidly decomposed. It was this architectural development which, until recently, Egyptologists regarded as the causative factor in the development of an intentional method of preserving the body ('true mummification'). The Egyptians had already evolved a concept of the afterlife in which a person's *ka* (spirit) passed into the next world, but then returned regularly to the tomb to partake of the food offerings; in order to obtain this sustenance, the spirit needed to be able to recognize and use the body of its owner, and it was therefore essential that a new

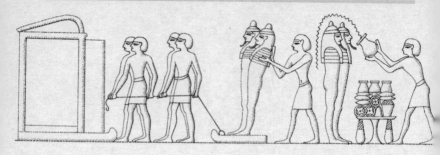

A tomb scene shows stages in a funeral: a man pours a libation over two mummies (*right*) and they are then dragged on sledges to a kiosk (*left*).

method was found to preserve the body. Previously, Egyptologists had proposed that there was a period of experimentation (probably a couple of hundred years), before true mummification became available, but that it was in use by Dynasty 4, at least for the royal family. However, excavations at Hieraconpolis have now revealed that true mummification was already being practised there in early predynastic times, and this will cause Egyptologists to re-evaluate the reason why intentional mummification was introduced in Egypt.

Eventually, true mummification became available to all who could afford it, but it was never practised universally: ordinary people continued to be buried in shallow desert graves where their bodies were naturally preserved. Nevertheless, mummification became quite widespread in the Graeco-Roman Period in particular when many more people were able to afford it. Even in the Christian era, it survived as an important funerary custom.

There is no extant Egyptian literary account of the techniques involved, but the earliest detailed descriptions have survived in the writings of Classical authors. The Greek historians Herodotus[11] (fifth century BCE), and Diodorus Siculus (first century BCE) provide many details, although their accounts were based on hearsay and written down centuries after the process had reached its zenith. Nevertheless, together with the physical evidence provided by the mummies, there is sufficient information to determine and describe the main stages of mummification.[12]

Herodotus states that three main methods were available according

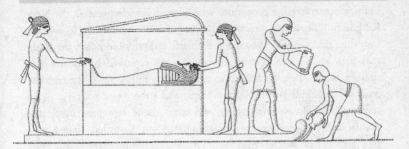

A tomb scene shows funerary preparations: men pour milk in front of a sledge that transports the owner's mummy on a bier, accompanied by two attendants.

to cost. The most expensive and elaborate method can perhaps be described as 'classic' mummification. The two main processes were (1) evisceration of the body, and (2) dehydration of the bodily tissues by means of a chemical agent, natron.[3] This is a natural deposit that occurs in a desert valley known today as the Wadi en-Natrun; it contains sodium carbonate and bicarbonate, and sometimes includes small amounts of sodium chloride and sulphate. In addition, the body was often anointed with oils, unguents and resins, but these were only cosmetic treatments: the basic and effective procedure always remained evisceration and dehydration of the body.

Evisceration involved making an incision in the abdominal left flank through which the viscera (except the heart and the kidneys) were removed from the thoracic and abdominal cavities. Sometimes, however, evisceration was not performed, or in some instances, the viscera were removed through the anus. The viscera were dehydrated by means of natron and, ultimately, either reinserted as packages inside the body cavities, or placed as a large packet on the legs of the mummy, or stored in canopic jars that formed part of the tomb equipment.

The body was then dehydrated by placing it in dry natron. The actual process probably lasted for a period of up to forty days; it is likely that the timespan of seventy days which Herodotus gives for the procedure included the associated religious rites. During its long history, there were only two major developments in the technique of Egyptian mummification. From the Middle Kingdom (c.1900 BCE) or earlier, the brain was extracted, a procedure which became widespread in the New Kingdom.[14] The usual practice involved the insertion of an iron hook into the cranial cavity through the nostril and ethmoid bone; the brain was then reduced to fragments, which were removed by means of a spatula. Sometimes, the brain was extracted by intervention through the base of the skull or through a trepanned orbit (eye socket). Brain removal was always incomplete and some tissue remained inside the cranial cavity. However, the extracted tissue was discarded, since Egyptians attached no special religious or ethical significance to the brain. They believed that the heart was the seat of the personality and the locus of the intellect and emotions, so this organ was left *in situ* in the body.

The second innovation was based on experiments first introduced in Dynasty 18 (1567–1320 BCE), which involved the subcutaneous packing of the body with linen, sawdust, earth, sand or butter through incisions made in the surface of the skin on the face, neck and elsewhere. The aim was to make the mummy appear more lifelike and to restore the shrunken body to some semblance of its plumper, original form. This method, apparently first employed for the mummy of Amenhotep III who ruled in Dynasty 18, was probably an attempt to restore his rounded bodily contours so that his spirit could recognize his mummy more easily.

The practice then lapsed but was reintroduced in Dynasty 21 (c. 1089–945 BCE) for all those who could afford the procedure. This was the period when mummification reached the zenith of technical skill: the embalmers sought to simulate the appearance of the living person as closely as possible, and in addition to subcutaneous packing of the face and neck, artificial eyes were often inserted into the eye sockets, and the natural hair was augmented by adding false locks. Also, the face or even the whole body was painted: yellow ochre was used for women and red ochre for men because, when they were alive, men had a darker complexion than women because they spent more time out of doors. However, after the Third Intermediate Period, mummification techniques declined, and by the Graeco-Roman Period, standards had deteriorated even further.

Although there were some changes and developments in this procedure over three thousand years, the basic principles of arresting bodily

A wooden coffin, of the transitional type between basket coffins or animals skins and body coffins, which represented a dwelling-place for the dead. From Tarkhan (*c*.2500 BCE).

A reed coffin – the type generally used for burials of the lower classes – containing the naturally preserved body of a baby. From Gurob (*c.*1450 BCE).

Body coffins from the Tomb of Two Brothers (Rifeh, c.1900 BCE). These stylized representations of the brothers are mummiform and carry vertical inscriptions that list food and other offerings for the deceased.

A mummy of a child, with a gilded cartonnage head and chest cover. It features inlaid stone eyes and moulded imitation jewellery set with glass. From Hawara (second century ACE).

A mummy of a young man (from Hawara, first century BCE). It incorporates elaborate geometrically patterned bandaging, and a panel portrait that probably represents a likeness of the owner.

A wooden statue of the god Osiris which would have received prayers and offerings. From Saqqara (c.380–343 BCE).

Left: A linen and stucco cover from the mummy of a child (early second century ACE).

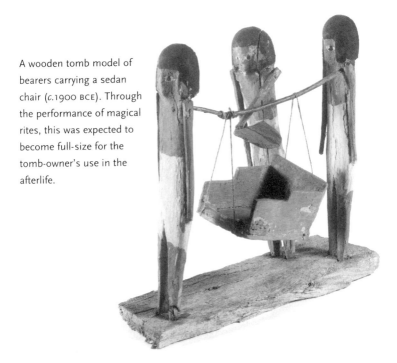

A wooden tomb model of bearers carrying a sedan chair (c.1900 BCE). Through the performance of magical rites, this was expected to become full-size for the tomb-owner's use in the afterlife.

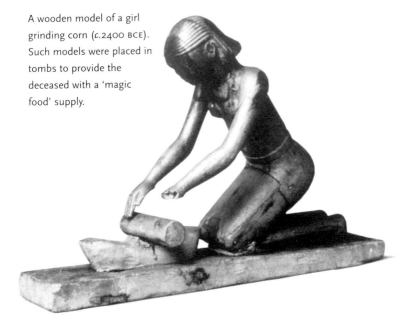

A wooden model of a girl grinding corn (c.2400 BCE). Such models were placed in tombs to provide the deceased with a 'magic food' supply.

A wooden boat model (*c.*1900 BCE) shows the owner's mummy accompanied by mourners and sailors; this was placed in the tomb for the deceased's journey to the sacred city of Abydos.

A wooden cat-shaped coffin (*c.*900 BCE) containing a mummified cat. This illustrates one aspect of the animal cults that flourished in ancient Egypt.

A stone *ushabti* belonging to Met-Mehy, Governor of the Southern Oasis (*c.*1350 BCE). *Ushabtis* were placed in the tomb to perform agricultural tasks in the afterlife for the deceased owner.

A painted wooden stela from a tomb (*c.*1450 BCE) shows the goddesses Isis (*left*) and Nephthys (*right*) worshipping the *Djed*-pillar which symbolized Isis' husband, Osiris.

Opposite: A wooden face from a coffin. The facial features were stylized and did not attempt to reproduce a person's individual appearance.

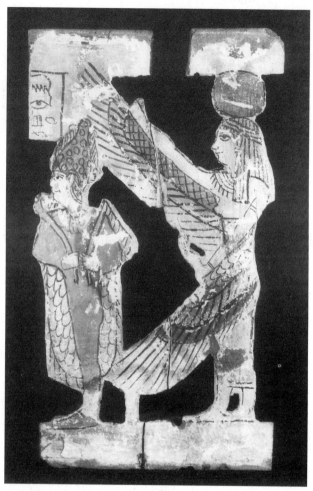

Painted wooden figurines of the god Osiris (*left*) and his wife Isis who protects him with her outstretched wings (*c.*600 BCE).

Opposite: A gilded cartonnage mask from a mummy that includes the representation of a feathered headdress and a bead collar. Ptolemaic Period (*c.*300 BCE).

A cartonnage head-piece from a mummy. It has a
gilded face and painted decoration which includes
a row of gods on the lappets of the headdress.
Ptolemaic Period (*c.*300 BCE).

A good example of realistic portraiture, this panel was placed over the face of a mummy. It probably represents a fairly accurate likeness of the owner. From Hawara (c.200 BCE).

A plaster head that was originally part of a mummy. From the cemetery at Mallawi, a Roman garrison town (second century ACE).

decomposition through evisceration and dehydration of the tissues remained the same. Today, palaeopathology (the study of disease in ancient populations) has opened up the possibility of detecting the existence and development of diseases in ancient Egypt. Unlike many early populations where only the skeletal remains have survived, in Egyptian mummies, the body tissues are also available for biomedical studies.[15] In addition, it is now possible to identify DNA in mummified remains, providing the opportunity to investigate familial relationships and population movements.

THE BUBASTITES[16]

The Bubastite Period consisted of Dynasties 22 (945–730 BCE) and 23 (c.818–715 BCE). Shoshenk I, the son-in-law of Psusennes II (the last ruler of Dynasty 21), inaugurated Dynasty 22, which is also known as the Libyan or Bubastite Dynasty. Previously, he had been the Chief and army commander of the descendants of the Meshwesh,[17] a Libyan group who fought against Merneptah and Ramesses III. Captured by the Egyptians, these people subsequently established themselves in the Delta and even served in the Egyptian army. Their numbers increased, and eventually they became totally integrated in the Egyptian system.

Shoshenk's marriage into the royal line, and his subsequent rulership of Egypt, were accepted throughout the country. The family centre of these rulers was the Delta city of Bubastis, and either this or nearby Tanis became their capital. In the south, the Theban High-priests continued to exercise considerable power, but the Bubastite rulers used royal appointments and marriage alliances to unify the north and south.

Shoshenk I was an able ruler: he made additions to the great temple at Tanis, and built the forecourt and gateway (the 'Bubastite Portal') at Karnak, between the Second Pylon and a small temple of Ramesses II. Here, scenes and inscriptions commemorated his campaigns in Palestine, and there is a partially destroyed list which gives the names of towns in Edom, Judah and Israel. Later rulers of this dynasty, however, were unable to sustain Shoshenk I's success, although the Tanis treasure indicates that well-equipped royal burials continued to be prepared. However, eventually it became impossible to hold the kingdom together, and the kings of Dynasty 23, centred at Leontopolis, probably ruled contemporaneously with Dynasty 22. Indeed, there were probably a number of semi-independent princelings (the descendants of Libyan chiefs) in the Delta, as well as other rulers in Upper Egypt. Dynasty 24 included a ruler named Bochchoris who ruled from Sais in the Delta and was captured and burnt alive by the Ethiopian ruler Sabacon (Shabaka) who inaugurated Dynasty 25.

THE ETHIOPIAN DYNASTY[18]

The rulers of Dynasty 25 (the so-called 'Ethiopian Dynasty') were foreigners who came from the south, where a substantial kingdom, whose capital city was situated at Napata, had developed. The culture that emerged here included many features characteristic of Egypt in Dynasty 18, including the worship of Amen-Re.[19] Although the Egyptians themselves had long since abandoned the custom of burying their kings in pyramids, the Napatans followed this practice, and major burial sites have been discovered and excavated.[20]

The Napatan ruler Piankhy initially marched north to stop the advance southwards of Tefnakht, a prince of Sais; Piankhy probably also wished to stabilize Thebes which was the centre of his own god, Amen-Re. This great campaign, recorded on a large stela which dates to Year 21 of his reign (c.730 BCE), was very successful; Piankhy captured cities and slaughtered many prisoners, before finally returning to his Napatan kingdom. However, it was his brother, Shabaka, who made himself ruler of the whole of Egypt. Succeeding Piankhy on the Napatan throne, he led a new campaign to Egypt, killed Bochchoris (Tefnakht's successor at Sais), and established the Egyptian Dynasty 25. As the first Nubian pharaoh, he briefly reversed the long tradition of Egyptian colonization of the south. He established his capital at Thebes, but ultimately returned south to be buried in a pyramid at Kurru.[21]

This dynasty was eventually driven out of Egypt by a new power – the Assyrians – who began to establish a great empire from their northern homeland. These people, with their formidable military force, advanced weapons, and compulsory military service, developed a new kind of empire. Unlike previous empires, which had consisted of semi-independent client-states, the Assyrian empire was constituted as one nation. The Assyrians were drawn into conflict with Egypt when their vassal-states in Syria/Palestine appealed to Egypt for help, and the Assyrian king Sennacherib met and defeated the Egyptian forces at el-Tekeh in 701 BCE.

Taharka, one of the most able kings of Dynasty 25, was crowned at Memphis, and undertook major building works throughout the kingdom, including the construction of a colonnade in the Bubastite forecourt at the Temple of Karnak. However, his policy of interference in Assyria's vassal-states again led to conflict with Esarhaddon, Sennacherib's successor, who successfully invaded Egypt and besieged and destroyed Memphis in 671 BCE. Taharka was driven back to the Napatan kingdom, and Esarhaddon replaced native rulers, governors and officials with new, local, pro-Assyrian men. One of these, Necho of Sais, managed to extend his influence throughout the western Delta, establishing a substantial kingdom and even adopting the pharaonic style in his own title. Esarhaddon confirmed him as a local ruler at Sais from 671 BCE, and his son, Psammetichus, eventually founded Dynasty 26.

Due to Esarhaddon's death, which occurred when he was en route from Assyria to Egypt to resolve further conflict, Taharka was able to briefly re-establish his rulership at Memphis, but he was soon driven out again (667/666 BCE) by the next Assyrian ruler, Ashurbanipal. He fled to Napata, where he finally died and was buried in a pyramid at Nuri. Although his successors continued the conflict against Assyria, they were also defeated and eventually returned south to Napata. The Assyrians themselves now faced a new threat from an alliance of the Medes who lived in northwest Iran and the Babylonians, and eventually their empire was overthrown by the Babylonian ruler Nabopolassar.

Far to the south, the 'Ethiopians' now developed an independent kingdom beyond the Third Cataract on the Nile, moving their capital from Napata to Meroë (hence the use of the term 'Meroïtic' for this society and culture). Here, their civilization developed in virtual isolation, retaining many features of Egyptian origin such as temples, religious practices and art styles. In the royal cemetery at Meroë, the rulers continued to be buried in pyramids from the third century BCE down to the fourth century ACE when King Aeizanes, ruler of the Ethiopian kingdom of Axum, finally destroyed Meroë.

God's Wife of Amun

The title and role of the 'God's Wife of Amun' became very important in the later pharaonic period. In the Old Kingdom, royal women were often priestesses of Hathor, and they were always significant as the feminine aspects of the creator.[22] The chief queen represented the main god's consort when she accompanied the king in various rituals and temple ceremonies. This role changed from one dynasty to another, according to which god was the supreme state god at any one time; for example, in the New Kingdom, when Amun was pre-eminent as the 'King of Gods', the chief queen would have enacted the role of his wife, the goddess Mut. Recently, however, the significance of the title *ḥmt-nṯr* (God's Wife) in terms of its cultic and dynastic associations has been reconsidered,[23] and an earlier suggestion that the bearer of this title was always the mother of the royal son and heir has been particularly discounted by one Egyptologist.[24] The argument is put forward that, because of a high infant mortality, the identity of the next 'king's mother' would have remained uncertain until the prince had actually ascended to the throne.

In Dynasty 21, however, the title came to have a different use and significance when it was transferred to the king's daughter who now became the wife of the chief state god, Amen-Re of Thebes. By Dynasty 25, the title was given a further political dimension when an adoption procedure was introduced whereby the royal daughter and God's Wife of Amun (daughter of the ruling king) adopted, as her successor, the daughter of the next king. The position of God's Wife of Amun now provided the kings with a tool of great political importance, and enabled them to retain direct control of Thebes through the status of their own daughters.

Although, politically, it was expected that the king's eldest daughter would marry in order to produce the next royal heir, as the consecrated wife of Amun, the princess could not take a human husband; she and her court of female attendants (regarded as Amun's concubines) had to obey the rule of chastity. This prevented any other man from seizing political power at Thebes by marrying the God's Wife, and thus rivalling the power of the king. Such measures ensured that the division which, in Dynasty 21, had occurred between the royal court and the Theban priesthood would not be repeated. As the God's Wife could not marry, the succession at Thebes was ensured by her adoption of the woman chosen by the next king (customarily his own daughter) as her heiress. Similarly, the women of the court of the God's Wife were celibate, and were therefore also expected to adopt their successors.

In 1904 ACE, in a cachette at Karnak, a statue was discovered of Ankhnesneferibre, daughter of Psammetichus II, together with a stela which records her adoption as 'heiress' by Nitocris, daughter of Psammetichus I; it also describes her enthronement as God's Wife of Amun.[25] This occasion in Dynasty 26, apparently marked by great national rejoicing, was the first investiture of a God's Wife for fifty years. As the only source that provides an extant account of the associated rituals, the inscription describes how Nitocris greeted the heiress and took her to the temple where her newly acquired titles were approved by the oracle of Amun. Subsequently, the god's statue was brought out into the temple forecourt to provide semi-public confirmation of this event.

The God's Wife had extensive power and wealth: at Thebes (where she was expected to reside and eventually die), she owned great endowments and possessions which equalled those of her royal father in many aspects, except that her influence was strictly limited to the city of Thebes and its vicinity. She was responsible for a substantial residence and household at Thebes, which consisted of the celibate devotees of Amun. She also enacted the functions which had previously been performed by the male 'First Prophet' of Amun. Ankhnesneferibre was the first woman known to have held the title of 'First Prophet', indicating that there was a significant transfer of the priests' powers to the God's Wife and her retinue. The redefined role of God's Wife in these later dynasties continued for many years, and successfully prevented male rivals from seizing power at Thebes and threatening the king's own supremacy.

THE LATE PERIOD: THE SAITE AND PERSIAN DYNASTIES (664–332 BCE)

The Saite Period

In Dynasty 26, there was a brief revival of Egyptian nationalism, which replaced the marked decline of the previous five dynasties when the kings had often ruled over a divided country at home and lost their claim of supremacy abroad. Prince Necho of Sais had developed the political opportunities which were afforded to him by the Assyrian rulers, and this prepared the way for his son, Psammetichus I, to establish the independent, native Dynasty 26. His daughter, Nitocris, was adopted as heiress by the God's Wife of Amun, thus ensuring the king's control over Thebes.

During this dynasty, there was a deliberate attempt to emphasize traditional Egyptian concepts such as animal worship. There is also strong evidence of 'archaism' which was expressed as an interest in archaeology and a conscious attempt to reproduce the dress, art, religion and writing of earlier times. For example, ancient titles of the nobility were revived, and Old Kingdom sculptures and reliefs were copied; in the tombs, the Pyramid Texts were inscribed on the walls, and once again, canopic jars were used to contain mummified viscera. Generally, the arts and crafts flourished, and this is particularly evident in the production of fine examples of ushabtis.

Archaism in art and religion and the nostalgia for traditional concepts were perhaps a reaction against the large influx of foreigners who now entered the country. The dynasty had been successfully established because of the military support provided by Greek mercenaries, and the Saite rulers continued to welcome the assistance of foreigners in pursuing both political and military aims, and economic development. Nevertheless, despite this external aid, the dynasty finally collapsed when the country was invaded in 525 BCE by Cambyses, King of Persia, who subsequently incorporated Egypt into the Persian Empire.

Egypt under Persian Rule[26]

An Aryan dynasty of Achaemenid rulers, which had arisen along the eastern side of the Persian Gulf under their new King Cyrus II (558–529 BCE), now set out to conquer the surrounding lands. By the time that Cyrus II died, they had established the greatest empire the world had yet seen. This vast empire was possible to manage effectively because it was organized into a number of satrapies (political divisions of land), which were each under the control of a satrap (governor) who was directly responsible to the king. However, the Persians realized that, if they wished to dominate the east, it was essential to secure the Egyptian ports and prevent Egypt from interfering in their foreign policy, and so they set out to conquer the country.

Cyrus II entrusted his son, Cambyses, with this task and, during the first period of Persian rule (Dynasty 27), Egypt was ruled by eight Persian kings. To some extent, the Persian rulers identified themselves with the Egyptian pharaoh, thus gaining some popular acceptance, and they also appear to have supported some Egyptian religious traditions, although there is conflicting evidence about this. For example, Herodotus claimed that Cambyses neglected his duties to the gods, and killed one of the sacred Apis bulls worshipped at Saqqara, but a dedicatory inscription attributed to Cambyses, which appears on the sarcophagus of one of the bulls in the Serapeum at Saqqara, suggests that he promoted the cult. Again, there are Classical accounts which stress his impiety to the gods, but these were probably generated by hostile propaganda put out by the priests because of certain fiscal restrictions he imposed[27]. In contrast, however, it was recorded that Darius I (King of Persia, 521–486 BCE) made additions to the Egyptian temples and performed his duties as a pharaoh.

When this first period of Persian domination ended in 401 BCE, the Egyptians briefly regained their independence, and their kings ruled from Sais (Dynasty 28), Mendes (Dynasty 29), and Sebennytos (Dynasty 30). A ruler of Dynasty 30, Nectanebo I, pursued an extensive building programme, including work at Karnak and the Temple of Hathor at Denderah. However, under his descendants, the Persians again briefly seized control of Egypt (Dynasty 31, 343–332 BCE).

SOURCES OF EVIDENCE FOR LATER HISTORY

In the final millennium of Egyptian history, there was a complex pattern of foreign conquest, internal decline, native resurgence and final destruction. The sources of evidence are far less comprehensive than in earlier times, and it is necessary to rely to a greater extent on non-Egyptian material. Literary sources therefore include not only Egyptian texts,[28] but also Classical writers such as Josephus and Herodotus,[29] cuneiform chronicles,[30] the Biblical Old Testament, and Aramaic writings.[31]

Most of the earlier types of Egyptian religious literature persist, including temple inscriptions, private autobiographies, and Wisdom Texts. However, there were marked differences: for example, the original purpose of the tomb Autobiography had been to record the successful events of the owner's life, but now there was greater emphasis on piety and less optimism that a good code of behaviour would ensure a happy and successful life. This was now thought to be totally dependent on the gods' will. One particularly interesting text preserves a Creation Myth which is known today as the 'Memphite Theology'. Inscribed on a black granite slab which was intended for erection in the Temple of Ptah at Memphis, this dates to the reign of Shabaka (c.715–701 BCE) (*see* p. 86). Other inscriptional evidence has also provided information about the religious customs of these later dynasties. For example, epithets of royal names in the late Third Intermediate Period such as 'son of Isis' or 'son of Bastet' may indicate dynastic affiliations, or simply reflect the place of origin where the inscribed object was discovered.[32] One series of fragments preserves a record of the inaugural lectures given by different grades of priests in Dynasties 21 to 23, providing information about another aspect of religion.[33]

There has been considerable interest in a collection of Aramaic papyri which were discovered on the island of Elephantine, situated near the First Cataract.[34] These indicate that a large garrison colony was housed there alongside a sizeable Jewish community during the Persian Period. Both groups lived and worshipped in the town, and evidence survives of a cult and a priesthood associated with the local ram-headed god Khnum, and a temple to Yahweh which the Jews were allowed to build.

However, this temple was burnt down and when they petitioned the Persian governor of Judah to permit them to rebuild it, there were considerable delays although eventually the project was completed.

In addition to such inscriptional evidence, archaeology has itself contributed to current knowledge of religion in this period. There have been studies of individual tombs, such as that of Harwa, the Great Steward who served the two God's Wives, Amenirdis I and Shepenopet.[35] Dating to Dynasty 25, this was built in the Assasif area of Thebes, where it established a 200-year tradition for burying high-ranking Theban officials at this site. One of the most important tombs belonged to Montuemhet, Fourth Priest of Amun and Mayor of Thebes in Dynasties 25 and 26. This provides a good example of the mixture of imitation and reinterpretation of earlier styles and innovatory ideas that characterized the Saite Period.[36]

The Saite artists made use of past styles for the new tombs, although there are few examples of 'direct copying'. Evidence suggests that they visited earlier cemeteries at Thebes and in Middle Egypt to study older models, and also drew heavily on Old Kingdom sources for details of clothing and methods of depicting the human figure.

Elsewhere, excavation of cemeteries has provided further information about funerary architecture. At Heracleopolis Magna (Ehnasya el-Medina), which was in use from the Third Intermediate Period to the Saite Period, the tombs of the resident nobles and priests (who had gained local, political and religious influence in the Third Intermediate Period) are being studied.[37] At Abusir, excavation of the tomb of Udjahorresnet, Chief Physician and one of the most influential officials at the beginning of the Persian Period, has revealed an intricate architectural system that was designed to prevent robbers from entering the burial chamber, although this was unfortunately not successful.[38] In a nearby tomb belonging to Iufaa, a lector-priest and Controller of Palaces in Dynasty 26, the sarcophagi, mummy of a young man, and an intact set of burial equipment have been found.[39]

Other buildings and religious objects from the Persian Period are the subject of continuing study. At the site of Tell el-Muqdam in the Delta, well-preserved remains have been discovered: Persian artistic influence is evident in the representations of lions found here, and the Persian kings, who identified with the strength of the lion, may have specially honoured Mihos, the chief god of the town.[40]

At Saqqara, the discovery of a stela, which may have originated in the principal state workshops at Memphis, is of considerable interest for the study of the Persian Period.[41] The owner of this stela may have had a Persian father and an Egyptian mother, and wished to reflect his background in this piece which was clearly produced by an artist who was familiar both with Egyptian traditions and the iconography of the Persian court. If the owner did have a mixed parentage, the stela nevertheless indicates that the owner chose to follow Egyptian funerary practices. Elsewhere, at Sebennytos (Samanud), there have been epigraphic studies of reliefs and architectural remains.[42] Here, within the precinct of a temple dating from at least Dynasty 26 and dedicated to Onuris-Shu and his consort Mehit, it is likely that the as-yet-undiscovered royal tombs of the native Dynasty 30 were built.

SOME IMPORTANT RELIGIOUS DEVELOPMENTS

In the last millennium of Egyptian civilization, political conditions were less stable, and it is possible that more widespread personal uncertainty led to a quest for new religious solutions which emphasized individual salvation. Generally, people were perhaps less optimistic that a virtuous life would bring them a blessed eternity, and more reliance was placed on the gods as a source of comfort. Traditional preparations for the afterlife continued, but people were also determined to enjoy their daily pleasures while they were still alive.

Although weak or foreign dynasties tried to revive the myth of the god-king in order to support their own royal status,[43] the political power of the king continued to decline, along with his influence on religion. However, there appears to have been an increased association between the temples and lay people. One noticeable feature was an increase in the custom of setting up personal statues inside the temples so that the owners could benefit from the regular rituals for the gods (which were the same as those performed in earlier periods), and thus receive sustenance from the divine food offerings. It also emphasized the owner's devotion to the god, and gave him a claim on the deity's attention.[44] This tradition emphasized the fact that the gods were now regarded as better guarantors of individual postmortem protection than the age-old mortuary cults.

A statue of the official Udjahorresnet, which was set up in the Temple of Neith at Sais in c.519 BCE, carries a text which provides important information about the Persian king Cambyses' role as pharaoh, who apparently performed the traditional rituals in this temple to sustain the deity.[45] Although they were foreign conquerors, the Persian rulers made themselves more acceptable to the Egyptians by identifying themselves as pharaohs who fulfilled their religious obligations.

Another interesting statue belonged to Djedhor whose career extended from Dynasty 30 down to the Ptolemaic Period. This is inscribed with a text that is important because it presents an Egyptian viewpoint in a period when most extant evidence comes from Greek sources.[46] The text gives details about contemporary religious practices: for example, Djedhor took the title of 'Saviour' to mark his role as a healer who could employ his magical powers against poisonous venom. This continued a tradition that stretched back to Imhotep and Amenhotep, son of Hapu, which accredited humans (most frequently royalty or physicians) with divine healing powers, and accordingly ensured that they would receive worship. Djedhor's good deeds were inscribed on his temple statue so that, according to custom, he could hope to gain rewards in the afterlife; in addition, the statue inscription would ask the living to repeat the owner's name, and thus keep his memory alive.

Generally, magic was of great importance in this later period. Spells were addressed to the gods, asking them to overthrow dangerous animals and protect the traveller from a variety of threats.[47] In the public areas of temple precincts, stone *cippi* were set up, to defeat scorpions, crocodiles and serpents, and to provide a means of curing those who had suffered from their bites or venom. A *cippus* (pl. *cippi*) is a statue-stela on which the figure of Horus is represented in three dimensions, and is inscribed with the appropriate spells against bites and venom.[48] Some *cippi* were also placed in houses and graves.

One of the most characteristic developments of this later period is the importance of animal cults.[49] In Predynastic times, evidence from the cemeteries indicates the importance of animal cults, and Herodotus claimed that animal worship had always been a tradition of Egyptian religion. Most gods had animal or part-animal forms, and the god's spirit was thought to enter and reside in the body of an animal in the same way that it occupied a cult-statue. Thus, the priests did not regard the individual animals as gods but as manifestations of the invisible power of the deity.

Sometimes, the god was present in the body of a single cult-animal (such as the Apis bull at Memphis), but in other cases, the divine spark was believed to inhabit all members of the species, thus extending the god's existence almost endlessly through a multitude of visible images.[50] In this way, the deity became more accessible to a multitude of worshippers than when the divine spirit rested only in the cult-statue. However, it is unclear if ordinary worshippers, unlike the priests, could actually differentiate between the god and his animal image.

Essentially, the Egyptians divided animals into three categories, and adopted different religious attitudes and procedures in relation to each group. First, they kept cats, dogs, monkeys, gazelles and birds as pets, which were depicted in tomb wall-scenes as part of the family group. There is evidence that some of these were given individual burials, and their mummified bodies placed in specially prepared coffins and tombs.[51]

Secondly, in the Late and Graeco-Roman Periods, a custom developed which involved the presentation of animals as votive offerings to some of the gods. Pilgrims to various temple sites could purchase animals that had been specially bred at these cult-centres; these creatures, which had no intrinsic divinity, would then be killed and mummified and placed in nearby catacombs as gifts for the resident god. At the various sites, the species of animal sacred to the particular local god was specially bred for this purpose. For example, at Tuna el-Gebel, ibises and baboons, associated with Thoth, the god of Hermopolis, were reared and buried, while at Abydos, there were dogs and jackals – the animal forms of a local deity, Khentiamentiu. At Bubastis, cult-centre of the feline goddess Bastet, vast cat cemeteries have been uncovered, while in the Delta, ibises were buried at Tell el-Zareiki, Tell el-Rub'a, and at Aboukir (near Alexandria).[52]

However, the most famous catacombs have been discovered at Saqqara where whole areas were devoted to animal burials: here, mummified dogs or jackals, cats, baboons, ichneumon, rams, ibises, monkeys, and bulls and cows have been found. From the method of burial, it is evident that some of these animals were votive offerings but others had once been the sacred cult-animals associated with particular temples.

W. B. Emery, the archaeologist who sought for the tomb of Imhotep at Saqqara, was disappointed in that particular quest, but during his investigations, he discovered a series of catacombs which had been built during the Late Period (664–332 BCE) and retained in use until Ptolemaic times (332–30 BCE). These housed the burials of animals, which included ibises, baboons, hawks, falcons, cows and bulls. Work has continued in the Sacred Animal Necropolis at Saqqara, revealing new information about these cults.[53] For example, some catacombs accommodated ibises and baboons, animals sacred to Thoth and therefore associated with Imhotep, the god of wisdom and medicine. Most of these ibis mummies contained complete birds rather than substitutes, but in the hawk mummies (the bird that represented Horus, the son of Osiris, and the sun-god Re), the embalmers frequently replaced the hawks with other material. On occasions, they used other birds, an ibis bill, another small part of a bird, or even a giant musk shrew, which were padded and wrapped to resemble hawks. This reflects what is known of the breeding habits of ibises and hawks: whereas the ibis can be easily bred in captivity, thus providing a readily available supply of birds for mummification, this is not the situation with birds of prey such as hawks. Since there would have been difficulty in obtaining specimens of these birds for mummification, it was usually necessary to trap the birds, but substitutes were also often used inside the hawk mummies.[54]

With regard to baboons,[55] only collective burials dating to the Late Period have been found in the Sacred Animal Necropolis at Saqqara, although individual examples are known from earlier times. Wrapped in linen, the mummified baboons were placed in wooden boxes and put inside niches in the walls of the catacombs at Saqqara, which were finally sealed with limestone slabs or masonry. At North Saqqara, the sacred baboons shared a brick temple enclosure, north of the Serapeum, with the Mother of Apis cows and the sacred falcons. Here, in a small limestone chapel situated at the gate of the enclosure, a squatting baboon statue was probably positioned to answer oracle questions. The baboon, as the cult animal of Thoth, the god of writing and wisdom, would have been regarded as a particularly knowledgeable source. At some sites, the sacred animal itself replaced the animal statue as an oracle through which the god's will could be sought and obtained.

In addition to those animals who were beloved companions or votive offerings, a third category included the creatures who were chosen to be cult symbols in the temples. Some of the baboons at Saqqara played this role, but the best example of these 'incarnation-animals' are the Apis bulls of Memphis. Each Apis bull was selected by the priests according to certain criteria: Herodotus[56] states that the sacred bull was not permitted to have a single black hair on its body, and the hair on its tail had to grow in a certain way. Regarded as the incarnation of the god Ptah, and also associated with Osiris and Harakhte,[57] the Apis bull was provided with a harem of sacred cows, and received a temple cult throughout its lifetime.

When it died, the bull, which was replaced by another, specially selected, living animal, was buried as Osiris-Apis (in Ptolemaic times, this was the god Serapis) in a vast subterranean structure known as the Serapeum. When it was first excavated, the Serapeum was found to contain the mummies of 64 Apis bulls, placed in great sarcophagi, which dated from the reign of Amenhotep III (Dynasty 18) down to the start of the Christian period. Thousands of the inscribed objects found associated with these burials have provided invaluable chronological evidence that relates particularly to the later periods of Egyptian history.

In Dynasty 30, it seems that a great national revival was marked by the construction of new temples at many ancient sites. At Saqqara, there were new endowments for the cults of the sacred animals at the Anubeion,[58] Bubasteion, and the burial places of the Apis bull and his mother, the cow Isis. The three establishments that functioned in connection with the Apis-bull cult included the 'Place of the Living Apis' where the bull had its living quarters, the *w'bt* where preparations were made for the bull's burial, and the Serapeum where the animal was finally buried. The living quarters and the $w'bt$ appear to have formed part of the Temple of Ptah.[59]

All the above categories of animals were mummified – a major industry which would have employed many people.[60] The second method of mummification for humans, described by Herodotus,[61] was probably also the basic technique that was used for animal mummification, but the procedure was by no means uniform. Radiological studies on cats[62] have shown that, in some cases, their necks were broken and the bodies were dehydrated using natron. Crocodiles were cured by means of salt or natron, but were not eviscerated, and these 'mummies' include either adult animals, juveniles, eggs with recognizable foetuses, or merely wrapped sticks.

The Apis bulls were more elaborately treated: they were eviscerated, probably by injecting a corrosive liquid through the anus, and then dehydrated with dry natron, before being wrapped in a shroud and adorned with a gold-leaf mask and artificial eyes. For hawks, there were two distinct techniques: in the simplest, the linen-wrapped bird was dipped in some kind of resin, but in other examples, resin was not used. These mummies were elaborately wrapped in linen bandages, on which details of the bird's feather markings and eyes were painted. At Tuna el-Gebel, a workshop has been discovered where animal mummification was carried out in the later periods.

Throughout the later historical periods, when Egypt's former political glory and military prowess had disappeared and the country was frequently ruled by dynasties of foreign kings, it was animal worship and the associated cults – so characteristic of the religious beliefs of the indigenous population – that enabled the Egyptians to retain a strong sense of their own cultural and spiritual identity. From earliest times, the gods had revealed themselves to their worshippers in the form of animals and thus, as the Egyptians' national pride was gradually eroded, they increasingly sought comfort and support from these ancient images of divinity.

CHAPTER 9

East meets West: Conflict and Co-operation in Graeco-Roman Egypt

332 BCE – 4th century ACE

HISTORICAL BACKGROUND[1]

Alexander the Great, King of Macedon, arrived in Egypt in the autumn of 332 BCE.[2] When his army and fleet reached Pelusium, the Persian satrap of Egypt surrendered without fighting, and the Egyptian people welcomed Alexander as their liberator from the Persians. In establishing his great empire, he had encouraged national individuality, although certain common ideas, based on Greek concepts, as well as economic growth and prosperity were key factors in holding the empire together. He ensured that the Egyptians were allowed to continue their own religious practices; he sacrificed to their gods and was invested as pharaoh by the Egyptian priests.

Alexander remained in Egypt for only six months, but made provision for the future government of the country by appointing a viceroy and six governors. He also founded a new city – Alexandria – on the Mediterranean coast, near the ancient village of Rhakotis,[3] which became the new capital of Egypt and the most important Mediterranean port.

Incorporating all the major elements of a Greek city, including temples to Greek gods, Alexandria soon became a great centre of Hellenistic knowledge, attracting scholars from many other parts of Alexander's empire.

A significant event during Alexander's stay in Egypt was the visit he made to the oracle of Jupiter Amun at the oasis of Siwa. Here, legend relates that when he entered the oracle alone, the god recognized him as his son and promised him world dominion. The priests, acting as the god's mouthpiece, would customarily have greeted any Egyptian ruler (who was the 'son of Re') in this way, but in this instance, the oracle was apparently interpreted as a special deification of Alexander, indicating that he had a divine nature. Although there is no convincing evidence that Alexander considered this 'deification' as anything different from the usual acknowledgement of an Egyptian king, or that he promoted himself as a god throughout the rest of his empire on the basis of the Siwa oracle, his recognition as legitimate divine heir would have assisted his foreign successors to be accepted as Egyptian pharaohs. A later tradition that Alexander was the physical son of Nectanebo II, the last native king of Egypt, by Olympias, the wife of Philip II of Macedon (his presumed father), exploited the Egyptian tradition that each pharaoh was the 'son of Re', based on the assumption that the god had visited the queen in the form of her husband.[4]

When Alexander died in Babylon in 323 BCE, one legend claims that his body was brought to Egypt and finally buried in a tomb at Alexandria where an official cult was established. The Roman Emperor Caracalla made the last recorded visit to the tomb in 215 ACE. After his death, Alexander's empire was divided between his generals.[5] Ptolemy, son of Lagos, the Macedonian general in charge of troops in Egypt, became satrap of Egypt, and then, as King Ptolemy I Soter, founded the Ptolemaic Dynasty in 305 BCE. As the regenerator of Egypt, he initiated a programme of reorganization: he appointed his son as his co-regent and revived the pharaonic tradition of consanguineous marriages; Macedonian and Greek administrators and soldiers now assisted him to sustain a Hellenistic monarchy; Greek cities were developed in Egypt; and Alexandria became the centre of a new type of Greek culture known as Hellenism.

Ptolemy I also restored the Egyptian temples, and established a divine cult for Alexander at Alexandria, thus creating a precedent for the official state cults of the later rulers of this dynasty. The Ptolemies ruled Egypt until the death of Cleopatra VII and the fall of the country to Rome in 30 BCE. Although they were Macedonian Greeks, they adopted the titles and role of pharaoh and upheld Egyptian traditions. By formally taking on the status of pharaohs, they acquired the religious and political legitimacy to rule the country, and in wall-scenes in contemporary Egyptian temples, they are shown worshipping the native gods and receiving divine acknowledgement as the rightful kings. However, unlike earlier kings, they primarily used their pharaonic powers to exact heavy taxes and drain the country's natural resources. Although Egypt became wealthy, the indigenous population received few rewards and their situation deteriorated under the Ptolemies. Their dissatisfaction was made evident in the native riots which erupted in the district of Thebes in 208–186 BCE and 88–86 BCE.[6]

As previously mentioned, the Ptolemies established a Hellenistic kingdom in Egypt: Greeks came to settle there, and the Greek language and customs were introduced. In addition to Alexandria, other, long-established Greek cities prospered in Egypt, but the Ptolemaic dynasty was unusual amongst the Hellenistic kingdoms that succeeded Alexander in not founding new Greek cities.[7] Until the foundation of Antinoopolis by the Roman Emperor Hadrian, the only other 'foreign' cities in Egypt were Naucratis and Ptolemais. Hellenistic culture predominated in the 'Greek' cities where theatres, gymnasia and temples were built, but at Ptolemais, in addition to cults to Dionysus and Zeus, there was still an Egyptian crocodile cult, as well as sanctuaries to other Egyptian deities. Outside of the cities, in the country areas, there was even more evidence of hybridization of Egyptian and Greek customs, because the Greeks who settled there more frequently adopted continuing Egyptian traditions.

Compared with other Hellenistic monarchies established elsewhere after Alexander's death, a wealth of literary, epigraphical, archaeological and papyrological evidence has survived in Egypt. Nevertheless, this material represents only a partial picture of Ptolemaic Egypt. The literary sources provide an uneven record in terms of chronology and geography, since the papyri date mainly to the reigns of Ptolemies II, III, VI and VII, and are mostly derived from the Fayoum, while the archaeological evidence, which is quite scarce, comes from relatively few sites. Nevertheless, the sources supply enough information to allow some conclusions to be drawn about the period. Cleopatra VII, who became joint ruler with her father and then with two of her brothers, was the last Macedonian to control Egypt. Her alliance with Mark Antony, the Roman Consul (44 BCE and 34 BCE) and Triumvir (43–38 BCE and 37–33 BCE), was a major factor that contributed to her eventual downfall, although initially both she and Mark Antony would have been aware of the mutually political advantages of their alliance. Cleopatra wanted Egypt to become a favoured client state of Rome, while Mark Antony regarded Egypt as a personal power base that he could use to counterbalance the influence of Rome.

However, Augustus (Octavian), the first Roman Emperor, saw Mark Antony's position as a threat to Roman supremacy, and also considered his liaison with Cleopatra as an insult to his own sister, Octavia, who was Mark Antony's wife. When Augustus captured Alexandria in 30 BCE, Antony and Cleopatra preferred to commit suicide than to face personal and political humiliation.

Augustus annexed Egypt as a province of the Roman Empire, and created a special status for the country which now became his personal possession: unlike other major provinces which were governed directly by the Roman Senate, Egypt was subject only to the Emperor who appointed a vice-regal governor (Prefect) to rule it. Augustus visited Egypt only once, but he established an administrative system, developed from that introduced by the Ptolemies (see below), which continued for some three hundred years. He adopted the role of pharaoh, and became Egypt's religious leader. Wall-scenes in Egyptian temples show him offering to the gods, and performing the same traditional rituals that had been enacted in these buildings for many centuries. He also made additions to some of the temples and founded others at Dendur and Kalabsha in Nubia.

However, although he employed these traditions to confirm himself and his successors as rightful rulers, he also introduced policies which firmly established Egypt as a Roman province, and provided a basis for stability and economic power. Expeditions were sent to the south to establish Roman control, and Egypt finally lost all independence as a kingdom. Instead, it became a supplier of commodities, particularly grain, for the Roman Empire. Although, from 30 BCE, the Romans were firmly in control of Egypt, they largely retained the administrative system that had been set up by the Ptolemies; however, they made some important innovations, such as the introduction of Roman law. The Greeks retained the status of a ruling minority, Greek still remained the official language, and Hellenistic culture predominated in the Greek cities. However, the Romans had no interest in supporting any one ethnic group in Egypt, and considered that their main task was to collect taxes and create conditions for the production of goods and materials such as corn, papyrus, and glass for Roman consumption. Although the economy flourished against a background of order and equilibrium, there was little attempt to invest in the country or improve the general conditions of the population. As a consequence, the Egyptians regarded the Romans as simply another line of foreign rulers who assumed the rights and powers of pharaohs to gain access to the country's wealth.

SOCIAL ORGANIZATION

During the periods when Egypt was ruled first by the Ptolemies (332–30 BCE) and then by the Romans (30 BCE – fourth century ACE) all aspects of Egypt's socio-economic life underwent profound change, producing far-reaching effects on the economy, government, demography and religion.[8] Although the Greeks were the most important and numerous of the new settlers, communities of Romans, Italians, Phrygians, Syrians, Jews and Indians also established themselves in Alexandria. In the Fayoum, hieratic papyri and Aramaic texts have revealed the presence of a Jewish community in the second century BCE, while nearby there was an Egyptian temple dedicated to Sobknebtunis that continued to function. As the site of an oracle that was still functioning in the third century BCE, this seems to have retained some of the judicial functions it performed in pharaonic times.[9]

In the Greek cities of Alexandria, Naucratis and Ptolemais, and in other areas where colonists had settled, the Greeks introduced the new Hellenistic culture. They also appropriated the top public offices and the best land. Meanwhile, alongside the Greeks in the cities and the countryside, the indigenous population continued its own traditions. The Egyptians, now mostly reduced to the lower levels of society, were employed to cultivate the royal lands or work in state factories, or were engaged as artisans, soldiers and traders. The changes that the Ptolemies and Romans introduced in relation to the political and socio-economic structure of the country were much more profound than any that the earlier Assyrian and Persian conquerors had instigated. The Assyrians and Persians had simply represented a change of dynastic rulers; there had been no major influx of new immigrants, and life for most Egyptians would have continued in the same way as under the native kings. However, the Ptolemies and the Romans set out to unravel the political and social hierarchy of pharaonic Egypt, and the indigenous population suffered to an unprecedented degree. The new political, legal and economic measures now undermined their status as individuals in their own country, and although the Greek settlers who arrived in Egypt were numerically insignificant in relation to the overall population, they were able to gain complete control because they had the full support of the early Ptolemaic rulers.

In the first part of the Ptolemaic dynasty, there seems to have been little direct interaction between the Greeks and Egyptians: intermarriage was rare, and although some Egyptians may have learnt to use Greek, they mainly retained their own language and scripts. The fate of the old Egyptian aristocracy is uncertain, but probably only the priests survived as an indigenous elite, largely because the kings needed their acceptance and support. However, the situation changed after the Battle of Raphia (217 BCE), when a national army defeated the Seleucid ruler, Antiochus III. Egyptians, who played a significant part in this conflict, became more confident as a result, and the Ptolemies recognized that they needed their support. Towards the end of the third century BCE, the waves of Greek settlers ceased to enter Egypt, and a new royal policy gradually emerged. Egyptians now began to hold high positions in the royal court, the civil service and the army, and Greek officials and farmers no longer received the king's gift of great country estates.

Although the Greek cities continued to promote Hellenism, the kings chose to develop a pro-Egyptian policy, and gradually the Greek and Egyptian communities grew closer together. Intermarriage did not become widespread, but there was an increase, particularly in marriages between Greek men and Egyptian women. In these families, Egyptian traditions prevailed, but some aspects of Hellenistic culture and education were acquired. Indeed, it was Greek education rather than birth that now gave a person the status of a 'Hellene', and some Egyptians now took additional Greek names, learnt Greek, and wore Greek clothes. However, this process of Hellenization was probably largely superficial and, for the most part, both communities continued to preserve their own traditions. A reverse process, Egyptianization, can also be observed (again this was probably superficial), with some Greeks taking Egyptian names and learning the Egyptian language. Some also accepted Egyptian gods; this was particularly evident in connection with funerary and burial procedures, where the Greeks adopted Egyptian customs such as mummification, and acknowledged the role of the traditional deities associated with death and resurrection.

RELIGIOUS CULTS

A diverse and complex religious experience developed in Egypt during the Graeco-Roman Period. Both communities of indigenes and settlers largely retained their own distinct beliefs and customs, but there was also some degree of hybridization. This took two forms: national cults were formally established with the aim of uniting both communities, and there was also a natural process whereby both communities adopted and fused elements from the two traditions.

The Cult of Living Kings

The Ptolemies adopted the role of Egyptian pharaoh, but they still felt the need to justify their reigns. Ptolemy I inaugurated a divine cult of Alexander the Great, and built a temple at Koptos for his own cult. His son and successor, Ptolemy II, established an official cult for himself and his sister-queen, thus creating a pattern for a dynastic cult. Although this was a Hellenistic innovation, it was closely associated with the Egyptian royal cult, and incorporated the dead deified Ptolemies into the Egyptian temples, where they shared the sanctuary with an Egyptian deity[10] and received the traditional royal rites and offerings which had always been presented to the living king and the ancestral rulers of Egypt.

The Ptolemaic queens played an important role in the royal cult, and are often shown in Egyptian temple reliefs as the royal spouse or co-regent. The pharaonic concept of the king as the embodiment of the state and his link with the gods were to some extent reflected in the Hellenistic ideology of kingship. However, there were greater dissimilarities between the concept of the Egyptian pharaoh and the Roman Emperor and, unlike the Ptolemies, the deified Roman ruler was not accompanied in the Egyptian temple scenes by his Empress.

National Cults[11]

The Greeks and Egyptians generally retained their own beliefs and customs, although there were areas where a hybridization of cultures occurred.[12] The rulers used some state cults as a means of uniting the two communities. The most important of these new cults, dedicated to the god Serapis, was introduced in an artificial attempt to unite Greeks and Egyptians. This deity combined some characteristics of the Egyptian god Osiris with the physical features of a Greek deity; his name was probably a derivation of 'Osiris-Apis', and he embraced characteristics of the Apis-bull cult which had flourished for centuries at Memphis (see pp. 315–16).[13] The cults of the new gods were given royal support and approval, and received widespread acclaim, but at a deeper level, they do not seem to have succeeded in uniting the two communities who, for the most part, continued to worship their own deities.[14]

In their own cities and communities, it is known that the Greeks built shrines to their own gods who included Apollo, Zeus, Demeter and Aphrodite, although there is little archaeological evidence to indicate the exact nature of this worship. The Greeks also accepted the new national gods because they had the physical appearance and many of the characteristics of their own gods. The Egyptians continued to worship their own traditional gods, and the new deities in their Egyptianized forms.

The cults of Osiris and Isis continued to be of considerable importance. As well as the continuing significance of Saqqara as a cult-centre for Serapis/Osiris, recent excavations have revealed structures at the Temple of Karnak enclosure, dating from the Third Intermediate Period to Ptolemaic times, which were associated with the worship of Osiris.[15] These include catacombs, dated to the reign of Ptolemy IV, where Osirid figures made during the Festival of Khoiakh were interred every year. Osiris, who was identified in Roman times with the Nile god Hapy, also became associated with a syncretic consort, Isis-Euthenia,[16] who played an active part in producing the inundation. According to one myth, this inundation was caused by the tears of Isis as she mourned her husband. In the fourth century ACE, the Nile deities became the cause of a controversy between the Christian authorities and the pagans in Alexandria, but with the triumph of Christianity, the Nile mythology was Christianized and the inundation was explained in terms of Christ's power.

However, the Egyptian deity who received most widespread acclaim was Isis. The Greeks identified her with Aphrodite and Hathor, and her cult was eventually disseminated throughout the Roman Empire. The Isis—Osiris Mysteries were celebrated at Rome and Corinth, and her cult reached Athens, the Danube region, Germania and Britain.[17] At Athens, the evidence for her cult spans some six centuries, down to the third century ACE.[18] In the Ptolemaic Period, her queenship was expressed iconographically for the first time, with particular emphasis on her crowns and insignia, and one of the Ptolemaic queens, possibly Cleopatra III, provided the prototype of an Isis-queen. Hymns to Isis inscribed on the walls of the temples at Philae and Kalabsha emphasized her role as the divine mother and her relationship to her son, Horus. Despite widespread acceptance, she remained entirely faithful to her Egyptian origins, as the devoted wife of Osiris who had helped to restore him to life, but she also adopted new forms and characteristics to suit her Greek and Roman worshippers.

She acquired additional powers as a universal supreme deity who was creator and sustainer of life, and she became the director of fate; as the 'Lady of Heaven, Earth and the Netherworld',[19] she was responsible for the annual inundation and for sustaining her creation.[20] She was also the 'Lady of Seafaring', and the goddess to whom many turned in a world of political and social change. Her importance amongst the religious and social elite is demonstrated in religious texts in tombs and temples, but most of her worshippers were illiterate and their beliefs are not recorded in writing. However, the numbers of terracotta figurines of Isis that have survived from this period demonstrate her popularity amongst all classes.[21] Generally, the Egyptians continued to worship a great variety of deities, and there was increased emphasis on personal piety.[22] While the state cults continued in the temples, there were religious festivals which involved the ordinary people in concepts such as the creation of the world and the continuing struggle to maintain the balance and order of the universe.[23]

TEMPLES IN GRAECO-ROMAN EGYPT[24]

Evidence of Greek temples in Egypt is relatively scarce. Apart from their presence in the cities of Alexandria, Ptolemais and Naucratis, the Greeks formed the minority population, and their temples were probably relatively modest in scale and structure. Little archaeological or literary evidence of their existence remains, although Greek temples are known to have been built for the worship of Greek deities in Alexandria, Ptolemais and Memphis. Only scanty remains of such buildings and some examples of the Greek columns which once formed part of these temples have survived, in addition to some inscribed stones and a long list of temples. However, it is generally assumed that the Greek temples that were built in Egypt would have followed the pattern of temples elsewhere, dedicated to the worship of Greek gods.

By contrast, traditional temples for Egyptian cults were increased and enhanced. This not only reflected the preponderance of Egyptians amongst the population during the Graeco-Roman Period, but was also the direct result of a policy pursued by both the Ptolemies and the

Romans to support the Egyptian gods and their priests. This enabled them, as foreign dynasts, to assume the role of pharaoh and adopt the associated political and economic rights and powers. These temples are among the largest and best-preserved examples, and are also the finest examples of architecture found in the Graeco-Roman Period.

Apart from some minor variations, all pharaonic temples conformed to an overall layout which was determined by religious and ritual factors (previously discussed, see pp. 186–98). The Egyptian temples of the Graeco-Roman Period retained all these features, but introduced some relatively minor innovations. In the earlier part of the Ptolemaic dynasty, the kings made partial restorations and additions to existing temples, including those at Karnak and Luxor and on the west bank at Thebes. However, magnificent new temples were also built, dedicated to Hathor at Denderah, Horus at Edfu, Sobek and Haroeris at Kom Ombo, Isis at Philae, and Khnum at Esna. There were also smaller temples dedicated to Hathor and Ma'at at Deir el-Medina, to Montu at Medamud, to Isis at Aswan, to Amun at Dabod, and to Mandulis, and Isis and Osiris, at Kalabsha. At Dendur, a new temple was dedicated to two deified brothers, Peteese and Pihor, who were local heroes. This extensive building programme was probably initiated by the Egyptian priests and supported by the rulers.

Common features shared by these temples include the basic layout of the rooms, and the addition of subterranean crypts and chapels or kiosks on the roof of the main building. The crypts were used for storing the god's sacred possessions and utensils employed in the rituals, while the chapels and kiosks acted as way-stations where the priests could rest the statue in the course of the processional rites, or where particular stages of the rituals could be carried out. The temples also have special features which identify them as a historical group, and these can be clearly demonstrated in the most completely preserved example of a temple, dedicated to the god Horus at Edfu.[25] Here, instead of restoring the existing temple, Ptolemy III laid the foundations for a new building in 237 BCE, which was completed in 57 BCE.

This temple has the traditional façade and pylon, but the entrance is not flanked by the colossal statues of a king or by the obelisks which were associated with the pharaonic temples. In the entrance or forecourt, there are lotiform, papyriform and composite capitals; the latter are a particular feature of this period. As in the pharaonic temples, these plant-form capitals symbolized the fertile landscape of the 'Island of Creation' which every temple was believed to represent. Between the forecourt and the columnar hall, there is a screen wall, decorated with a frieze and ritual scenes. This wall, which is solidly constructed in the lower part but open at the top to provide both privacy and natural daylight, replaced the solid partition found in most pharaonic temples. Within the temple, the central sanctuary now formed a separate structure with its own roof, and was surrounded by a corridor.

The clerestory lighting found in pharaonic temples was replaced by another method of illumination. This consisted of small shafts inserted at intervals in the roof that allowed natural light to pass into the chambers below. An additional building known as a 'Mammisi' (Birth-house) was also included in the Ptolemaic temple complex.[26] These small, subsidiary temples (again, showing no Greek influence) reflected the general features of the main building. They were sanctuaries where the birth of the child in the divine family triad was celebrated by means of special rituals, which included various presentations of food and other offerings, and also where rites were enacted to assert and emphasize the king's divine birth when he succeeded to the throne. The rituals carried out in the Birth-houses confirmed the identification of the king with the divine child, and thus gave him the right to rule Egypt. This building was a departure from the arrangement in the pharaonic temples, where the god's birth was celebrated in special halls or chambers within the main building.

The temples became the chief repositories of Egyptian wisdom and religious lore in the Graeco-Roman Period, and the texts on the walls included extracts and summaries from books in the temple archive. At Edfu, the room that once housed the temple library has been identified, although no parallel has yet been found in the pharaonic temples. Some of the subject matter found on the Ptolemaic temple walls includes scenes and inscriptions that occurred in earlier buildings, but other material is unique to these later edifices.

The scenes and inscriptions generally record the traditional daily rites and festivals (discussed previously, *see* pp. 194–7), although they are often recorded here more fully than in the pharaonic buildings; there are also depictions of processions, the temple foundation ceremony (discussed previously, *see* pp. 189–96), victories of the gods, and the creation of the world. The latter is described at Edfu in a series of important inscriptions known as the 'Building Texts'. In scenes that decorate the ambulatory walls around Edfu, there is a vivid depiction of the mythological 'Conflict between Horus and Seth'. In this period, myths were presented in this way as a comprehensive narrative, to ensure that they could be transmitted to later generations in the form of a permanent written record.[27] Ptolemaic temples promoted the myth of divine kingship, as in the engagement between Horus and Seth. They also included unique decoration that emphasized the cultic role of the queen (shown with the king, making offerings to the gods), and also the dynastic role of the pharaohs.

Astronomy played an important part in Egyptian religion. There were astronomical texts and charts of the heavens painted on the ceilings in temples and some tombs;[28] in the temples, these were often placed in rooms with natural light or rooms with a mortuary significance.[29] In the temples, the priests studied the movements of the heavenly bodies, and succeeded in observing and recording five planets, including Mars. However, following the Babylonian tradition, they grouped their stars in a different way from our own system, and so it is difficult to identify their constellations, although some, including the Great Bear, are evident. Astral observations were carried out at the start of all building procedures involving major religious monuments, in order that the correct orientation of the building could be determined. Also, according to some Ptolemaic texts, protective deities associated with astronomy were believed to defend the cosmic order against the forces of chaos. At Edfu, sixty of these deities, created by the principal gods, performed this function through the agency of cosmic magic, and it was believed that magic could also enhance and extend this role to protect the whole universe.[30] As well as the sky charts in the tombs and temples, additional information about astronomy is preserved in tables that refer to the movement of stars at night, astronomical treatises, and references to astronomical lore in religious literature such as the Pyramid Texts.

Despite their interest and involvement in astronomy, however, and although there are some modern claims that astrology and occult studies originated in Egypt, the Egyptians did not in fact initiate or develop the idea that the positions of the stars influenced individual destiny. There are a few references to this belief, but they only occur in late demotic texts, and the concept was originally introduced to Egypt from Meso-potamia. However, hemerology – a system of determining whether a particular day would be lucky or unlucky – was widely practised in ancient Egypt, but these horoscopes were not based on the position of the stars. Such predictions were reached by studying the various mythological events which had occurred on particular days and which therefore, according to their belief, were likely to have an influence on future events.

Thus, in the Ptolemaic temples, the ritual scenes and inscriptions, selected from those found in earlier temples or from documents deposited in temple archives, were modified and adapted as required.[31] Although the content of scenes and inscriptions was essentially the same as in pharaonic times, inscriptions were usually written in Ptolemaic Egyptian, a late stage of Egyptian hieroglyphs, which is still not completely understood or readily translated.

The role of the priests in the great Ptolemaic temples was crucial to the survival of this knowledge and the continuation of Egyptian religion.[32] Information about the priesthood in the Ptolemaic Period has survived from hieroglyphic, demotic and Greek sources. In addition to the 'Prophets' (the full-time, top-level priests) there were part-time priests. The High-priest at Memphis, who performed the king's coronation ceremony, held the most important position in the religious hierarchy at this time. His wife was also prominent in her role as priestess; she formed part of the body of women priests whose most senior members acted as the gods' consorts, protectresses, and mothers. Succession to the priesthood was hereditary, and priests continued to be subject to a range of prohibitions while they were on duty; for example, they were forbidden to eat beans, fish, beef, pork, mutton, pigeon and garlic. Although the priesthood was still primarily regarded as a secure and lucrative post rather than a vocation, there may have been some attempt to 'spiritualize' the cult so that priests were now expected to develop powers of contemplation and a vision of the divine,[33] in order to become pious and gain honour and security. The priests also played major roles in transmitting knowledge, and in ensuring the development and prosperity of the temple estates.

The senior priests ('Prophets') often exercised great influence, while the deputies and specialists carried out a multitude of cultic and other duties within the temples. Some priests were acquainted with the Greek language, and had contact with Greek scholars. The temples were totally integrated into the society and economy of Egypt, both through their role as major landowners, and by the attendance of priests at the annual synods where they met state officials and had the opportunity to discuss religious and political matters. Although ordinary people played no direct part in the temple functions, they shared the view of the world that was promoted by the temples. They came to the temple gates to pray and seek help from the oracles,[34] to receive dream interpretations, or try to obtain medical help, and it was through these subsidiary activities that the priests had direct contact with the people. On other occasions, ordinary people also participated regularly in the gods' festivals.

In this period, the temple was primarily regarded as a microcosm of the universe where the rituals, as the main channel of 'state magic' (see pp. 283–4), were believed to transform chaos into order and life into death. The temple was the home and locus of the Creator where he became accessible to mankind. However, in addition to this cultic role, the temples were the one surviving base and focus of native influence during Graeco-Roman times and played an essential role in enabling the king to rule Egypt. It was for this reason that the Ptolemies and the Romans ensured that they functioned and flourished.

FUNERARY CUSTOMS

Tomb Architecture

In Ptolemaic Egypt, patterns of tomb architecture amongst the indigenous population and the immigrants also followed separate paths. From the evidence of cemeteries at Alexandria, Naucratis, Abusir and the Fayoum, it appears that Greek burials in Egypt derived most of their inspiration from Greece. The two main types were pit graves and underground tombs. Pit tombs, resembling similar burials in Greece, were cut into the rock or sunk in the soil and then covered with earth or stone slabs. The underground tombs included loculus and kline tombs. The loculus tombs, discovered at Alexandria and in the Fayoum towns, were used for middle-class burials and included two types which accommodated either single or mass burials. However, kline tombs, found only in Alexandria and used for the aristocracy, were similar to those in Macedonia. They consisted of an open court, a *prostas* (anteroom), where there was an offering altar and bench for mourners, and an *oikos* (main room), where the burial was usually accommodated in a sarcophagus, although sometimes burials were also put in the *prostas*. This practice of dividing the tomb into the *prostas* and *oikos* is only found in Macedonia and Alexandria.

Although there is no evidence of any fusion of Greek and Egyptian tomb architecture here, there are some cross-influences in the funerary decorative features. For example, carved sphinxes placed outside the tomb to guard the dead were derived from an old Greek idea, but sometimes the tomb façade copied Egyptian temple architecture, and some Egyptian motifs such as crowns and pillar decoration were also employed. The tombs also contained stelae, statues, columns and massive quadrangular monuments on a base of three steps, which were probably sacrificial altars. Because of the population growth in Alexandria, only limited space was available for burials, and to alleviate the problem, there was an increased re-use of old tombs. Also, because it could be built to accommodate more bodies than the kline tomb (which it eventually replaced), the loculus tomb was increasingly employed for mass burials. For single burials, the loculus tomb incorporated a shaft with a flight of steps that descended to a landing where the burial was placed, but when this type of tomb was used as a mass grave, the burial area consisted of a long, narrow corridor where the bodies were laid in holes cut into the walls.

Little remaining evidence of Egyptian burials has been found in Alexandria, possibly because the tombs were destroyed by subsequent building, but also perhaps because they were simple structures, since most of them belonged to poor residents. Some Egyptians may also have used old tombs, and in other cemeteries, there was re-use of tombs that had been plundered and abandoned. For example, there is evidence that New Kingdom tombs at Thebes and Hawara, and Third Intermediate Period tombs elsewhere, were reoccupied at this time. At Thebes,[35] a range of different burial practices occurred, although relatively few studies have been made of this area in the Graeco-Roman Period.[36] It is evident that large numbers of bodies were sometimes interred in one tomb (one catacomb contained at least sixty Roman mummies, including a large number of women and children). Also, some tombs were re-opened to deposit bodies brought home from other parts of Egypt or, as at Hawara, mummies from several generations, originally kept elsewhere, were finally interred in mass graves. Since the end of the New Kingdom, there was a continuing decline in the quantity of tomb-goods, and less emphasis was placed on the provision of individual tombs. However, in the Graeco-Roman Period, this was offset by giving increased attention to the preparation of elaborately wrapped and decorated mummies.

A wide range of burial practices seem to have occurred at each site, and also any available tomb space was utilized in a variety of ways. However, two main types of tomb can be determined: the shaft tomb, where the burials were interred either in shafts open to the sky or in shafts that descended from the pavement of a chapel; and chamber tombs, which consisted of one or two chambers that either were cut into the rock and reached by steps or an inclined plane, or were built underground and reached by a shaft. Most shaft tombs were designed for single burials, and have been found at many sites including Gurob, Hawara and the Fayoum, where they continued a long-established Egyptian tradition. More elaborate examples also existed, such as one limestone tomb at Atfih where the walls of the burial chamber were decorated with Egyptian scenes painted on to a layer of stucco. The chamber tombs had a very similar design to earlier pharaonic examples. They were used for family burials, particularly those of the middle classes, but a rare and more expensive type had wall-scenes with funerary subjects and painted inscriptions. These had shafts and burial chambers but no chapels, thus following the pattern of Middle Kingdom and Saite tombs.

Generally, Egyptian tombs of the Ptolemaic Period continued the pharaonic traditions, but they reflected the demoted status of the indigenous population. Roughly built, with small or non-existent chapels, they generally accommodated multiple burials. Indeed, individual preference for any particular type of tomb was generally dictated by the owner's wealth and status, and the number of burials the tomb was intended to accommodate. In these tombs, the style, decoration and evidence of funerary practices are purely Egyptian: the decoration (which only occurred on the walls of the burial chamber and on coffins) was traditional, the inscriptions were written in Hieroglyphs, and the bodies were preserved with traditional mummification.[37] Funerary customs, such as the banquet held at the tomb, also seem to have survived.[38]

Where the mythology of Greek and Egyptian deities overlapped, the god's support was sometimes sought by worshippers who were beyond the ranks of the deity's immediate community. One such deity, Demeter, was a rare example of a Greek goddess who occurred in the Egyptian countryside in her Hellenistic form. As the Greek mother-goddess who had successfully restored her daughter to earth from Hades, there were parallels between her mythology and the Osiris story, and in the Roman Period, she appears with the Egyptian deities Isis, Serapis and Harpocrates on terracotta lamps and coins.

In the catacombs of Kom el-Shuqafa in Alexandria, in two niches decorated with frescoes, the Osirian cycle of death and rebirth is shown in one niche, represented in the Egyptian style, while in the other, the Demeter myth is depicted according to the Greek tradition. This cult was unusual in that it flourished in both Greek and Egyptian contexts.[39] Another example where Egyptian and Graeco-Roman motifs are combined occurs in a painting found on a linen shroud; this may have belonged to an Egyptian owner who had married into the Greek community.[40]

One remarkable exception to the tradition that the Egyptian-style tombs showed no evidence of Greek influence is found at Tuna el-Gebel. Here, a tomb was built for Petosiris, a priest of Thoth, and his family,[41] which probably dates to the early Ptolemaic Period. It is built in a style that is neither entirely Egyptian nor Greek. The tomb façade is totally

Egyptian in concept and style but, uniquely, it resembles the front of an Egyptian temple. Inside, the walls of a large, rectangular chamber (*pronaos*) are decorated with scenes, arranged in horizontal registers. Egyptian in content and artistic technique but combining Greek and Egyptian styles of representation, these scenes depict agricultural and other activities found in traditional Egyptian tombs.

In the chapel, the content of the scenes is also Egyptian, showing funerary ceremonies and Petosiris and his family in the presence of the gods. However, in both the *pronaos* and the chapel, Greek features also appear in the treatment of the dress and the appearance of the figures. Therefore, in this tomb, the style is neither entirely Egyptian nor Greek: the figures in the scenes retain the profile pose typical of Egyptian art, and the themes and content are almost exclusively Egyptian, continuing the pharaonic traditions found in Memphite and Theban tombs, but some Greek features are also evident. In aesthetic terms, this unique attempt at hybridization was not entirely successful – perhaps one reason why the experiment was not repeated.

Mummification

'Mummy labels' incorporated intercessory formulae – short texts written on mummy bandages, papyrus or coffins, which were intended to accompany the deceased to the underworld. They sought to provide the gods and the blessed dead with the assurance that the newcomer was worthy to join them, and as such, they provide an insight into some of the mortuary beliefs that were current in the Graeco-Roman Period.[42]

One aspect of Egyptian religion that some immigrants adopted during the Graeco-Roman Period was mummification.[43] As increasing numbers of people chose this practice, there was a consequent decline in the standards of mummification, since commercial rather than religious criteria now dictated the procedures. In some mummies, the viscera were removed, treated, and then returned to the body cavities, but in other cases, the body was either packed with balls of resin-soaked linen, mud or broken pottery, or with molten resin or bitumen. In some examples, no incision was made and the viscera remained in the body.

Resin, now used in its molten form as the main embalming agent, was poured into the body cavities through the flank incision, and into the skull through the nostril or foramen magnum after removal of the brain, although, in many cases, there was no attempt to remove the brain. Linen and mud, or sometimes resin and wax, were also packed inside the body, and the mouth and orbits were filled with mud and linen. This widespread use of resin ensured that all the mummies of this period have a darkened skin colour, and are frequently hard and shiny.

Also, they were often in an advanced state of decomposition by the time embalming was carried out, and maggots and beetles, already feeding off the decomposing tissues, were frequently killed and trapped in the molten resin. X-rays of some of these mummies indicate that partial decomposition had already set in when embalming commenced. Sometimes, the head had become detached from the body, or limbs were missing, indicating that the body had fallen apart during embalming, and some mummies even incorporate the bones of more than one individual. The general decline in mummification can be explained by the existence of a more widespread and commercially orientated enterprise, which resulted in delays in starting work on the cheaper burials and in a fall in the standards of craftsmanship. However, in some instances, the explanation may be more sinister. Herodotus[44] claimed that the bodies of beautiful women or the wives of eminent men were only handed over to the embalmers several days after death, when decomposition had already started, presumably in an attempt to inhibit necrophilia.

In the Roman Period, mummification procedures deteriorated still further: a basic treatment to prevent decay involved the application of a thick coating of resinous substances to the body surface; and it is usually impossible to determine if the viscera and brain have been removed. This decline in standards was counterbalanced by the provision of increasingly elaborate outer wrappings. Earliest examples from the Ptolemaic Period incorporate a gilded face mask in which the eyes and eyebrows are often inlaid with glass or semi-precious stones.

In later, more elaborate mummies, the outermost bandages were often finely pleated in a series of geometrical patterns interspersed with gilded studs. The mummy now also incorporated three separate units of cartonnage (a combination of stucco and cloth or waste paper which sometimes includes fragments of papyrus documents). One unit covered the head and shoulders; another, decorated with representations of amulets, jewellery and religious scenes, was placed over the chest; and a foot-piece, painted to resemble a pair of sandals, covered the feet. Next, the portrait cartonnage or bust piece was developed which fitted over the head and chest of the mummy. On this, the decorative details were moulded in the cartonnage; the face, arms and front were usually gilded and the head area was painted. The eyes were also painted or, more often, inlaid with opaque glass or white marble and obsidian. A wreath (usually of red flowers) is shown in the right hand, while the left one is placed beneath it, across the chest. The shapes of different kinds of jewellery – serpent bracelets, armlets, earrings and finger rings – are moulded in the cartonnage, and these are often set with cut-stones and glass, to create a realistic effect.

The final stage was the inclusion of a panel portrait as part of the head-piece. Examples from the cemeteries of the Roman Period provide unparalleled information about Classical portrait painting, although they represent the art of a remote provincial district.[45] This custom of portrait painting undoubtedly existed in other parts of the Empire, but in Egypt, the uniquely favourable environmental conditions and the adaptation of the portraits for funerary customs ensured their survival. The first examples of the portraits to reach Europe were brought back from Saqqara in 1615 ACE. Later, from 1887 ACE, many other portraits were acquired by the collector Graf; these reputedly came from the cemetery which served the town Arsinoe, established in the Fayoum in the second century BCE. Petrie's excavations at the Roman cemetery of Hawara in 1888 ACE and 1911 ACE[46] revealed more portraits of the inhabitants of Arsinoe, and others have been found elsewhere at sites including Antinoopolis.

Although they do not all come from the same area,[47] the term 'Fayoum portraits' is sometimes applied to them. The Fayoum was the area where the Greeks and Romans pursued land reclamation schemes to provide settlement areas for their veterans, and the local mixed population of Greeks, Egyptians, and other Mediterranean peoples is reflected in the portraits. The earliest examples date to the first half of the first century ACE, but most come from the second and third centuries; they continued into the fourth century, finally ceasing when the spread of Christianity brought about a decline in mummification.

Criteria used by scholars to establish the date of each portrait include details of the clothing, hairstyles, and women's jewellery, as well as the painting techniques.[48] Unlike the earlier cartonnage masks, which feature mass-produced, stylized faces bearing no specific likeness to the individual owners, these portraits usually capture a personal image. The idea of such portraits originated in the Classical world (examples also occur in the wall-scenes of houses at Pompeii in Italy), but in Egypt they developed a unique funerary use. The portraits may have been painted by itinerant artists during the owner's lifetime, a theory supported by Petrie's discovery of a portrait at Hawara which still retained its square wooden frame with a cord for hanging on the wall. When the owner died, the portrait was cut to shape and incorporated in the mummy so that it could act as an image of the owner, as well as protecting the mummy's head and providing his spirit with a focus to which it could return at will.

The portraits generally depict young, good-looking individuals,[49] continuing the Egyptian funerary tradition of representing the deceased in an idealized way. However, in these portraits, the faces are no longer shown in profile, and unlike Egyptian traditional art, techniques such as shading, highlighting and the use of depth and perspective are all used to give realism to the face. Generally, the portraits represent the wealthy, Hellenized, racially mixed population of Roman Egypt, and uniquely they combine an Egyptian funerary purpose with Classical art-style and technique. They demonstrate how, in the important area of funerary customs and beliefs, Egyptian and foreign ideas became entwined; they also provide a unique source for the study of the origins of 'Western-style' portraiture.

RELIGION IN THE ARTS

Religious beliefs were expressed in various other art forms throughout the Graeco-Roman Period. In sculpture, examples of Egyptian, Greek and hybridized forms have survived.[50] The custom of placing private statues inside the temples, which started in pharaonic times, continued until the Roman Period. From the First Persian Period, there had been an attempt to represent true rather than idealized portraits of the owners, and some fine examples of these private statues have survived.

Under the Ptolemies, a local Greek style of sculpture developed at Alexandria, which was used for statues of gods and goddesses, and funerary and honorary figures of men and women. Indigenous Egyptian art is best exemplified by the Ptolemaic Period wall-reliefs in the Egyptian temples. Here, although the subject matter continued the pharaonic tradition, the human figures were now shown with contemporary physical characteristics – including a pouting mouth and a protruding abdomen – which were probably modelled on the physique of the Ptolemaic rulers. Some sculpture combined Greek and Egyptian concepts: there are statues which represent Ptolemaic princesses as Isis in the Alexandrian style, and one statue of Isis is carved in the Egyptian style but incorporates a Greek dress. Many Egyptian gods, such as Horus and Bes, are shown in the Greek style, but only statues of Ptolemaic kings and queens are represented with a totally Egyptian appearance.

Some examples of stelae, which incorporate bright colours and formal funerary texts, continue the earlier Egyptian tradition, whereas Greek stelae were usually decorated in the Greek style, although a few examples exhibit some Egyptian influence. Other art forms that mainly followed their individual Egyptian or Greek traditions include painted funerary reliefs and tombstones, and the Greek gems and cameos. In the latter, however, there is occasionally a mixed influence, when Egyptian gods are depicted in the Greek style but incorporate some Egyptian features and details of dress and hairstyle. Generally, the art of the two communities was inspired by very different traditions and religious beliefs, and the two styles remained distinct, reflecting the social pattern of the country in which the Greeks and Egyptians co-existed but did not mingle.

In literature, certain types of Egyptian text continued from earlier times. These included the wall inscriptions in the Egyptian temples, the autobiographical inscriptions and the Wisdom Texts. However, the original purpose of the Autobiography – to record the successful events of the owner's life and thus prove him worthy of a blessed eternity – was changed to some extent. It now included a lament over the owner's too-early death which brought it closer to the Greek epitaphs where biographical details are combined with statements of mourning.

The Wisdom Instruction of Ankhsheshonq (Pap. British Museum 10508) is of uncertain date, although it possibly belonged to the late Ptolemaic Period. The text, written as practical, commonsense advice for an ordinary person, follows earlier examples. However, the personal circumstances of the writer are unique: Ankhsheshonq, finding himself in prison with time to write and think, took this opportunity to set down advice for his son.[51] Generally, the Egyptian texts of this period, like other art forms, perpetuated many of the earlier beliefs and ideas but also reflected the influence of the many profound political and economic changes that had affected the country.

THE COMING OF CHRISTIANITY

The Egyptians eagerly adopted Christianity as early as the first century ACE. The religion was introduced through Alexandria, having been brought there from Jerusalem by friends and relatives of the Alexandrian Jewish community.[52] Christianity, which promoted some concepts that were already familiar to the Egyptians from their ancient religion, was readily accepted by many people. In particular, the religion held an immediate appeal for the poor, with its message of disinterest in worldly goods and mutual support. However, wealthy people at first clung to their old beliefs, and the Roman rulers regarded Christianity as a subversive movement since it refused to acknowledge the divinity of the Emperor.

The Romans carried out a systematic persecution of the Christians in Egypt, but this only encouraged the masses to embrace the new faith as a sign of their antagonism to the Roman state, and by the end of the second century ACE, Christian communities in Alexandria and Lower Egypt were flourishing. Ultimately, the Emperor Constantine I (the son of Saint Helena), the first ruler who supported Christianity, put an end to the persecutions by issuing his Edict of Toleration (311 ACE). In a later Edict (384 ACE), Theodosius I (379–95 ACE), who was baptized a Christian soon after his accession, formally declared that Christianity was the official religion of the Roman Empire. He also ordered the closure of all temples dedicated to the old gods. There was now widespread persecution of heretics and pagans, and a systematic destruction of temples was pursued throughout Egypt, with the result that the old faith was largely destroyed. However, the temple of Isis on the island of Philae continued to function alongside the Christian churches, until it was closed in c.535 ACE in the reign of Justinian, and despite the official change in religion, many old customs nevertheless survived.[53]

With the establishment of Christianity, the nature of the Alexandrian patriarch's ecclesiastical position and his far-reaching influence on political and economic matters reflected the role that had once been played by the pharaoh.[54] Some earlier rites and ideas were also carried over into Egyptian Christianity, including saints' cults, pilgrimages, dreams, healing oracles and mortuary traditions.[55] Mummification continued in parts of Egypt and Nubia: although evisceration was discontinued, the surface of the body was spread with natron and other substances to make the skin soft and pliable. The body was elaborately dressed in embroidered clothes and boots, and wrapped in linen sheets. The Egyptian Christians did not disapprove of the preservation of the body after death, and the practice even survived amongst members of monastic communities.[56] Mummification only ceased to be practised after the Arab invasion of Egypt in 641 ACE, and the subsequent introduction of Islam.

Even the custom of holding funerary banquets at the tomb survived the onset of Christianity, although attempts were made to suppress it. For example, the Theodosian Code stated that tombs should be located outside the city walls, and forbade the celebration of funerary meals within the necropolis.[57] Even today, in Egypt, there are at least two funerary occasions whose origins can be traced to antiquity. On one of these – known as el-Arbeiyin – the deceased's family take food to his grave and present it to the poor who gather there. This can only take place once a period of forty days has elapsed since death, and it recalls the ancient Egyptian burial service when relatives gathered at the tomb for ceremonies that culminated in a funerary banquet. Another ancient custom is recalled in the contemporary annual visit that many people make to the family grave, carrying food specially prepared for the occasion which they present to the poor.

The contribution of the Egyptian temple to Christianity has never been extensively explored,[58] although there has been a brief study of the possibility that the concept of the Trinity was transmitted from ancient Egypt.[59] Other ideas have filtered down from Egyptian religion to both the Old and New Testaments and, as one writer states,[60] 'The influence of Egyptian religion on posterity is mainly felt through Christianity and its antecedents.' Associations have also been noted between the Egyptian Wisdom Texts and the Biblical Books of Psalms and Proverbs, and the Judaic and Christian doctrine of creation 'through the word' has parallels in the Egyptian creation myths. Also, the idea of a 'Day of Judgement' occurs in both Egyptian and Judaeo-Christian traditions, while the Osiris myth, with its emphasis on death, rebirth and resurrection, may have prepared the Egyptian mind for a ready acceptance of Christianity. Links have also been drawn between the Isis cult and Mariolatry, and it is evident that Egyptian religion influenced Christianity not only through the Old and New Testaments but also through the Egypto-Hellenistic traditions of Alexandria where Christianity first took root. However, the development of Christianity in Egypt was slower than is sometimes recognized, and the disappearance of paganism occurred over a long period, providing the opportunity for both traditions to influence each other.

In terms of popular religion, many customs have also survived.[61] In modern times, these ancient influences include such diverse elements as folk medicine,[62] and festivals in which pharaonic traditions survive in a recognizable form.[63] Today, the festival of Sham el-Nessim celebrates the coming of spring, when families take part in outings and give each other presents of coloured eggs. This continues an ancient festival that marked the rebirth of the vegetation and the renewal of life. Similarly, at the festival of Awru el-Nil, when the population of modern Egypt enjoys a national holiday and throws flowers into the Nile, they are recalling the ancient celebration of the inundation, when the god was requested to bestow an adequate flood and grant prosperity to the land and its inhabitants.

For thousands of years, the religion of ancient Egypt provided a sophisticated and brilliant people with ideas and institutions that supported them and apparently met their spiritual needs. Today, it is interesting to observe that some of these customs have survived as national traditions; most importantly, however, we can recognize that ancient Egyptian deliberations on immortality, monotheism, ethics and morals have made their own indelible imprint on the three great faiths of Judaism, Christianity and Islam.

Selected Passages from Egyptian Religious Texts

The following conventions have been observed in the translations: square brackets [ ] enclose restorations of the text; parentheses ( ) enclose additions in the English translations; a question mark (?) indicates a tentative translation; and a row of dots . . . indicates a lacuna in the Egyptian text or an omission in the English translation.

A THE COFFIN TEXTS

A good example of the Coffin Texts occurs on the coffins found in the Middle Kingdom tomb of 'Two Brothers' (named Khnum-Nakht and Nekht-Ankh) which was discovered at Der Rifeh in 1905 ACE. This large, unsculptured tomb (c.1900 BCE) was cut into the cliffs about eight miles south of Assiut in Middle Egypt. It was part of the cemetery for the ancient town of Shas-hotep, dedicated to the ram-headed god Khnum. Previously undisturbed, the tomb was found to contain the mummies of the brothers, their anthropoid and rectangular painted wooden coffins, Nekht-Ankh's canopic chest and jars, and their tomb models, statuettes, and other funerary goods. The complete tomb-group was acquired from the excavator, W. M. F. Petrie, by the Manchester University Museum in England in 1907 ACE. Petrie described the group as one of the best examples of a non-royal burial of the Middle Kingdom which had ever been discovered.

The two brothers, residents of Shashotep, would have enjoyed a moderately wealthy lifestyle. Nekht-Ankh held the priesthood of Khnum, a position he inherited from his father and grandfather. The tomb-group, including the texts painted on the rectangular wooden coffins, is typical of the provincial style of the period.

Coffin of Nekht-Ankh

Lid Inscription

Utterance,[1] may you sit upon the *pesekh* seat[2] of turquoise at the prow of the barque of Re. May you purify yourself in the Cool Lake. May Anubis fumigate the incense for you, revered one, son of a local prince, Nekht-Ankh, offspring of Khnum-Aa.[3]

A-boon-which-the-King-gives[4] and boon which Anubis, Lord of Sep, gives in front of the divine booth, that he may ferry across, that he may be interred, that he may ascend to the great god,[5] lord of heaven, in peace (twice), upon the beautiful ways of the West.

Utterance. Your mother Nut has shared with you in her name of Shetpet. She has caused you to be a god without enemies, in your name of Great God. She protects you against all evil things, in her name of Khnumet.

Right-side (horizontal)

A-boon-which-the-King-gives and which Anubis gives, he who is upon his mountain, he who is in the place of embalming, lord of the Sacred Land,[6] may he give a good burial in the western necropolis, in his tomb of the underworld, revered one, son of a local prince, Nekht-Ankh, justified.

Utterance. The gates of the horizon are opened, its doorbolts are drawn back. He has come before the Red Crown, he has come before the Great One, he has come before Great-of-Magic.[7] Pure things (are) for you, many (things) (are) for you, may you be satisfied concerning it, may you be satisfied concerning the pure things.

Right-side (vertical)

Utterance. You shine forth as the two feathers of Soped.

Revered before Hapy, Nekht-Ankh, justified.

Revered before Tefnut, Nekht-Ankh, born of Khnum-Aa.

Utterance. May the donkeys come down to you.

Utterance. May the Sem-priest perform the ceremonies for you at the Going-forth.[8]

Revered before Nut who has borne the gods.

Revered before Qebehsenuef.

Utterance. Birds and oxen, 450 head of the estate (?) are slaughtered for you.

Head End

Revered before Nephthys, Nekht-Ankh, justified.

Utterance. May you be clothed with the sacred robes of Ptah, Nekht-Ankh.

Revered before the Little Ennead.

Revered before the Great Ennead.

Foot End

Revered before Isis the goddess, Nekht-Ankh.

Utterance. May this your father go forth from your house, Horus, may he embrace you.

Revered before Selket.

Revered before Neith, Nekht-Ankh, born of Khnum-Aa.

Left-side (horizontal)

A-boon-which-the-King-gives (to) Osiris, Lord of Busiris,[9] the Great God, Lord of Abydos, in all his places, that he may give invocation-offerings (consisting of) bread and beer, oxen and fowl, alabaster, clothing and incense, all things good and pure on which a god lives, to the spirit of the revered Nekht-Ankh, born of Khnum-Aa.

Utterance. The Great Ennead praises you, the Little Ennead worships you, the Upper Egyptian Conclave praises you, the Lower Egyptian Conclave names you, your poison is destroyed, the Nine Bows[10] follow you.

Left-side (vertical)

May your place be broad in the bark.
Revered before Imset, Nekht-Ankh, justified.
Revered before Shu, son of Re, lord of Heaven.
[?] in (your) limbs, may the sky approach you.
Eating a cake which comes forth from Letopolis.
Revered before Geb, father of gods, Nekht-Ankh, justified.
Revered before Duamutef, Nekht-Ankh, justified.
Utterance by Re: I make your name Horus.

Coffin of Khnum-Nakht

Lid inscription

Utterance. Your mother Nut has spread herself over you in her name of 'Veil-of-heaven'. She makes you exist as a god, without enemies, in your name of Great God, lord of the sky. Welcome, welcome, your mother, Nut, as she exists.

A boon-which-the-King-gives and which Anubis gives in front of the divine booth, Lord of Sep, that he may ferry across the sky, that he may be interred in the Pure Place which is in the sky, the revered one, great *w'b*-priest, son of the local prince, Khnum-Nakht, born of Khnum-Aa, justified.

Right side

A boon-which-the-King-gives and which Anubis gives, he who is upon his mountain, lord of *R-krrt*[11] he who is in the place of embalming, lord of the Sacred Land,[12] may he have a good burial in the necropolis amongst the revered ones of the necropolis, the revered one, son of the local prince, Khnum-Nakht, born of Khnum-Aa, justified.

Utterance. It is the voice (of) the revered ones who come in peace to the beautiful West from the Island of Flame. This Osiris Khnum-Nakht comes in peace from the Island of Flame. Prostrate yourselves to him upon your bellies, make jubilation for him, create for him the protection of the book.

Left side

A-boon-which-the-King-gives (to) Osiris, Lord of Busiris, the Great God, Lord of Abydos, in all his places, that he may give invocation-offerings (consisting of) bread and beer, oxen and fowl, clothing, incense and ointment, all things good and pure which the sky creates, which the earth produces, in abundance, on which a god lives, to the spirit of the revered great *w'b*-priest, lord of Shashotep,[13] son of the local prince, Khnum-Nakht.

Utterance. A cry comes forth from the mouth of all the Great Ones, a call falls from the mouth of the Wrapped Ones.[14]

B THE DAILY TEMPLE RITUAL

This ritual was performed every day in every divine cult complex and every royal cult complex throughout Egypt. No complete list of the episodes of this ritual has yet been discovered, but the Berlin Papyrus (Dynasty 22) provides a total of sixty-six episodes of the ritual which was performed for Amun in his temple at Karnak. Also, several temples preserve wall-scenes with accompanying inscriptions which represent some of the same episodes. The most complete set (twenty-nine episodes) occurs in the six chapels of the sanctuary area in the Temple of King Sethos I at Abydos (*c.*1300 BCE). However, neither source provides a complete version of the ritual. These episodes probably formed part of an original, as yet undiscovered, service book. This translation is a condensed version of the episodes on the walls of the Chapel of Re-Harakhte in the Temple of Sethos I at Abydos.

Entry

Episode 1
'Spell for entering in order to uncover the face in the interior of the palace and the chapels which are beside the Sanctuary.'

(Sethos says to Atum:)

I have come before thee, the Great One following me, my purification upon my arms. I have passed by Tefnut, Tefnut having purified me. Assuredly, I am a prophet, the son of a prophet of this temple. I shall not linger, I shall not turn back. I am a prophet. I have come to perform the ritual. Indeed, I have not come to do that which is not to be done.

Opening the Shrine

Episode 3
'Spell for unfastening the seal.'

(The King is breaking the string, removing the seal, in order to open this door. He says:)

For I have completely cast out all evils that pertained to me. I have come and I have brought your eye; Horus, your eye belongs to you. Oh, Horus, I am Thoth who assesses the sound eye.

Episode 4
'Spell for pulling back the bolt.'

(The King says to Re-Harakhte:)

The finger of Seth[15] is withdrawn from the Eye of Horus, and it is well. The finger of Seth is unloosed from the Eye of Horus, and it is well. The cord is undone from Osiris, the sickness is unloosed from the god. Re-Harakhte, receive for yourself your two white plumes, [your] right one on your right,

[your] left one on your left. Oh, naked one, dress yourself, oh, bandaged one, bandage yourself.

. . . Indeed, I am a prophet; it is the king who has commanded me to see the god. I am that great phoenix who is in Heliopolis.[16]

Adoring the God

Episode 9
'Spell for entering the Great Place.'[17]

(The King says to Re-Harakhte:)

May the god be in peace (twice), living spirit who strikes his enemies. Your *ba* is with you, your power is at your side. I have brought for you, the King, Lord of the Two Lands, Menmaetre,[18] given life, your living image associating with you.

Episode 10
'Spell for kissing the ground; putting oneself upon one's belly in order to touch the ground with one's fingers.'

(The King says to Atum:)

I kiss the ground, my face bowed. I offer Ma'at to its lord, and offerings to their Maker. There is no god who has made what you have made, Re-Harakhte, and I will not present my face towards the sky, and I will not commit impurity and I will not make your grace like that of any other god. Greetings to you! I have brought your heart for you in your body. I have placed (it) for you in its place.

Purification of the God

Episode 11
'Spell for cleansing the Sanctuary.'

(The King to Atum:)

I am Horus; I have come seeking for my two eyes; I shall not allow that it should be far from you, Re-Harakhte. Atum, Lord of the Great Mansion, who resides in the Mansion of Menmaetre,[19] behold me carrying it! May you come in peace! It has driven out all your impurities, for you have assembled it, Atum, father of the gods, who resides in the Mansion of Menmaetre.

Preparing the God

Episode 13
'Spell for laying hands upon the god.'

(The King says to Re-Harakhte:)

Thoth is come to see you, his *nms*-cloth[20] at his throat, his tail at his buttocks. Awake you, that you may hear his voice. Oh, greetings to you, Re-Harakhte, with that which your father Atum has judged you.

My arms are upon you as Horus, my arms are upon you as Thoth, my fingers are upon you as Anubis.

Episode 14
'Spell for wiping off the *md*-ointment.'[21]

(The King to the god:)

I am come, and anoint you with unguent which came out of the Eye of Horus. May it bind your bones, may it re-unite your limbs, may it reassemble your flesh. It releases all your evil fluids.

Episode 15
'Spell for taking off the clothing.'[22]

(The King to the god:)

Your beauty belongs to you, your *m'r*-cloth[23] is around you, Re-Harakhte, who resides in the Mansion of Menmaetre. I have seized for you this Eye of Horus. Adorn yourself with it. You possess your beauty, you possess your raiment, you are a god, oh Re-Harakhte.

Robing: outside the Shrine

Episode 17
'Spell for arraying with the White Cloth.'

(The King to the god:)

Oh, Re-Harakhte, take for yourself this your shining cloth! Take for yourself this your beautiful cloth! Take for yourself this your *m'r*-garment! Take for yourself this your *mnht* cloth![24]

Take for yourself this Eye of White Horus, coming forth from Nekhen, that you may shine in it, that you may be splendid in it, in this its name of *mnht*, that it may cleave to you, in this its name of *idmi*.[25]

Episode 18
'Making purification with 4 pellets of *bd*-natron.'

(The King to Re-Harakhte:)

Making purification with 4 pellets of *bd*-natron.[26] Your natron is the natron of Horus; the natron of Horus is your natron; your natron is the natron of Thoth and vice versa; your natron is the natron of Soker and vice versa. You are established amongst them. To be recited 3 times. You are pure (twice), Re-Harakhte.

(Episodes 19 and 21 are spells for arraying with the green and red cloths. Episodes 20 and 22 are spells for purification with Upper and Lower Egyptian natron.)

Episode 23
'Spell for presenting the broad collar.'[27]

(The King to Atum:)

Hail to you, Atum! Hail to you, Khepri! You are elevated upon the stairway, you rise in the Benben, in the House of the Benben in Heliopolis.

(The King asks the god to protect Atum, and then invokes the Ennead:)

Oh, Great Ennead of gods who are in Heliopolis, Atum, Shu, Tefnut, Geb, Nut, Osiris, Isis, Seth and Nephthys, children of Atum, who turns his heart to his children in these their names of the Nine Bows,[28] let him not turn his back to you, in order that your name of the Ennead may be pronounced. May he protect Atum from his enemies, and when he protects, no evil thing shall come to him forever and ever.

Robing: inside the Shrine

Episode 27
'Fixing the two plumes upon the head.'[29]

(The King to Atum:)

The great crown is on the head of Atum who resides in the Mansion of Menmaetre. Isis establishes it for you upon your head, Soker adorns it for you, and Re glorifies it, when he makes you triumphant over your enemies, for Atum is more sacrosanct than gods and spirits. Your two plumes are on your head, having appeared on your forehead.

Episode 28
'Spell for giving the *w3s*-sceptre,[30] crook, flail, bracelets and anklets.'

(The King to Re-Harakhte:)

I have given you your Horus Eye, I have bound for you your bones, I have made your limbs to grow for you. May he give the lifespan of his body in the sky, and love of him in the hearts of the patricians to the Sons of Re . . .

Episode 31
'Spell for arraying the body with the *nms*-cloth.'[31]

(The King to the goddess Hathor-Nebet-Hetepet:)

The White Cloth comes (twice), the White Eye of Horus comes, having left El Kab, the cloth in which the gods are covered, in this its own name of adornment.

May you array Nebet-hetepet[32] . . . May you adorn her, may you assume your position on her arms in [this name of yours of White One] of Nekhen, Nekhbet, who has come forth from Nekhen.

Episode 33
'Spell for putting on the great cloth after these.'

(The King to the goddess *Iw.s-'3.s*:)

His raiment is the cloth which *Iw.s-'3.s*, who resides in the Mansion of Menmaetre, received. Her raiment is the *idmi*-cloth from the arms of Tait[33] . . . the god approached his god, that he may array the god in this his own name of *idmi* . . .

Isis has woven it, Nephthys has spun it. May you make the cloth to shine on the day of *Iw.s-'3.s*. May you triumph against your enemies.

Exit

Episode 35
'Spell for wiping out the footprint, with the *hdn*-plant.'[34]

(The inscription reads:)

Thoth comes, he has rescued the Eye of Horus from his enemies, and no enemy, male or female, enters into this sanctuary. Closing the door by Ptah, fastening the door by Thoth, closing the door and fastening the door with a bolt.

Post-exit Purification

Episode 36
'Making purification with incense upon the fire, walking around 4 times.'[35]

(The King to Atum:)

Take to thee the Eye of Horus, [its perfume comes towards you, the perfume of the Eye of Horus comes towards you. Spoken 4 times. You are pure (twice)].

C THE RITUAL OF THE ROYAL ANCESTORS

This ritual was performed in every royal cult complex from the New Kingdom onwards. It took the form of a daily presentation of food to the Royal Ancestors (dead kings of Egypt), which had been previously removed from the god's altar at the culmination of the Daily Temple Ritual, in the rite known as the 'First Reversion of Offerings'. At the end of the Ritual of the Royal Ancestors, when the 'Second Reversion of Offerings' was performed, the food was removed from the Ancestors' altar and divided amongst the priests as daily rations. The ritual was preserved in various papyri (Chester Beatty IX, Cairo and Turin), as well as on the walls of several temples. In the Temple of Sethos I at Abydos (*c.*1300 BCE), the rites occur consecutively in several areas of the building, depicted in scenes arranged in horizontal registers on the interior walls. The two Reversions of Offerings are translated below.

The First Reversion of Offerings
Title: 'Spell for entering for the Reversion of Offerings to the King, Lord of the Two Lands, Menmaetre, given life.'

(The god *Iwn-mwt.f* and Thoth stand before the bark. A priest representing Thoth would have spoken the following words:)

Hail, Son of Re, Sety Merenptah, your enemies are turned back, your father Atum has repelled them. Horus turns himself on account of his Eye, in its name of Reversion of Offerings.

Your perfume belongs to you, oh gods; your sweat belongs to you, oh gods. [I am Thoth] and I have come to perform the ritual for King Menmaetre, given life, and his Ennead.

Oh, that the Eye of Horus that is before you might flourish for you . . .

Making-a-boon-which-the-king-gives for the King Menmaetre, given life, by Horus *Iwn-mwt.f*, Lord of the Great Mansion, with bread and beer, and [oxen] and all kinds of fowl, and every pure thing.[36]

The Second Reversion of Offerings

Title: 'Making-a-boon-which-the-king-gives, the Reversion of Offerings by his beloved son, the King's eldest bodily son, hereditary prince, Ramesses, life prosperity, health.'

(Sethos I (still alive) and Prince Ramesses (who performs the rite as though Sethos were already a dead king) stand before an offering list. Above the list of offerings are the words:)

Making-a-boon-which-the-King-gives for Ptah-Soker-Osiris, Foremost of the Westerners, who resides in the Mansion of Menmaetre, and the Ennead who are in attendance upon him, by the King Menmaetre, Son of Re, Sety Merenptah.

Come to me, Ptah-Soker-Osiris . . . oh, ranger of the gods, come, at your invocation, oh, you swift gods, come to me; oh, Ptah-Soker-Osiris, come, oh ranger of the gods, to King Menmaetre, thy Majesty, thy servant, who does not forget your body, with all these your provisions.

You enter into this your bread, into this your beer, namely choicest meat portions of cattle and fowl, in millions and hundred thousands, tens of thousands, thousands and hundreds. You have filled your house with all good things.

Thoth is pleased with the White Eye of Horus, that your face may be white thereby, in its name of bread.

D THE ATEN HYMNS

The most complete statement of the doctrine of Atenism is to be found in 'The Great Hymn to the Aten', which may owe its authorship or inspiration to King Akhenaten. The hymn (translated below) was inscribed on the west wall in the tomb of Ay at Amarna, above figures of Ay and his wife. Other short hymns and prayers have also been found, addressed either jointly to the Aten and the king or to the Aten alone. Their similarity to each other indicates that they were probably derived from a common source compiled by a royal scribe. 'The Shorter Hymn to the Aten' was inscribed on the west wall in the tomb of the courtier Ahmes at Amarna.

The Great Hymn to the Aten

You appear in splendour in the horizon of heaven,
O living Aten who originates life!
When you shine forth in the eastern horizon
You fill every land with your beauty.
You are beautiful, you are great,
You are radiant, you are high over every land.
Your rays encompass the lands
To the limit of all that you have made.
You are Re and you reach their limits.
You subdue them (for) your beloved son.[37]
You are far away, but your rays are on earth.
You are in sight, but your movements are unseen.

When you set in the western horizon,
The Earth is in darkness as in the state of death;
They[38] sleep in chambers, their heads covered
And no eye catches sight of another.

If their possessions were stolen,
Although they are under their heads,
Yet they would not perceive it.
Every lion comes forth from its den
And all serpents bite.

The darkness hovers, and
The earth is silent
While their creator rests in his horizon

The earth grows bright when you arise in the horizon,
When you shine as the Aten by day;
As you dispel the darkness,
As you shed your beams,
The Two Lands make festival.

Awakened, they stand on their feet,
For you have raised them up.
Their bodies cleansed, they assume their clothes,
Their hands are upraised in praise of your appearance,

The entire land goes about its work,
All beasts are content on their pastures,
Trees and herbs become verdant.
Birds fly from their nests,
Their wings giving praise to your spirit.

All flocks frisk on their feet,
All that take wing,
They live, when you arise for them.

Ships fare north and also fare south.
Every route is opened when you appear.
The fish in the river leap before your face,
Your rays are in the midst of the sea.

Who makes seed to grow in women
Who makes life-fluid in mankind,
Who gives life to the son in his mother's womb,
Who soothes him so that he does not cry.

Nurse in the womb,
Who gives breath
To keep alive all that he has made.

When he comes forth from the womb
To breath, on the day of his birth,
You open wide his mouth
And supply his needs.

When the chick in the egg chirps in the shell,
You give him air in it to sustain him.
When you have made him complete
To break out from the egg,
He comes out from the egg
To speak of his completion;
Walking on his two feet,
He comes forth from it.

How manifold are your deeds!
They are hidden from sight,
O Sole God, like whom there is no other!
You made the earth as you desired, you alone.

All people, herds and flocks,
All that is on earth that walks on legs,
All that soars above, that fly on wings,
The lands of Khor and Kush[39]
And the land of Egypt.

You set every man in his place,
You supply their needs,

Each one has provision,
His lifetime is reckoned.[40]

Their tongues are diverse in speech,
And their characters likewise;
Their skins are distinct,
For you have distinguished the peoples.

You made the Nile in the netherworld,[41]
You bring it when you so desire,
To sustain the people,
Even as you have given them life.

You are lord of them all,
Who toils for them,
The lord of all lands,
Who shines for them,
Aten of the daytime, great of majesty.

All far-off lands, you have made their life,
You made a Nile in the sky[42]
That it may descend for them
That it may make waves on the hills like the sea,
To drench their fields and their towns.

How excellent are your plans, O Lord of Eternity!
A Nile flood in the sky, you appoint it for the foreign peoples,
And all animals of every country that walk on legs.
But the Nile comes forth from the underworld for Egypt.

Your rays give sustenance to all fields,
When you shine forth, they live and they grow for thee.

You make the seasons to nurture all that you have made,
The winter to cool them,
The heat that they may taste you.

You made the distant sky to shine in it,
In order to see all that you have made.

You are alone, shining in your form of living
Aten, risen, radiant, distant, near.[43]
(But) you make millions of forms from yourself alone,
Towns and villages, fields, roads and river.
Every eye sees you ahead of them,
For you are the Aten of the daytime on high,
You are in my heart,
There is no other who knows you
Except your son, Neferkheprure,[44] Sole-One-of-Re,
You have made him skilled in your ways and in your strength.
The earth comes into being as the result of your hand,
For you have created them.

When you have arisen, they live,
When you set, they die.

You yourself are lifetime and men live in you.
All eyes look upon your beauty until you set,
All work ceases when you set in the West.

When you rise, you make everyone prosper for the king,
Every leg is in action since you founded the earth.

You raise them up for your son who came forth from your body, the King of
Upper and Lower Egypt, who lives on truth, the Lord of the Two Lands,
Neferkheprure, Sole-One-of-Re, Son of Re, living on Truth, Lord of Dia-
dems, Akhenaten, great in his duration; and for the King's Great Royal Wife
whom he loves, Lady of the Two Lands, Nefernefruaten-Nefertiti, may she
live and flourish for ever and ever.

The Shorter Hymn to the Aten[45]

Beautiful you arise, oh Harakhti-who-rejoices-in-the-horizon-in-his-name-Shu-who-is-in-Aten.[46] You living sun beside whom there is no other, who gives health to the eyes with his rays, who has created everything that exists.

You arise in the horizon of heaven to give life to all that you have created, to all men, [all animals], all that flies and soars, and to all reptiles that are on earth. They live when they see you, they sleep when you rest.

You cause your son Neferkheprure-Sole-One-of-Re,[47] to live with you forever, and (to do what) your heart (wishes), and to see what you have made every day. He makes jubilation when he sees your beauty.

Grant him life, joy and happiness so that all that you encompass may be under [his feet]. He administers them for your spirit.

Your son, whom you have yourself begotten. [?] the south as the north, the west and the east. The Isles in the midst of the Great Green[48] make jubilation to his spirit. His southern boundary stretches as far as the wind blows, the northern (boundaries) as far as the Aten shines.

All their rulers are made supplicant and rendered weak because of his power, this beautiful essence that makes the Two Lands festive and meets the requirements of the entire country. Let him be with you forever and ever, as he loves to gaze upon you; grant him very many jubilees[49] and many years of peace; give him of that which your heart loves, even as the multitude of sand is on the shore, as the fish in the rivers have scales, and cattle have hair.

Let him reside here[50] until the [swan?] turns black, until the [raven?] becomes white, until the hills arise to depart, until water flows upstream, while I continue to attend the good god[51] until he allocates me the burial which he grants.[52]

A Selective List of Major Religious Sites in Egypt and Nubia

Many Egyptian sites have more than one name; sometimes, there are modern (Arabic), ancient Egyptian, and Classical (Greek or Graeco-Roman) names. In this list, the sites are generally arranged under the modern name (this often refers to a village near the archaeological site), and the ancient Egyptian and Classical names (if known) are given in brackets. In some cases, the site is better known by a name other than the modern one, and this is then given in small capitals (e.g. San el-Hagar; *Eg*: Dja'net; *Cl*: TANIS)

1 LOWER EGYPT: DELTA SITES

Kom Abu Billo (*Eg*: Tarrana; *Cl*: Tereruthis)

Town where serpent goddess Renenutet was probably worshipped. Temple to Hathor, and necropolis with burials ranging from Dynasty 6 to the fourth century ACE.

Kom el-Hisn (*Eg*: Imu)

Capital of the Third Lower Egyptian nome from New Kingdom. Temple to Sekhmet-Hathor. Cemeteries of Middle and New Kingdoms.

Naukratis

Site of Greek trading post from Dynasty 26. Several Greek temples, and Egyptian temple to Amun and Thoth.

Alexandria

Chief city and port of the Hellenistic world, founded by Alexander the Great. Important buildings included the Serapeum, the centre for the cult of Serapis; and catacombs of Kom el-Shuqafa (first to second century ACE).

San el-Hagar (*Eg*: Zau; *Cl*: SAIS)

Capital of the Fifth Lower Egyptian nome; in Dynasty 26, capital of Egypt, with temples and royal tombs. Centre of goddess Neith since earliest times.

Tell el-Fara'in (*Eg*: Per-Wadjit; BUTO)

Ancient capital of the Red Land; cult centre of goddess Wadjet. Remains of a temple enclosure.

Behbeit el-Hagar (near SEBENNYTOS)

Site of important temple of Isis (Late Ptolemaic period).

Tell Atrib (*Eg*: Hut-hery-ib; *Cl*: ATHRIBIS)

Capital of the Tenth Lower Egyptian nome. Crocodile- or falcon-god Khentekhtai worshipped here in pharaonic times. Although occupied since at least Dynasty 4, the archaeological evidence dates from Dynasty 26 and the Graeco-Roman Period. Temples and tombs have been discovered here.

Tell el-Muqdam (*Cl*: LEONTOPOLIS)

Capital of the Eleventh Lower Egyptian nome in Ptolemaic Period. Burial place of Queen Kamama, mother of Osorkon IV. May be royal cemetery of Dynasty 23. Temple of lion-god Mihos.

Samannud (*Eg*: Tjebnutjer; *Cl*: SEBENNYTOS)

Capital of the Twelfth Lower Egyptian nome. Home of Manetho. Possibly centre of rulers of Dynasty 30. Temple of Onuris-Shu (Dynasty 30 and Ptolemaic Period).

El-Baqliya (*Eg*: Ba'h; *Cl*: Hermopolis Parva)

Capital of the Fifteenth Lower Egyptian nome; temple of Thoth, and necropolis, including ibis cemetery.

Tell el-Rub'a and Tell el-Timai (*Eg*: Per-banebdjedet; *Cl*: MENDES (el-Rub'a) and Thmuis (el-Timai)

Both the site of capital of the Sixteenth Lower Egyptian nome. Most important local cult of the ram; cemetery of sacred rams. Tombs of Dynasty 4; temple of Dynasty 26 is attested by foundation deposits. Tell el-Rub'a was possibly capital of Dynasty 29.

Heliopolis (*Cl*) (*Eg*: Iunu; Arabic: Tell Hisn)

Capital of the Thirteenth Lower Egyptian nome. Modern suburb of Cairo. Centre of cult of sun god. Temple (now destroyed) to Re-Atum. Tombs of High-priests (Dynasty 5); also burials of New Kingdom and Late Period, and Ramesside Period tombs of Mnevis bulls.

Tell el-Yahudiya (*Eg*: Nay-ta-hut; *Cl*: LEONTOPOLIS)

Massive enclosure walls, possibly built by Asiatics during the Hyksos Period; building may have had religious use. Temple of Ramesses II probably built inside enclosure. Another temple built (reign of Ptolemy VI) by exiled Jewish priest Onias. Cemeteries from Middle Kingdom.

Tell Basta (*Eg*: Per-Bastet; *Cl*: BUBASTIS)

Capital of the Eighteenth Lower Egyptian nome in Late Period. Cult-centre of lioness-goddess Bastet. Centre of kings of Dynasty 22. Temple of Bastet. Other temples and religious buildings cover the period from the Old Kingdom to Roman times.

Saft el-Hinna (*Eg*: Per-Sopdu)

Capital of the Twentieth nome of Lower Egypt. Soped was worshipped here. Remains of local temple.

Qantir

Pi-Ramesse (residence of the Ramessides and the Biblical Ramses) is probably near Qantir.

Tell el-Dab'a (*Cl*: AVARIS)

To the south of Qantir, Tell ed-Dab'a (probably Avaris, the Hyksos capital) has evidence of Aegean presence or influence during the Hyksos Period. In the later New Kingdom, a temple was built, dedicated to Seth.

Tell Nabasha (*Eg*: Imet)

Temple enclosure of Wadjet, with at least two temples (probably Ramesside and Dynasty 26).

San el-Hagar (*Eg*: Dja'net; *Cl*: TANIS)

Royal residence and necropolis during Dynasties 21 and 22. Great temple of Amun and royal tombs and treasure. Building material from earlier Ramesside monuments re-used here in Dynasty 21. Later chapels and temples, down to Graeco-Roman Period.

Tell el-Maskhuta (*Eg*: Tjeku; Biblical: PITHOM)

Capital of the Eighth Lower Egyptian nome. Might be city of Pithom mentioned in connection with the Exodus. Temple excavated here.

2 LOWER EGYPT: THE PYRAMID AREA

Mit Rahina (*Eg*: Ineb-hedj ('White Wall'); later, Mennufer; *Cl*: MEMPHIS)

Little remains of Memphis, royal residence and capital in Archaic Period and Old Kingdom, and centre of the First Lower Egyptian nome. Temple of Ptah enclosure; alabaster sphinx. Other religious buildings included embalming house of Apis bulls, temple of Tuthmosis IV, and other temples to Hathor and Ptah. Tombs of First Intermediate and Late Periods.

The necropolis of Memphis included Dahshur, Saqqara, Abusir, Zawiyet el-'Aryan, Giza, and Abu Rawash.

Dahshur

Important pyramids demonstrate the transition to the true pyramid form: Bent Pyramid (Dynasties 3/4) and Northern Stone Pyramid (Red Pyramid) which was the first true pyramid (Dynasty 4). Dynasty 12: pyramids of Amenemhet II (White Pyramid), Senusret III, and Amenemhet III (Black Pyramid).

Saqqara

Extensive necropolis includes world's first great stone monument, Step Pyramid of Djoser (Dynasty 3). There are also pyramids of Userkaf, Isesi, and Unas (all Dynasty 5), and of Teti, Pepy I and Pepy II (all Dynasty 6). Royal 'tombs' of Archaic Period, and officials' tombs from Old Kingdom onwards, including late New Kingdom courtiers Horemheb, Tia and Maya. Sacred animal complexes including Serapeum for Apis-bull burials.

Abusir

Sun temple of Userkaf (Dynasty 5). Three pyramid complexes of Sahure, Neferirkare and Niuserre (Dynasty 5). Mastabas, including tomb of Vizier Ptahshepses (Dynasty 5).

Abu Gurob

Sun temples of Userkaf and Niuserre (Dynasty 5).

Zawiyet el-'Aryan

Incomplete pyramids – 'Layer Pyramid' (Dynasty 3) and 'Unfinished Pyramid' (Dynasty 4).

Giza

Pyramid complexes (Dynasty 4) of Cheops (Khufu), Chephren (Khaefre) and Mycerinus (Menkaure). Complex of Chephren is most complete, with pyramid, valley building, causeway and royal cult-temple; Great Sphinx is situated near the valley building. Tomb of Queen Hetepheres (Dynasty 4) near Cheops' pyramid. Extensive cemeteries of mastabas for members of the royal family and officials. Egypt's most famous archaeological site.

Abu Rawash

Early dynastic necropolis. Pyramid of Djedefre (Dynasty 4).

3 THE FAYOUM AND ASSOCIATED AREA

The Fayoum (*Eg*: She-resy)

Important centre in Dynasty 12 and Graeco-Roman Period; location of Lake Moeris (Arabic: Birket Qarun). Site of royal cemeteries (Lahun, Hawara) in Dynasty 12, and Greek and Macedonian immigrants settled there in Graeco-Roman Period. Cult centre of Sobek (Suchos), the crocodile-god.

Hawara

Pyramid of Amenemhet III (Dynasty 12) and his mortuary temple (the 'Labyrinth'). Cemeteries from Middle Kingdom to Graeco-Roman Period (discovery of many of the mummy panel portraits). Temples of both periods.

El-Lahun

Pyramid of Senusret II (Dynasty 12), and royal jewellery in associated shaft tomb.

Kahun (*Eg*: Hetep-Senusret)

Town of royal workers who built Lahun pyramid. Source of domestic religious artifacts and famous papyri.

Kom Medinet Ghurab (GUROB)

New Kingdom royal residence town, particularly in reign of Amenhotep III. Remains of two temples, cemeteries and domestic quarters.

Meydum

Pyramid built for Huni or Sneferu (Dynasty 4): first attempt (unsuccessful) to construct a true pyramid. Cemeteries (Dynasty 4) for Sneferu's courtiers, including famous tombs of Ra-hotep and Nefert, Nefermaat and Itet.

El-Lisht (*Eg*: It-towy)

Capital city of Dynasty 12 has never been located, but it was served by the cemeteries at el-Lisht, el-Lahun and Hawara. Pyramids of Amenemhet I and Senusret I. Private tombs of Old and Middle Kingdoms.

4 MIDDLE EGYPT

Ihnasya el-Medina (*Eg*: Henen-nesut; *Cl*: HERACLEOPOLIS MAGNA)

Capital of the Twentieth Upper Egyptian nome. Chief god, ram-headed Herishef, became Greek Herakles. Temple to god, enlarged in New Kingdom, and used until Late Period. Important city in First Intermediate Period; tombs of contemporary officials. Main necropolis probably at nearby Sidmant el-Gebel.

El-Bahnasa (*Eg*:Per-medjed; *Cl*: OXYRHYNCHUS)

Capital of the Nineteenth Upper Egyptian nome. Known in Graeco-Roman Period as Oxyrhynchus, after species of mormyrus fish worshipped there. Substantial Roman remains. Source of major archive of Greek papyri.

Beni Hasan

Most important Middle Kingdom provincial necropolis in Middle Egypt. Necropolis of town of Monet-Khufu. Large rock-cut tombs of great provincial rulers of Oryx Nome (Sixteenth nome of Upper Egypt) in Dynasties 11 and 12. Rock-cut temple (Speos Artemidos) to south, dedicated to lioness-goddess Pakhet (Dynasty 18).

El-Sheikh 'Ibada (*Cl*: Antinoopolis)

City founded by Emperor Hadrian (130 ACE) in memory of favourite Antinous who drowned here. Temple of Ramesses II.

El-Ashmunein (*Eg*: Khmun; *Cl*: HERMOPOLIS MAGNA)

Capital of Fifteenth Upper Egyptian nome. Cult-centre of Thoth, place of origin of major creation myth. Greeks identified Thoth with their god Hermes. Graeco-Roman remains included Temple of Thoth. Pylon of temple built by Ramesses II was found to contain over fifteen hundred decorated blocks brought from dismantled temples dedicated to the Aten at Amarna.

Tuna el-Gebel

Necropolis of Hermopolis Magna; also catacombs with ibis and baboon burials (mostly Graeco-Roman). Tomb of Petosiris (*c.*300 BCE), and others (the first centuries ACE), including that of Isadora. Northwestern stela in group of six erected by Akhenaten (Dynasty 18) to mark the boundary of Akhetaten and its environs.

Deir el-Bersha

Rock-cut tombs, mostly Dynasty 12, of governors of Fifteenth Upper Egyptian nome, in desert ravine. Most famous belonged to provincial governor Djehutihotep.

Tell el-Amarna (AMARNA; *Eg*: Akhetaten)

Capital city of Akhenaten (Dynasty 18) and cult-centre of the Aten. Aten temples, courtiers' tombs, and the Royal Tomb (nine kilometres distant, in remote mountain valley) provide evidence about Atenism. Workmen's village: continuing traditional domestic worship.

Meir

Rock-cut tombs of local governors of Fourteenth Upper Egyptian nome in Dynasties 6 and 12.

Deir el-Gebrawi

Rock-cut tombs of local governors of Twelfth Upper Egyptian nome in Dynasty 6.

Assiut (*Eg*: Zawty; *Cl*: Lycopolis)

Capital of Thirteenth nome of Upper Egypt. Cult-centre of god Wepwawet. Tombs of First Intermediate Period, Middle Kingdom and Ramesside times. Important town in First Intermediate Period.

5 UPPER EGYPT (NORTH)

Qau el-Kebir (*Eg*: Tjebu; *Cl*:Antaiopolis or Panopolis)

Tombs of officials of Dynasty 12, and later periods.

Akhmim (*Eg*: Ipu or Khent-min; *Cl*: Khemmis)

Capital of Ninth Upper Egyptian nome. Extensive cemeteries. Cult of Min (rock-chapel, Dynasty 18). Rock-cut tombs nearby at el-Hawawish and el-Salamuni.

Beit Khallaf

Five mastabas of officials (Dynasty 3).

Abydos (*Eg*: Abedju)

Egypt's most important religious centre. Cult-centre of Khentiamentiu, and later of Osiris. Royal tombs/cenotaphs of Archaic Period at Umm el-Ga'ab. Possibly early funerary enclosure at Shunet el-Zebib. Temple at Kom El-Sultan. Tombs of Old, Middle and New Kingdoms and later periods. Royal cult temples of Sethos I (Dynasty 19), with associated Osireion or 'Cenotaph of Osiris'; and of Ramesses I and II.

Hu (*Eg*: Hut-sekhem; *Cl*: DIOSPOLIS PARVA)

Cult-centre of goddess Bat. Extensive human (all periods) and animal (Graeco-Roman Period) cemeteries.

Denderah (*Eg*: Iunet; *Cl*: Tentyris)

Capital of Sixth nome of Upper Egypt. Cult-centre of Hathor, and her husband Horus and son Ihy. Tombs from Archaic to First Intermediate periods. Major Temple of Hathor (Graeco-Roman Period).

Quft (*Eg*: Gebtu; *Cl*: KOPTOS)

Capital of Fifth Upper Egyptian nome. Cult-centre of Min, and also of Isis and Osiris in Graeco-Roman periods.

Naqada

Cemeteries of Predynastic Period for inhabitants of nearby town, Nubt (Greek: Ombos), cult-centre of Seth. Burials represented last two cultures of predynastic era (Naqada I and II).

6 THEBES (*EG*: WASET; *CL*: THEBAI)

Capital city of Egypt and its empire in New Kingdom. Major archaeological site which includes main part of city on the East Bank, and cemeteries and royal cult temples on the West Bank.

The East Bank

Divine cult complex of Karnak, with centres of Amun, Montu, Mut and Khonsu. (Dynasty 12 foundation, major additions in New Kingdom, and further work in later periods.) Temple of Luxor, dedicated to Mut (New Kingdom and later).

The West Bank

Royal cult temples: Mentuhotep Nebhepetre (Dynasty 11) and Hatshepsut (Dynasty 18) at Deir el-Bahri; the Ramesseum (Ramesses II) and Qurna (Sethos I) (both Dynasty 19); Tuthmosis III (Dynasty 18) and Ramesses III (Dynasty 20) at Medinet Habu. Royal tombs: at El-Tarif (Dynasty 11), Dra'abu el-Naga' (Dynasties 17 and early 18), Valley of the Kings (Biban el-Moluk) (Dynasties 18–20), Valley of the Queens (Dynasties 19–20). Private tombs: areas include Dra'abu el-Naga', Deir el-Bahri, el-Khokha, Assasif, Sheikh Abd el-Qurna, Deir el-Medina and Qurnet Mura'i (from Dynasty 6 to the Graeco-Roman Period). Royal necropolis workmen's village at Deir el-Medina: votive stelae, and evidence of personal religion; temples (New Kingdom to Graeco-Roman Period).

7 UPPER EGYPT (SOUTH)

Armant (*Eg*: Iuny; *Cl*: Hermonthis)

Important cult-centre of Montu. Original site of temple. The Bucheum, burial site of Sacred Buchis bulls (Dynasty 30 to Roman Period); also burial place of 'Mother of Buchis' cows. Large human cemeteries.

Tod (*Eg*: Djerty; *Cl*: Tuphium)

Local cult of Montu from Dynasty 11. Temple of Graeco-Roman Period.

Gebelein (*Eg*: Per-Hathor; *Cl*: Aphroditopolis)

Tombs of First Intermediate Period. A temple existed here from Dynasty 3, but now destroyed.

Esna (*Eg*: Iunyt; *Cl*: Latopolis)

Cult-centre of the *Lates*-fish (fish and human cemeteries nearby, dating from Middle Kingdom to Late Period). Main temple (Graeco-Roman Period), dedicated to Khnum and companion deities Neith, Heka, Satit and Menheyet.

El-Kab (*Eg*: NEKHEB; *Cl*: Eileithyiaspolis)

Nekheb (east bank) was a very important predynastic and early dynastic settlement. Nekhbet (local goddess) was royal patroness deity of the White Land in predynastic times, who was later identified with the Greek goddess Eileithyia. Temples of Nekhbet (New Kingdom), Shesmetet (Ptolemaic Period), Hathor and Nekhbet (Dynasty 18), and a chapel for Re-Harakhte, Hathor, Amun, Nekhbet and Ramesses II (Dynasty 19). Cemeteries date to the Old, Middle and New Kingdoms; inscriptions in the tombs of Ahmose Pennekheb and Ahmose, son of Ebana, are a particularly important source for the wars against the Hyksos and during Dynasty 18.

Kom el-Ahmar (*Eg*: NEKHEN; *Cl*: HIERACONPOLIS)

On the west bank of river, opposite Nekheb, with which Nekhen formed the capital of Upper Egypt in predynastic times. Chief god was falcon Nekheny (identified with Horus). Temple where main deposit of votive offerings, including Narmer Palette, was found. Extensive predynastic cemeteries, including the now-lost Decorated Tomb 100, and rock-cut tombs from Dynasties 6 to 18.

Edfu (*Eg*: Dbot; *Cl*: Apollopolis Magna)

This town was capital of the Second nome of Upper Egypt. Site of tombs of Old Kingdom and First Intermediate Period. Most important monument is temple dedicated to Horus, Hathor of Denderah, and the young Horus (built and decorated from 237 to 57 BCE, on a site that goes back to Old Kingdom). Best-preserved temple in Egypt. Important texts (Building Texts) about temple mythology, and scenes and inscriptions of Sacred Drama (conflict between Horus and Seth).

Gebel es-Silsila

Originally regarded as source of Nile; later, festivals celebrated here for Nile-god Hapy. Rock stelae and graffiti recall presence of men who worked quarries here between New Kingdom and Graeco-Roman Period. Rock-cut shrines and cenotaphs to rulers and officials. Great Speos (rock-cut chapel) of Horemheb. Other cenotaphs of Sethos I, Ramesses II and Merneptah, and Stela of Akhenaten.

Kom Ombo (*Eg*: Ombos)

Unique double temple (Graeco-Roman Period), dedicated to Sobek, with Hathor and Khonsu, and to Haroeris, with Tasenetnofret and Panebtawy.

Aswan and Elephantine (*Eg*: Yebu; *Cl*: Syene)

The district around modern Aswan, including island of Elephantine, was ancient capital of the First Upper Egyptian nome. Important garrison town and trading centre because of its vicinity to First Cataract.

On island of Elephantine: temples of Trajan and Alexander II, and remains of New Kingdom buildings; burials of rams, sacred to Khnum; Nilometer; remains of Jewish colony of Persian Period.

Granite quarries to south of Elephantine. Rock-cut tombs of local governors and officials of Elephantine at Qubhet el-Hawa (Old Kingdom to New Kingdom).

8 MAJOR UNESCO SALVAGE OPERATIONS

With the construction of dams in the twentieth century ACE, many archaeological sites were threatened by the resulting increased water level. Action was taken, first by the Archaeological Survey of Nubia (early twentieth century ACE) and then by the UNESCO Salvage Campaign (1960s ACE), to rescue some of the affected monuments and archaeological remains. Two rescue missions at Abu Simbel and Philae removed the temples to safe locations near the original sites; some monuments were removed and rebuilt in an open-air museum at New Kalabsha near Aswan, or at other sites in Egypt; and other temples were donated to countries in Europe and the USA, as gestures of goodwill for their contributions to the rescue programme.

Island of Philae (Eg: Pi-lak)

Situated at the First Cataract, but became submerged for most of year with the building of the first dam at Aswan. With construction of the High Dam at Aswan, the temples were dismantled and rebuilt on the neighbouring island of Agilkia. The oldest buildings date to Late Period, but temples (main one to Isis) date mostly to Graeco-Roman Period. Ancient cults still existed here until Emperor Justinian (527–65 ACE) discontinued them.

Abu Simbel

Two rock-cut temples built by Ramesses II, and moved in 1964–8 ACE to avoid them being submerged by Lake Nasser, as the result of construction of the High Dam. The Great Temple was dedicated to Ptah, Amen-Re, Re-Harakhte and the deified Ramesses II; and the Smaller Temple to Queen Nefertari and Hathor.

Temples Rebuilt at New Kalabsha

Temples transported from original sites and relocated on promontory near Aswan: Beit el-Wali, rock-cut temple built by Ramesses II and dedicated to Amen-Re and other gods; Kalabsha, constructed in reign of Emperor Augustus, and dedicated to Mandulis.

Monuments Rebuilt Elsewhere in Egypt

Amada: temple, Dynasty 18, dedicated to Amen-Re and Re-Harakhte; moved to new location near original site.

El-Derr: temple built by Ramesses II and dedicated to Re-Harakhte. Dismantled and rebuilt near Amada.

Aniba: capital of Wawat district in New Kingdom; rock-cut tomb of Penniut, Viceroy of Wawat under Ramesses VI, moved to site near Amada.

El-Sebu'a: two temples built in New Kingdom, and relocated near to original site.

El-Dakka: temple built in Graeco-Roman Period, and relocated near to el-Sebu'a.

Nubian Temples Transported Abroad

Dabod: built by Meroitic king Adikhalamani (third century BCE) and enlarged by Ptolemies. Dedicated to Amun. Dismantled and re-erected in Madrid, Spain.

Tafa: two temples (Roman Period); one dismantled and presented to Rijksmuseum Van Oudheden, Leiden, Holland.

Dendur: built by Emperor Augustus, and dedicated to several gods. Dismantled and re-erected in Metropolitan Museum of Fine Art, New York, USA.

El-Lessiya: rock-cut chapels (New Kingdom). One (reign of Tuthmosis III) now in Turin Museum, Italy.

9 SITES IN UPPER NUBIA

This area spans the southernmost district of Egypt and the northern part of Sudan. Religious buildings include:

(i) temples built by New Kingdom rulers to demonstrate their power to the local population: these include Faras, Serra West, Dibeira East and West, Amarna West, Sedeinga, Soleb, Sesebi, Nauri and Tombos. Temples of Amenhotep III at Sedeinga and Soleb are especially important, and also Aten temple at Sesebi;

(ii) the pyramid fields and temples built by rulers of Dynasty 25 and their descendants (rulers of Napatan and Meroitic kingdoms): many sites located between Third and Sixth Cataracts. Most important excavations are at Kawa (temples of Amun), el-Kurru (pyramids of Dynasty 25, together with horse burials), and Napata (table-mountain, known today as Gebel Barkal, believed to be home of god Amun), where there are temples and chapels built to Amun by rulers of New Kingdom, Dynasty 25, and Napatan and Meroitic kingdoms. Extensive pyramid sites at Napata, and also Nuri (Dynasty 25, and rulers of Napatan and Meroitic kingdoms);

(iii) Meroë: capital of Napatan kingdom after rulers were overwhelmed by Abyssinians and moved south (c.300 BCE to 350 ACE); pyramids, and temples and sanctuaries to Amun and local lion-god Apedemak.

Notes

1 The Creation of Egyptian Civilization

1. Baines (1989).
2. Herodotus, Bk. II (transl. by de Sélincourt (1961)).
3. Cockburn and Reyman (1998).
4. Gaillard and Daressy (1905); Armitage and Clutton-Brock (1981).
5. Smith and Jones (1910).
6. Smith (2000).
7. Smith and Dawson (1991).
8. Murray (1910).
9. Balout and Roubet (1985).
10. Harrison (1966); Harrison *et al.* (1969); Leek (1972) and (1977).
11. Davis (1910); Derry (1931); Reeves (1981).
12. David (1979).
13. Ibid. (2000).
14. Herodotus, Bk. II, para. 86–88 (transl. by de Sélincourt (1961)), pp. 133–4; David (1979); Lucas (2000).
15. Sandison (1963); Dawson (1927); David (1979).

2 The Emergence of Religion

1. Petrie (1920), pp. 3–4; Kemp (1982).
2. Hassan (1983).
3. Derry (1956); Engelbach (1943); Kantor (1942 and 1952); Emery (1972), pp. 30–31, 40.

4. Hassan (1983), p. 139.

5. Ibid., p. 140.

6. Wilson (1955).

7. Case and Payne (1962); Payne (1973); Kemp (1973).

8. Quibell and Green (1900–1902).

9. Morenz (1990), p. 17; Hornung (1983), pp. 101–9.

10. For example, Jéquier (1946).

11. Shafer (1991), pp. 13ff; Hornung (1983), pp. 33–41.

12. Hornung (1983).

13. Shafer (1991), p. 33.

14. Bard (1986).

15. Friedman (1997).

16. *Nekhen News* (1999).

17. Frankfort (1948); O'Connor and Silverman (1995).

18. Shafer (1991), pp. 34–9.

19. Petrie (1900–1901), II, pl. x. 2.

20. Hendrickx (1996).

21. Emery (1963), pp. 128–64.

22. Wood (1987).

23. Emery (1949 and 1954); (1972), pp. 38–103.

24. Dreyer (1993).

25. O'Connor (1995(i)).

3 The Rise of the Sun-Cult

1. Moret (1902(i)); Posener (1960); Hornung (1983); Shafer (1991); O'Connor and Silverman (1995(ii)).

2. Allen (1988), p. 62.

3. Hornung (1983), pp. 172–80.

4. Allen (1988), p. 8.

5. Ibid., pp. 25–6.

6. Herodotus, Bk. II, para. 73 (transl. by de Sélincourt (1961)), p. 130.

7. Utterance 527. *See* also Faulkner (1969).

8. Allen (1988), pp. 42–3.

9. British Museum No. 498 (Shabaka Stone), lines 53–4. *See* Lichtheim (1973), p. 54.

10. Ibid., line 56. *See* Lichtheim (1973), p. 54.

11. Faulkner (1966); Bradshaw (1990); Quirke (2001).

12. *See* Lichtheim (1973), p. 33.

13. Thompson (1990).

14. Mercer (1952: the first complete translation and commentary in English); Faulkner (1969).

15. For a selection of passages, *see* Lichtheim (1973), pp. 29–50.

16. *See* Erman (1927), p. 2.

17. Faulkner (1924).

18. *See* Erman (1927), p. 6.

19. Burnt as incense. Ibid., p. 6, note 7.

20. Used as fuel. Ibid., p. 6, note 8.

21. Edwards (1992), pp. 278–80.

22. Ibid., p. 277.

23. Arnold in Shafer (1997), pp. 40–44.

24. Ibid.

25. Ibid., p. 46.

26. Mendelssohn (1973).

27. Herodotus, Bk. II, para. 125 (transl. by de Sélincourt (1961)), p. 150.

28. Ibid., para. 128, p. 152.

29. Arnold in Shafer (1997), pp. 51–3.

30. Posener-Kriéger and Cenival (1968).

31. Kemp in Trigger *et al* (1983), p. 85.

32. Kemp (1995(i)), p. 5.

33. Siliotti (1997), p.45.
34. Jordan (1998); Lehner and Hawass (1994).
35. Herodotus, Bk. II, para. 131 (transl. by de Sélincourt (1961)), p. 153.
36. Borchadt (1910–13).
37. Piankoff (1968).
38. Awad (1973); Hassan (1955).
39. Firth and Gunn (1926).
40. A translation is given in Lichtheim (1973), pp. 215–23.
41. Ricke et al. (1965).
42. Limme et al. (1997)
43. Blackman (1916(ii)).
44. Roth (1992) and (1993).
45. Harpur (1981).
46. Schäfer (1974).
47. Iversen (1955).
48. Simpson (1982).
49. Lichtheim (1973), pp. 58–80; Gardiner (1914(i)).
50. Gardiner (1946).
51. Cf. translations in Lichtheim (1973), pp. 63–80, and Erman (1927), pp. 54–66.
52. Ibid.
53. Ibid.
54. Ibid.
55. See translation in Lichtheim (1973), pp. 149–63.

4 Osiris, The People's God

1. Lichtheim (1973), pp. 97–109; Gardiner (1914(ii)).
2. A version of the translation of the text is given in Lichtheim (1973), pp. 139–45.

3. Possibly a reference to fasting observed by people at the time of death, see Erman (1927), p. 114, note 2.
4. Ta-seti is the Egyptian name for Nubia.
5. The two goddesses, Nekhbet and Wadjet, who were patrons of the southern and northern Predynastic kingdoms; their union represented the unification of Egypt.
6. The two gods, Horus and Seth, who protected the Two Lands.
7. A version of the translation is given in Lichtheim (1973), pp. 149–63; for further commentary, see Gardiner (1969).
8. Because of deprivation, children are exposed and left to die.
9. A version of the translation is given in Lichtheim (1973), pp. 163–9; further commentary, Faulkner (1956).
10. The land of the dead.
11. The soul was frequently depicted in the form of a bird which perched on the body of the supine mummy.
12. Lichtheim (1945) and (1973), pp. 193–7; Wente (1962).
13. Fox (1977).
14. Ibid.
15. The oils that the gods used.
16. A version of the translation is given in Lichtheim (1976), pp. 115–16.
17. Winlock (1947).
18. Simpson (1963).
19. Quirke (1991).
20. A version of the translation is given in Lichtheim (1973), pp. 135–9; further commentary, Goedicke (1968).

21. Foster (1981).
22. Pendlebury (1930).
23. Hall (1914).
24. Wainwright (1963).
25. Shafer (1997), p. 5.
26. Malek (1992).
27. Griffiths (1980).
28. Ibid. (1980).
29. Ibid. (1980).
30. Leahy (1989).
31. Winlock (1940).
32. Naville and Hall (1907–13).
33. Arnold (1979).
34. Edwards (1992), p. 200.
35. Shafer (1997), p.75.
36. Arnold (1988).
37. Shafer (1997), p.80.
38. Edwards (1992), pp. 211–14.
39. Petrie (1889 and 1890(ii)).
40. Petrie et al. (1912); Lloyd (1970).
41. Edwards (1992), pp. 216–17.
42. Petrie (1890(i)).
43. Brunton (1920); Winlock (1934).
44. Winlock (1940 and 1947).
45. Garstang (1904); Newberry (1893–1900).
46. Newberry and Griffith (1892).
47. Griffith (1889).
48. Kanawati (1980–92 and 1993).
49. von Bissing (1915).
50. Abdalla (1992).
51. Quirke (1991).
52. Murray (1910).
53. de Buck and Gardiner (1935–61).
54. Faulkner (1973–8).
55. Thompson (1990).
56. Dodson (1994).
57. Winlock (1955).

58. Aldred (1971); Andrews (1999).
59. Wilkinson (1994).
60. Lucas (1999).

5 Religion and Empire

1. Quirke (1991).
2. Shafer (1997), pp. 82–3.
3. Leahy (1989).
4. Lichtheim (1988).
5. Van Seters (1966); Engelbach (1939).
6. Säve-Soderbergh (1951).
7. Van Seters (1971).
8. Bietak (1992).
9. Ibid. (1992).
10. Ibid. (1992).
11. Hankey (1993).
12. Bietak (1992).
13. Ibid (1997).
14. Allen (1988), pp. 55–6.
15. Ibid., p. 48.
16. Ibid., p. 49.
17. Ibid., p. 52.
18. Erman (1927), p.286.
19. Allen (1988), p. 62.
20. Ibid., p. 62.
21. Kákosy (1980).
22. Shafer (1997).
23. Ibid., p.2.
24. Ibid., pp. 4–5.
25. Ibid., p. 29.
26. Simpson (1989), p. 56.
27. Kaper (1995).
28. David (1981).
29. Fairman (1954).
30. Simpson (1982), p. 270.
31. Gardiner (1950).
32. Schulz (1992); Quirke (1990).

33. Nelson (1949).

34. Lichtheim (1973), pp. 123–5.

35. Graindorge (1996).

36. Janssen (1991).

37. Redford (1976), p. 123.

38. Sauneron (2000).

39. Shafer (1991), p. 11.

40. Galvin (1984).

41. Thomson (1998).

42. Herodotus (1961).

43. Maystre (1992).

44. Reeves (1990(ii)).

45. Polz (1995).

46. Yoshimura (1995).

47. Wilkinson (1835); Porter and Moss (1927–99).

48. Carter (1972).

49. Hornung (1990); Piankoff (1954).

50. Budge (1898); Allen (1960).

51. Gardiner and Weigall (1913).

52. Mackay (1921).

53. Davies (1938); Davies and Davies (1915–33); Davies and Gardiner (1915).

54. Blackman (1927), pp. 117–20; 263–7.

6 The Amarna Heresy

1. McGovern (1997).

2. Aldred (1957(i), 1973 and 1988).

3. Ibid. (1959); Engelbach (1940–41); Redford (1959).

4. Redford (1984).

5. Smith and Redford (1976).

6. Ibid.

7. Shafer (1997), pp. 180–83.

8. Pendlebury (1933, 1934 and 1936).

9. Davies (1903–8); Frankfort and Pendlebury (1933).

10. Kemp (1984–5).

11. Ibid. (1987).

12. Ibid. (1980).

13. Ibid. (1983).

14. Shaw (1994).

15. Bakhry (1972).

16. Uphill (1963 and 1970); Gohary (1992).

17. Ikram (1989).

18. Martin (1989).

19. Davies (1903–8).

20. Sandman (1938); Murnane (1995).

21. Moran (1992); Mercer (1939).

22. Campbell (1964).

23. Davies (1903–8), vol. 6, pls. XXVII–XLI; Sandman (1938), pp. 93–6; Gardiner (1961), pp. 225–7; Lichtheim (1976), pp. 96–9.

24. Davies (1903–8), vol. 3, pl. XXIX; Erman (1927), p. 292.

25. Stewart (1960); Redford (1976).

26. A full version of the translation of the text is given in Erman (1927), p. 139.

27. Assmann (1983).

28. Zandee (1992).

29. Hornung (1983), p.246.

30. Ibid., p. 246.

31. Junker (1934), pp. 47–57.

32. Junker (1961), p. 134.

33. Morenz (1990), p. 190.

34. Hornung (1983), p. 191.

35. Johnson (1996).

36. Harris (1973, 1974(i) and 1977); Samson (1977).

37. Varille (1940).

38. Helck (1939), p. 74.

39. Hornung (1964), pp. 89 ff.

40. Kadry (1982).
41. Hornung (1964), pp. 89 ff.
42. Aldred (1961).
43. Gardiner (1957); Thomas (1961).
44. For a summary, *see* Reeves (1981).
45. Davis (1910).
46. Derry (1931).
47. Harrison (1966 and 1969).
48. Harris (1973, 1974(i) and 1977).
49. Samson (1973).
50. Arnold (1996).
51. Hayes (1959), p. 294.
52. Harris (1974(ii)).
53. Reeves (1988).
54. Frankfort (1929); Davies (1921).
55. Simpson (1982), p. 268.
56. Weatherhead (1992).
57. Ghalioungui (1947).
58. Aldred (1957).
59. Kadry (1982).
60. Ibid.
61. Eaton-Krauss and Graefe (1985).
62. Leek (1977).
63. Reeves (1990(i)); Carter (1972).
64. Leek (1972).
65. Harrison (1979).
66. British Museum (1972).
67. Piankoff (1955).
68. Kitchen (1962).
69. Seele (1955); Newberry (1932).
70. Schaden (1984).
71. Gardiner (1953); Martin (1976–9).
72. Pfluger (1946).
73. Redford (1984).
74. Hornung (1983), p. 230.
75. Shafer (1991), p. 187.
76. Ibid.
77. Hornung (1983), p. 86.

7 The Return to Orthodoxy

1. Shafer (1991), pp. 191–3.
2. Gardiner (1961), p. 247.
3. Fox (1977).
4. Kitchen (1974).
5. Faulkner (1947).
6. Kitchen (1974).
7. Breasted (1903); Kitchen (1964).
8. Langdon and Gardiner (1920).
9. Balout and Roubet (1985).
10. Shafer (1991), p. 111.
11. Calverley and Broome (1933–58); Baines (1984).
12. Baines (1989).
13. Frankfort *et al.* (1933); Murray (1904).
14. David (1981).
15. Fairman (1954).
16. Greener (1962).
17. Chicago University (1932–40).
18. Edgerton and Wilson (1936).
19. Kaper (1995).
20. Piankoff (1954).
21. Le Blanc (1997).
22. Weeks (1998).
23. Ibid. (1994).
24. Ibid. (1992).
25. Egyptian Antiquities Organization/Getty Conservation Institute (1987).
26. Martin (1991).
27. Martin *et al.* (1988(ii)).
28. Martin (1984).
29. Martin *et al.* (1988(ii)).
30. Martin (1987).
31. Lichtheim (1976), pp. 119–32.
32. Munro (1987).
33. Lichtheim (1976), pp. 135–46.

34. Ibid., pp. 146–63.

35. Ibid., p. 154.

36. Ibid., p. 152.

37. Ibid., p. 151.

38. Ibid., pp. 167–78; Gardiner (1935), vol. I, pp. 38–9; vol. II, pls. 18–19.

39. Kitchen (1966); Wilson (1986); Rainey (1987); Bimson (1978).

40. Genesis, Chapters 37–50; Redford (1970).

41. Exodus, Chapters 1–20.

42. Freud (1967); Osman (1990).

43. Naville (1924).

44. For a discussion, see Rainey (1987).

45. Redford (1972).

46. Baines (1987).

47. Shafer (1991), p. 129.

48. Ibid., pp. 144–5.

49. Ibid., p. 173.

50. Ibid., p. 174.

51. David (1996).

52. Petrie (1890(i and ii)).

53. Griffith (1897–8).

54. El-Aguizy (1987).

55. Černy (1973); Bierbrier (1995).

56. Friedman (1985).

57. Ibid.

58. Kamel (1983).

59. Giveon (1980).

60. Sadek (1987).

61. Gunn (1916).

62. Baines (1982).

63. Černy (1962).

64. Baines (1987).

65. Shafer (1991), p. 149; Blackman (1925).

66. Fischer-Elfert (1996).

67. Ryholt (1993).

68. Černy (1939), p. 28, lines 3–6.

69. Bohleke (1997).

70. Shafer (1991), p.178.

71. Bohleke (1997); Edwards (1960).

72. Baines (1987).

73. Ray (1976).

74. Shafer (1991), pp. 153–5.

75. Baines (1987).

76. Friedman (1985).

77. Sadek (1987).

78. Janssen (1982).

79. Sadek (1987).

80. Jacq (1985).

81. Faulkner (1973), pp. 199–200.

82. Allen (1988), p. 36.

83. Hornung (1983), p. 209.

84. Pinch (1994), p. 9; Borghouts (1978).

85. Gardiner (1955), pp. 1–2.

86. Quibell (1898), p.3.

87. Pinch (1994), p. 131.

88. Ibid.

89. David (1996), p. 136.

90. Shafer (1991), p. 169.

91. Lacau (1921–2).

92. Ghalioungui (1963); Nunn (1996); Worth Estes (1989); Sigerist (1951).

93. Miller (1990); Gilbert (1988).

94. Grafton Milne (1914).

95. Dawson (1932–5).

96. Blackman (1925).

97. Allam (1991).

98. Assmann (1992).

99. For an alternative explanation, see Willems (1990).

100. Eyre (1992).

101. Eyre (1984); Parkinson (1995).

102. Sweeney (1994).

103. Goedicke (1963); de Buck (1937).

104. Peet (1925); (1930); Capart *et al.*
(1936).
105. Goelet (1996).

8 Kings and Priests: The Final Conflict

1. Kitchen (1996); Bierbrier (1975).
2. Montet (1947, 1951 and 1960).
3. Petrie (1885 and 1888).
4. For some of these discussions, *see*
Montet (1947, 1951 and 1960); Bietak
(1981).
5. Coutts (1988); Brissaud (1998).
6. Shafer (1991), p. 111.
7. Niwinski (1984).
8. Smith (2000).
9. Smith and Jones (1910).
10. Smith and Dawson (1991).
11. Herodotus, Bk. II, para. 86–8
(trans. by de Sélincourt, (1961)),
pp. 133–4.
12. Dawson (1927).
13. Sandison (1963).
14. Leek (1969).
15. Cockburn and Reyman (1998);
David (1979 and 2000).
16. Kitchen (1996).
17. Wainwright (1962).
18. Von Zeissl (1944).
19. Laming Macadam (1949 and 1955).
20. Dunham (1950–57).
21. Ibid.
22. Troy (1986).
23. Gitton (1984).
24. Robins (1993).
25. Leahy (1996).
26. Posener (1936).
27. Lloyd (1982).
28. Lichtheim (1980).
29. Herodotus, Bk. II (trans. by de
Sélincourt (1961)).
30. Luckenbill (1968); Wiseman
(1956).
31. Kraeling (1953); Driver (1957).
32. Muhs (1998).
33. Kruchten (1989).
34. Gordon (1969).
35. Tiradritti (1998).
36. Manuelian (1985).
37. Pérez Die (1995).
38. Verner (1995).
39. Verner (1999).
40. Redmount and Friedman (1993).
41. Mathieson *et al.* (1995).
42. Spencer (1999).
43. Shafer (1991), p.111.
44. Ibid., p. 198.
45. Lloyd (1982).
46. Sherman (1967).
47. Bohleke (1997).
48. Kákosy (1998); Andrews
(1998).
49. Houlihan (1996).
50. Hornung (1983), p. 137.
51. Tooley (1988).
52. Mohammed (1987).
53. Nicholson (1994(i)), (1994(ii)).
54. Nicholson (1994(ii)).
55. Perizonius *et al.* (1993).
56. Herodotus, Bk. II (trans. by de
Sélincourt (1961)), p. 117.
57. Vos (1998).
58. Smith and Jeffreys (1980).
59. Jones (1990).
60. Gaillard and Daressy (1905).
61. Herodotus, Bk II, para. 87
(transl. by de Sélincourt (1961)),
pp. 133–4.

62. Armitage and Clutton-Brock (1981).

9 East meets West: Conflict and Co-operation in Graeco-Roman Egypt

1. Bell (1956); Austin (1981); Bowman (1986); Hoffmann (1986).
2. Wilcken (1932).
3. Fraser (1972).
4. Lloyd (1982).
5. Bevan (1927).
6. Grafton Milne (1928).
7. Bagnall (1998).
8. Rostovtzeff (1920).
9. Gallazzi (1999).
10. Shafer (1997), p. 229.
11. Bell (1953).
12. Thompson (1998).
13. Fraser (1960).
14. Hope (1998).
15. Leclere (1996).
16. Kákosy (1982).
17. Ellis (1926); Witt (1971); Solmsen (1979).
18. Walters (1988).
19. Delia (1998).
20. Zabkar (1983).
21. Dunand (1979).
22. Bell (1948).
23. Montserrat (1996).
24. Shafer (1997), pp. 185–237.
25. Reymond (1963), (1965); Blackman and Fairman (1946).
26. Badawy (1963).
27. Sternberg (1985).
28. Depuydt (1998).
29. Kaper (1995).
30. Goyon (1985).
31. Zabkar (1980).
32. Maystre (1992).
33. Shafer (1997), p. 214.
34. Bianchi (1998); Dominique (1998).
35. Montserrat and Meskell (1997(i)).
36. Bataille (1952); Vleeming (1995).
37. Niwinski (1998).
38. Montserrat (1992).
39. Thompson (1998).
40. Griffiths (1982).
41. Cavaignac (1931).
42. Quaegebeur (1978); Vleeming (1998).
43. Niwinski (1998).
44. Herodotus, Bk. II, para. 90 (transl. by de Sélincourt (1961)), p. 134.
45. Doxiadis (1995); Walker (1997 and 2000).
46. Montserrat (1997); Schwabe (1985).
47. Walker (1997).
48. Shore (1962).
49. Montserrat (1993).
50. Davis (1967).
51. Lichtheim (1980), pp. 159–84.
52. Watterson (1988).
53. Rémondon (1952).
54. Hauben (1998).
55. Blackman (1916); Wainwright (1949).
56. Jeffreys and Strouhal (1980).
57. Montserrat (1992).
58. Coquin (1972).
59. Morenz (1973), pp. 270–73.
60. Ibid., p. 251.
61. Rees (1950).
62. Ghalioungui (1969); Sobhy (1937–8); Walker (1934).
63. Murray (1921).

APPENDIX A

1. Alternatively, this could be translated as 'Words spoken' or 'Incantation'. It introduced a specific spell from the Coffin Texts.
2. This was the prime seat in the god's barque. The spell sought to ensure that Nekht-Ankh was allocated a foremost position when he accompanied the gods on their celestial journey.
3. Mother of Nekht-Ankh and Khnum-Nakht.
4. This was the formula used in funerary texts to confirm that all the offerings presented on behalf of the deceased were granted through the beneficence of the king.
5. Here, the three types of afterlife envisaged by the Egyptians – in the land of Osiris, in the tomb, and in the sky – are mentioned together.
6. The necropolis.
7. Goddess of Magic.
8. The funeral.
9. Cult centres of Osiris.
10. Egypt's enemies.
11. The necropolis of Assiut.
12. The necropolis.
13. The town where the brothers lived.
14. The mummies.
15. The door-bolt is identified with Seth's finger.
16. The Bennw-bird.
17. The 'Great Place' was the shrine.
18. Name of King Sethos I.
19. King Sethos' temple.

20. This cloth, wrapped around the statue, gave it magical protection.
21. The king wipes the special ointment from the uraeus-serpent on the god's brow.
22. The king unwinds the clothing from the god's body.
23. Another type of cloth, to bring good fortune to the wearer.
24. A cloth of costly material. There is a play on words here, since *mnht* also means 'potent' or 'excellent' – qualities that the cloth would transfer to the wearer.
25. Red linen cloth. All the cloths were believed to imbue the wearer with different powers and abilities. This one was identified with the fiery uraeus goddess Wadjet, and thus protected the god.
26. A particular type or quality of natron. This fumigated the god and removed any impurity from him.
27. The god, clothed and fumigated, was now presented with special jewellery and insignia, to give him additional powers.
28. Egypt's enemies.
29. The Double Plumes were attached to the god's crown, which gave him the ability to triumph over his enemies, rule Egypt and receive his offerings.
30. A special sceptre that symbolized power and dominion.
31. *See* Note 20.
32. A form of the goddess Hathor.
33. Goddess of weaving.
34. The withdrawal of the priest from the sanctuary, backwards, facing the

statue. As he exited, he used a plant (unidentified) to brush away his last footprint.

35. A final fumigation outside the sanctuary.

36. The food-offerings.

37. Akhenaten.

38. Mankind.

39. Syria and Nubia; expressing the universality of the Aten as a god of all peoples, not just the Egyptians.

40. Everyone's lifespan is ordained.

41. The creation of the river occurs in the underworld.

42. Egypt's water comes primarily from the Nile as there is little rainfall, whereas rain in foreign lands was envisaged as descending from a 'Nile in the Sky'.

43. The appearance of the sun in the sky at different times of the day.

44. Name of Akhenaten.

45. Originally composed to be recited by the king, the hymn was subsequently adapted for the use of the courtiers.

46. The official name of the Aten.

47. Akhenaten.

48. The Aegean Islands.

49. A long reign.

50. At Amarna.

51. The king.

52. Until the courtier dies. As in the Old Kingdom, provision for burial was considered to emanate from the king's personal bounty during the Amarna Period.

Glossary

1 MAJOR KINGS AND QUEENS MENTIONED IN THE BOOK

Kings

Akhenaten
(*See* Amenhotep IV)

Akhtoy (Achthoes III) (c.2160 BCE)
Also known as 'Khety', Akhtoy III was a king during Dynasty 9. This dynasty originated with the governors of the Heracleopolitan nome. Akhtoy was accredited as the author of the 'Instruction for King Merikare'.

Alexander the Great (ruled Egypt 332–323 BCE)
Son of Philip II, King of Macedon, Alexander conquered Egypt and made it part of his empire.

Amenemhet I (1991–1962 BCE)

Founder of Dynasty 12 and inaugurator of Middle Kingdom. Reorganized internal adminstration and consolidated the power of the monarchy.

Amenemhet II (1929–1895 BCE)

Grandson of Amenemhet I. Built a pyramid at Dahshur.

Amenemhet III (1842–1797 BCE)

Very prosperous reign. Two pyramids at Dahshur and Hawara; also built the Labyrinth (funerary temple and administrative centre).

Amenhotep I (1546–1526 BCE)

Helped to establish Egypt's empire at start of Dynasty 18. Campaigned in Nubia and Syria. Received a cult at Deir el-Medina.

Amenhotep II (1450–1425 BCE)

Great royal sportsman. Campaigned in Nubia and Syria. Temple-building programme. One cache of royal mummies buried in his tomb at Thebes.

Amenhotep III (1417–1379 BCE).

Ruled Egypt's empire at its zenith. Replaced military expeditions with diplomacy. Major temple-building programme. Restricted power of god Amun and promoted cult of the Aten.

Amenhotep IV (Akhenaten) (1379–1362 BCE)

Son of Amenhotep III. Unique contribution was to change the Aten's cult to a form of monotheism. Established new capital and religious centre at Akhetaten (Tell el-Amarna).

Amosis I (1570–1546 BCE)

Founder of Dynasty 18 who drove the Hyksos rulers out of Egypt. Fostered cult of his local Theban god, Amun.

Ay (1352–1348 BCE)

Close adviser of Akhenaten, and vizier to Tutankhamun whom he succeeded as king. Assisted return to religious orthodoxy after the Amarna Period.

Bochchoris (c.718 BCE)
Ruler of Dynasty 24 who was taken captive and deposed by Shabaka.

Cambyses (525–522 BCE)
King of Persia who conquered and ruled Egypt. Some accounts state that he neglected the Egyptian gods but other evidence does not bear this out.

Cheops (Khufu) (c.2589–2566 BCE)
Absolute ruler who, in Dynasty 4, used his country's resources to build the Great Pyramid at Giza.

Chephren (Khafre) (2558–2533 BCE)
Son of Cheops who built second pyramid at Giza, with its associated complex, and the Great Sphinx. Herodotus stated that both Cheops and Chephren were tyrants.

Darius I (521–486 BCE)
King of Persia who ruled Egypt as part of Persian Empire. Encouraged and promoted Egyptian religion.

Djedefre (2566–2558 BCE)
Son and successor of Cheops.

Esarhaddon (681–669 BCE)
King of Assyria who besieged and conquered Egypt. Destroyed Memphis and drove Taharka back to the south.

Herihor (1100–1094 BCE)
Inaugurated line of High-priests of Amun who ruled virtually independently at Thebes in Dynasty 21.

Horemheb (1348–1320 BCE)
Army commander under Akhenaten, who succeeded Ay as king and re-established orthodox religious beliefs after the Amarna interlude.

Huni (2637–2613 BCE)
King of Dynasty 3 who may have initiated construction of Bent Pyramid at Medum.

Ibi (c. 2137 BCE)
A king of Dynasty 8 who ruled from Memphis.

Isesi (c. 2414–2375 BCE)
King of Dynasty 5.

Kamose (c. 1570–1567 BCE)
A Theban prince, ruler of Dynasty 17, who helped to drive the Hyksos out of Egypt.

Menes (c. 3100–? BCE)
Founder of historic Egypt, who established Dynasty 1 and united the northern and southern kingdoms. Most probably to be identified with Hor-'aha (however, *see* 'Narmer').

Mentuhotep II (Nebhepetre) (2060–2010 BCE)
He united Egypt after the troubled internal dissension of First Intermediate Period. Built unique funerary monument at Thebes.

Merenre (2283–2269 BCE)
King of Dynasty 5 who sent an important expedition to Nubia.

Merikare (c.2100 BCE)
King of the First Intermediate Period who is known from the 'Instruction for King Merikare', the earliest extant treatise on kingship.

Merneptah (1236–1223 BCE)
Son and successor of Ramesses II who campaigned against attacks of the Sea-peoples.

Mycerinus (Menkaure) (c. 2528–2500 BCE)
Grandson of Cheops and builder of the third pyramid at Giza.

Narmer (c. 3100–? BCE)
Has been identified with Menes, although Menes is now usually identified with Hor-'aha. The so-called Narmer Palette, found in Temple of Hierakonpolis, probably commemorates the unification of Egypt.

Nectanebo I (380–363 BCE)
Ruler of Dynasty 30 who supported temple-building and forced the Persians to retreat.

Nectanebo II (360–343 BCE)
Last ruler of Dynasty 30 (the last native dynasty) who was defeated by the Persians.

Neferirkare (2473–2463 BCE)
King of Dynasty 5, mentioned in the Westcar Papyrus, who built a pyramid complex at Abusir.

Nesbenebded (Smendes) (1089–1063 BCE)
Ruler of northern part of Egypt who became first king of Dynasty 21. Capital at Tanis.

Niuserre (2453–2422 BCE)
King of Dynasty 6 who built sun-temple at Abu Gurob and pyramid complex at Abusir.

Pepy I (2332–2283 BCE)
King of Dynasty 6 who had a pyramid at Saqqara.

Pepy II (2269–2175 BCE)
During his long reign, royal power diminished. Built pyramid at Saqqara. Reign marked end of the Old Kingdom.

Piankhy (747–716 BCE)
Ruler of Kingdom of Napata who conquered Egypt. Pyramid at Kurru in Nubia.

Pinudjem I (1044–1026 BCE)
High-priest of Amun at Thebes in Dynasty 21 who 'ruled' southern part of the country while kings reigned from Tanis in the north.

Pinudjem II (985–969 BCE)
High-priest of Amun at Thebes in Dynasty 21. Rescued and reburied royal mummies of the New Kingdom.

Psammetichus I (664–610 BCE)
Prince of Sais who founded Dynasty 26. Revival of Egyptian religious customs, and special emphasis on animal cults.

Psammetichus II (595–589 BCE)
Ruler of Dynasty 26 who campaigned in Nubia.

Psusennes I (1063–1037 BCE)
King of Dynasty 21 who ruled from Tanis where his tomb and treasure were discovered.

Psusennes II (959–945 BCE)

Son of High-priest Pinudjem II, Psusennes II took over kingship of entire land when the king at Tanis died, once again uniting the north and south.

Ptolemy I (305–283 BCE)

Macedonian general under Alexander the Great, he became governor and then king of Egypt, inaugurating the Ptolemaic Dynasty.

Ptolemy II (283–246 BCE)

Ptolemaic dynasty reached its zenith during his reign. Established a royal dynastic cult of himself and his queen, Arsinoe, and patronized the arts, especially the enhancement of Alexandria.

Ptolemy III (246–221 BCE)

Great benefactor of the Egyptian temples and cults, inaugurating the construction of the Temple of Horus at Edfu.

Ptolemy IV (221–204 BCE)

The Battle of Raphia (217 BCE) against Antiochus III of Syria was the watershed in relations between Ptolemaic rulers and native population of Egypt.

Ramesses I (1320–1318 BCE)

Founder of Dynasty 19.

Ramesses II (1304–1237 BCE)

Noted warrior and prolific builder; his temples include the Ramesseum, Abydos and Abu Simbel. Campaigned against the Hittites.

Ramesses III (1198–1166 BCE)

Last great warrior king of Egypt. Fought against the Sea-peoples. Major temple at Medinet Habu. Latter part of reign was troubled by strikes of the royal necropolis workforce, and the unsuccessful harem conspiracy to kill the king.

Ramesses V (1160–1156 BCE)

A troubled reign in which there were many thefts and crimes.

Ramesses IX (1140–1121 BCE)

High-priests of Amun acquired considerable degree of power during this reign. Royal necropolis workforce at Deir el-Mederia went on strike and there was a series of famous tomb robberies.

Ramesses XI (1113–1085 BCE)

Last king of Dynasty 20 in whose reign the country became virtually divided; he continued to rule in the north, but the High-priest of Amun at Thebes gained considerable power over the south.

Sahure (2487–2473 BCE)

Mentioned in the Westcar Papyrus, he continued the policy of his father, Userkaf, in promoting the sun-cult. He inaugurated the royal cemetery at Abusir, where he built a fine pyramid and a funerary complex.

Scorpion (before 3100 BCE)

A southern ruler of the Predynastic Period whose name is preserved on the Scorpion Macehead. He probably took early steps to conquer the northern kingdom.

Senusret I (1971–1928 BCE)

A major king of Dynasty 12, he helped to restore the power of the monarchy, carried out a prodigious programme of building religious monuments, and received a personal divine cult.

Senusret II (1897–1878 BCE)

Promoted trade with Syria/Palestine and the Aegean Islands. Built pyramid of Lahun where royal treasure was found in the enclosure; the pyramid workmen's town of Kahun is nearby.

Senusret III (1878–1843 BCE)

A major ruler of Dynasty 12 who curtailed the power of the provincial nobility, and consolidated Egypt's annexation of Nubia. Pyramid at Dahshur, where royal treasure was discovered in associated royal tombs.

Seqenenre Ta'o II (c.1575 BCE)

Theban prince and ruler of Dynasty 17 who helped to expel the Hyksos from Egypt.

Sethos I (1318–1304 BCE)

Major ruler of Dynasty 19 who restored Egypt's military might and empire in Syria; his campaigns are recorded on the walls of the Hypostyle Hall at Karnak. Fine tomb in the Valley of the Kings, and unique temple at Abydos.

Shabaka (716–702 BCE)

Ethiopian king who established Dynasty 25 in Egypt. He was the first Nubian pharaoh to rule the whole of Egypt.

Shepseskaf (2500–2496 BCE)

Last ruler of Dynasty 4. Broke with the tradition of pyramid building by constructing a mastaba tomb. Known as the Mastabat Fara'un. This may have been an attempt to break away from the cult of Re and its priesthood.

Shoshenk I (c.945–924 BCE)

Descendant of the Libyan chiefs who had attacked and then settled in Egypt, Shoshenk became the first king of Dynasty 22 and restored unity after the division of Egypt between the kings and High-priests in Dynasty 21.

Smenkhkare (c. 1364–1361 BCE)

Possibly half-brother and co-regent of Akhenaten, Smenkhkare briefly ruled alone. He may have been involved in the early stages of the return to religious orthodoxy after the Amarna interlude. He was possibly buried in Tomb 55 in the Valley of the Kings.

Sneferu (c.2613–2589 BCE)

Inaugurator of Dynasty 4, Sneferu received a personal divine cult. Possibly built two pyramids at Dahshur and one at Medum.

Taharka (690–664 BCE)

Ethiopian king of Egypt who carried out an extensive building programme. Repulsed the Assyrians in 674 BCE, but they succeeded in driving him from Memphis in 671 BCE. Although he re-established his rulership, the Assyrians eventually drove Taharka to the south where he died at Napata.

Teti (c.2345–2333 BCE)

First king of Dynasty 6, Teti ruled a peaceful and stable country. He had a pyramid at Saqqara that is famous for the Pyramid Texts inscribed inside.

Tutankhamun (Tutankhaten) (1361–1352 BCE)

Famous for his tomb and treasure discovered in the Valley of the Kings, Tutankhamun succeeded to the throne while still a child. He was involved in the restoration of orthodox religion after the Amarna Period.

Tuthmosis I (1525–1512 BCE)

Great military pharaoh of Dynasty 18 who laid the foundations for Egypt's empire in Syria.

Tuthmosis III (1504–1450 BCE)

Reigned first as a minor under the regency of Queen Hatshepsut, followed by period of sole rule. The greatest military pharaoh who expanded Egypt's empire in Syria/Palestine at the expense of the Hittites.

Tuthmosis IV (1425–1417 BCE)

Probably married to a foreign queen, Tuthmosis IV seems to have introduced the concept of the Aten as a separate deity.

Unas (2375–2345 BCE)

Built a pyramid at Saqqara with famous Pyramid Texts inscribed inside; it is also noted for its well-preserved causeway.

Userkaf (2494–2487 BCE)

First king of Dynasty 5, he promoted the sun-cult and introduced the sun-temples at Abu Gurob.

Queens

Ankhesenamun (Ankhesenpaaten) (1361–1352 BCE)

Daughter of King Akhenaten who married, in addition to her father, the kings Smenkhkare, Tutankhamun and Ay. Together with Tutankhamun, she was involved in the early stages of restoring religious orthodoxy.

Cleopatra VII (51–30 BCE)

Last ruler of the Ptolemaic Dynasty, she reigned jointly with her father, and then her two brothers. Her liaisons with Caesar and Mark Antony brought her notoriety; Augustus, Rome's first Emperor, defeated the troops of Antony and Cleopatra, which led them both to commit suicide.

Gilukhepa (c.1407–1379 BCE)
Daughter of the king of Mitanni, she married Amenhotep III to consolidate the diplomatic ties between the two countries.

Hatshepsut (1503–1482 BCE)
Queen who seized sole rulership of Egypt after death of her husband, Tuthmosis II. Fine temple at Deir el-Bahri.

Kiya (c.1375 BCE)
Secondary wife of King Akhenaten.

Meritaten (c.1370–1360 BCE)
Daughter of King Akhenaten, whom she married, as well as King Smenkhkare.

Mutemweya (1425–1417 BCE)
Possibly identified as the daughter of Artatama I, King of Mitanni, who married Tuthmosis IV and became his chief queen and mother of his heir, Amenhotep III.

Nefertari (1304–1237 BCE)
A principal queen of Ramesses II, she had the finest tomb in the Valley of the Queens, and Ramesses II built the smaller rock-cut temple at Abu Simbel for her.

Nefertiti (1379–1362 BCE)
Chief queen of Akhenaten and mother of his six daughters, Nefertiti's parentage remains obscure. She appears to have played a leading role in his religious 'revolution'.

Sitamun (c.1400 BCE)
Daughter of Amenhotep III and Queen Tiye, Sitamun married her own father and may have been the mother of Tutankhamun.

Sobeknefru (1789–1786 BCE)
The daughter of Amenemhet III and sister of Amenemhet IV, she also became the last sole ruler of Dynasty 12.

Tadukhepa (1417–1379 BCE)
Daughter of King Tushratta of Mitanni, she was sent to Egypt to become the bride of Amenhotep III and was subsequently transferred to the harem of his son, Akhenaten.

Tiye (1417–1379 BCE)

Amenhotep III made Tiye his Chief Queen, although she was the daughter of commoners, Yuya and Thuya. This broke with political and religious traditions and may have been intended to curb the powers of the priest of Amen-Re. Tiye became mother of the royal heir, Akhenaten, and wielded great influence at the royal court.

2 DEITIES

Aesculapius

Greek physician whom the Greeks identified with Imhotep, a deified Egyptian vizier credited as the founder of medical science. A temple at Saqqara dedicated to Imhotep was called the Aesculapion by the Greeks.

Amenhotep, son of Hapu

Royal architect who served Amenhotep III. After death, he was deified and received a cult at his temple in western Thebes. Later, revered as a great sage and healer, he was worshipped as a god of healing and had a sanatorium in the Temple of Deir el-Bahri.

Amun (Amen-Re)

Originally one of the Ogdoad worshipped at Hermopolis, Amun had a cult at Thebes in Dynasty 12. In Dynasty 18, Amun and Re were combined to form the deity Amen-Re who was worshipped as the 'King of Gods' and supreme deity of the Egyptian empire. His main cult centre was at Karnak.

Anath

A western Semitic war-goddess who became the wife of Seth at Avaris in the Hyksos Period. She reached her peak of popularity during the Ramesside Period.

Anta

A form of the goddess Mut, worshipped at Tanis as the consort of Amen-Re.

Anubis

God of the dead, the cemeteries and mummification, Anubis is usually represented as a jackal-headed man. According to mythology, he mummified the body of Osiris. He also guarded the scales at the Day of Judgement.

Anukit

A wife of Khnum, Anukit was goddess of the cataract on Egypt's southern border. Her chief shrine was on the island of Seheil. She may have originated in the Sudan.

Apedemak

Lion-god worshipped at Meroë.

Aphrodite

Greek goddess of love whom the Greeks identified with Hathor.

Apollo

Greek sun-god whom the Greeks identified as Horus.

Apophis

A monster serpent who was an ever-present threat to the sun-god. Every morning, Re cut off his head with a knife, but at the end of each night, Apophis was ready to assault the god's sailing barque again.

Astarte

A western Semitic war-goddess, identified with Sekhmet and, as goddess of love, with Hathor; she was one of Seth's wives at Avaris during the Hyksos Period.

Aten

The Aten or 'sun's disc' was promoted by King Akhenaten as a monotheistic cult. However, it had appeared as an aspect of Re since the Middle Kingdom, but it was increasingly promoted by Akhenaten's immediate predecessors, Amenhotep III and Tuthmosis IV. It is represented as the sun disc in heaven, from which rays descend, terminating in hands, which bestow bounty on the royal family and Egypt.

Atum

A great creator-god worshipped at Heliopolis where he was united with Re (Re-Atum) to become a sun-god. Mythology states that he was self-created and made the whole universe out of his own being.

Baal

A Semitic god introduced by the Hyksos, whom they identified with Seth, worshipped at Avaris by the name of Sutekh.

Bastet

Cat-goddess who represented the benevolent aspect of Sekhmet, the lioness deity. Worshipped as a woman with a cat's head, her major cult centre was at Bubastis.

Bat

The personification of the sistrum of Hathor, who was worshipped in the Temple of Hathor at Hu.

Bes

A dwarf-god who protected children and women in childbirth, Bes was worshipped in people's homes. He had two wives – Tauert and Beset.

Beset

A female counterpart of Bes who played an important role in magical ceremonies.

Demeter

Greek goddess of the earth whom the Greeks identified with Isis.

'The Devourer'

Composite animal who appears in scenes of the Day of Judgement, crouching beside the scales. The hearts of those found unworthy of immortality were cast to this creature to be eaten and devoured.

Dionysus

Greek god. Some of his characteristics were incorporated in the god Serapis.

Ennead, Great

Group of nine gods worshipped at Heliopolis as creator deities. Led by Re-Atum, they also included Shu, Tefnut, Geb, Nut, Osiris, Isis, Seth and Nephthys.

Ennead, Little

Group of nine lesser deities, also worshipped at Heliopolis.

Four Sons of Horus

Minor deities Imset, Hapy, Duamutef and Qebehsenuef who guarded the visceral contents of the four canopic jars.

Geb

The earth-god, husband of Nut, who is sometimes shown as a goose or goose-headed man.

Great-of-Magic
(*See* Weret-Hekau)

Hapy
The essence of the Nile, and part of Nun (primordial ocean). Depicted as a hermaphrodite figure, he guaranteed life and food for Egypt.

Hardedef
Son of King Cheops, Hardedef was accredited with the authorship of an early Instruction in Wisdom; he probably received a personal cult and was esteemed by later generations.

Haroeris
The Greek name used to describe one aspect of the sky god Horus – the 'Great Horus' or 'Horus the Elder'. In this form, he appeared on earth as a falcon.

Harpocrates
The Greek version of 'Horus-the-child', the son of Osiris and Isis. He was represented in this form as a young boy wearing the Sidelock-of-Youth and sucking the finger of his right hand.

Hathor
Cow-goddess who symbolized fertility. She was also worshipped as the goddess of beauty, love and foreign lands and as a personification of the sky. She had major temples at Deir el-Bahri and Denderah.

Hathor-Nebet-Hetepet
Goddess of Heliopolis; she represented the god's hand, and was both a mother-goddess and an intellectual concept.

Heket
Primordial creator-goddess depicted as a frog, consort of Khnum; she was a goddess of childbirth and also helped Osiris to rise from the dead.

Heqaib
Governor of Aswan in reign of Pepy II who received a personal cult.

Herishef
Ram-god of Heracleopolis, whom the Greeks identified with their deity Arsaphes.

Horus

At first, Horus was a sky-god, represented on earth as a falcon; he was the earliest state god, and had already become the royal god and patron in Predynastic times. Ousted from that position by Re of Heliopolis in the Old Kingdom, Horus then coalesced with Re to become a sun-god, Re-Harakhte. However, he was incorporated into the Heliopolitan mythology not as a sun-god or sky deity but as Horus, son of Osiris and Isis. Each reigning king came to be regarded as Horus incarnate.

Ihy

Son of Hathor, a god of music who was worshipped with Hathor at Denderah where his divine birth is recorded in wall-scenes in one of the Birth-houses.

Imhotep

A high official of King Djoser, accredited as the architect of the Step Pyramid at Saqqara and the founder of medical science in Egypt. He later received a personal cult, and was identified by the Greeks with their own deity, Aesculapius. Regarded as a god of healing, his cult was celebrated at Saqqara and other sites.

Isis

Most popular Egyptian goddess whose cult spread to many other lands. A universal deity and mother-goddess, she was wife of Osiris and mother of Horus, and played a crucial role in the resurrection of Osiris. Her most famous temple was at Philae.

Isis-Eutheria

A syncretic goddess of Graeco-Roman Egypt; when she mourned Osiris' death, her tears were believed to cause the inundation.

Iw.s-ʿ3.s

Heliopolitan goddess, associated with Hathor-Nebet-Hetepet; feminine counterpart of the sun-god whom the theologians invented in order to explain creation.

Jupiter-Amun

The Greeks continued to worship Amun as Zeus-Amun (he had a major oracle in the Siwa oasis), and the Romans called him Jupiter-Amun.

Kagemni

Vizier during Dynasty 6 who received a personal cult. A Wisdom Text also carries his name, in which the vizier of King Huni was instructed to write down his experiences as a guide for the royal children, including Kagemni.

Khentekhtai

Crocodile-god worshipped at Athribis; as early as Dynasty 4, Horus syncretized with this god and took over his name.

Khentiamentiu

Local god of Abydos whose name means 'First (or Foremost) of the Westerners.' The most important god in the west where mankind went after death, Khentiamentiu replaced Wepwawet at Abydos. A god of the dead, he was eventually absorbed by Osiris.

Khepri

A manifestation of the creator-god, appearing as the rising sun. Associated with the scarab (dung-beetle).

Khnum

Worshipped in the form of a ram, Khnum's cult-centre was at Elephantine. Closely connected with the inundation, he also modelled mankind on a potter's turntable.

Khonsu

The son of Amun and Mut, Khonsu was worshipped with them at Thebes. He was a moon-god and was also regarded as a healing deity.

Lates-fish

The Nile perch (*Latus niloticus*), sacred to the goddess Neith, was worshipped at Esna.

Ma^cat

Daughter of Re, and personification of Truth and Justice, Ma^cat represented the equilibrium of the universe. Depicted wearing a feather on her head, Ma^cat (Order) was constantly threatened by Chaos.

Mandulis

A Nubian god worshipped at the Temple of Kalabsha

Menheyet

A lioness-goddess who appears as a companion to Khnum in his temple at Esna.

Mertetseger

A local cobra-goddess worshipped at Deir el-Medina

Meskhenet

Goddess of fate, consort of Shay ('Fate') and personification of the birth stool, she assisted with childbirth and predicted the future of each newly born child.

Mihos

A lion-god, the son of Bastet, who had a temple at Bubastis.

Min

Ithyphallic god of fertility, with important cult centres at Koptos and Akhmim, where he was worshipped in the form of a sacred white bull.

Montu

Falcon-god of war worshipped by rulers of Dynasty 11. At Armant, he took the form of a sacred Buchis-bull.

Mut

Probably worshipped in Predynastic times in the form of a vulture, Mut was a mother-goddess who became Amun's consort at Thebes in the New Kingdom.

Neith

A goddess of hunting and warfare whose main cult centre was at Sais. She was a mother-goddess and patroness of the north.

Nekhbet

Vulture-goddess associated with Predynastic city of Hierakonpolis, Nekhbet became protectress of Upper Egypt, while Wadjet was patroness of the north. They were entitled 'The Two Ladies'.

Nekheny

Chief god of the Predynastic town of Nekhen, he is shown as a falcon with two feathers on his head; Nekheny was eventually assimilated by Horus.

Neper

The son of goddess Renenutet, Neper personified the corn and was equated with Osiris.

Nephthys

The wife of Seth, and sister of Osiris and Isis, Nephthys was part of the Heliopolitan mythology, participating in the protection and resurrection of Osiris, but she apparently had no personal cult or temple.

Nut

The personification of the vault of heaven, Nut was worshipped as a sky-goddess. She is sometimes depicted as a cow straddling the earth. She was the wife of Geb, and mother of Osiris, Isis, Seth and Nephthys.

Onuris

A warrior-god, with major sanctuaries at This, near Abydos, and Sebennytos.

Orion

The constellation that is sometimes identified with Osiris.

Osiris

The great god of the dead; originally a human king who brought civilization to Egypt, Osiris was murdered by Seth, and was ultimately resurrected to become King of the Dead and judge of the underworld. He was originally a vegetation god, and later acquired roles as a moon-god and corn deity. His wife was Isis, and their son, Horus, fought Seth to avenge Osiris' murder. Osiris offered his followers the chance of immortality. His major centres were at Abydos and Busiris.

Osiris-Apis

The Apis bull, already worshipped at Memphis as an animal sacred to Ptah, was identified with Osiris in the later periods. A major cult existed at Saqqara, where the sacred bulls were ultimately mummified and buried in the Serapeum.

Pakhet

Lioness-goddess, a form of Sekhmet, worshipped locally at Speos Artemidos, Beni Hasan.

Panebtawy

He shared the left-hand side of the Temple of Kom Ombo with his father Haroeris and mother Tasenetnofret. His name means 'Lord of the Two Lands'.

(The) Peak

Also known as 'Peak-of-the-West', this goddess personified the highest point of the cliffs behind the Valley of the Kings. She was particularly worshipped at Deir el-Medina.

Peteese and Pihor

Deified local heroes and sons of Quper; the Temple of Dendur was dedicated to several gods including these brothers.

Ptah

Always shown as a mummiform, human figure, Ptah had united with Soker, a funerary god, and Ta-tenen, an earth-god, to become the supreme god at Memphis. Regarded as a creator-god, Ptah was also patron deity of crafts and artisans. Apis, the local sacred bull, became Ptah's cult-animal when his worship was established at Memphis.

Ptah-hotep

Vizier, and author of a famous Wisdom Text, he was highly regarded and probably received a personal cult.

Ptah-Sokar-Osiris

By the Middle Kingdom, these three gods had coalesced to become one deity, associated with creation and death.

Qudshu

A Syrian goddess of love, incorporated into the Egyptian pantheon in the New Kingdom when she became the consort of Resheph.

Re

Sun-god of Heliopolis whose cult spread throughout Egypt during the Old Kingdom, when he became royal patron and supreme deity. Closely associated with the pyramids, his cult reached its zenith in Dynasty 5, when the kings constructed special solar temples. At Heliopolis, Re combined with Atum to become the great creator-god of Heliopolitan mythology. Later, in the New Kingdom, he joined with Amun to become Amen-Re, supreme god of Egypt's empire.

Re-Harakhte

The sun had various forms: Re represented the noonday sun, Khepri symbolized the rising sun, and Atum was the setting sun. Harakhte ('Horus-of-the-Horizon') was a falcon-god who coalesced with Re to become Re-Harakhte, another form of the sun in which the god represented the two horizons of sunrise and sunset, and was shown as a man with a hawk's head surmounted by the sun's disc.

Renenutet

A goddess of fertility whose name meant 'the provider of nourishment', she took the form of a cobra. Her son was Neper, a corn deity.

Resheph

A Canaanite-Phoenician god of thunder and war, introduced into the Egyptian pantheon in the New Kingdom and then associated with Min. His wife was Qudshu.

Satit

Consort of Khnum, whom the Greeks identified with Hera, wife of Zeus. She was also the daughter of Khnum and Anukit, and probably a local hunting goddess. Her cult-centre was on the Island of Seheil, and she became a goddess of the inundation.

Sekhmet

A lioness-goddess, usually shown as a lion-headed woman, Sekhmet's chief centre was at Memphis. She was goddess of warfare, strife, and healing. She was also identified with Hathor, Bastet, Mut and Pakhet. As Mut, she received an important cult at Karnak.

Serapis

Ptolemy I, in a largely unsuccessful attempt to provide his Greek and Egyptian subjects with an acceptable deity, introduced the cult of Serapis. He was a god who combined elements of Osiris, the sacred Apis bull, and the Greek deities Zeus, Aesculapius, and Dionysos. He was a god of fertility and the underworld, with a main cult-centre at Alexandria, known as the Serapeum, which attracted many pilgrims. At Saqqara, the long-established burial site of the Apis bulls also came to be known as the Serapeum.

Serket

A scorpion-goddess, sometimes known as Selket or Selkis, who helped to protect and guard the mummified viscera in the canopic jars.

Seshat

Goddess of writing and books. The female counterpart of Thoth, she wrote the king's name on the Persea tree, each leaf representing a year in his allotted lifespan, and she assisted him with the measurements in temple foundation ceremonies.

Seth

A Predynastic god worshipped at Ombos, he was later identified with the losing side when the 'Followers of Horus' became the kings of Egypt, and he became the embodiment of evil. In the Myth of Osiris, he was identified as Osiris' murderer. However, the Hyksos promoted his worship at Avaris, under the name of Sutekh, and the early Ramesside rulers also emphasized his importance.

Shesmetet

A goddess for whom a temple was built at Nekheb in the Ptolemaic Period.

Shu

God of light and air, Shu was the son of Atum and the husband of Tefnut; he played an important role in the Heliopolitan creation myth.

Sobek

A crocodile-god who was worshipped at many centres including the Fayoum and Kom Ombo. Sobek was a form of Sutekh (Seth).

Soker

A hawk-god who originated in the area of Memphis, he was a guardian of the local cemetery. Once Ptah became established at Memphis, he was united with Soker.

Soped

A falcon-god who became identified with Horus; he guarded Egypt's eastern border, and was lord of foreign lands.

Sothis

At Elephantine, Isis was identified with Sothis, the Dog-star who, as a goddess responsible for the inundation, was represented as a woman with a five-pointed star on her head. She was also identified with Satit.

Sutekh

The Semitic name under which the Hyksos worshipped the god Seth, whom they identified with their own god Baal, Sutekh later became the warlike form of Seth in the Ramesside Period.

Tait

Goddess of weaving. She provided the cloths for adorning the cult-statue during the Daily Temple Ritual; the cloths assumed the same magical properties that she herself possessed, and conveyed these to the wearer.

Tasenetnofret

A special form of Hathor, the name means 'the Good Sister'; with her husband and son, she shared the section of the Temple of Kom Ombo which was dedicated to Haroeris.

Tauert
Hippopotamus-goddess of fertility and fecundity. The wife of Bes, Tauert was worshipped in households throughout the land.

Tefnut
The daughter of Re-Atum, and wife of Shu, Tefnut represented moisture and played an important role in the Heliopolitan creation mythology.

Thoth
A lunar god whose main cult-centre was at Hermopolis. Worshipped as the god of wisdom and writing, Thoth was a royal god and also played an important role in the Day of Judgement. He was the scribe and messenger of the gods whom the Greeks identified with their god, Hermes; the baboon and ibis were Thoth's sacred animals, and he is depicted as a man with an ibis-head.

Wadjet
Sometimes translated as 'Edjo', this Predynastic goddess was worshipped in the form of a cobra at Buto. She was the counterpart of Nekhbet, and became the patron of northern Egypt; together, these goddesses became the royal protectresses.

Wepwawet
The earliest known god at Abydos, his name meant 'the Opener of the Ways'. Shown as a jackal, he directed the dead along the paths of the underworld. In fact, he probably represented a wolf rather than a jackal, and was also worshipped in this form at Assiut. At Abydos, he was eventually ousted by Khentiamentiu.

Weret-hekau
A goddess whose name means 'Great-of-Magic', she was a manifestation of the eye of the sun, who protected the sun-god. Sometimes, she took the form of a snake.

Yahweh
The Jehovah of the Bible, worshipped by the community of Jews at Elephantine.

Zeus
The supreme Greek god, some of his characteristics were incorporated in the god Serapis.

3 GENERAL TERMS

Abydene Symbol

Cult-image of Osiris in which the god's spirit could reside. Its original meaning is obscure, but it may have represented a stylized head and wig.

Akh

An invisible power or spirit which could be used to enhance the abilities of gods and men; represented in Hieroglyphs by a tufted ibis.

Amulets

Pieces of jewellery that were believed to provide the owner with magical powers and protection.

Ankh

The Egyptian word for 'life', frequently used in religious and magical rituals.

Anthropomorphism

A process by which animal gods acquired human or part-human physical characteristics.

Anubeion

Centre established at Saqqara for the sacred animal cult of Anubis, god of cemeteries and mummification.

Archaism

An interest in archaeology and traditional customs, especially evident in Dynasty 26, when there was a conscious attempt to reproduce the art, dress, religion and writing of earlier times.

Asiatics

Traditional northern enemies of Egypt; a collective term for peoples from Syria/Palestine and those who live on Egypt's north-eastern borders.

Atenism

The cult of the Aten, as developed and fostered by Akhenaten during the Amarna Period.

Autobiography
An inscription on the wall of a non-royal tomb that provided an idealized and self-laudatory summary of the owner's characteristics and achievements, to substantiate and support his request for immortality.

Ba
The soul, represented with a human head and a bird body.

Baptism
A part of the coronation ritual in which the gods baptized, purified and acknowledged the king as their son and the rightful ruler.

Barque
Special portable boat in which the god's statue was carried during religious processions.

Benben Stone
Cult symbol of the sun-god at Heliopolis, a squat stone obelisk topped by a pyramidion.

Bennu-bird
Divine bird that alighted on the Benben Stone; later described as the phoenix.

Birth-house
(See Mammisi)

Book of the Dead
A New Kingdom funerary text which contained a series of spells and instructions to enable the deceased owner to achieve immortality. The Books of Gates and Caverns provided other, similar texts.

Boundary Stela
An inscribed stone used, as one of a series, to delineate the perimeter of a particular site.

Bubasteion
Centre established at Saqqara for a sacred animal cult.

Buchis-bull
A sacred bull that represented Montu at Armant; it was buried in a nearby special catacomb known as the Bucheum.

Building Texts
Wall inscriptions in the Temple of Edfu that relate the creation mythology.

Busirite Symbol
(*See* Djed-pillar)

Cache
Collection of buried material; for example, the groups of reinterred royal mummies.

Cannibal Hymn
A section of the Pyramid Texts which describes how the king ate and absorbed the gods' powers.

Canopic Chest
A special chest which contained the canopic jars.

Canopic Jars
A set of four containers which stored the eviscerated organs removed during mummification.

Cartonnage
A composition of papyrus and gum or glue used to manufacture masks and other pieces of funerary equipment.

Cartouche
The Egyptian definition of the universe, meaning 'that which the sun encircles'. Shown as a loop of rope with a knot at the base, this was elongated so that the king's name could be written inside the cartouche, indicating that he owned the world.

Cenotaph
A symbolic funerary monument which does not actually contain a burial.

Chamber Tomb
A type of tomb found in Graeco-Roman Egypt.

Cippus (pl. Cippi)

A statue-stela in which the figure of Horus is carved in three dimensions. Shown as a child, he grapples with snakes, scorpions and dangerous animals. Set up in temples, houses or tombs, the cippi were inscribed with anti-venom spells, and protected against dangerous creatures, and cured those who had been bitten.

Coffins

Used to house and protect the body, coffins were usually either rectangular or anthropoid (body-shaped).

Coffin Texts

Spells derived from the Pyramid Texts, they were inscribed on coffins to provide magical assistance for the owner to achieve immortality.

Colossi of Memnon

Pair of large statues which once flanked the entrance to the temple of Amenhotep III on the west bank at Thebes.

Columns

A major feature of Egyptian temples, they were decorated with lotiform (lotus), papyriform (papyrus), palmiform (palm) or composite (mixed plants) capitals.

Concubine-figure

Special type of model figurine placed in tomb to provide sexual pleasure for the owner in the next world.

Consecration Ceremony

Rituals performed when a new temple was handed over to its resident god.

Cosmogony

Creation myth, describing how the universe came into existence.

Cult animal

Sacred animal in which the god's spirit resided; kept at the temple.

Cult-centre

Temple where the god's worship was carried out.

Cult-statue

A god's statue that received temple rituals.

Cultus temple
(*See* Divine cult complex)

Daily Temple Ritual
Rites performed daily in the temples to supply the god's basic needs.

Day of Judgement
Trial before the divine tribunal, which each deceased person faced in order to attain eternity.

Demotic
Script derived from Hieroglyphs, used after *c.*700 BCE for legal, business and literary texts.

Deshret
The Egyptian name, 'Red Land', for the desert.

Divine cult complex
Sometimes referred to as a 'cultus temple', this was where rituals were performed on behalf of the god.

Djed-pillar
Symbol of Osiris, sometimes believed to represent the god's backbone, it came to mean resurrection and stability.

Duat (Amduat)
The underworld kingdom of Osiris, which was inhabited by non-royal persons who had successfully achieved eternity.

Dynastic Race
A hypothetical ethnic group who, according to some scholars, may have entered Egypt during the Predynastic era. Their actual existence is now disputed.

Ennead
Group of nine gods, as in the Great Ennead of Heliopolis.

Execration Texts
Magical inscriptions intended to destroy both an individual's personal enemies and those of Egypt.

Eye of Horus
The *wedjat*-eye, symbolizing health and completeness; it belonged to Horus and was plucked out when he fought with Seth.

False beard
A beard of woven fabric which was attached to the face by means of straps; it was worn by the gods, kings and the blessed dead.

False door
Carved into the wall of a tomb, this represented a door, to allow the deceased owner's spirit to enter and leave the tomb, in order to partake of the food offerings.

Father of the God
Title of a high-ranking priest.

Fayoum portrait
Painted panel portrait, dating to Roman Egypt, which was placed over the face of a mummy.

Field of Offerings
The land of Osiris, the underworld.

Field of Reeds/Rushes
Land of Osiris, situated somewhere in the west.

First Occasion
The time when the universe was created, and the gods handed over all knowledge to mankind.

Followers of Horus
Early supporters of the god Horus who probably established his cult in Egypt.

Foundation Ceremony
The ritual in which the foundations of a new temple were measured out.

Foundation Deposit
A set of magical objects placed in the foundations of a temple to give it protection.

Funerary Books

The New Kingdom funerary texts (for example, the Book of the Dead) that protected the deceased owner.

Gods

Chief god: main resident in a temple or a cult; *subsidiary god*: companion or minor god in a temple or myth; *state god*: deity who received universal worship and received a temple cult; *local god*: deity who received worship only in particular places and had a temple cult; *'household' or personal god*: deity worshipped in the home, who did not receive a temple cult.

God's Son

The king; he first took the additional title 'son of the god' in the Old Kingdom.

God's Wife of Amun

Originally used for the chief queen, in later periods this title was given to the king's daughter who performed special functions at Thebes.

Great Royal Daughter

Eldest daughter of the reigning king and queen; it was the tradition for the male heir apparent to marry her.

Great Royal Wife

Chief queen of the reigning king.

Hemerology

A system of determining whether a particular day would be lucky or unlucky, based on information derived from mythical events.

Henotheism

Belief in one god, but not excluding the worship of others.

Hieratic

A cursive script derived from hieroglyphs, used for many secular and religious texts.

Hieroglyphs

The picture script developed to convey the language of ancient Egypt. Traditionally used for religious texts.

House of the ka
The tomb, where the *ka* (spirit) was believed to reside.

House of Life
A section of the temple where religious texts were composed and edited. Some teaching may also have been carried out here.

Htp-di-nsw
The formula, translated as the 'Boon-which-the-king-gives', used when the menu and funerary goods were offered at commoners' tombs; it ensured that these became efficacious through the king's bounty.

Hypostyle Hall
The columned reception area of a temple.

Incantation
Spell recited during religious or magical rituals or rites.

Incarnation-animal
The sacred animal kept in the temple, through which the god's spirit was made manifest.

Inundation
The annual rising and flooding of the Nile.

Island of Creation
According to mythology, this was the place where creation had occurred; each temple claimed to symbolize this island.

Jubilee Festival
Celebrated after thirty years' reign, or sometimes more frequently, this reaffirmed the coronation and renewed the king's ability and power to rule.

Ka
The spirit or 'double', represented by a pair of upraised arms, the *ka* was believed to be part of an individual's personality before and after death.

Ka-servant
Priest who performed a man's mortuary rites.

Ka-settlement

Part of a man's estate allocated to pay for a priest to attend to his mortuary cult.

Kamares ware

Minoan pottery found at some Egyptian sites as well as at Kamares in Crete.

Keftians

Foreigners shown in New Kingdom tomb scenes, who possibly came from Crete and the Aegean Islands.

Kemet

The Egyptian name, the 'Black Land', for the Nile valley and Delta.

Kenbet

A local law court.

King List

List of the legitimate rulers of Egypt that was placed in the temple so that the 'Royal Ancestors' (former kings) could receive a cult.

Kline tomb

A type of tomb found in Graeco-Roman Egypt.

Labyrinth (The)

A renowned building at Hawara, which is now destroyed but originally housed the pyramid temple and administrative headquarters of Amenemhet III.

Letters to the Dead

Letters written to the dead and placed at the tomb, requesting their intercession on behalf of the living.

Libation

A liquid offering presented to the god or the dead, as part of a temple or funerary ritual.

Loculus tomb

A type of tomb found in Graeco-Roman Egypt.

Lower Egypt

Northernmost part of Egypt, including the Delta and part of the Nile Valley, which formed a separate kingdom before *c.*3100 BCE.

Mammisi

The 'Birth-house' found in Egyptian temple complexes of the Graeco-Roman Period where the god's birth and the king's identification with the god were celebrated.

Mansion of the God

Egyptian name for the temple, where the god resided.

Mariolatry

The cult of Mary, mother of Jesus.

Mastaba tomb

Burial place (usually non-royal) that combined a burial chamber and offering chapel. The word *mastaba* (Arabic: bench, bench-shaped) describes its bench-like outer structure.

Medical Papyrus

A text that includes medical and magical prescriptions and treatments for the sick.

Menu

List of food and other offerings presented to the gods or the dead.

Model

Miniature figurine, ship or building included in tomb equipment.

Monotheism

Exclusive worship of one god.

Mortuary cult

Performance of rites and the presentation of offerings carried out on behalf of the deceased, in order to obtain particular benefits on his behalf.

Mother of Apis

Mother of the calf selected by the priests to become the Sacred Bull. This cow was looked after by the priests, and, after death, was mummified and interred in a special catacomb.

Mummification

Method of preserving the body by means of evisceration and dehydration using natron.

Mummy

A preserved body. The word 'mummy' is derived from the Arabic *mumia*, meaning a type of pitch or bitumen. It was believed (erroneously) that this substance had been used in the preparation of mummies.

Mysteries

The secret initiation into the cult of a god, and some of the temple rituals performed for the god.

Mystery Plays

Interpretations of events in a god's life, enacted in public as part of ceremonies at festivals that were attended by pilgrims.

Natron

Naturally occurring salt compound found in the Wadi en-Natrun, used for cleaning and purification purposes as well as mummification.

Necropolis

A cemetery, usually situated on the west bank of the Nile.

Nilometer

A device for measuring the levels of water in the river.

Nine Bows

The collective term for Egypt's traditional enemies.

Nome

A geographical district in Egypt.

Nubia

The land to the south, colonized by Egypt from earliest times; a major source of gold and hard stone.

Nun

The great primeval ocean from which the Island of Creation emerged, Nun represented darkness and non-existence.

Obelisk

Upright stone, topped by a pyramidion, which was a symbol of the sun-cult.

Offering chapel

Part of a tomb where the priest made offerings on behalf of the deceased.

Offering list

Inscribed on the wall of a tomb or temple, this included the food, clothing and other commodities presented to the dead or gods as part of mortuary or divine cults.

Offering tray

Stone or pottery tray placed in a tomb and used for the presentation of food offerings to the deceased owner.

Ogdoad

Group of eight gods; for example, the Hermopolitan Ogdoad who featured in a creation myth.

Oikos

Main room and burial chamber in the *kline* tombs of the Graeco-Roman Period.

Opening-of-the-Mouth Ceremony

Performed by a priest on the mummies, statues and figures in tomb and temple wall-reliefs, this ritual was believed to 'bring them to life' by means of magic.

Oracle

A sacred statue or animal used by a god to give advice to petitioners.

Osireion

Monument behind the Temple of Sethos I at Abydos, probably regarded as the cenotaph of Osiris.

Osirid

Type of column found in some temples which represented the upright, bodily form of Osiris.

Osiris Complex at Abydos
Set of rooms in the Temple of Sethos I, where secret rites were performed as part of the annual festival of Osiris.

Ostracon (pl. Ostraca)
A limestone flake or pottery sherd used as a writing or drawing surface.

Overseer figure
A model figurine that accompanied and supervised the sets of *ushabtis* (models of agricultural workers) placed in tombs.

Paddle-doll
A fertility figurine with a paddle-shaped body that emphasized the genitalia, which was placed in the tomb.

Palaeopathology
The study of disease in ancient human remains.

Pantheon
The whole group of gods found in one religious tradition.

Papyrus
A plant processed to provide writing material.

Pectoral
An ornament, usually rectangular in shape, that was worn on the chest.

Pessimistic Literature
A genre of writing that expressed doubt and unhappiness about contemporary conditions.

Phyle
A group of priests who served in the temple on a regular rota system.

Place-of-Truth
Part of the Theban necropolis or royal workmen's village at Deir el-Medina

Polytheism
The worship of many gods.

Priest

Lector: recited the liturgy; *sem*: performed the burial service; *High-*: headed the temple hierarchy; *w^cb*: ordinary level of priest in the temple; *mortuary*: performed the mortuary cult, presenting offerings at the tomb; *lay*: combined his part-time temple duties with a secular profession.

Private

Non-royal or commoner, as in 'private tomb' or 'private statuary'.

Pronaos

Area in front of the sanctuary or shrine in a temple or tomb.

Prostas

Anteroom with an offering altar and a bench for mourners, in the *kline* tombs of Graeco-Roman Egypt.

Ptolemaic Egyptian

A late stage of Egyptian hieroglyphs used in the temple inscriptions of the Ptolemaic Period.

Pylon

Two massive stone towers flanking the doorway that formed a gateway into or between the various sections of a temple.

Pyramid

Probably derived from the Greek word *pyramis* (meaning 'wheaten cake'); the Egyptian word for this monument was *Mer* or 'Place of Ascension'. The pyramid was closely associated with the sun-cult and, as the king's burial place, it provided him with a means of ascent to heaven.

Pyramid Texts

Magical texts inscribed on the interior walls of some pyramids to assist the king to reach heaven.

Pyramidion

Small gilded pyramid-shaped stone that crowned the obelisk; this was lit by the sun from dawn to dusk.

Raising the Djed-pillar
Rite in the annual Osiris Festival when the *Djed*-pillar (Osiris' symbol) was erected in the upright position, signifying the god's resurrection.

Repeater-of-Births
Ruler who inaugurated a new era.

Reed and papyrus
The symbols of Upper and Lower Egypt.

Report
The 'Report' or 'Bulletin' was inscribed on some New Kingdom temple walls and provided a summary of the king's military successes.

Reversion of Offerings
Stages in the temple ritual when the food offerings were taken from the god's altar and offered to the Ancestors (kings) (First Reversion), and then removed from the Ancestors and divided amongst the priests (Second Reversion).

Ritual of the Royal Ancestors
This followed the Daily Temple Ritual in some temples, and affirmed the previous kings' acceptance of the current ruler. It is also known as the Ritual of Amenhotep I.

Rock-cut tomb
Special type of tomb in which the offering chapel and burial chamber are cut into the cliff side or rock.

Royal Ancestors
All the legitimate, previous kings of Egypt; they were honoured in a daily temple ritual.

Royal Cult (personal)
Some kings were deified and received individual worship, in addition to their role as Royal Ancestors.

Royal Cult Complex
Sometimes referred to as a 'mortuary temple', this was where rituals were performed on behalf of the gods, the Royal Ancestors, and to ensure the continuation of the current ruler during his lifetime and after death.

Sacred Lake
Situated in the temple precinct, this was where the priests performed their daily ablutions and all the gods' utensils were washed.

Saff-tomb
A special type of tomb that was built in rows.

Sarcophagus
Rectangular, outer coffin, usually made of stone.

Satrap
Persian governor.

Satrapy
Province of the Persian Empire.

Scarab
The dung-beetle; a symbol of rebirth and renewal.

School boy Exercises
Model texts composed in the form of letters exchanged between teachers and pupils, which extolled the virtues of teachers and the educational system.

Screen Wall
In the Egyptian temples of the Graeco-Roman Period, this separated the outer court from the hypostyle hall.

Scribe
State official whose duties extended far beyond the ability to write.

Scriptorium
A section of the temple where the sacred texts were composed and copied.

Sea-peoples
A confederation of peoples or tribes from the north who attacked Egypt in the reigns of Merneptah and Ramesses III.

Second death
The final obliteration of an individual soul; a state faced by those who did not meet the requirements of the Day of Judgement.

Sed-festival
(*See* Jubilee Festival)

Serapeum
Burial complex of the Apis bulls at Saqqara.

Serdab
Cell-like chamber in the tomb, which housed the deceased's statue.

Servant-of-the-god
General term for a priest, who was responsible for attending to the god's spiritual and physical requirements.

Settlement site
Archaeological site: a city, town or village once occupied by a living community.

Shaduf
A water-lifting device.

Shaft-tomb
Special type of tomb found in pharaonic and Graeco-Roman Periods, in which a shaft provides access to the burial chamber.

Sidelock-of-Youth
A hairstyle worn in childhood, in which the head was shaved except for a plait left at the side. This was also cut off when a boy reached puberty.

Sistrum (pl. *sistra*)
A tinkling rattle used in temple rituals and dances.

Solar barque
Boat in which the sun sailed across the heavens.

Solar/sun cult
Worship of the sun-god; he had several forms of which Re was the most important.

Soul-house
Pottery model of a house placed in the tomb to act as an offering tray.

Spell
Incantation recited in order to bring about a desired result.

Speos
Rock-cut temple or shrine.

Sphinx
Stone carving of a lion with the head of pharaoh, representing the sun-god or a king. The finest example — the Great Sphinx at Giza — was guardian of the sacred buildings in the locality.

Star-cults
The worship of certain stars and constellations, which probably predated the solar cult.

Stela (pl. stelae)
Inscribed stone block placed in the tomb or at another religious place, to provide the deceased with a biography, prayers and offering scenes, in order to ensure his eternal life.

Step Pyramid
A stepped structure which predated the geometrically true pyramid with its smooth, sloping sides. The most famous example, built by Imhotep for King Djoser, is at Saqqara.

Story of Sinuhe
Literary masterpiece of the Middle Kingdom that relates the imaginary adventures of a royal official, Sinuhe.

Subcutaneous packing
Materials inserted under the skin during the mummification process in Dynasty 21, to give the body a more rounded, realistic appearance.

Syncretism
The process whereby the deities of victorious people assimilated or absorbed the gods of conquered or subordinated groups; in this way, a successful god could embrace and adopt any desirable features and characteristics of a lesser deity.

Taboo
A sacred interdiction upon the use of certain things, words, or the performance of certain actions.

Theocracy
Government of the state by priests or ministers as the gods' representatives.

Tomb-chapel
Offering place attached to the tomb.

Tomb-model
(*See* Model)

Tomb robberies
Desecration and despoliation of the burial places; these reached a peak in Dynasty 20.

Triad
Group of three gods that often consisted of a father, mother and child.

Two Ladies
Wadjet and Nekhbet, Predynastic goddesses of Lower and Upper Egypt.

Two Lands
Egypt: the two separate kingdoms of Upper and Lower Egypt, united in *c.*3100 BCE by King Menes.

Two Lords
Horus and Seth, gods of the two kingdoms of Egypt.

Upper Egypt
Southernmost part of Egypt, the Nile Valley. A separate kingdom before unification in *c.*3100 BCE.

Uraeus
Serpent which sat on the royal brow and spat venom at the king's enemies.

Ushabti (shabti)
Mummiform figurine of an agricultural worker, placed in the tomb to assist the deceased in the next world.

Viceroy of Nubia
Official appointed to govern Nubia, directly responsible to the king.

Vizier
King's Chief Minister.

Votive Hymns
Hymns petitioning the gods for mercy.

Votive Offerings
Personal gifts that people placed at cult-centres to request favours from the god.

Wa'abet
Literally, the 'Place of Purification'; the building or possibly the tent where the mummification procedure was carried out.

Wadi
Dry desert valley.

Way-station
Place on the processional route where the priests rested briefly when carrying the god's statue.

Wedjat-eye
(*See* Eye of Horus)

West, The
Land of the dead, situated below the horizon where the sun sets.

Westcar Papyrus
A text which relates a propagandist version of the divine origin of the earliest rulers of Dynasty 5; it provides an early example of public story-telling.

Wisdom Literature
Also known as 'Instructions in Wisdom', these texts provided moral and ethical teaching for upper- and middle-class boys.

Zoolatry
Deification and worship of animals.

Bibliography

ABBREVIATIONS

AJSL	*American Journal of Semitic Languages and Literatures*
ASAE	*Annales du Service des Antiquités de l'Égypte*
Bib. Arch.	*Biblical Archaeology*
BIFAO	*Bulletin de l'Institut français d'Archéologie orientale*
BJRLM	*Bulletin of the John Rylands Library, Manchester*
Bull. Inst. Ég.	*Bulletin de l'Institut de l'Égypte*
Chr. d'Ég.	*La Chronique d'Égypte*
Eg. Arch.	*Egyptian Archaeology. The Bulletin of the Egypt Exploration Society*
JARCE	*Journal of the American Research Center in Egypt*
JAS	*Journal of Archaeological Science*
JEA	*Journal of Egyptian Archaeology*
JNES	*Journal of Near Eastern Studies*
ZÄS	*Zeitschrift für ägyptische Sprache und Altertumskunde*

A. Abdalla, 'A Group of Osiris-cloths of the 21st Dynasty in the Cairo Museum', *JEA* 74 (1988), pp. 157–64.

—, 'The Cenotaph of the Sekwashet Family from Saqqara', *JEA* 78 (1992), pp. 93–112.

F. Abitz, *Ramses III in den Gräbern seiner Söhne* (Freiburg and Gottingen, 1986).

B. Adams, *Ancient Hierakonpolis* (Warminster, 1974).

O. el-Aguizy, 'Dwarfs and Pygmies in Ancient Egypt', *ASAE* 71 (1987), pp. 53–60.

C. Aldred, 'Year 12 at El-Amarna', *JEA* 43 (1957(i)), pp. 114–17.

—, 'The End of the Amarna Period', *JEA* 43 (1957(ii)), pp. 30–41.

—, 'The Beginning of the Amarna Period', *JEA* 45 (1959), pp. 19–33.

—, 'The Tomb of Akhenaten at Thebes', *JEA* 47 (1961), pp. 41–59.

—, *Jewels of the Pharaohs* (London, 1971).

—, *Akhenaten and Nefertiti* (Brooklyn, 1973).

—, *Akhenaten: King of Egypt* (London, 1988).

S. Allam, 'Egyptian Law Courts in Pharaonic and Hellenistic Times', *JEA* 77 (1991), pp. 109–27.

J. P. Allen, *Genesis in Egypt. The Philosophy of Ancient Egyptian Creation Accounts* (New Haven, Connecticut, 1988).

T. G. Allen, *The Egyptian Book of the Dead* (Chicago, 1960).

C. Andrews, *Amulets of Ancient Egypt* (London, 1994).

—, 'A Stone Vessel with Magical Scenes and Texts', in Clarysse *et al.*, *Egyptian Religion* (1998), pp. 297–310.

—, *Ancient Egyptian Jewellery* (London, 1999).

P. L. Armitage and J. Clutton-Brock, 'A Radiological and Histological Investigation into the Mummification of Cats from Ancient Egypt', *JAS* 8 (1981), pp. 185–96.

D. Arnold, *The Temple of Mentuhotep at Deir el Bahari* (New York, 1979).

—, *The South Cemeteries of Lisht. I. The Pyramid of Senwosret I* (New York, 1988).

—, *The Royal Women of Amarna* (New York, 1996).

J. Assmann, *Re and Amun* (Freiburg and Gottingen, 1983).

—, 'When Justice Fails: Jurisdiction and Imprecation in Ancient Egypt and the Near East', *JEA* 78 (1992), pp. 149–78.

—, *Egyptian Solar Religion in the New Kingdom* (London, 1995).

—, *Moses the Egyptian: The Memory of Egypt in Western Monotheism* (Harvard, Mass., 1997).

M. M. Austin, *The Hellenistic World from Alexander to the Roman Conquest* (Cambridge, 1981).

R. M. Awad, 'The Causeway of the Ounas Pyramid', *ASAE* 61 (1973), p. 151.

A. Badawy, *A History of Egyptian Architecture*, 3 vols (Cairo, Berkeley and Los Angeles, 1954–68).

—, 'The Ideology of the Superstructure of the Mastaba-tomb in Egypt', *JNES* 15 (1956), pp. 180–83.

—, 'The Architectural Symbolism of the Mammisi-chapels of Egypt', *Chr. d'Ég.* 38 (1963), pp. 78–90.

R. S. Bagnall, 'Cults and Names of Ptolemais in Upper Egypt', in Clarysse *et al.*, *Egyptian Religion* (1998), pp. 1093–1101.

J. Baines, 'Interpreting Sinuhe', *JEA* 68 (1982), pp. 31–44.

—, 'Abydos, Temple of Sethos I: Preliminary Report', *JEA* 70 (1984), pp. 13–22.

—, 'Practical Religion and Piety', *JEA* 73 (1987), pp. 79–98.

—, 'Techniques of Decoration in the Hall of the Barques in the Temple of Sethos I at Abydos', *JEA* 75 (1989), pp. 13–30.

—, 'Merit by Proxy: The Biographies of the Dwarf Djeho and His Patron Tjai-harpta', *JEA* 78 (1992), pp. 241–57.

H. K. S. Bakhry, 'Akhenaten at Heliopolis', *Chr. d'Ég.* 47 (1972), pp. 55–67.

L. Balout and C. Roubet, *La Momie de Ramsès II* (Paris, 1985).

K. Bard, 'A Quantitative Analysis of the Predynastic Burials in Armant Cemetery 1400–1500', *JEA* 74 (1988), pp. 39–55.

A. Bataille, *Les Memnonia: recherches de papyrologie et d'épigraphie grecques sur la nécropole de la Thèbes d'Égypte aux époques hellénistique et romaine* (Cairo, 1952).

E. Baumgartel, *The Cultures of Predynastic Egypt* (Oxford, 1955).

H. I. Bell, 'Popular Religion in Graeco-Roman Egypt. I. The Pagan Period', *JEA* 34 (1948), pp. 82–97.

—, *Cults and Creeds in Graeco-Roman Egypt* (Liverpool, 1953; repr. 1957).

—, *Egypt from Alexander the Great to the Arab Conquest* (Oxford, 1956).

E. Bevan, *A History of Egypt under the Ptolemaic Dynasty* (London, 1927).

R. S. Bianchi, 'The Oracle at the Temple of Dendur', in Clarysse *et al.*, *Egyptian Religion* (1998), pp. 773–80.

M. Bierbrier, *The Late New Kingdom in Egypt (c. 1300–664 BC)* (Warminster, 1975).

—, *The Tomb-builders of the Pharaohs* (London, 1995).

M. Bietak, *Avaris and Piramesse: Archaeological Exploration in the Eastern Nile Delta* (Oxford, 1981; reprinted from *Proceedings of the British Academy*, London, vol. lxv (1979)).

—, 'Minoan Wall-paintings Unearthed at Ancient Avaris', *Eg. Arch.*, No. 2 (1992), pp. 26–8.

—, *Avaris, the Capital of the Hyksos. Recent Excavations at Tell el-Dab'a* (London, 1996).

—, 'Avaris, Capital of the Hyksos Kingdom: New results of Excavations' in E. Oren (ed.), *The Hyksos: New Historical and Archaeological Perspectives* (Philadelphia, 1997).

J. Bimson, *Relating the Exodus and Conquest* (London, 1978).

F. W. F. von Bissing, 'Les tombeaux d'Assouan', *ASAE* 15 (1915), pp. 1–14.

A. M. Blackman, 'Libations to the Dead in Modern Nubia and Ancient Egypt', *JEA* 3 (1916(i)), pp. 31–4.

—, 'The Ka-house and the Serdab', *JEA* 3 (1916(ii)), pp. 250–54.

—, 'Oracles in Ancient Egypt', *JEA* 11 (1925), pp. 249–55; 12 (1926), pp. 176–85.

— and H. W. Fairman, 'The Consecration of an Egyptian Temple According to the Use of Edfu', *JEA* 32 (1946), pp. 75–91.

W. S. Blackman, *The Fellahin of Upper Egypt* (London, 1927).

C. Le Blanc, 'The Tomb of Ramesses II and Remains of His Funerary Treasure', *Eg. Arch.*, No. 10 (1997), pp. 11–13.

B. Bohleke, 'An Oracular Amuletic Decree of Khonsu in the Cleveland Museum of Art', *JEA* 83 (1997), pp. 155–67.

L. Borchadt, *Das Grabdenkmal des Königs Sa-hu-re*, 2 vols (Leipzig, 1910–13).

J. Borghouts, *Ancient Egyptian Magical Texts* (Leiden, 1978).

A. Bowman, *Egypt after the Pharaohs* (London, 1986).

P. Boylan, *Thoth, the Hermes of Egypt* (Oxford, repr. 1999).

J. Bradshaw, *The Imperishable Stars of the Northern Sky in the Pyramid Texts* (published privately, London, 1990).

J. H. Breasted, *The Battle of Kadesh* (Chicago, 1903).

P. Brissaud, 'An Enigma at Tanis', *Eg. Arch.*, No. 12 (1998), pp. 33–6.

British Museum, *Treasures of Tutankhamun. Catalogue of the Exhibition Held at the British Museum* (London, 1972).

G. Brunton, *Lahun I, the Treasure* (London, 1920).

— and W. Caton-Thompson, *The Badarian Civilisation* (London, 1928).

A. de Buck, 'The Judicial Papyrus of Turin', *JEA* 23 (1937), pp. 152–64.

— and A. H. Gardiner (eds), *The Egyptian Coffin Texts* (Chicago, 1935–61).

E. A. W. Budge, *The Book of the Dead*, 3 vols (London, 1898).

A. Burridge, 'Did Akhenaten Suffer from Marfan's Syndrome?', *Bib. Arch.* 59 (1996), pp. 127–8.

A. M. Calverley and M. F. Broome, *The Temple of King Sethos I at Abydos*, 4 vols (London, 1933–58).

E. F. Campbell, *The Chronology of the Amarna Letters, with Special Reference to the Hypothetical Co-regency of Amenophis III and Akhenaten* (Baltimore, 1964).

J. Capart, A. H. Gardiner and B. van der Walle, 'New Light on the Ramesside Tomb-robberies', *JEA* 22 (1936), pp. 169–93.

H. Carter, *The Tomb of Tut-Ankh-Amen*, 3 vols (London, 1923–33; repr. London, 1972).

H. Case and J. C. Payne, 'Tomb 100: The Decorated Tomb at Hierakonpolis', *JEA* 48 (1962), pp. 5–18.

E. Cavaignac, 'La date du tombeau de Pétosiris: Grèce ou Perse?', *BIFAO* 30 (1931), pp. 201–7.

J. Černy, *Late Ramesside Letters* (Brussels, 1939).

—, 'Egyptian Oracles' in R. A. Parker (ed.), *A Saite Oracle Papyrus from Thebes in the Brooklyn Museum* (Providence, R.I., 1962), pp. 35–48.

—, *A Community of Workmen at Thebes in the Ramesside Period* (Cairo, 1973).

Chicago University, Oriental Institute, *Medinet Habu*, 4 vols (Chicago, 1932–40).

W. Clarysse, A. Schoors and H. Willems (eds), *Egyptian Religion. The Last Thousand Years*, 2 vols (Louvain, Belgium, 1998).

E. Cockburn and T. A. Reyman (eds), *Mummies, Disease and Ancient Cultures*, 2nd ed. (Cambridge, 1998).

J. D. Cooney, 'Three Early Saite Tomb Reliefs', *JNES* 9 (1950), pp. 193–203.

—, 'Persian Influence in Late Egyptian Art', *JARCE* 4 (1965), pp. 39–48.

R. G. Coquin, 'La Christianisation des temples de Karnak', *BIFAO* 72 (1972), pp. 169–78.

H. Coutts (ed.), *Gold of the Pharaohs. Catalogue of the Exhibition of Treasures from Tanis* (Edinburgh, 1988).

P. T. Crocker, 'Status Symbols in the Architecture of El-Amarna', *JEA* 71 (1985), pp. 52–65.

A. R. David (transl.), *A Guide to Religious Ritual at Abydos, c. 1300 BC* (Warminster, 1981).

—, *The Manchester Museum Mummy Project* (Manchester, 1979).

—, 'Mummification' in P. T. Nicholson and I. Shaw (eds), *Ancient Egyptian Materials and Technology* (Cambridge, 2000).

R. David, *The Pyramid Builders of Ancient Egypt* (London, 1996).

N. de Garis Davies, *The Rock Tombs of El-Amarna* (London, 1903–8).

—, 'Mural Paintings in the City of Akhenaten', *JEA* 7 (1921), pp. 1–7.

— and A. H. Gardiner, *The Tomb of Amenemhet* (London, 1915).

Nina de Garis Davies, 'Some Representations of Tombs from the Theban Necropolis', *JEA* 24 (1938), pp. 25–40.

— and N. de Garis Davies, *The Theban Tomb Series* (London, 1915–33).

T. M. Davis, *The Tomb of Queen Tiyi* (London, 1910).

W. M. Davis, 'Egypt, Samos, and the Archaic Style in Greek Sculpture', *JEA* 81 (1967), pp. 61–81.

W. R. Dawson, 'Making a Mummy', *JEA* 13 (1927), pp. 40–49.

—, 'Studies in the Egyptian Medical Texts', I. *JEA* 18 (1932), pp. 150–54; II. 19 (1933), pp. 133–7; III. 20 (1934), pp. 41–6; IV. 20 (1934), pp. 185–8; V. 21 (1935), pp. 37–40.

D. Delia, 'Isis, or the Moon', in Clarysse *et al.*, *Egyptian Religion* (1998), pp. 539–50.

L. Depuydt, 'The Demotic Mathematical Astronomical Papyrus Carlsberg 9 Reinterpreted' in Clarysse *et al.*, *Egyptian Religion* (1998), pp. 1276–97.

D. E. Derry, 'Note of the Skeleton Believed To Be That of Akhenaten', *ASAE* 31 (1931), pp. 115–19.

—, 'The Dynastic Race in Egypt', *JEA* 42 (1956), pp. 80–85.

M. del Carmen Pérez Die, 'Discoveries at Heracleopolis Magna (Ehnasya el-Medina)', *Eg. Arch.*, No. 6 (1995), pp. 23–5.

A. Dodson, *The Canopic Equipment of the Kings of Egypt* (London, 1994).

—, 'A Funerary Mask in Durham and Mummy Adornment in the Late Second Intermediate Period and Early Dynasty 18', *JEA* 84 (1998), pp. 93–100.

V. Dominique and H. Geneviève, 'Les questions oraculaires d'Égypte: histoire de la recherche nouveautés et perspectives', in Clarysse *et al.*, *Egyptian Religion* (1998), pp. 1055–71.

E. Doxiadis, *The Mysterious Fayoum Portraits: Faces from Ancient Egypt* (London, 1995).

G. Dreyer, 'A Hundred Years at Abydos', *Eg. Arch.*, No. 3 (1993), pp. 10–12.

G. R. Driver, *Aramaic Documents of the Fifth Century BC* (Oxford, 1957).

F. Dunand, *Études préliminaires aux religions orientales dans l'empire romain* (Leiden, 1979).

D. Dunham, *The Royal Cemeteries of Kush*, 4 vols (Oxford, 1950–57).

W. Edgerton and J. A. Wilson, *Historical Records of Ramesses III* (Chicago, 1936).

I. E. S. Edwards, 'Some Early Dynastic Contributions to Egyptian Architecture', *JEA* 35 (1949), pp. 123–8.

—, *Hieratic Papyri in the British Museum, 4th series: Oracular Amuletic Decrees of the Late New Kingdom* (London, 1960).

—, 'The Collapse of the Meidum Pyramid', *JEA* 60 (1974), pp. 251–2.

—, *The Pyramids of Egypt* (Harmondsworth, repr. 1992).

Egyptian Antiquities Organization/Getty Conservation Institute, *Wall Paintings of the Tomb of Nefertari: Scientific Studies for Their Conservation* (Cairo, 1987).

H. W. Fischer-Elfert, 'Two Oracle Petitions Addressed to Horus-Khau with Some Notes on the Oracular Amuletic Decrees', *JEA* 82 (1996), pp. 129–44.

L. B. Ellis, 'Isis at Cologne and Aix', *Ancient Egypt* IV (1926), pp. 97–101.

W. B. Emery, *Great Tombs of the First Dynasty*, 2 vols (Cairo, 1949; Oxford, 1954).

—, *Archaic Egypt* (Harmondsworth, 1972).

J. Y. Empereur, *Alexandria Rediscovered* (London, 1998).

R. M. Engelbach, *The Hyksos Reconsidered* (Chicago, 1939).

—, 'Material for a Revision of the History of the Heresy Period of the XVIIIth Dynasty', *ASAE* 40 (1940–41), pp. 133–83.

—, 'An Essay on the Advent of the Dynastic Race in Egypt and Its Consequences', *ASAE* 42 (1943), pp. 193–221.

A. Erman (transl. by A. Blackman), *The Literature of the Ancient Egyptians* (London, 1927).

J. Worth Estes, *The Medical Skills of Ancient Egypt* (Canton, Mass., 1989).

C. J. Eyre, 'Crime and Adultery in Ancient Egypt', *JEA* 70 (1984), pp. 92–105.

—, 'The Adoption Papyrus in Social Context', *JEA* 78 (1992), pp. 207–21.

H. W. Fairman, 'Worship and Festivals in an Egyptian Temple', *BJRLM* 37 (1954), pp. 165–202.

R. O. Faulkner, 'The Cannibal Hymn from the Pyramid Texts', *JEA* 10 (1924), pp. 97–103.

—, 'The Wars of Sethos I', *JEA* 33 (1947), pp. 34–9.

—, 'The Man Who was Tired of Life', *JEA* 42 (1956), pp. 21–40.

—, 'The King and the Star-religion in the Pyramid Texts', *JNES* 25 (1966), pp. 153–61.

—, *The Ancient Egyptian Coffin* Texts, 3 vols (Warminster, 1973–78).

—, *The Ancient Egyptian Pyramid Texts* (Oxford, 1969).

C. M. Firth and B. Gunn, *The Teti Pyramid Cemeteries*, 2 vols (Cairo, 1926).

J. L. Foster, 'The Contribution to the Testament of Ammenemes, King of Egypt', *JEA* 67 (1981), pp. 36–47.

M. V. Fox, 'A Study of Antef', *Orientalia* 46 (1977), pp. 393–423.

H. Frankfort (ed.), *The Mural Paintings of El-Amarnah* (London, 1929).

—, *Ancient Egyptian Religion* (New York, 1948).

—, *Kingship and the Gods: A Study of Ancient Near Eastern Religion as the Integration of Society and Nature* (Chicago, 1978).

—, A. de Buck and B. Gunn, *The Cenotaph of Seti at Abydos*, 2 vols (London, 1933).

—and J. D. S. Pendlebury, *The City of Akhenaten*, vol. 2 (London, 1933).

D. Frankfurter, *Religion in Roman Egypt: Assimilation and Resistance* (Princeton, New Jersey, 1998).

P. M. Fraser, *Two Studies on the Cult of Sarapis in the Hellenistic World* (London, 1960).

—, *Ptolemaic Alexandria* (Oxford, 1972).

R. Freed, Y. Markowitz and S. D'Auria (eds), *Pharaohs of the Sun. Akhenaten, Nefertiti and Tutankhamun* (London, 1999).

S. Freud, *Moses and Monotheism* (New York, 1967).

F. Friedman, 'On the Meaning of Some Anthropoid Busts from Deir el-Medina', *JEA* 71 (1985), pp. 82–97.

F. D. Friedman, *Beyond the Pharaohs: Egypt and the Copts in the 2nd to 7th centuries AD* (Providence, R.I., 1989).

R. Friedman, 'Hierakonpolis: A New Look at an Old Site', Eg. Arch., No. 11 (1997), pp. 12–14.

C. Gaillard and G. Daressy, *La Faune momifiée* (Cairo, 1905).

C. Gallazzi, 'Further Surprises from Tebtunis', *Eg. Arch.*, No. 14 (1999), pp. 16–17.

M. Galvin, 'The Hereditary Status of the Titles of the Cult of Hathor', *JEA* 70 (1984), pp. 42–9.

A. H. Gardiner, 'New Literary Sources from Ancient Egypt', *JEA* 1 (1914(i)), pp. 20–35.

—, 'The Instruction for King Merykare', *JEA* 1 (1914(ii)), pp. 20–36.

—, *Hieratic Papyri in the British Museum*, 2 vols (London, 1935).

—, 'The Instructions Addressed to Kagemni and His Brethren', *JEA* 32 (1946), pp. 71–6.

—, 'The Baptism of Pharaoh', *JEA* 36 (1950), pp. 3–12.

—, 'The Memphite Tomb of the General Horemheb', *JEA* 39 (1953), pp. 3–12.

—, *The Ramesseum Papyri* (Oxford, 1955).

—, 'The So-called Tomb of Queen Tiye', *JEA* 43 (1957), pp. 10–25.

—, 'Was Osiris an Ancient King Subsequently Deified?', *JEA* 46 (1960), p. 104.

—, *Egypt of the Pharaohs* (Oxford, 1961).

—, *The Admonitions of an Egyptian Sage* (Leipzig, 1909, repr. Hildesheim, 1969).

— and A. Weigall, *A Topographical Catalogue of the Private Tombs of Thebes* (London, 1913).

J. Garstang, 'Excavations at Beni Hasan (1902–4)', *ASAE* 5 (1904), pp. 215–28.

P. Ghalioungui, 'A Medical Study of Akhenaten', *ASAE* 47 (1947), pp. 29–46.

—, *Magic and Medical Science in Ancient Egypt* (London, 1963).

—, 'Ancient Egyptian Remedies and Medieval Arabic Writers', *BIFAO* 68 (1969), pp. 41–6.

A. S. Gilbert, 'Zooarchaeological Observations on the Slaughterhouse of Meketre', *JEA* 74 (1988), pp. 69–89.

M. Gitton, *Les Divines Épouses de la 18e dynastie* (Paris, 1984).

R. Giveon, 'Resheph in Egypt', *JEA* 66 (1980), pp. 144–50.

H. Goedicke, 'Was Magic Used in the Harem Conspiracy against Ramesses III?', *JEA* 49 (1963), pp. 71–92.

—, 'The Beginning of the Instruction of King Amenemhet', *JARCE* 7 (1968), pp. 15–22.

O. Goelet, Jr., 'A New "Robbery" Papyrus: Rochester MAG 51.346.1', *JEA* 82 (1996), pp. 107–27.

J. Gohary, *Akhenaten's Sed-festival at Karnak* (London, 1992).

C. E. Gordon, 'The Religion of the Jews of Elephantine in the Light of the Hermopolis Papyri', *JNES* 28 (1969), pp. 116–21.

J-C. Goyon, *Les Dieux-Gardiens et la genèse des temples*, 2 vols (Cairo, 1985).

C. Graindorge, 'La Quête de la Lumière au Mois de Khoiak: une Histoire d'Oies', *JEA* 82 (1996), pp. 83–105.

L. Greener, *High Dam over Nubia* (New York, 1962).

F. Ll. Griffith, *The Inscriptions of Siut and Der Rifeh* (London, 1889).

—, *Hieratic Papyri from Kahun and Gurob*, 3 vols (London, 1897–8).

J. G. Griffiths, *The Origins of Osiris and His Cult* (Leiden, 1980).

—, *De Iside et Osiride* (Cardiff, 1970).

—, 'Eight Funerary Paintings with Judgement Scenes in the Swansea Wellcome Museum', *JEA* 68 (1982), pp. 228–52.

C. W. Griggs, *Early Christianity from Its Origins to 451 C.E.*, 2nd edn. (Leiden, 1991).

B. Gunn, 'Religion of the Poor in Ancient Egypt', *JEA* 3 (1916), pp. 81–94.

L. Habachi, 'Sais and Its Monuments', *ASAE* 43 (1942), pp. 369–416.

H. R. Hall, 'The Relations of Aegean with Egyptian Art', *JEA* 1 (1914), pp. 110–18.

V. Hankey, 'Egypt, the Aegean and the Levant', *Eg. Arch.*, No. 3 (1993), pp. 27–9.

Y. M. Harpur, 'Two Old Kingdom Tombs at Giza', *JEA* 67 (1981), pp. 24–35.

—, *Decoration in Egyptian Tombs of the Old Kingdom. Studies in Orientation and Scene Content* (London, 1987).

J. R. Harris, 'Nefertiti Rediviva', *Acta Orientalis* 35 (1973), pp. 5–14.

—, 'Nefernefruaten Regnans', *Acta Orientalis* 36 (1974(i)), pp. 11–22.

—, 'Kiya', *Chr. d'Ég.* 49 (1974(ii)), pp. 25–30.

—, 'Akhenaten or Nefertiti?', *Acta Orientalis* 38 (1977), pp. 5–10.

R. G. Harrison, 'An Anatomical Examination of the Pharaonic Remains Purported to be Akhenaten', *JEA* 52 (1966), pp. 95–119.

— *et al.*, 'The Kingship of Smenkhkare and Tutankhamun Demonstrated Serologically', *Nature* 224 (1969), pp. 325–6.

— *et al.*, 'A Mummified Foetus from the Tomb of Tutankhamun', *Antiquity* 53, No. 207 (1979), p. 21.

F. A. Hassan, 'The Origins of the Egyptian Civilisation: A Working Model', *ASAE* 65 (1983), pp. 135–48.

S. Hassan, *Excavations at Giza*, 8 vols (Oxford and Cambridge, 1932–53).

—, 'The Causeway of Wnis at Saqqara', *ZÄS* 80 (1955), pp. 136–9.

H. Hauben, 'The Alexandrian Patriarch as Pharaoh. From Biblical Metaphor to Scholarly Topos', in Clarysse *et al.*, *Egyptian Religion*, 1998, pp. 1341–52.

W. C. Hayes, *The Scepter of Egypt* (New York, 1959).

—, 'Most Ancient Egypt', *JNES* 23 (1964), pp. 74–273.

W. Helck, *Der Einfluss der Militärführer in der 18 ägyptischer Dynastie* (Leipzig, 1939).

S. Hendrickx, 'Two Protodynastic Objects in Brussels and the Origin of the Bilobate Cult-sign of Neith', *JEA* 82 (1996), pp. 23–42.

Herodotus (transl. by A. de Sélincourt, Penguin Classics), *The Histories*, Book II (Harmondsworth, 1961).

A. K. Hoffmann, *Egypt after the Pharaohs: 332 BC – AD 642 from Alexander to the Arab Conquest* (London, 1986).

C. Hope, 'Objects from the Temple of Tutu', in Clarysse *et al.*, *Egyptian Religion* (1998), pp. 803–58.

G. D. Hornblower, 'Predynastic Figures of Women and Their Successors', *JEA* 15 (1939), pp. 29–47.

E. Hornung, *Untersuchungen zur Chronologie und Geschichte des Neuen Reiches* (Wiesbaden, 1964).

—, *Conceptions of God in Ancient Egypt: The One and the Many* (London, 1983).

—, *The Valley of the Kings* (New York, 1990).

P. Houlihan, *The Animal World of the Pharaohs* (London, 1996).

S. Ikram, 'Domestic Shrines and the Cult of the Royal Family at Amarna', *JEA* 75 (1989), pp. 89–101.

E. Iversen, *Canon and Proportions in Egyptian Art* (London, 1955).

C. Jacq, *Egyptian Magic* (Warminster, 1985).

J. J. Janssen, 'Gift-giving in Ancient Egypt as an Economic Feature', *JEA* 68 (1982), pp. 253–65.

—, 'Requisitions from Upper Egyptian Temples', *JEA* 77 (1991), pp. 79–94.

D. G. Jeffreys and E. Strouhal, 'North Saqqara 1978–9: The Coptic Cemetery Site at the Sacred Animal Necropolis. Preliminary Report', *JEA* 66 (1980), pp. 28–35.

G. Jéquier, *Considérations sur les religions égyptiennes* (Neuchâtel, 1946).

J. H. Johnson, 'The Role of the Egyptian Priesthood in Ptolemaic Egypt', in L. H. Lesko (ed.), *Egyptian Studies in Honor of Richard A. Parker* (Hanover and London, 1986), pp. 70–84.

W. R. Johnson, 'Amenhotep III and Amarna: Some New Considerations', *JEA* 82 (1966), pp. 65–82.

M. Jones, 'The Temple of Apis in Memphis', *JEA* 76 (1990), pp. 141–7.

P. Jordan, *Riddles of the Sphinx* (Stroud, Glos., 1998).

H. Junker, *Giza*, vol. 2 (Vienna, 1934).

—, *Die Geisteshaltung der Ägypter in der Frühzeit* (Graz, 1961).

A. Kadry, 'Semenkhkare, the Ephemeral King', *ASAE* 68 (1982), pp. 191–4.

L. Kákosy, 'A Memphite Triad', *JEA* 66 (1980), pp. 48–53.

—, 'The Nile, Euthenia, and the Nymphs', *JEA* 68 (1982), pp. 290–98.

—, 'A Horus Cippus with Royal Cartouches', in Clarysse *et al.*, *Egyptian Religion* (1998), pp. 125–38.

I. M. Kamel, 'Foreign Deities in the Eastern Delta', *ASAE* 65 (1983), pp. 83–9.

N. Kanawati, *The Rock Tombs of el-Hawawish: The Cemetery of Akhmim*, 10 vols (Sydney, 1980–92).

—, *The Tombs of El-Hagarsa*, 2 vols (Sydney, 1993).

H. Kantor, 'The Early Relations of Egypt with Asia', *JNES* 1 (1942), pp. 174–213.

—, 'Further Evidence for Early Mesopotamian Relations with Egypt', *JNES* 11 (1952), pp. 239–50.

O. E. Kaper, 'The Astronomical Ceiling of Deir el-Haggar in the Dakhleh Oasis', *JEA* 81 (1995), pp. 175–95.

H. Kees, *Der Götterglaube im alten Ägypten* (Leipzig, 1941; 2nd edn. Berlin, 1956).

B. J. Kemp, 'Abydos and the Royal Tombs of the First Dynasty', *JEA* 52 (1966), pp. 13–22.

—, 'Merimda and the Theory of House Burial in Prehistoric Egypt', *Chr. d'Ég.* 43 (1968), pp. 313–24.

—, 'Photographs of the Decorated Tomb at Hierakonpolis', *JEA* 59 (1973), pp. 36–43.

—, 'Preliminary Report on the El-Amarna Expedition, 1979', *JEA* 66 (1980), pp. 5–16.

—, 'Automatic Analysis of Predynastic Cemeteries: A New Method for an Old Problem', *JEA* 68 (1982), pp. 5–15.

—, 'Preliminary Report on the El-Amarna Expedition, 1981–2', *JEA* 69 (1983), pp. 5–24.

—, 'Report on the Tell El-Amarna Expedition, 1977–82', *ASAE* 70 (1984–5), pp. 83–98.

—, 'The Amarna Workmen's Village in Retrospect', *JEA* 73 (1987), pp. 21–50.

K. A. Kitchen, *Suppiluliuma and the Amarna Pharaohs* (Liverpool, 1962).

—, 'Some New Light on the Asiatic Wars of Ramesses II', *JEA* 50 (1964), pp. 47–70.

—, *Ancient Orient and Old Testament* (London, 1966).

—, *Pharaoh Triumphant: The Life and Times of Ramesses II* (Warminster, 1974).

—, *Ramesside Inscriptions, Translated and Annotated*, vols 1 and 2 (Oxford, 1993–9).

—, *The Third Intermediate Period in Egypt (1100–650 BC)* (Warminster, 1996).

E. G. Kraeling, *The Brooklyn Museum Aramaic Papyri* (New Haven, 1953).

M. Eaton-Krauss and E. Graefe, *The Small Golden Shrine from the Tomb of Tutankhamun* (Oxford, 1985).

P. Posener-Kriéger and J. L. de Cenival, *Hieratic Papyri in the British Museum. 5th Ser., The Abu Sir Papyri* (London, 1968).

J-M. Kruchten, *Les annales des prêtres de Karnak (XXI–XXIIIièmes Dynasties) et autres textes contemporains relatif à limitation des prêtres d'Amon* (Louvain, 1989).

P. Lacau, 'Les statues "guérisseuses" dans l'ancienne Égypte', in Fondation Eugène Piot, *Monuments et Mémoires* 25 (1921–2), pp. 189–209.

S. Langdon and A. H. Gardiner, 'The Treaty of Alliance between Hattusili, King of the Hittites, and Pharaoh Ramesses II of Egypt', *JEA* 6 (1920), pp. 179–205.

K. Lange and M. Hirmer, *Egypt: Architecture, Sculpture and Painting in Three Thousand Years* (London, 1956).

J-P. Lauer, 'Sur la pyramide de Meidoum et les deux pyramides du roi Snefrou à Dahchour', *Orientalia* 36 (1967), pp. 239–54.

—, 'À propos du pretendu désastre de la pyramide de Meidoum', *Chr. d'Ég.*, 101 (1976), pp. 72–89.

A. Leahy, 'A Protective Measure at Abydos in the 13th Dynasty', *JEA* 75 (1989), pp. 41–60.

—, 'The Adoption of Ankhnesneferibre at Karnak', *JEA* 82 (1996), pp. 145–66.

F. Leclere, 'A Cemetery of Osirid Figurines at Karnak', *Eg. Arch.*, No. 8 (1996), pp. 9–12.

F. F. Leek, 'The Problem of Brain Removal during Embalming by the Ancient Egyptians', *JEA* 55 (1969), pp. 112–16.

—, *The Human Remains from the Tomb of Tutankhamun* (Oxford, 1972).

—, 'How Old Was Tutankhamun?', *JEA* 63 (1977), pp. 112–15.

M. Lehner, *The Complete Pyramids* (London and New York, 1997).

—, and Z. Hawass, 'The Sphinx – Who Built It and Why?', *Archaeology* 47, No. 5 (Sept-Oct 1994), pp. 30–47.

R. J. Leprohon, 'The Offering in the First Intermediate Period', *JEA* 76 (1990), pp. 163–4.

M. Lichtheim, 'Songs of the Harpers', *JNES* 4 (1945), pp. 178–212.

—, *Ancient Egyptian Literature*, 3 vols (California, 1973, 1976 and 1980).

—, *Ancient Egyptian Autobiographies, Chiefly of the Middle Kingdom: A Study and an Anthology* (Freiburg and Gottingen, 1988).

L. Limme, S. Hendrickx and D. Huyge, 'El Kab: Excavations in the Old Kingdom Rock Necropolis', *Eg. Arch.*, No. 11 (1997), pp. 3–6.

A. B. Lloyd, 'The Egyptian Labyrinth', *JEA* 56 (1970), pp. 81–100.

—, 'The Inscription of Udjahorresnet. A Collaborator's Testament', *JEA* 68 (1982), pp. 166–80.

A. Lucas, *Ancient Egyptian Materials and Industries* (London, 1962; rev. edn. New York, 1999).

D. D. Luckenbill, *Ancient Records of Assyria and Babylonia*, 2 vols (Chicago, 1926–7; rev. edn. 1968).

E. Mackay, 'The Cutting and Preparation of Tomb-chapels in the Theban Necropolis', *JEA* 7 (1921), pp. 154–68.

J. Malek, 'The Annals of Amenemhet II', *Eg. Arch.*, No. 2 (1992), p.18.

P. der Manuelian, 'Two Fragments of Relief and a New Model for the Tomb of Montuemhet at Thebes', *JEA* 71 (1985), pp. 98–121.

G. T. Martin, *The Royal Tomb at El-Amarna*, 2 vols (London, 1974 and 1989).

—, 'Excavation Reports on the Tomb of Horemheb at Saqqara', *JEA* 62 (1976), pp. 5–13; 63 (1977), pp. 13–19; 64 (1978), pp. 5–9; 65 (1979), pp. 13–16.

—, 'The Tomb of Tia and Tia: Preliminary Report on the Saqqara Excavations, 1983', *JEA* 70 (1984), pp. 5–12.

—, 'The Saqqara New Kingdom Necropolis Excavations, 1986: Preliminary Report', *JEA* 73 (1987), pp. 1–9.

—, *The Hidden Tombs of Memphis: New Discoveries from the Time of Tutankhamun and Ramesses the Great* (London, 1991).

—, M. J. Raven, B. G. Aston and J. Van Dijk, 'The Tomb of Maya and Meryt: Preliminary Report on the Saqqara Excavations, 1987', *JEA* 74 (1988(i)), pp. 1–14.

—, M. J. Raven and D. A. Aston, 'The Tomb-chambers of Iurudef: Preliminary Report on the Saqqara Excavations, 1985', *JEA* 74 (1988(ii)), pp. 15–22.

I. Mathieson, E. Bettles, S. Davies and H. S. Smith, 'A Stela of the Persian Period from Saqqara', *JEA* 81 (1995), pp. 23–41.

C. Maystre, *Les grands prêtres de Ptah de Memphis* (Freiburg and Gottingen, 1992).

P. E. McGovern, 'Wine of Egypt's Golden Age: An Archaeochemical Perspective', *JEA* 83 (1997), pp. 69–108.

D. Randall-McIver and A. C. Mace, *El-Amrah and Abydos* (London, 1902).

K. Mendelssohn, 'A Building Disaster at the Meidum Pyramid', *JEA* 59 (1973), pp. 60–71.

S. A. B. Mercer, *The Tell El-Amarna Tablets*, 2 vols (Toronto, 1939).

—, *Horus, Royal God of Egypt* (Grafton, Mass., 1942).

—, *The Pyramid Texts* (New York, 1952).

R. L. Miller, 'Hogs and Hygiene', *JEA* 76 (1990), pp. 125–40.

J. Grafton Milne, 'The Sanatorium of Deir El-Bahri', *JEA* 1 (1914), pp. 96–8.

—, 'Egyptian Nationalism under Greek and Roman Rule', *JEA* 14 (1928), pp. 226–34.

A-Q. Mohammed, 'An Ibis Catacomb at Abu-kir', *ASAE* 66 (1987), pp. 121–3.

P. Montet, *La nécropole royale de Tanis*, 3 vols (Paris, 1947, 1951, 1960).

D. Montserrat, 'The Kline of Anubis', *JEA* 78 (1992), pp. 301–7.

—, 'The Representations of Young Males in "Fayoum Portraits"', *JEA* 79 (1993), pp. 215–25.

—, *Sex and Society in Graeco-Roman Egypt* (London, 1996).

—, 'Heron "Bearer of Philosophia" and Hermione Grammatike', *JEA* 83 (1997(ii)), pp. 223–6.

— and L. Meskell, 'Mortuary Archaeology and Religious Landscape at Graeco-Roman Deir el-Medina', *JEA* 83 (1997(i)), pp. 179–97.

W. L. Moran, *The Amarna Letters* (Baltimore, 1992).

S. Morenz, *Gott und Mensch im alten Ägypten* (Leipzig, 1964; Heidelberg, 1965).

—(trans. A. Keep), *Egyptian Religion* (London, 1973; repr. New York, 1990).

A. Moret, *Du caractère religieux de la royauté pharaonique* (Paris, 1902(i)).

—, *Le rituel de culte divin journalier en Égypte* (Paris, 1902, (ii)).

B. Muhs, 'Partisan Royal Epithets in the Late 3rd Intermediate Period and the Dynastic Affiliations of Pedubast I and Iuput II', *JEA* 84 (1998), pp. 220–23.

I. Munro, *Untersuchungen zu den Totenbuch-Papyri der 18. Dyn. Kriterien ihrer Datierung* (London and New York, 1987).

W. J. Murnane, *Texts from the Amarna Period in Egypt* (Atlanta, Georgia, 1995).

M. A. Murray, *The Osireion at Abydos* (London, 1904).

—, *The Tomb of Two Brothers* (Manchester, 1910).

—, 'Nawruz, or the Coptic New Year', *Ancient Egypt*, III (1921), pp. 79–81.

—, 'Burial Customs and Beliefs in the Hereafter in Predynastic Egypt', *JEA* 42 (1956), pp. 86–96.

H. Mustapha, 'The Surveying of the Bent Pyramid at Dahshur', *ASAE* 52 (1954), pp. 595–602.

E. Naville, 'The Geography of the Exodus', *JEA* 10 (1924), pp. 18–39.

—, and H. R. Hall, *The XIth Dynasty Temple of Deir el-Bahri*, 3 vols (London, 1907–13).

Nekhen News, vol. 11 (1999), pp. 4–5.

H. H. Nelson, 'Certain Reliefs at Karnak and Medinet Habu and the Ritual of Amenophis I', *JNES* 8 (1949), pp. 201–32, 310–45.

P. E. Newberry, *Beni Hasan*, 4 parts (London, 1893–1900).

—, 'The Set Rebellion of the Second Dynasty', *Ancient Egypt*, vol. 2 (1922), pp. 40–46.

—, 'King Ay, the Successor of Tutankhamun', *JEA* 18 (1932), pp. 50–52.

— and F. Ll. Griffith, *El-Bersheh*, 2 parts (London, 1892).

P. T. Nicholson, 'Archaeology beneath Saqqara', *Eg. Arch.*, No. 4 (1994(i)), p. 8.

—, 'Preliminary Report on Work at the Sacred Animal Necropolis, North Saqqara, 1992', *JEA* 80 (1994(ii)), pp. 1–10.

— and I. Shaw, *Ancient Egyptian Materials and Technology* (Cambridge, 2000).

A. Niwinski, 'The Bab el-Gusus Tomb and the Royal Cache in Deir el-Bahri', *JEA* 70 (1984), pp. 73–81.

—, 'Some Unusual Amulets Found on the Late Period Mummies in Warsaw and Cracow', in Clarysse, *Egyptian Religion* (1998), pp. 178–90.

J. Nunn, *Ancient Egyptian Medicine* (London, 1996).

D. O'Connor, 'The Earliest Royal Boat Graves', *Eg. Arch.*, No. 5 (1995(i)), pp. 3–7.

— and D. P. Silverman (eds), *Ancient Egyptian Kingship* (Leiden, New York, Cologne, 1995(ii)).

A. Osman, *Moses, Pharaoh of Egypt* (London, 1990).

R. B. Parkinson, '"Homosexual" Desire and Middle Kingdom Literature', *JEA* 81 (1995), pp. 57–76.

J. C. Payne, 'Tomb 100: The Decorated Tomb at Hierakonpolis Confirmed', *JEA* 59 (1973), pp. 31–5.

T. E. Peet, 'Fresh Light on the Tomb-robberies of the 20th Dynasty at Thebes', *JEA* 11 (1925), pp. 162–4.

—, *The Great Tomb-Robberies of the Twentieth Egyptian Dynasty*, 2 vols (Oxford, 1930).

J. D. S. Pendlebury, 'Egypt and the Aegean in the Late Bronze Age', *JEA* 16 (1930), pp. 75–92.

—, 'Excavated at Tell El-Amarna', *JEA* 19 (1933), pp. 129–36; 20 (1934), pp. 113–18; 22 (1936), pp. 194–8.

R. Perizonius, M. Attia, H. Smith and J. Goudsmit, 'Monkey Mummies and North Saqqara', *Eg. Arch.*, No. 3 (1993), pp. 31–3.

W. M. F. Petrie, *Tanis I* (London, 1885).

—, *Tanis II* (London, 1888).

—, *Hawara, Biahmu and Arsinoe* (London, 1889).

—, *Illahun, Kahun and Gurob* (London, 1890(i)).

—, *Kahun, Gurob and Hawara* (London, 1890(ii)).

—, *The Royal Tombs of the First Dynasty* (London, 1900).

—, *Royal Tombs of the Earliest Dynasties*, 2 vols (London, 1900–1901).

—, *Diospolis Parva* (London, 1901; repr. 1973).

—, *Prehistoric Egypt* (London, 1920).

—, *Prehistoric Egypt Corpus* (London, 1921).

—, *The Making of Egypt* (London, 1939).

—, *Ceremonial Slate Palettes* (London, 1953).

— and J. E. Quibell, *Naqada and Ballas* (London, 1896).

—, G. A. Wainwright and E. Mackay, *The Labyrinth, Gerzeh and Mazghuneh* (London, 1912).

K. Pfluger, 'The Edict of King Haremhab', *JNES* 5 (1946), pp. 260–68.

A. Piankoff, *The Tomb of Ramesses VI* (New York, 1954).

—, *The Shrines of Tut-ankh-Amon* (New York, 1955).

—, *The Pyramid of Unas* (Princeton, 1968).

G. Pinch, *Magic in Ancient Egypt* (London, 1994).

D. Polz, 'Excavations in Dra Abu el-Naga', *Eg. Arch.*, No. 7 (1995), pp. 6–8.

B. Porter and R. Moss (eds), *Topographical Bibliography of Ancient Egyptian Hieroglyphic Texts, Reliefs and Paintings*, 8 vols (Oxford, 1927–99).

G. Posener, *La première domination Perse en Egypte* (Cairo, 1936).

—, *De la divinité du pharaon* (Cahier de la Société Asiatique 15) (Paris, 1960).

J. Quaegebeur, 'Mummy Labels: An Orientation', in E. Boswinkel and P. W. Pestman (eds), *Textes grecs, démotiques et bilingués* (Pap. Lugd. - Bat. 19) (Leiden, 1978), pp. 232–59.

J. E. Quibell, *The Ramesseum* (London, 1898).

— and F. W. Green, *Hierakonpolis*, 2 vols (London, 1900–1902).

S. Quirke, 'Kerem in the Fitzwilliam Museum', *JEA* 76 (1990), pp. 170–74.

—, *The Cult of Ra* (London, 2001).

— (ed.), *Middle Kingdom Studies* (New Malden, 1991).

— and A. J. Spencer, *The British Museum Book of Ancient Egypt* (London, 1992).

A. F. Rainey (ed.), *Egypt, Israel, Sinai - Archaeological and Historical Relationships in the Biblical Period* (Tel Aviv, 1987).

J. D. Ray, *The Archive of Hor, Texts from Excavation*, 2 (London, 1976).

D. B. Redford, 'Some Observations on Amarna Chronology', *JEA* 45 (1959), pp. 34–7.

—, *A Study of the Biblical Story of Joseph, Genesis 37–50* (Leiden, 1970).

—, *Egypt, Canaan and Israel in Ancient Times* (Princeton, 1972).

—, 'The Sun-disc in Akhenaten's Program: Its Worship and Antecedents, I', *JARCE* 13 (1976), pp. 47–62.

—, *Akhenaten. The Heretic King* (Princeton, 1984).

C. A. Redmount and R. Friedman, 'Tell El-Muqdam: City of Lions', *Eg. Arch.*, No. 3 (1993), pp. 37–8.

B. R. Rees, 'Popular Religion in Graeco-Roman Egypt: II The Transition to Christianity', *JEA* 36 (1950), pp. 86–100.

C. N. Reeves, 'A Reappraisal of Tomb 55 in the Valley of the Kings', *JEA* 67 (1981), pp. 48–55.

—, 'New Light on Kiya from Texts in the British Museum', *JEA* 74 (1988), pp. 91–101.

—, *The Complete Tutankhamun* (London, 1990(i)).

—, *Valley of the Kings: The Decline of a Royal Necropolis* (London, 1990(ii)).

G. A. Reisner, *The Development of the Egyptian Tomb down to the Accession of Cheops* (Cambridge, Oxford, London, 1936).

—, *A History of the Giza Necropolis*, 2 vols (Cambridge, 1942 and 1955).

R. Rémondon, 'L'Égypte et la suprême résistance au christianisme (Ve – VIIe siècles)', *BIFAO* 51 (1952), pp. 63–78.

P. le Page Renouf, *Lectures on the Origin and Growth of Religion as Illustrated by the Religion of Ancient Egypt* (London, 1880; 4th ed. London, 1897).

E. A. E. Reymond, 'Worship of the Ancestor Gods at Edfu', *Chr. d'Ég.*, 38 (1963), pp. 49–70.

—, 'A Late Edfu Theory on the Nature of the God', *Chr. d'Ég.*, 40 (1965), pp. 61–71.

H. Ricke *et al.*, *Das Sonnenheiligtum Des Königs Userkaf*, 2 vols (Cairo, 1965).

G. Robins, 'The God's Wife of Amun in the 18th Dynasty in Egypt', in A. Cameron and A. Kuhrt (eds), *Images of Women in Antiquity* (London, 1983), pp. 70–78.

—, *Women in Ancient Egypt* (London, 1993).

—, *Proportion and Style in Ancient Egyptian Art* (London, 1994).

—, *The Art of Ancient Egypt* (London, 1997).

M. Rostovtzeff, 'The Foundations of Social and Economic Life in Hellenistic Times', *JEA* 6 (1920), pp. 161–78.

A. M. Roth, 'Fingers, Stars and the "Opening of the Mouth": The Nature and Function of Ntrwy-blades', *JEA* 79 (1993), pp. 57–80.

—, 'The *Pss-kf* and the "Opening of the Mouth" Ceremony: A Ritual of Birth and Rebirth', *JEA* 78 (1992), pp. 113–47.

K. Ryholt, 'A Pair of Oracle Petitions Addressed to Horus-of-the-Camp', *JEA* 79 (1993), pp. 189–98.

A. I. Sadek, *Popular Religion in Egypt during the New Kingdom* (Hildesheim, 1987).

J. Samson, 'Amarna Crowns and Wigs', *JEA* 59 (1973), pp. 47–59.

—, 'Nefertiti's Regality', *JEA* 63 (1977), pp. 88–97.

A. T. Sandison, 'The Use of Natron in Mummification in Ancient Egypt', *JNES* 22 (1963), pp. 259–67.

M. Sandman, *Texts from the Time of Akhenaten* (Brussels, 1938).

S. Sauneron, *The Priests of Ancient Egypt* (London, 1960; rev. edn. New York, 2000).

T. Säve-Soderbergh, 'The Hyksos Rule in Egypt', *JEA* 37 (1951), pp. 53–71.

O. J. Schaden, 'Clearance of the Tomb of King Ay', *JARCE* 21 (1984), pp. 39–64.

H. Schäfer, *Principles of Egyptian Art* (ed. with epilogue by E. Brunner-Traut; transl. and ed. by J. R. Baines) (Oxford, 1974).

R. Schulz, *Die Entwicklung und Bedeutung des kuboiden Statuentypus* (Hildesheim, 1992).

L. C. Schwabe, 'Hawara Portrait Mummy No. 4', *JEA* 71 (1985), pp. 190–93.

K. C. Seele, 'King Ay and the Close of the Amarna Age', *JNES* 14 (1955), pp. 168–80.

J. Van Seters, *The Hyksos: A New Investigation* (New Haven, 1966).

—, 'The Hyksos Burials in Palestine: A Review of the Evidence', *JNES* 30 (1971), pp. 110–17.

B. E. Shafer (ed.), *Religion in Ancient Egypt. Gods, Myths and Personal Practice* (New York and London, 1991).

— (ed.), *Temples of Ancient Egypt* (New York, 1997).

I. Shaw, 'Balustrades, Stairs and Altars in the Cult of the Aten at El-Amarna', *JEA* 80 (1994), pp. 109–27.

E. J. Sherman, 'Djedhor the Saviour Statue Base 01 10589', *JEA* 81 (1967), pp. 82–102.

A. F. Shore, *Portrait Painting from Roman Egypt* (London, 1962).

H. E. Sigerist, *A History of Medicine, vol. 1. Primitive and Archaic Medicine* (New York, 1951).

A. Siliotti, *Guide to the Pyramids of Egypt* (Cairo, 1997).

W. K. Simpson, 'Studies in the Twelfth Egyptian Dynasty: 1. The Residence of Ittowy. 2. The Sed Festival in Dynasty 12', *JARCE* 2 (1963), pp. 53–64.

—, 'Egyptian Sculpture and Two-dimensional Representation as Propaganda', *JEA* 68 (1982), pp. 266–71.

— (ed.), *Religion and Philosophy in Ancient Egypt* (New Haven, 1989).

G. E. Smith, *The Royal Mummies* (Cairo, 1912; repr. London, 2000).

— and W. R. Dawson, *Egyptian Mummies* (London, 1924; repr. London, 1991)

— and F. W. Jones, *Archaeological Survey of Nubia 1907–8 (2). Report on the Human Remains*, 2 vols (London, 1910).

H. S. Smith and D. G. Jeffreys, ' "The Anubeion", North Saqqara. Preliminary Report, 1978–9', *JEA* 66 (1980), pp. 17–27.

R. S. Smith and D. B. Redford, *The Akhenaten Temple Project, vol 1: Initial Discoveries* (Warminster, 1976).

W. S. Smith, *A History of Egyptian Sculpture and Painting in the Old Kingdom* (Oxford, 1946).

—, *The Art and Architecture of Ancient Egypt* (London, 1958).

G. P. G. Sobhy, 'Remains of Ancient Egyptian Medicine in Modern Domestic Treatment', *Bull. Inst. Ég.* 20 (1937–8), pp. 9–18.

F. Solmsen, *Isis among the Greeks and Romans* (Cambridge, Mass., 1979).

A. J. Spencer, *Death in Ancient Egypt* (London, 1982).

N. Spencer, 'The Temple of Onuris-Shu at Samanud', *Eg. Arch.*, No. 14 (1999), pp. 7–9.

H. Sternberg, *Mythische Motive und Mythenbildung in den ägyptischen Tempeln und Papyri der Griechisch-Romischen Zeit* (Wiesbaden, 1985).

W. Stevenson Smith, *A History of Egyptian Sculpture and Painting in the Old Kingdom* (Oxford, 1946).

H. M. Stewart, 'Some Pre-Amarnah Sun Hymns', *JEA* 46 (1960), pp. 83–90.

D. Sweeney, 'Henuttawy's Guilty Conscience (Gods and Grain in the Late Ramesside Letter No. 37)', *JEA* 80 (1994), pp. 208–12.

S. A. Takacs, *Isis and Seraphis in the Roman World* (Leiden, 1995).

E. Thomas, 'The Plan of Tomb 55 in the Valley of the Kings', *JEA* 47 (1961), p. 24.

D. J. Thompson, 'Demeter in Graeco-Roman Egypt', in Clarysse *et al.*, *Egyptian Religion* (1998), pp. 699–707.

S. E. Thompson, 'The Origin of the Pyramid Texts Found on Middle Kingdom Saqqara Coffins', *JEA* 76 (1990), pp. 17–25.

J. K. Thomson, 'A First Acolyte of Amun', *JEA* 84 (1998), pp. 215–20.

F. Tiradritti, 'Three Years of Research in the Tomb of Harwa', *Eg. Arch.*, No. 13 (1998), pp. 3–6.

A. Tooley, 'Osiris Bricks', *JEA* 82 (1996), pp. 167–79.

A. J. Tooley, 'Coffin of a Dog from Beni Hasan', *JEA* 74 (1988), pp. 207–11.

B. G. Trigger, B. J. Kemp, D. O'Connor and A. B. Lloyd, *Ancient Egypt: A Social History* (Cambridge, 1983).

L. Troy, *Patterns of Queenship in Ancient Egyptian Myth and History* (Uppsala, 1986).

E. Uphill, 'The Sed Festivals of Akhenaten', *JNES* 22 (1963), pp. 123–7.

—, 'The Per Aten at Amarna', *JNES* 29 (1970), pp. 151–66.

A. Varille, 'Toutankhamon: est-il fils d'Amenophis III et de Satamon?', *ASAE* 40 (1940), pp. 651–7.

R. Ventura, 'The Largest Project for a Royal Tomb in the Valley of the Kings', *JEA* 74 (1988), pp. 137–56.

J. Vergote, 'La notion de Dieu dans les livres de sagesse égyptiens', in *Les sagesses du Proche-Orient ancien, Colloque de Strasbourg* 17–19 mai, 1962 (Paris, 1962).

M. Verner, 'Forgotten Pyramids, Temples and Tombs of Abusir', *Eg. Arch.*, No. 7 (1995), pp. 19–20.

—, 'The Tomb of Iufaa at Abusir', *Eg. Arch.*, No. 14 (1999), pp. 39–40.

S. P. Vleeming, *Hundred-gated Thebes* (Leiden, 1995).

—, 'Some Mummy Labels in the Metropolitan Museum of Art, New York', in Clarysse *et al.*, *Egyptian Religion* (1998), pp. 476–515.

R. L. Vos, 'Varius Coloribus Apis. Some Remarks on the Colours of Apis and Other Sacred Animals', in Clarysse *et al.*, *Egyptian Religion* (1998), pp. 709–18.

G. A. Wainwright, 'Pharaonic Survivals between Lake Chad and the West Coast', *JEA* 35 (1949), pp. 170–75.

—, 'The Meshwesh', *JEA* 48 (1962), pp. 89–92.

—, 'The Origin of Amun', *JEA* 49 (1963), pp. 21–3.

J. Walker, *Folk Medicine in Modern Egypt* (London, 1934).

S. Walker, 'Ancient Faces: An Exhibition of Mummy Portraiture at the British Museum', *Eg. Arch.*, No. 10 (1997), pp. 19–23.

— (ed.), *Ancient Faces. Mummy Portraits from Roman Egypt* (London, 1997 and New York, 2000).

E. J. Walters, *Attic Grave Reliefs That Represent Women in the Dress of Isis* (New Jersey, 1988).

B. Watterson, *Coptic Egypt* (Edinburgh, 1988).

F. Weatherhead, 'Painted Pavements in the Great Palace at Amarna', *JEA* 78 (1992), pp. 179–94.

K. R. Weeks, 'The Theban Mapping Project and Work in KV5', in C. N. Reeves (ed.), *After Tutankhamun: Research and Excavation in the Royal Necropolis at Thebes* (London, 1992).

—, 'Protecting the Theban Necropolis', *Eg. Arch.*, No. 4 (1994), p. 23.

—, *The Lost Tomb. The Greatest Discovery at the Valley of the Kings since Tutankhamun* (London, 1998).

E. F. Wente, 'Egyptian "Make Merry" Songs Reconsidered', *JNES* 21 (1962), pp. 118–28.

S. Whale, *The Family in the Eighteenth Dynasty of Egypt* (Sydney, 1989).

C. Wilcken, *Alexander the Great* (London, 1932).

D. Wildung, *Egyptian Saints: Deification in Pharaonic Egypt* (New York, 1977).

J. G. Wilkinson, *Topography of Thebes and General View of Egypt* (London, 1835).

R. Wilkinson, *Reading Egyptian Art* (London, 1992).

—, *Symbol and Magic in Egyptian Art* (London, 1994).

—, *The Complete Temples of Ancient Egypt* (London, 2000).

T. A. H. Wilkinson, 'A New King in the Western Desert', *JEA* 81 (1995), pp. 205–10.

H. Willems, 'Crime, Cult and Capital Punishment (Mo'alla Inscription 8)', *JEA* 76 (1990), pp. 27–54.

I. Wilson, *The Exodus Enigma* (London, 1986).

J. A. Wilson, 'The Artist of the Egyptian Old Kingdom', *JNES* 6 (1947), pp. 231–49.

—, 'Buto and Hierakonpolis in the Geography of Egypt', *JNES* 14 (1955), pp. 209–36.

H. E. Winlock, 'The Theban Necropolis in the Middle Kingdom', *AJSL* 32 (1915), pp. 1–37.

—, *The Treasure of El-Lahun* (New York, 1934).

—, 'Neb-hepet-Re and Mentu-hotpe of the Eleventh Dynasty', *JEA* 26 (1940), pp. 116–19.

—, *The Rise and Fall of the Middle Kingdom in Thebes* (New York, 1947).

—, *Models of Daily Life in Ancient Egypt from the Tomb of Meket-Re* (Cambridge, Mass., 1955).

D. J. Wiseman, *Chronicles of Chaldean Kings* (London, 1956).

R. E. Witt, *Isis in the Graeco-Roman World* (London, 1971).

W. Wood, 'The Archaic Stone Tombs at Helwan', *JEA* 73 (1987), pp. 59–70.

S. Yoshimura, 'Excavations at the Tomb of Amenhotep III', *Eg. Arch.*, No. 7 (1995), pp. 17–18.

L. V. Zabkar, 'Adaptation of Ancient Egyptian Texts to the Temple Ritual at Philae', *JEA* 66 (1980), pp. 127–36.

—, 'Six Hymns to Isis in the Sanctuary of Her Temple at Philae, and Their Theological Significance', *JEA* 69 (1983), pp. 115–37.

J. Zandee, *Studies in Egyptian Religion* (Leiden, 1982).

—, *Der Amunhymnus des Papyrus Leiden I 344, verso. Band I–III* (Leiden, 1992).

H. von Zeissl, *Athiopen und Assyrer in Ägypten* (Gluckstadt, 1944).

Index